The Limits of British Colonial Control in South Asia

This book assesses British colonialism in South Asia in a transnational light, with the Indian Ocean region as its ambit, and with a focus on subaltern groups and actors. It breaks new ground by combining new strands of research on colonial history.

Thinking about colonialism in dynamic terms, the book focuses on the movement of various underclasses in the context of imperial ventures. Challenging the assumed stability of colonial rule, it considers social spaces that threatened the racial, class and moral order instituted by British colonial states. By elaborating on the colonial state's strategies to control perceived disorder and the modes of resistance and subversion that subaltern subjects used to challenge state control, the book presents a picture of the British Empire as an ultimately precarious, shifting and unruly formation, which is quite distinct from its self-projected image as an orderly entity.

Thoroughly researched and innovative in its approach, this book will be a valuable resource for scholars of Asian, British imperial/colonial, transnational and global history.

Ashwini Tambe is Assistant Professor of Women's Studies at the University of Toronto, Canada. Her research interests include gender and sexuality in South Asia, colonial history and globalization, and specifically the history of the sex trade in colonial Bombay.

Harald Fischer-Tiné is Professor of History at Jacobs University, Bremen. He holds a PhD in South Asian History from Heidelberg University (2000) and has published extensively on the social and cultural history of the British Raj and varieties of Hindu reform and Hindu nationalism in 19th and 20th century India.

Routledge Studies in the Modern History of Asia

1. **The Police in Occupation Japan**
   Control, corruption and resistance to reform
   Christopher Aldous

2. **Chinese Workers**
   A new history
   Jackie Sheehan

3. **The Aftermath of Partition in South Asia**
   Tai Yong Tan and Gyanesh Kudaisya

4. **The Australia–Japan Political Alignment**
   1952 to the present
   Alan Rix

5. **Japan and Singapore in the World Economy**
   Japan's economic advance into Singapore, 1870–1965
   Shimizu Hiroshi and Hirakawa Hitoshi

6. **The Triads as Business**
   Yiu Kong Chu

7. **Contemporary Taiwanese Cultural Nationalism**
   A-chin Hsiau

8. **Religion and Nationalism in India**
   The case of the Punjab
   Harnik Deol

9. **Japanese Industrialisation**
   Historical and cultural perspectives
   Ian Inkster

10. **War and Nationalism in China 1925–45**
    Hans J. van de Ven

11. **Hong Kong in Transition**
    One country, two systems
    Edited by Robert Ash, Peter Ferdinand, Brian Hook and Robin Porter

12. **Japan's Postwar Economic Recovery and Anglo-Japanese Relations, 1948–62**
    Noriko Yokoi

13. **Japanese Army Stragglers and Memories of the War in Japan, 1950–75**
    Beatrice Trefalt

14. **Ending the Vietnam War**
    The Vietnamese Communists' perspective
    Ang Cheng Guan

15. **The Development of the Japanese Nursing Profession**
    Adopting and adapting Western influences
    Aya Takahashi

16. **Women's Suffrage in Asia**
    Gender nationalism and democracy
    Louise Edwards and Mina Roces

17 **The Anglo-Japanese Alliance, 1902–22**
Phillips Payson O'Brien

18 **The United States and Cambodia, 1870–1969**
From curiosity to confrontation
Kenton Clymer

19 **Capitalist Restructuring and the Pacific Rim**
Ravi Arvind Palat

20 **The United States and Cambodia, 1969–2000**
A troubled relationship
Kenton Clymer

21 **British Business in Post-Colonial Malaysia, 1957–70**
'Neo-colonialism' or 'disengagement'?
Nicholas J. White

22 **The Rise and Decline of Thai Absolutism**
Kullada Kesboonchoo Mead

23 **Russian Views of Japan, 1792–1913**
An anthology of travel writing
David N. Wells

24 **The Internment of Western Civilians under the Japanese, 1941–45**
A patchwork of internment
Bernice Archer

25 **The British Empire and Tibet**
1900–922
Wendy Palace

26 **Nationalism in Southeast Asia**
If the people are with us
Nicholas Tarling

27 **Women, Work and the Japanese Economic Miracle**
The case of the cotton textile industry, 1945–75
Helen Macnaughtan

28 **A Colonial Economy in Crisis**
Burma's rice cultivators and the world depression of the 1930s
Ian Brown

29 **A Vietnamese Royal Exile in Japan**
Prince Cuong De (1882–1951)
Tran My-Van

30 **Corruption and Good Governance in Asia**
Nicholas Tarling

31 **US–China Cold War Collaboration, 1971–89**
S. Mahmud Ali

32 **Rural Economic Development in Japan**
From the nineteenth century to the Pacific War
Penelope Francks

33 **Colonial Armies in Southeast Asia**
Edited by Karl Hack and Tobias Rettig

34 **Intra Asian Trade and the World Market**
A J H Latham and Heita Kawakatsu

35 **Japanese–German Relations, 1895–1945**
War, diplomacy and public opinion
Edited by Christian W. Spang and Rolf-Harald Wippich

36 **Britain's Imperial Cornerstone in China**
The Chinese maritime customs service, 1854–1949
Donna Brunero

37 **Colonial Cambodia's 'Bad Frenchmen'**
The rise of French rule and the life of Thomas Caraman, 1840–87
Gregor Muller

38 **Japanese-American Civilian Prisoner Exchanges and Detention Camps, 1941–45**
Bruce Elleman

39 **Regionalism in Southeast Asia**
Nicholas Tarling

40 **Changing Visions of East Asia, 1943–93**
Transformations and continuities
R. B. Smith
(Edited by Chad J. Mitcham)

41 **Christian Heretics in Late Imperial China**
Christian inculturation and state control, 1720–1850
Lars P. Laamann

42 **Beijing – a Concise History**
Stephen G. Haw

43 **The Impact of the Russo-Japanese War**
Edited by Rotem Kowner

44 **Business–Government Relations in Prewar Japan**
Peter von Staden

45 **India's Princely States**
People, princes and colonialism
Edited by Waltraud Ernst and Biswamoy Pati

46 **Rethinking Gandhi and Nonviolent Relationality**
Global perspectives
Edited by Debjani Ganguly and John Docker

47 **The Quest for Gentility in China**
Negotiations beyond gender and class
Edited by Daria Berg and Chloë Starr

48 **Forgotten Captives in Japanese Occupied Asia**
Edited by Kevin Blackburn and Karl Hack

49 **Japanese Diplomacy in the 1950s**
From isolation to integration
Edited by Iokibe Makoto, Caroline Rose, Tomaru Junko and John Weste

50 **The Limits of British Colonial Control in South Asia**
Spaces of disorder in the Indian Ocean region
Edited by Ashwini Tambe and Harald Fischer-Tiné

The Limits of British Colonial Control in South Asia

Spaces of disorder in the Indian Ocean region

Edited by
Ashwini Tambe and Harald Fischer-Tiné

LONDON AND NEW YORK

First published 2009
by Routledge
2 Park Square, Milton Park, Abingdon, Oxon OX14 4RN

Simultaneously published in the USA and Canada
by Routledge
711 Third Avenue, New York, NY 10017

*Routledge is an imprint of the Taylor & Francis Group,
an informa business*

First issued in paperback 2012

Transferred to Digital Printing 2009

© 2009 Editorial selection and matter, Ashwini Tambe and Harald Fischer-Tiné; individual chapters, the contributors

Typeset in Times New Roman by
Taylor & Francis Books Ltd

All rights reserved. No part of this book may be reprinted or reproduced or utilised in any form or by any electronic, mechanical, or other means, now known or hereafter invented, including photocopying and recording, or in any information storage or retrieval system, without permission in writing from the publishers.

British Library Cataloguing in Publication Data
A catalogue record for this book is available from the British Library

Library of Congress Cataloging in Publication Data
 The limits of British colonial control in South Asia : spaces of disorder in the Indian Ocean Region / edited by Ashwini Tambe and Harald Fischer-Tiné.
  p. cm. – (Routledge studies in the modern history of Asia series ; 50)
 Includes bibliographical references and index.
 1. South Asia–Politics and government–19th century. 2. South Asia–Politics and government–20th century. 3. South Asia–Social conditions–19th century. 4. South Asia–Social conditions–20th century. I. Tambe, Ashwini. II. Fischer-Tiné, Harald.
  DS340.L56 2008
  325'.410954–dc22

2008006850

ISBN: 978-0-415-45257-1 (hbk)
ISBN: 978-0-203-89244-2 (ebk)
ISBN: 978-0-415-53323-2 (pbk)

Contents

List of contributors ix

Introduction 1
ASHWINI TAMBE AND HARALD FISCHER-TINÉ

PART I
Subaltern mobility and the problem of control and containment 11

1 Networks of subordination – networks of the subordinated: The ordered spaces of South Asian maritime labour in an age of imperialism (*c.* 1890–1947) 13
   RAVI AHUJA

2 Passport, ticket, and india-rubber stamp: 'The problem of the pauper pilgrim' in colonial India *c.* 1882–1925 49
   RADHIKA SINGHA

3 Do not destroy our honour: Wartime propaganda directed at East African soldiers in Ceylon (1943–44) 84
   KATRIN BROMBER

PART II
Subalternity, race and the transgression of moral boundaries 103

4 Discourses of exclusion and the 'convict stain' in the Indian Ocean (*c.* 1800–1850) 105
   CLARE ANDERSON

5 Flotsam and jetsam of the Empire?: European seamen and spaces of disease and disorder in mid-nineteenth century Calcutta 121
   HARALD FISCHER-TINÉ

6 'Degenerate whites' and their spaces of disorder: Disciplining racial and class ambiguities in colonial Calcutta (*c.* 1880–1930)   155
SATOSHI MIZUTANI

7 Hierarchies of subalternity: Managed stratification in Bombay's brothels, 1914–1930   192
ASHWINI TAMBE

Index   208

Contributors

Ravi Ahuja is Professor of Modern South History at the School of African and Oriental Studies, University of London. He gained his PhD at Heidelberg University in 1999 and has published widely on labour history and the history of transport in South Asia and the Indian Ocean.

Clare Anderson is Reader in the Department of Sociology, University of Warwick. She gained her PhD at the University of Edinburgh in 1997 and has taught at the University of Leicester. Her work focuses on the history of convicts and issues of migration in South Asia and the Indian Ocean region.

Katrin Bromber is a senior research fellow at the Centre for Modern Oriental Studies, Berlin. She was trained in African studies and linguistics at the University of Leipzig, from where she gained her PhD in 1993. She has taught at the Universities of Berlin and Vienna and published on various aspects of the history, society and culture of East Africa.

Harald Fischer-Tiné is Professor of History at Jacobs University, Bremen. He holds a PhD in South Asian History from Heidelberg University (2000) and has published extensively on the social and cultural history of the British Raj and varieties of Hindu reform and Hindu nationalism in nineteenth and twentieth century India.

Satoshi Mizutani is Assistant Professor at the Institute for Language and Culture, Doshisha University, Kyoto. He holds a DPhil from Oxford University (2005) and has published on the history of Eurasians and working class Europeans in colonial India.

Radhika Singha is Associate Professor of History at Jawaharlal Nehru University, New Delhi. She gained her PhD from Cambridge University and has published widely on the legal and penal history of colonial India.

Ashwini Tambe is Assistant Professor of Women's Studies and History at the University of Toronto. Her research interests include gender and sexuality in South Asia, colonial history and globalization, and specifically the history of the sex trade in colonial Bombay.

Introduction

Ashwini Tambe and Harald Fischer-Tiné

The historiography of colonial South Asia has witnessed important paradigm shifts in the past three decades. The turn away from elite historiography and the subsequent focus on marginal or lower class actors, led most prominently by the Marxist and Subaltern Studies schools in the 1980s, has been widely heralded and refined through internal critiques.[1] While both these schools have robustly challenged the effect of nationalism on history writing, recent research in colonial studies has been animated by calls to think beyond the very category of the nation.[2] Scholars recognize and critique the power of nation-state boundaries to structure both what is studied, and how it is approached. There is now a considerable wealth of research on transnational circuits of labour, capital and communication in the colonial period,[3] as well as a growing criticism of the limits that state-bound archives impose on knowledge formation.[4] Inspired by such currents, this volume brings together a set of chapters that present British colonialism in South Asia in a transnational light, with the Indian Ocean region as its ambit, and with a focus on subaltern groups and actors.

The dominant optic for understanding colonial formations has been dyadic, focused on the relationship between a metropole and a colony. Most authors associated with the otherwise quite innovative current of 'new imperial history' have not questioned the purportedly closed character of the imperial system, and have limited their analysis to the study of imperial core and colonial periphery.[5] Yet colonial regimes themselves were sustained by networks of transportation and communication that exceeded the territorial units of the colonial and metropolitan states.[6] Using a maritime optic allows us to view colonialism in broader, more dynamic terms. Indeed, if one takes seriously the role of maritime movement in shaping the history of this region, colonial political boundaries recede into the background. The Indian Ocean has been remarkable for its role in facilitating contact between the Arab world, East Africa, coastal India, the Malay world and Australia for millennia. As Pearson and Bose discuss, the Indian Ocean is one of the oldest and most striking spaces of cross-cultural interaction, in part as a result of how the monsoon winds have fostered contact between its various coasts. In the late colonial period, such mobility intensified with the advent of steamships and the opening of the Suez Canal in 1869, and more regular and predictable interaction between Europe and the Indian Ocean world occurred. People from a greater range of social groups began to travel these waters. It is this era that the present volume highlights; its chronological scope covers almost the entire period of British colonialism in India starting from the late eighteenth century, with a clear emphasis on the 'high noon of the Raj' in the second half of the nineteenth and the early years of the twentieth century.

Studies of maritime mobility in the Indian Ocean have predominantly focused on merchant networks and the movement of commodities.[7] Our volume, by contrast, concentrates on the movement of subaltern groups. In using the term 'subaltern', we do not claim to be continuing the project of the Subaltern Studies Collective; some of our contributors, indeed, would strenuously resist such a label. The term 'subaltern' is, nonetheless, a useful descriptor of the social groups our authors discuss: underclasses who were problem populations in the official imagination. The chapters present the social milieus of poor Europeans, Australians and East Africans within South Asia, as well as Indian pauper pilgrims travelling abroad in the *Hijaz* and Indian seamen employed in the British merchant marine. This focus also departs from other scholarship on mobile subalterns in specific ways. When scholarly attention has been given to mobile underclasses, it has been for the most part to indentured or enslaved labour in colonial plantations, mines and factories.[8] The circumstances of such itinerant figures as sailors, soldiers, prostitutes, escaped convicts, or pilgrims have been relatively less studied.[9] The present chapters focus on subjects for whom moving between port cities was a regular activity, and who thus travelled between India, Australia, Ceylon, Kenya, and the Arabic peninsula. Some of them travelled constantly, as in the case of seamen or brothel workers in Bombay and Calcutta, while others went on pilgrimage to fulfil their religious duty or were transported during wars, such as military personnel recruited in East Africa and stationed in Ceylon. Such groups often passed through port cities or they constituted a specific and permanent stratum of the inhabitants of these cities. Port cities, the bridgeheads of mercantile imperialism, thus form the setting of many of our studies.[10]

A major contention of this volume is that focusing on such social groups allows us to contest the assumed stability of colonial rule. The social spaces featured in this volume are those that threatened the racial, class and moral order instituted by British colonial states. These spaces include unruly maritime, military and convict labour, and prostitutes who occupied the interstices of racial and legal categories. Frequently, it was the mobility of these social groups that was regarded as causing disorder. In other cases, their mere existence provoked debates about moral values and social or racial hierarchies. Because of their perceived 'in-between' and unruly character, these groups created problems for both the privileged European and non-European elites, and also entered into conflicts with other 'subaltern' layers of the population. Our contributors both elaborate the colonial state's strategies to control perceived disorder, and the modes of resistance and subversion that subaltern subjects used to challenge state control. Taken together, the chapters present a picture of the British Empire as an ultimately precarious, shifting and unruly formation, quite distinct from its self-projected image as an orderly behemoth.

Many of the chapters deal with the general question of colonial classification, particularly with respect to race and class. The grammar of difference initiated under colonial rule has been a topic of scholarship in a variety of fields in the past two decades.[11] Postcolonial literary studies, transnational feminist studies, historical anthropology, and subaltern studies are prominent sites where scholars have explored the question of how European colonial regimes defined the categories of the rulers and the ruled. They now acknowledge that these categories were neither monolithic nor static, that lines defining differences between peoples shifted and that the infamous 'colour line' sometimes turned out to be rather elusive.[12] By focusing on social groups that were located in interstitial spaces, and whose presence threatened the fixity of categories, our authors problematize the certainties of a dichotomous categorization of the rulers and the ruled.

Several contributors highlight the manner in which the incorporation of soldiers and sailors into a nexus of capitalist and military relations occurred in tandem with expanding forms of racial, ethnic and cultural differentiation. As wage labourers, sailors and soldiers experienced class formation within the broad language of colonial racial and cultural distinctions. Thus, Ravi Ahuja's study in this volume of Indian sailors, or lascars, on British merchant steamships underlines how ethnic definitions of Indian sailors were critical to their networks of recruitment. Correspondingly, Radhika Singha's chapter analyzes how the category of the Indian pauper pilgrim was constructed in the context of *Hajj*-related traffic in the Indian Ocean. She offers insights into the play between local protocols of scrutinizing bodies and recording identity and the international conventions of travel shaped by European powers. Katrin Bromber's chapter on East African soldiers in Ceylon underlines how racial categories of the African, the Indian and the Ceylonese were naturalized in wartime propaganda material.

While these studies acknowledge the reification of racial and ethnic categories under British colonialism, they also point to ways in which these categories were subverted. Singha, for instance, describes the manifold difficulties entailed in the adoption of the category 'pauper pilgrim' for the British administration. By the same token, Bromber's analysis also points out how soldiers used their status as strangers in Ceylon to gain access to literacy and English education.

The idea that colonizers and colonized were inherently different, a cornerstone of colonial order, required constant tending. There was a great deal of work that went into elaborating and maintaining racial distinctions, as the chapters in the second part of this volume explore. In particular, those chapters describing white underclasses in a colonial setting attest to the anxieties that accompanied the notion of monolithic whiteness. Satoshi Mizutani's treatment of the impoverished domiciled British class, partly inspired by the growing body of critical whiteness studies,[13] underscores how tenuous the notion of white racial solidarity across class lines was. The bonds of kith and kin between settled and transient white populations in India were constantly invoked as a means to justify action against pauperism among the domiciled. In a similar vein, Clare Anderson's study of Australian escaped convicts living in India and Harald Fischer-Tiné's exploration of European seamen on the fringes of white society in Calcutta demonstrate that the language colonial officials used to characterize colonized peoples – the references to dirt and disease, so closely associated with 'native' life-worlds, for example – was also utilized in descriptions of white underclasses. Along the same lines, Ashwini Tambe's chapter describes how non-British European prostitutes likewise embodied a lesser form of whiteness within a stratified sexual order in colonial Bombay. These chapters, then, argue against the notion of self-evident and monolithic whiteness, by exploring fissures of class and nation within the category. Read together, therefore, they provide a useful corrective against a simplistic understanding of colonial power relations based on an insurmountable racial divide.

Several of our authors advance the intellectual agenda of transnational colonial history through their critiques of prevailing tendencies within the field. Ravi Ahuja, for instance, argues that the 'network approach' to studying subaltern maritime labour in the Indian Ocean region has tended to underrate structural limitations on network development. His chapter focuses on such limitations and argues that in the case of South Asian maritime labour, the political and economic context of British imperialism preconditioned the emergence and many of the structural properties of networks of recruitment and labour control.

A specific strength of the present collection is our authors' responsiveness to Dipesh Chakrabarty's recent imperative to write "ambivalences, contradictions, [...] tragedies and ironies" into the history of colonial modernity.[14] Both Harald Fischer-Tiné and Satoshi Mizutani explore ambiguities in the way that elite British communities in Calcutta dealt with groups on the fringes of white society. In presenting examples of how 'white' sailors were both 'orientalized' and celebrated, and how 'domiciled classes' were simultaneously stigmatized and recuperated, they argue for a more nuanced, and internally contradictory, understanding of privileged European classes in colonies. The contradictory impulses of the colonial police force form the focus of Ashwini Tambe's chapter on prostitution in Bombay. By analyzing the manner in which police officials responded to international anti-trafficking conventions, she argues for an understanding of the variegated character of the colonial state.

Another significant contribution to wider historiographical debates is how our authors point to more fruitful approaches to an understanding of subaltern experiences. Rather than writing off the endeavour of recovering subaltern voices as doomed because of the state-circumscribed nature of official archives,[15] our authors present a more agentic view of such subjects. Several of our chapters feature the mobility of subaltern figures, and their capacity to shape their own circumstances. In studying the escape and migration of convicts and ex-convicts from Australian penal settlements to India, Anderson demonstrates the extent to which knowledge about subaltern spaces circulated during this period. Radhika Singha addresses similar questions with a focus on Indian subaltern groups – she explores how Indian 'pauper pilgrims' made maximal use of the limited room for manoeuvre that they had. Katrin Bromber, attending to 'subalterns' in the original military sense of the term, presents a reading of war time propaganda that suggests the ways in which East African soldiers' needs were being met through the pressure they posed on their authorities, during their Ceylonese sojourn.

A final transnational dimension of this volume, we are tempted to add, is that of its authors, who collaborated across regions: the contributors live and work in Canada, Germany, Japan, UK, India and the United States, reflecting the diverse profile and strengths of scholarship on South Asia around the world. In multiple ways, then, this volume proposes a more expansive vision of South Asian studies.

Acknowledgements

Ashwini Tambe gratefully acknowledges the excellent research assistance of Rachel Levee, and the support of a WGSI SSHRC Institutional Grant.

Notes

1 See in particular, *Subaltern Studies* volumes I–VI. For a review of Marxist critiques of elite historiography, see S. Sarkar, *Writing Social History*, Delhi: Oxford University Press, 1998.
2 See C.A. Bayly, 'Beating the Boundaries: South Asian History, *c.* 1700–1850' in *South Asia and World Capitalism*, ed. S. Bose, Delhi: Oxford University Press, 1990; A. Burton, ed., *After the Imperial Turn: Thinking With and Through the Nation*, Durham, NC: Duke University Press, 2003; P. Levine, *Prostitution, Race, and Politics: Policing Venereal Disease in the British Empire*, Oxford: Routledge, 2003; K. Verdery 'Whither "Nation" and "Nationalism"?' in *Mapping the Nation*, ed. G. Balakrishnan, London: Verso, 1996, pp. 226–34. For critiques of nationalist historiography in Subaltern Studies influenced by postcolonial thought, see Dipesh Chakrabarty, 'Postcoloniality and the Artifice of History: Who Speaks for "Indian" Pasts?' *Representations* 37, 1992: 1–26; P. Chatterjee, 'Whose Imagined Community?' in *Mapping the Nation*, ed. Gopal Balakrishnan, London: Verso, 1996, pp. 214–44. For a critique from a more traditional Marxist vantage point see Sumit Sarkar, *Beyond Nationalist Frames: Postmodernism, Hindu Fundamentalism, History*, Delhi: Permanent Black, 2003.
3 See for instance D. Ghosh and D. Kennedy (eds), *Decentering Empire: Britain, India and the Transcolonial World*, New Delhi: Orient Longman, 2006; C. Markovits,

6 Introduction

J. Pouchepadass and S. Subramanyam, eds, *Society and Circulation: Mobile People and Itinerant Cultures in South Asia, 1750–1950*, Delhi: Permanent Black, 2003; T. Ballantyne, *Orientalism and Race: Aryanism in the British Empire*, Houndmills, Basingstoke-New York: Palgrave Macmillan, 2002; and C. Bates (ed.), *Community, Empire and Migration: South Asians in Diaspora*, Hyderabad: Orient Longman, 2001.

4 S. Bose, *A Hundred Horizons: The Indian Ocean in the Age of Global Empire*, Cambridge, MA: Harvard University Press, 2006. Bose's work uses state archives and literary sources that integrate different approaches to Indian Ocean history. For a critique of reliance on official archives, see A. Burton, *Dwelling in the Archive: Women Writing, House, Home and History in Late Colonial India*, New Delhi: Oxford University Press, 2003.

5 See for example K. Wilson (ed.), *A New Imperial History: Culture, Identity and Modernity in Britain and the Empire, 1660–1840*, Cambridge: Cambridge University Press, 2004; J. Marriott, *The Other Empire: Metropolis, India and Progress in the Colonial Imagination*, Manchester: Manchester University Press, 2003; and S. Sen, *Distant Sovereignty: National Imperialism and the Origins of British India*, New York and London: Routledge, 2002.

6 C.A. Bayly, 'Archaic and Modern Globalization in the Eurasian and African Arena, c. 1750–1850,' in *Globalization in World History*, ed. A. G. Hopkins, London: Pimlico, 2002, pp. 47–73. Bayly's work calls for moving beyond the centre/periphery dichotomy characteristic of world systems theory. Bose's *One Hundred Horizons* and M. Pearson's *The Indian Ocean*, London: Routledge, 2003 also speak to this dynamic, elaborating the role of interactions across the Indian Ocean. See also: R. Blyth, *The Empire of the Raj: India, Eastern Africa and the Middle East, 1858–1947*, New York: Palgrave Macmillan, 2003; J.-G. Deutsch and B. Reinwald (eds), *Space on the Move: Transformations of an Indian Ocean Seascape in the Nineteenth and Early Twentieth Centuries*, Berlin: Klaus Schwarze Verlag, 2002; and K.S. Mathew (ed.), *Mariners, Merchants and Oceans: Studies in Maritime History*, New Delhi: Manohar, 1995.

7 Pearson in *The Indian Ocean* makes the critique that studies of the Indian Ocean have focused too much on politics and trade, and not enough on the movement of tourists, information, religion, and disease. On merchant networks, see C. Markovits, *The Global World of Indian Merchants: Traders of Sind from Bukhara to Panama*, Cambridge: Cambridge University Press, 2000, as well as V. Padayachee and Robert Morell, 'Indian Merchants and Dukanwallahs in the Natal Economy, c. 1875–1914,' *Journal of Southern African Studies* 17, 1, 1991: 71–102. On the Indian Ocean as an economic space: N. Steengaard, 'The Indian Ocean Network and the Emerging World-Economy, circa 1500–1750' in *The Indian Ocean: Explorations in History, Commerce and Politics*, ed. S. Chandra, New Delhi: Sage, 1987.

8 For a global perspective on indentured labour see: D. Northrup, *Indentured Labor in the Age of Imperialism, 1834–1922*, Cambridge: Cambridge University Press, 1995. The work on Indian indentured labour is extensive. To name but a few of the more important titles: M. Carter, *Voices from Indenture: Experiences of Indian Migrants in the British Empire*, London-New York: Leicester University Press, 1996; M. Carter, *Servants, Sirdars and Settlers: Indians in Mauritius 1834–1874*, Delhi: Oxford University Press, 1995; R. Hoefte, *In Place of Slavery: A Social History of British Indian and Javanese Laborers in Suriname*, Gainesville, FL: University Press of Florida, 1998; Hugh Tinker, *A New System of Slavery: The Export of Indian Labour Overseas, 1830–1920*, 2nd ed., London: Hansib, 1993.

9 Soldiers have been mentioned by Bose in *One Hundred Horizons*, see chapter 4. On sailors, see J. E. Ewald, 'Crossers of the Sea: Slaves, Freedmen and Other Migrants in the Northwestern Indian Ocean, c. 1750–1914', *The American Historical Review* 105, 1, 2000: 69–91.

Introduction 7

10 An important precursor to this work, linking trade, religion and maritime power is S. Subrahmanyam, 'Of Imarat and Tijarat: Asian Merchants and State Power in the Western Indian Ocean, 1400 to 1750,' *Comparative Studies in Society and History* 37, 4, 1995: 750–80. On moving beyond landmasses to transnational maritime networks see P. Hulme, 'Subversive Archipelagos: Colonial Discourse and the Break-up of Continental Theory,' *Dispositio*, 14, 1989: 1–23.

11 This theme is beautifully conceptualized in F. Cooper and A. L. Stoler, *Tensions of Empire: Colonial Cultures in a Bourgeois World*, Berkeley, CA and London: University of California Press, 1997. For detailed discussions of the intersections between race, class and gender in colonial settings see also D. Ghosh, *Sex and the Family in Colonial India: The Making of Empire*, Cambridge: Cambridge University Press, 2004; P. Levine, ed., *Gender and Empire*, Oxford: Oxford University Press, 2004; A. L. Stoler, *Carnal Knowledge and Imperial Power: Race and the Intimate in Colonial Rule*, Berkeley, Los Angeles, CA and London, 2002; H. Fischer-Tiné, 'Britain's other Civilising Mission: Class-prejudice, European "Loaferism" and the Workhouse-system in Colonial India,' *Indian Economic and Social History Review* 42, 3, 2005: 295–338; T. Hubel, 'In Search of the British Indian in British India: White Orphans, Kipling's Kim and Class in Colonial India,' *Modern Asian Studies* 38, 1, 2004: 227–51; K. Ballhatchet, *Race, Sex and Class under the Raj: Imperial Attitudes and Policies and their Critics 1793–1905*, London: Weidenfeld and Nicholson 1980 and D. Arnold, 'European Orphans and Vagrants in India in the Nineteenth Century,' *Journal of Imperial and Commonwealth History* 7, 2, 1979: 104–27.

12 See E. Buettner, 'Problematic Spaces, Problematic Races: Defining Europeans in Late Colonial India,' *Women's History Review* 9, 2 2000: 277–99; S. Mizutani, 'Constitutions of the Colonising Self in Late British India: Race, Class and Environment', *Zinbun: Annals of the Institute for Research in Humanities, Kyoto University* 38, 2005: 21–75; and S. P. Mohanty, 'Drawing the Color Line: Kipling and the Culture of Colonial Rule,' in *The Bounds of Race: Perspectives on Hegemony and Resistance*, ed. D. La Capra, Ithaca, NY: Cornell University Press, 1991, pp. 311–43.

13 Birgit B. Rasmussen, ed., *The Making and Unmaking of Whiteness*, Durham, NC: Duke University Press, 2001; T. K Nakayama, ed., *Whiteness: The Communication of Social Identity*, Thousand Oaks, CA: Sage, 1999; M. Hill, ed., *Whiteness: A Critical Reader*, New York-London: New York University Press, 1997; R. Frankenberg, *White Women, Race Matters: the Social Construction of Whiteness*, Minneapolis, MN: University of Minnesota Press, 1994; and Idem ed., *Displacing Whiteness: Essays in Social and Cultural Criticism*, Durham, NC: Duke University Press, 1997.

14 D. Chakrabarty, *Provincialising Europe: Postcolonial Thought and Historical Difference*, Princeton, NJ: Princeton University Press, 2000, p. 43.

15 G.C. Spivak, 'Can the Subaltern Speak?' in *Marxism and the Interpretation of Culture*, ed. C. Nelson and L. Grossberg, Urbana: University of Illinois Press, 1988, 271–313. See also the discussion in A. Loomba, *Colonialism/Postcolonialism*, London: Routledge, 1998, pp. 231–44.

Bibliography

Printed material

Arnold, D., 'European Orphans and Vagrants in India in the Nineteenth Century,' *Journal of Imperial and Commonwealth History*, 7 (2) 1979: 104–27.

8 Introduction

Ballantyne, T., *Orientalism and Race: Aryanism in the British Empire*, Houndmills, Basingstoke and New York: Palgrave, 2002.
Ballhatchet, K., *Race, Sex and Class under the Raj: Imperial Attitudes and Policies and their Critics 1793–1905*, London: Weidenfeld and Nicolson, 1980.
Bates, C., (ed.), *Community, Empire and Migration: South Asians in Diaspora*, Hyderabad: Orient Longman, 2001.
Bayly, C. A., 'Archaic and Modern Globalization in the Eurasian and African Arena, c. 1750–1850,' in *Globalization in World History*, ed. A. G. Hopkins, London: Pimlico, 2002, pp. 47–73.
——, 'Beating the Boundaries: South Asian History, c. 1700–1850' in *South Asia and World Capitalism*, ed. S. Bose, Delhi: Oxford University Press, 1990, pp. 27–39.
Blyth, R., *The Empire of the Raj: India, Eastern Africa and the Middle East, 1858–1947*, New York: Palgrave Macmillan, 2003.
Bose, S., *A Hundred Horizons: The Indian Ocean in the Age of Global Empire*, Cambridge, MA : Harvard University Press, 2006.
Buettner, E., 'Problematic Spaces, Problematic Races: Defining Europeans in Late Colonial India,' *Women's History Review*, 9 (2) 2000: 277–99.
Burton, A., *After the Imperial Turn: Thinking With and Through the Nation*, Durham, NC: Duke University Press, 2003.
——, *Dwelling in the Archive: Women Writing, House, Home and History in Late Colonial India*, New Delhi: Oxford University Press, 2003.
Carter, M., *Servants, Sirdars and Settlers: Indians in Mauritius 1834–1874*, Delhi: Oxford University Press, 1995.
——, *Voices from Indenture: Experiences of Indian Migrants in the British Empire*, London-New York: Leicester University Press 1996.
Chakrabarty, D., *Provincialising Europe: Postcolonial Thought and Historical Difference*, Princeton, NJ: Princeton University Press, 2000.
——, 'Postcoloniality and the Artifice of History: Who Speaks for 'Indian' Pasts?', *Representations*, 37 (Winter 1992): 1–26.
Chatterjee, P., 'Whose Imagined Community?' in *Mapping the Nation*, ed. Gopal Balakrishnan, London: Verso, 1996, pp. 214–44.
Cooper, F., and Stoler, A. L., *Tensions of Empire: Colonial Cultures in a Bourgeois World*, Berkeley, CA and London: University of California Press, 1997.
Deutsch, J. G. and Reinwald, B., eds, *Space on the Move: Transformations of an Indian Ocean Seascape in the Nineteenth and Early Twentieth Centuries*, Berlin: Klaus Schwarze Verlag, 2002.
Ewald, J. E., 'Crossers of the Sea: Slaves, Freedmen and Other Migrants in the Northwestern Indian Ocean, c. 1750–1914', *The American Historical Review*, 105, No. 1. 2000: 69–91.
Fischer-Tiné, H., 'Britain's other Civilising Mission: Class-prejudice, European 'Loaferism' and the Workhouse-system in Colonial India,' *Indian Economic and Social History Review*, 42 (3), 2005: 295–338.
Frankenberg, R., *White Women, Race Matters: the Social Construction of Whiteness*, Minneapolis, MN: University of Minnesota Press, 1994.
——, *Displacing Whiteness: Essays in Social and Cultural Criticism*, Durham, NC: Duke University Press, 1997.
Ghosh, D., *Sex and the Family in Colonial India: The Making of Empire*, Cambridge: Cambridge University Press, 2004.

Ghosh, D., and Kennedy, D., eds, *Decentring Empire: Britain, India and the Transcolonial World*, New Delhi: Orient Longman, 2006.
Hill, M., ed., *Whiteness: A Critical Reader*, New York and London: New York University Press, 1997.
Hoefte, R., *In Place of Slavery: A Social History of British Indian and Javanese Laborers in Suriname*, Gainesville, FL: University Press of Florida, 1998.
Hubel, T., 'In Search of the British Indian in British India: White Orphans, Kipling's Kim and Class in Colonial India,' *Modern Asian Studies*, 38 (1), 2004: 227–51.
Hulme, P., 'Subversive Archipelagos: Colonial Discourse and the Break-up of Continental Theory,' *Dispositio*, 14, 1989: 1–23.
Levine, P., *Prostitution, Race, and Politics: Policing Venereal Disease in the British Empire*, Oxford: Routledge, 2003.
——, ed, *Gender and Empire*, Oxford: Oxford University Press, 2004.
Loomba, A., *Colonialism/Postcolonialism*, London: Routledge, 1998.
Markovits, C., Pouchepadass, J. and Subramanyam, S., eds, *Society and Circulation: Mobile People and Itinerant Cultures in South Asia, 1750–1950*, Delhi: Permanent Black 2003.
Markovits, C., *The Global World of Indian Merchants: Traders of Sind from Bukhara to Panama*, Cambridge University Press, 2000.
Marriott, J., *The Other Empire: Metropolis, India and Progress in the Colonial Imagination*, Manchester: Manchester University Press, 2003.
Mathew, K. S., ed., *Mariners, Merchants and Oceans: Studies in Maritime History*, New Delhi: Manohar, 1995.
Mizutani, S., 'Constitutions of the Colonising Self in Late British India: Race, Class and Environment', *Zinbun: Annals of the Institute for Research in Humanities, Kyoto University*, 38, 2005: 21–75.
Mohanty, S. P., 'Drawing the Color Line: Kipling and the Culture of Colonial Rule,' in *The Bounds of Race: Perspectives on Hegemony and Resistance*, ed. D. La Capra, Ithaca, NY: Cornell University Press, 1991, pp. 311–43.
Nakayama, T. K., ed., *Whiteness: The Communication of Social Identity*, Thousand Oaks, CA: Sage, 1999.
Northrup, D., *Indentured Labor in the Age of Imperialism, 1834–1922*, Cambridge: Cambridge University Press, 1995.
Padayachee, V. and Morell. R., 'Indian Merchants and Dukanwallahs in the Natal Economy, *c.* 1875–1914,' *Journal of Southern African Studies*, 17, No 1, 1991: 71–102.
Rasmussen, B. B., ed., *The Making and Unmaking of Whiteness*, Durham, NC: Duke University Press, 2001.
Sarkar, S., *Writing Social History*, Delhi: Oxford University Press, 1998.
——, *Beyond Nationalist Frames: Postmodernism, Hindu Fundamentalism, History*, Delhi: Permanent Black, 2003.
Sen, S., *Distant Sovereignty: National Imperialism and the Origins of British India*, New York and London, 2002.
Spivak, G. C., 'Can the Subaltern Speak?' in *Marxism and the Interpretation of Culture*, Cary Nelson and Lawrence Grossberg eds, Urbana, IL: University of Illinois Press, 1988, pp. 271–313.
Steengaard, N., 'The Indian Ocean Network and the Emerging World-Economy, circa 1500–1750' in *The Indian Ocean: Explorations in History, Commerce and Politics*, ed. Chandra, S., New Delhi: Sage, 1987.

Stoler, A. L., *Carnal Knowledge and Imperial Power: Race and the Intimate in Colonial Rule*, Berkeley, Los Angeles, CA and London, 2002.

Subrahmanyam, S., 'Of Imarat and Tijarat: Asian Merchants and State Power in the Western Indian Ocean, 1400 to 1750,' *Comparative Studies in Society and History*, 37, No. 4, 1995: 750–80.

Tinker, H., *A New System of Slavery: The Export of Indian Labour Overseas, 1830–1920*, 2nd ed., London: Hansib, 1993.

Verdery, K., 'Whither 'Nation' and 'Nationalism'?' in *Mapping the Nation*, ed. G. Balakrishnan, London: Verso, 1996, pp. 226–34.

Wilson, K., ed., *A New Imperial History: Culture, Identity and Modernity in Britain and the Empire, 1660–1840*, Cambridge: Cambridge University Press, 2004.

Wolf, E.R., *Europe and the People Without History*, Berkeley, Los Angeles, CA and London: University of California, 1997.

Part I
Subaltern mobility and the problem of control and containment

1 Networks of subordination – networks of the subordinated
The ordered spaces of South Asian maritime labour in an age of imperialism (c. 1890–1947)
Ravi Ahuja

Introduction: the 'lascar' and the Empire

South Asian sailors had toiled on sailing ships of the English East India Company even before the nineteenth century, but it was the combined expansion of British imperialism and steam navigation in the Indian Ocean region that boosted employment figures. As early as in 1855, it was estimated that between 10,000 and 12,000 'lascars' or 'native seamen' were engaged in the British merchant marine on ships plying the seas of Africa and Asia and about 60 per cent of them originated from South Asia.[1] The five decades between the opening of the Suez Canal and the end of the First World War were not only the age of 'high imperialism' but also a period when 'lascar' employment rose continuously. '[T]he lascar is a fairly good sailor, is cheaper in respect of both food and wages, requires less forecastle accommodation, is more alienable to discipline, and, as a matter of course, is gradually working his way against the British seamen', noted the Calcutta Shipping Master in 1896.[2] The last assertion is confirmed by maritime census figures that are available from 1886, when 16,673 or 8.2 per cent of 204,470 sailors on British merchant vessels were said to be lascars. In 1914, the British merchant marine's total employment figures had risen to 295,652, of which 51,616 or 17.5 per cent were lascars.[3] Thus, if total employment had increased by about 50 per cent, lascar employment had trebled. However, many more lascars were actually engaged in Indian ports than those mentioned in British maritime censuses: As early as in 1899, they were estimated at 45,000 in each of Bombay and Calcutta, the two major ports of recruitment.[4] More reliable port statistics are available for the early 1920s, when about 33,000 and 44,000 Indian seamen were annually shipped from Bombay and Calcutta respectively.[5] From about the turn of the century, the Indian Ocean labour market was also tapped by shipping companies of other European states. Most prominent was the German 'Hansa Linie' who reportedly engaged 4,000 lascars on average in the early 1900s, while official sources quoted a figure of approximately 3,000 South Asian seamen who had annually been recruited in Bombay alone by 'foreign' companies before the First World War.[6] When a long-drawn crisis of British merchant shipping, as well as technological changes, resulted in a drastic decline of maritime employment in the 1920s and 1930s, the figures for lascars remained more stable. Hence in 1938, 50,700 or 26.4 per cent of the 192,375 sailors employed on British merchant vessels were lascars.[7] In 1960, more than a decade after the end of British rule in India, seamen 'under Asian agreements' still made up about a quarter of the British merchant fleet's labour force.[8] Yet India's independence and partition in 1947, and the emergence of air passenger traffic and container shipping, transformed South Asia's maritime labour scene fundamentally in the two decades after the Second World War.[9] Thus, the 'age of the lascar' lasted from about the 1890s until the mid-twentieth century. This chapter focuses on employment of Indian Ocean seafarers on British merchant steamships in this period.

Let us ask first what precisely was a 'lascar' and what rendered these maritime workers so attractive to European shipping companies? In the eighteenth century, the Persian word 'las(h)kar' had been used by the British as a denomination of South Asian sailors as well as of non-fighting military personnel (such as 'tent-pitchers' or the 'gun lascars' who moved artillery equipment).[10] By the nineteenth century, the phrase had entered the European maritime language as a generic term for sailors from colonies of the Indian Ocean region. In Indian languages, there are various words to designate a sailor, and in nineteenth- and twentieth-century sources it appears that South Asian seamen preferred to call themselves 'jehazis/jehajis' (ship people) or, more often, 'khalasis' (another word of Persian origin, literally meaning 'freed person' and referring to maritime labourers of a superior status).[11] On steamers, however, these designations seem to have been used only for deckhands. In the engine rooms, workers appear to have referred to themselves not as seamen but rather as 'ag-wallahs' (Hindustani: agvala, a direct translation of the English 'fireman') in clear distinction to the 'panivalas' ('water men').[12] The term 'lascar', on the other hand, being one of several categories for colonial, 'native' labour, carried connotations of a low, subordinated status and of inferiority to 'white' workers. If an 'unskilled' Asian labourer was not a worker but a 'coolie' and an Indian infantryman not a soldier but a 'sepoy', an Indian Ocean sailor was not a seaman but merely a 'lascar'. This discriminating label stuck to Indian seamen even after the end of colonial rule when it was ordered, without much success, not to use it in official correspondence.[13]

This 'inferiority' became legally inscribed from 1814 when the first laws regulating the employment of Indian Ocean seamen on British ships were enacted. It was at this point that the generic expression 'lascar' was turned into a legal term distinguishing 'native' maritime labour from white 'seamen'.[14] Discriminating legislation concerning South Asian seamen was passed by British governments until well after the end of the colonial period reflecting and reinforcing the attractions the employment of lascars held for British shipping companies.[15] These attractions were mainly that lascars were much cheaper and had fewer rights than their European colleagues. Their cheapness was not only a matter of lower wages that have consistently amounted only to between a third and a fifth of the pay of European sailors from the nineteenth century up to the 1980s,[16] engaging crews under so-called Asiatic or Lascar Articles, the special contracts for 'lascars and other native seamen', had further material advantages for employers. According to these legal instruments, a 'lascar' 'required' only about half the accommodation space on board to which a 'seaman' was entitled (36 instead of 72 cubic feet before 1914; afterwards 72 instead of 120 cubic feet).[17] Criticism was regularly countered with the argument that the lascars' 'accommodation is infinitely superior to anything they are accustomed to their own homes on shore, while on boardship [sic] they have the additional advantage of pure air, pure water and good food'.[18] As for the 'good food', their regulated rations were, too, considerably cheaper than those of Europeans and complaints appear to have been frequent though rarely recorded.[19] When occasionally an inspection declared a ship's food supplies 'unfit for human consumption', 'lascars' received less compensation than 'seamen'.[20] Though workmen's compensation in case of an accident was provided for by law, lascars and their families often found it difficult to enforce their claims.[21] 'War Risk Compensations' paid to dependents of drowned lascars after the First World War were very much lower than those granted to the families of deceased British sailors.[22] Moreover, shipping officials and colonial bureaucrats succeeded well into the 1920s in defending the practice to recruit adolescent (and therefore cheaper) workers as agvalas and lascars against criticism from different quarters. The standard argument was that 'Indians mature much more rapidly than Europeans'.[23] The lascars' inferior legal status further reduced the cost of their labour power. For instance, they were not engaged for single voyages, but for fixed periods not extending 24, later 12 months. Recruitment costs and lay days were thus cut back, as was the lascars' freedom to claim their discharge.[24] Moreover, Indian seamen were to be returned to a port in India at the end of their contract and were not entitled to terminate their agreement outside South Asia. In British ports, they could be 'transferred' to any other vessel including those of different companies even against their will.[25] When in port, they were often denied the right to shore leave, especially in the USA and South Africa.[26] Hence, while a promoter of lascar employment on British ships pointed out in the early 1900s that Indian seamen were 'more completely the servants of the shipowner [...] than any other group of men doing similar work',[27] social reformers contended in 1940 that the lascars' legal status was a 'form of servitude'.[28] This critique was insofar appropriate as 'Lascar Articles' restricted the labourers' freedom to terminate a contract with their employer. They were another specific colonial application of 'master and servant law', i.e. of a type of labour law that inscribed a legal inferiority of workers to their employers.[29] That lascars were 'more completely the servants of the shipowner' was also perceivable from their working hours. The so-called khalasi watch system, an experienced shipmaster explained, simply meant:

'all hands at all times'.³⁰ A standard command formula in simple Hindustani, published in a 'Lascari' dictionary designed for the use of officers of P&O steamers thus read: 'Yih log, hamesha taiyar hona, rat-ko, din-ko' ('These people are to be always ready, day and night').³¹ No law regulated working hours, neither the duration of shifts nor of periods of recovery, and colonial administrators resisted the 'riotous extravagance of social legislation',³² in this respect successfully until the end of the colonial period. There were, of course, some informal arrangements regulating the working time of the ship's departments (firemen, whose working conditions were exceedingly strenuous, had shorter watches than khalasis, while stewards had to be in almost permanent attendance). The lack of any formal regulation, however, did not merely imply that lascars worked longer hours than 'white' seamen, but also that they were more comprehensively at their officers' disposal.³³ The khalasi's labour relations, therefore, resembled not so much those of formally free labourers who, on the basis of (largely fictional, but by no means inconsequential) legal equality, had surrendered for a wage the utilisation of their labour power to an employer for a certain, clearly defined period of the day. Lascars' employment relations were (despite major and important differences) structurally more akin to those of plantation labourers whose 'indenture' contracts subordinated them under their employer *as persons* for the whole duration of their contract.

Reduced labour costs enabled shipping companies to hire lascar crews that were at least 50 but more often 100 per cent larger than a European crew would have been on a comparable vessel. This manning scale was justified in official and unofficial documents, like many other special arrangements for the regulation of lascar labour, in terms of a racially determined inferior efficiency of 'Asiatics'. Experienced shipmasters admitted, however, that the quotidian tasks on a steamship could be handled at much greater ease with a larger 'lascar crew'. On a lascar-manned steamer, wrote Captain W. H. Hood, '[t]he work gets done, and decently done, without the officers having to off coats and bustle about like a b'osn's mate', while several witnesses had assured the Manning Committee of 1896 that 'with the much larger number of lascars which such ships are able to carry they are worked and kept better than they would be by a European crew, and the men are always attentive and obedient and never give trouble'.³⁴

The main attractions of 'lascar' labour for employers – low cost and greater controllability – were not only due to economic factors like chronic underemployment and low wage levels that would have also characterised other subregions of the Indian Ocean during the period under review; ultimately, it was the political control over the 'sources' of maritime labour recruitment that rendered South Asian seamen even 'cheaper' and more 'docile' than Chinese and Malay seafarers. India's colonial status facilitated the control over the movements of a potentially highly mobile workforce: South Asian steamship labour did not freely wander about the Indian Ocean region and much less so beyond. Lascars had to return to South Asia and, before 1956, most of them appear to have done so. This prevented them from achieving higher pay and superior rights either by signing on in western ports under regular articles or by entering the non-maritime labour market in metropolitan countries.[35] It was in this context that the loose descriptive label 'lascar', which had earlier designated Indian Ocean maritime labour in general, was in the course of the nineteenth century turned into a legal term covering *colonial* maritime labour only. The legal definition of who exactly was a 'lascar' became a highly contentious issue between British Indian and metropolitan social forces and was repeatedly changed. Ultimately, under the influence of anti-migrant policies in post-First World War Britain, the term came to apply exclusively to seamen born on the Indian subcontinent or residing in Aden.[36]

The problem: maritime labour networks in the Indian Ocean

'Lascars' on European steamships were among the first industrial wage labourers of the Indian Ocean region. They moved between cosmopolitan port cities and organized themselves, at least in South Asia, in trade unions earlier and in greater proportion than most occupational groups in modern industry.[37] So, one might easily be led to the assumption that the age of the steamship moulded maritime labour into a socially and culturally integrated (if not homogenous then at least syncretistic) industrial workforce, into a nucleus of an integrated Indian Ocean working class. This was, however, not the case. The 'modern sector' of the maritime labour market was created along ethnic lines and remained highly exclusive and segmented. By far, not all communities of seafarers of the Indian Ocean region gained access to this sector and some were apparently sidelined in the period under review. Moreover, new entrants into the world of steamship labour were not usually recruited from supposedly cosmopolitan lower classes of the port cities but, at least in the case of South Asia, from a surprisingly restricted range of rural 'labour catchment areas'. There is no denying that the massive expansion of European merchant shipping in the age of high imperialism incorporated a very considerable number of working men of the Indian Ocean region into an increasingly international maritime labour market, but there is little evidence for the emergence of a socially and culturally homogenous class of Indian Ocean seamen and port labourers. Consider for instance the case of Sylhet, then a rural district in eastern Bengal (now in Bangladesh) and one of the most important recruitment areas of the British merchant marine in the period under review. If Sylhetis are today one of the major South Asian immigrant groups in Britain, the terrain of their immigration was prepared by lascars since the late nineteenth century. The incorporation of Sylheti smallholders into an international labour market has, however, not resulted in any 'rubbing off' of Sylheti 'identity' but rather, as Katy Gardner has pointed out, in a redefinition and even in a heightened awareness of this subregional 'identity'.[38]

Similar processes have, of course, been discussed extensively in many other fields of labour and migration history. But how do we conceptualise this dual phenomenon of expanding incorporation and simultaneous differentiation? More often than not, historians and anthropologists have dealt with this duality in rather vague terms – 'on the one hand' incorporation, 'on the other' differentiation – without examining the interdependence of the two processes. Others ascribe the persistence of cultural difference to an alleged 'homeostasis' of 'primordial identities' that proved to be immune against the onslaught of colonial state intervention and market incorporation.[39] Yet others, more aware of the formative role of quotidian social experience in processes of cultural reproduction and transformation, have considered the assertion and/or redefinition of 'difference' as reactive, as well as proactive, subaltern strategies of coping with incorporation into the modern state (empire or nation) and into the capitalist world market.[40] According to the latter view, the various and culturally distinct networks of maritime labourers in the Indian Ocean would appear as modes of resistance against the levelling modern forces of commodification and territorialization (or at least as appropriations of the new realities created by these forces). By virtue of their transterritoriality, these networks could thus be perceived, in spatial terms, as generators of 'spaces of disorder', as counter-forces subverting the dominant spaces of market and state.

Much evidence can be marshalled in support of this view, which catches, however, only one side of the interdependence of the dual processes of incorporation and differentiation. Any exaggeration of the subversive momentum bears the risk, however, of concealing the violence of domination. Let us reconsider, therefore, some suggestions by Eric R. Wolf that hint at a more comprehensive and dialectical framework of analysis. 'Capitalist accumulation [...] continues to engender new working classes in widely dispersed areas of the world', wrote Wolf in his *Europe and the People Without History* and continued:

> It recruits these working classes from a wide variety of social and cultural backgrounds, and inserts them into variable political and economic hierarchies. The new working classes change these hierarchies by their presence, and are themselves changed by the forces to which they are exposed. On one level, therefore, the diffusion of the capitalist mode creates everywhere a wider unity through the constant reconstitution of its characteristic capital–labour relationship. On another level, it also *creates diversity, accentuating social opposition and segmentation even as it unifies* [emphasis added].[41]

In one of his theoretical essays, Wolf identified the forces creating this interdependence of the processes of differentiation and incorporation more clearly. He argued that the continuously reproduced 'division of the capitalist labor market into segments *both creates and feeds on* [emphasis added] differentiations of identity by gender, ethnicity, and social race among the labor force'.[42] In other words, when various groups were incorporated into an international labour market, they were incorporated into a segmented and continuously re-segmented structure, which integrated differential ethnic or other identities and even created new ones – Justin Willis' study of the changing labour system in the port of colonial Mombasa and its impact on the formation of a new Mijikenda ethnicity is a particularly impressive illustration of the latter case.[43] To sum up the argument, 'differentiation' will be understood in this paper not as being inconsistent with 'incorporation', but as the very process in which incorporation is articulated and materialized in an infinite variety of concrete forms.

In order to understand how this 'differential incorporation' into an international maritime labour market worked in the case of South Asian seamen, we need to look closely at various institutional arrangements. We have already referred to the role of colonial law in defining the lascars' position in the international maritime labour market. However, other institutions such as kinship, locality and debt also contributed to connecting rural hinterlands of the Indian Ocean region with the world of imperial steam shipping (and hence to the 'production' of an ordered social space). The specific combination of such institutional arrangements that linked a particular group of maritime labourers to the international labour market will, in this paper, be called a 'network'. The phrase 'network' is thus used in the sense of an *infrastructure of differential incorporation* that is produced and reproduced by historical actors over a longer time-span.[44] Such networks should, however, not be understood as unidirectional conductors in a smooth functional system of labour supply; 'subaltern networks' were constituted through strained and contradictory relations between historical actors with widely differing interests and could, therefore, be used for a variety of conflicting purposes.[45]

This becomes clearer if we look at one of the key actors in maritime labour networks, the so-called serang. Derived from the Persian word 'sarhang' (commander, overseer), this term was used almost everywhere in the Indian Ocean region from Mombasa via Bombay and Calcutta to Singapur as a denomination for intermediaries in the maritime labour market, for labour subcontractors, recruiters and foremen of seamen and port workers.[46] On steamships, the serang was the Indian equivalent of a European boatswain. Yet, as Balachandran has shown, colonial records and other sources describe the serang in strikingly ambivalent terms. He is represented as a crimp, who was said, however, to be often related to members of his gang or to hail from the same village. He figures as an exploitative moneylender or 'corrupt' middleman at one time and as the lascars' spokesman at another. He was obstinately defended by employers and officials as indispensable for imposing discipline and 'harmony' on lascar crews and simultaneously decried as a potential strike leader. He was believed to be a traditional, pre-capitalist institutional form of organizing social labour in South Asia but if trade union leaders emerged at all from among the lascars, they were likely to have established their standing by functioning as serangs or as butlers (the equivalent of the serang in the saloon department).[47] We will return to this interesting social figure in greater detail below, but what should be underscored here is this: the serang's ambivalent position reflects the fact that maritime labour networks functioned in both ways – as an organizational infrastructure for the recruitment and subordination of labour and as an organizational infrastructure used by the lascars to appropriate their employment conditions to their own purposes and even as a means of combining against their employers. Networks of subordination could thus, at least temporarily, be turned into networks of the subordinated.

Infrastructures of differential incorporation can be studied in various ways, but the remainder of this chapter focuses on aspects of *social space*, on the changing 'seascape' of the Indian Ocean in so far as it was constituted by maritime labour networks.[48] It is argued that this 'seascape' was spatially reorganized (or, to use the phraseology of this volume, 'reordered') under British imperialism during the six decades before South Asia's partition and independence when modern colonial port cities emerged as novel 'gateways' to the ocean, when areas in the interior of the subcontinent were newly connected to the sea while some coastal regions' maritime links deteriorated. The networks under research extended from India's interior regions well beyond the subcontinent, to ports elsewhere on the Indian Ocean Rim and further on to the metropolises of global capitalism. Yet, for practical reasons, this chapter examines only those sections of maritime labour networks that lay within South Asia.[49] The next section identifies the relocation of maritime labour networks under colonialism, and the following sections examine the rural origins of lascars and analyse household strategies combining agriculture and seafaring. The emergence of networks that spanned the distance between recruitment ports and 'labour catchment areas' is then discussed and the final section draws preliminary conclusions and sketches perspectives of further research.

Redirecting maritime labour networks: colonial recruitment ports

One of the most permanent and irreversible effects of colonial rule in South Asia was, in the words of the geographer David Sopher, the 'spatial reorganization' of the subcontinent.[50] This included a changed pattern of urban development according to which many older centres, usually located in the interior, declined, while large colonial metropolises like Bombay, Calcutta and Madras emerged on (or at least not too far from) the shores of the Indian Ocean. According to the needs of the imperial economy (such as extraction of natural resources and tropical products, establishment of markets for English industrial products) the communications infrastructure was not only technologically revolutionized and quantitatively expanded but also spatially redirected towards these imperial port cities, which came to be the termini of trunk roads and railway lines. Yet for all contemporary prophecies of a 'disappearance from the Eastern seas of the Country-wallah, Buggalow, Dhow, and all other crazy country craft',[51] Indian sailing vessels continued to be a major factor in the subcontinent's maritime economy even after the rise of imperial steam navigation. Indian coasters were, for instance, rather successful in opening up a space for themselves within the imperial transport system, especially in Western India where the total tonnage of 'native craft' merely declined by ten per cent between the 1870s and 1915.[52] During the following decades, thousands of Indian sailing vessels continued to ply the Western Indian Ocean (according to one official estimate as many as 15,000) and their number even appears to have increased during the Second World War, when shipping capacity was scarce.[53] However, the rise of steam navigation in the Indian Ocean region, no less connected to the exigencies and institutions of imperialism than railway construction,[54] resulted in a massive centralization of trade and shipping in a small number of colonial port cities. This was also due to the technological transformations of the steam age, as intercontinental steamshipping required large investment in harbour and dock facilities, which were provided in the late nineteenth century in only a few colonial port cities.[55] Correspondingly, the recruitment of lascars was not organized along the established lines of South Asian ocean transport. While dhonis, phatemaris, baghalahs and other Indian sailing vessels were based at and continued to draw their (still very sizeable) workforce from numerous small ports along the subcontinent's coastline, the recruitment of steamship crews was highly centralized and relied fully on Calcutta and Bombay. Such crews were almost exclusively hired in these two colonial metropolises, while other South Asian ports were (with the temporary exception of Karachi) only used to replace lascars who had died, become incapacitated or jumped ship during the voyage. To give an idea of the quantitative dimensions, it may be mentioned that lascar recruitment amounted from 1926 to 1929 on average to annually 58,300 in Calcutta and to 34,600 in Bombay.[56] Underemployment was notoriously high among lascars. Seamen's organizations thus estimated in 1930 the total number of seamen 'belonging' to (but not necessarily always present at) the ports of Calcutta, Bombay and Karachi at 140,000, 70,000 and 25,000 respectively.[57]

Spatial centralization of lascar recruitment was paralleled by centralization in organizational terms. Before the foundation of the Scindia Steam Navigation Company in 1919, transcontinental and even coastal steam vessels were almost invariably owned by large British liners. The Peninsular and Oriental Steam Navigation Company (P&O), which dominated shipping between South Asia and Europe, was the largest recruiter of Indian seamen in Bombay, while about half of the crews hired in Calcutta worked on vessels of the British India Steam Navigation Company (BI), which controlled much of the steamship business across the Indian Ocean and along South Asia's coasts.[58] These two giant shipping firms merged into a single, almost monopolistic company in 1914, but even earlier both had been deeply interwoven with the imperial state who subsidized them heavily by means of mail contracts.⁵⁹ Both companies had their own recruitment organizations, which were left largely unchecked by any state agency. The other liners provided themselves with crews with the assistance and under the supervision of colonial officials, the Shipping Masters of Bombay and Calcutta, who had sometimes been shipmasters for many years of P&O or BI steamers before their appointment.⁶⁰ Lascar recruitment was a profitable and, once again, highly centralized business in itself. In Bombay, a Parsi entrepreneurial family, the Chichgars, reportedly entered this line of business as early as in the mid-nineteenth century, established themselves as the only legal recruitment agency for the merchant marine and continued to operate as 'licensed shipping brokers' up to the 1930s.⁶¹ In Calcutta, recruitment was organized on slightly less monopolistic lines. Here a number of 'licensed shipping brokers' who were usually designated as 'ghat serangs' (i.e. port serangs) had divided up the recruitment business between themselves.⁶²

Villages and steamships: the lascars' rural origins

If lascar recruitment was focused on Bombay and Calcutta, it should not be assumed that maritime labour networks originated in these cities. South Asian sailors were, as a rule, no permanent city dwellers and the social networks that connected them to the maritime labour market extended to minor port towns and rural villages sometimes hundreds of miles away. Before we turn to identifying the major 'catchment areas', it is necessary to point out that steam navigation created somewhat different demands on skill and organization of labour than sail navigation. On a steamship, only a part of the crew required some of the hereditary occupational knowledge of seafaring communities, while those working in the engine room as trimmers and stokers or the numerous stewards, cooks and 'pantrymen' of large passenger vessels needed rather different skills. Moreover, along with the bridge, the engine room emerged as a second centre of authority on steamers, and in order to avoid conflicts between shipmaster and chief engineer, the navigational crew was strictly divided into a 'deck' and an 'engine' department, while the 'purser's' (or 'saloon') department formed a third distinct element. Accordingly, the workers of the three departments were often recruited from different social and ethnic groups in South Asia. While most lascars hired in Calcutta were Muslims from the districts of Sylhet, Chittagong and Noakhali in Eastern Bengal and could, therefore, communicate with some difficulty, the Bombay crews were far more segregated in religious, linguistic and ethnic terms: Punjabi Muslim 'ag-wallahs' of the engine department would have found it difficult to make themselves understood with the Christian Goanese stewards who would in turn have had little in common with Hindu khalasis from Gujarat. This ethnic heterogeneity was, however, of a controlled kind – 'mixed crews' were not appreciated and suspected to be troublesome by shipmasters.⁶³ Within each of the three departments of a steamship, cultural homogeneity was preferred (and often achieved for at least the core of the departmental crew).[64] Their work places and even their living quarters were apart on board ship. Every department had its own cook and ate separately. Thus, crews were segmented, rather than heterogenous, in terms of ethnicity.[65]

Turning to the sources of recruitment, it is clear that only the 'deckhands' or khalasis were predominantly (but not exclusively) recruited from seafaring communities. Many of these workers had already acquired navigational skills either on coasters or, especially in Bengal, on riverboats.[66] However, not all of the communities plying South Asian sailing vessels were represented on steamships indicating again a major transformation of the maritime labour market and of the Indian Ocean 'seascape' in general. Hence, the Coromandel Coast in the subcontinent's Southeast that had been a main area of shipbuilding, and coastal as well as transcontinental shipping for many centuries, is rarely mentioned as a recruitment area for Calcutta in contrast, for instance, to the Lakhadive and Maldive islands which are at an even greater distance.[67] Calcutta deckhands were, however, predominantly Muslims from Noakhali and Chittagong, the coastal districts of eastern Bengal.[68] About three-quarters of the Bombay khalasis were reported to be Muslims, too, though a Gujarati Hindu fishing caste, the Kharwas, was also among the communities most favoured by recruiting agents and shipmasters. On the west coast, recruitment focused on specific coastal settlements. North of Bombay, recruitment towns were in the region of Gujarat and included Diu and Ghogha on the peninsula of Kathiawar as well as Surat and Daman on the opposite side of the Gulf of Khambhat. The most important recruitment area for khalasis was, however, the Konkani coast south of Bombay and more specifically a number of coastal towns in the Ratnagiri and Kolaba districts and in the princely state of Janjira.[69] The two communities of Konkani Muslims who are reported to have migrated to Bombay to be employed as seamen both claimed Arabic descent and combined seafaring with agriculture. High-status Jama'tis, however, also engaged in trade, while Daldis appear to have relied more heavily on fishing for their subsistence.[70] Ratnagiri district was one of the major recruitment areas for industrial labour in Western India; about twenty per cent of the population of Bombay originated from this area in the early decades of the twentieth century.[71] The specific pressures created by the system of land tenure in this district may also have induced members of its Muslim communities to seek employment with the Royal Indian Marine and the British merchant navy as a supplementary source of income.[72]

The connection between local systems of land tenure and maritime recruitment is, however, more apparent when we turn to the 'catchment areas' for stewards and engine room crews. Catholic villagers from Goa appear to have been the first non-seafaring people who gained access to the newly emerging market for steamship labour as early as in the middle of the nineteenth century. The Portuguese colonial administration increasingly interfered with corporate land rights of the 'communidades' (village communities) and created a growing fragmentation of the land held by Catholics through new inheritance laws, thus inducing them to seek supplementary sources of income elsewhere. Being Christians, they had distinct advantages over Hindus and Muslims in getting jobs in the service sector of British colonial settlements.[73] A large majority of the Catholic migrants who found work in Bombay as stewards on steamships or in various other, often domestic service occupations originated from the 'velhas conquistas', the 'old conquest' areas of coastal Goa.[74] By the turn of the century, Goan Catholics had succeeded in almost totally excluding all competitors from this segment of the city's maritime labour market and British shipmasters labelled Goa a 'land of servants'.[75] In 1927–28, 10,480 Goanese were signed on in Bombay, 'almost all in the steward's department'.[76] Even in distant Calcutta, 2,060 Goan Christians were hired for the 'purser's department' of British steamships in 1922–23, though the majority of stewards appears to have been recruited here from Muslim inhabitants of Dacca and Calcutta as well as from the community of 'Anglo–Indians'.[77]

As for coal trimmers and firemen, they were clearly not recruited from the urban poor. They were typically Muslims from rural areas where a fragmented structure of property coincided with low agricultural productivity and they were much more often small landholders than agricultural labourers. Thus, the Deputy Commissioner of Sylhet stressed in 1913 that lascars were recruited in this district from an 'independent class' of Muslims 'who are by no means poor and not forced to go abroad in search of labour like the coolies who are recruited for tea gardens from districts which are liable to periodic famines'.[78] It has been argued that the absence of a 'permanent' revenue settlement and, correspondingly, of big landlords as well as the need of smallholding households to open up supplementary sources of income distinguished Sylhet district from other districts of Bengal and rendered its less fertile parts into the main 'catchment area' for Calcutta lascars.[79] While at least river navigation was extensive in Sylhet, the firemen and coal trimmers hired in Bombay originated increasingly from Northern Punjab or the North-West Frontier Provinces, where no link to seafaring had ever existed. These 'ag-wallahs' were Punjabis or Pashtuns, mostly Muslims and, again, often the younger sons of smallholding families in arid agricultural tracts. Syed Rasul, a former fireman from this area, may have expressed the experience of many when he remembered: 'I had only enough land to grow a little food – not enough for next season food'.[80] From the early twentieth century onwards, men from India's Northwest appear to have sidelined the previously dominating 'Sidis' (or 'Africans') from Somalia and Zanzibar in engine rooms of the Western Indian Ocean: The 'Punjabi [...] has even ousted the Seedie boy from favouritism', asserted Captain W. H. Hood in 1903.[81] Correspondingly, twentieth-century reports on seamen and dock workers in Bombay mentioned only few Africans, while their number was said to have amounted to about 1,000 in 1864.[82] Though Somalis continued to be recruited in Aden for British steamers, the main recruitment areas of the colonial Indian Army for Punjabi and Pashtun Muslims, namely the districts of Rawalpindi, Jhelum, Attock and Peshawar, were increasingly preferred as recruitment grounds for Bombay engine room crews especially during the First World War, and many demobilized sepoys found employment with the British Merchant Marine in the post-war period.[83] However, a sizeable proportion of the Bombay agvalas also originated from other parts of Punjab and especially from Mirpur, an area belonging to the princely state of Kashmir.[84] In sum, it is clear that access to the maritime labour markets of Bombay and Calcutta was restricted to workers from certain regions. Such 'labour catchment areas' were neither solely determined by the availability of specific seafaring skills nor necessarily by spatial proximity. The colonial political economy of the recruitment areas (and particularly their revenue system and agrarian structure), its administrative infrastructure (e.g. the recruitment officers of the colonial army in northern Punjab) and cultural framework (such as the prevalence of Catholicism in many villages of coastal Goa) were other determinants of the propensity and ability of specific socio-cultural groups in a certain town or area to gain access to the maritime labour market.

Agriculture and seafaring: tracing lascar household strategies

Thus, we have identified sets of nodal points between which recruitment networks for South Asian steamship labour were established: First, a number of coastal and inland districts, and second, the colonial port cities Bombay and Calcutta. Recruitment networks between these nodal points often displayed a remarkable durability, for instance in the case of Goan catholic villages, some of which have apparently been continuously linked for one and a half centuries to the Bombay maritime labour market.[85] This stability reflects the enduring village links of maritime labourers and the efforts of kinship groups and village communities to exclude 'outsiders' from the labour market segment to which they had gained access – the reason being, of course, that a reduction of competition turned maritime labour into a more reliable source of income. Strategies of specific kinship groups or (stratified) village communities of combining rural and urban income sources could, however, only be successful because they coincided with employer interest. As in other colonial industries, shipping companies preferred labourers who had additional yet insufficient means of subsistence, which rendered higher wages and more permanent labour relations dispensable.[86]

The availability of agricultural income sources, the question of whether the lascar was 'essentially a peasant' or an industrial worker who strove for regular employment on steamships was, however, a constant matter of dispute between employers and colonial state agencies on the one side, and seamen's trade unions on the other. There is unfortunately, though perhaps not accidentally, little documentary evidence concerning the economic activities and situation of lascars outside maritime employment. Shipping companies and colonial administration made little effort in screening this segment of the labour market, which was usually well supplied and created few problems despite low material standards. For them, unspecific references to agricultural resources of the lascars sufficed to 'prove' the redundancy and inapplicability of social security measures, such as unemployment insurance, in the context of Indian maritime labour.[87] It was, therefore, predominantly left to social reformers and trade unionists to closely examine the situation of Indian seamen.[88] In most of their reports, they stressed that a majority of Indian seamen had 'become a permanent part of the working-classes [...] and are not prone to give up their vocation unless under the stress of adverse circumstances'.[89] Such observations apparently reflect a *tendency* towards 'de-peasantization' and are corroborated by evidence indicating that a significant minority of the maritime labour force did 'follow the sea constantly and [... does] not go away from the sea for long periods'.[90] However, Dinkar Desai's statement in 1940 that the 'agrarian moorings of the Indian sailor have long been snapped' is clearly exaggerated.[91] Trade unionists like Desai were likely to underplay their clients' non-maritime and rural income sources in order to strengthen their case for subsistence wages, more regular employment and social insurance schemes. Yet even Balachandran's otherwise excellent studies on Indian seamen tend to perpetuate this image of the lascar as a fully proletarianized worker who had no means of subsistence other than steamship wage labour. Thus, according to his view, the 'context of contestation' or field-of-force, where maritime labour relations were forged, was formed by three agencies: 'capital, the state and the working-class'.[92] Fragmentary evidence from colonial records together with published memories of Sylheti lascars and several anthropological studies indicate, however, that sections of the smallholding peasantry need to be included, too.

First, it is evident that even for the lascar as an individual the income from steamship labour was way below a subsistence wage. Hence, trade union representatives stated to the 'Royal Commission on Labour in India' (RCLI) in 1929 that Bombay seamen could live off the wages of a year of maritime employment for four to six months after the end of their contract in their villages, but that they succeeded in being hired as lascars, on average, only every third year.[93] Working on steamships thus covered only about half of their subsistence and forced them to look for other sources of income both in their home villages and in town. Information concerning Calcutta points in the same direction: of an estimated 140,000 seamen 'belonging' to the port, less than 60,000 succeeded in being employed in 1929. But, for the remaining 80,000 lascars, shipping master and trade unionists agreed that only a minority, between 12,000 and 20,000, stayed in Calcutta in search of maritime employment at one time.[94]

Second, and this is where the networks come in, Indian seamen cannot be construed to have been autonomous economic actors but have to be understood as parts of households combining multiple subsistence strategies. For one, lascars had parents, siblings, wives and children who were usually living in their home village where they tilled family land, were employed as field labourers, or processed agricultural produce.[95] As can be demonstrated most clearly for the 'agvalas', Indian seamen were often younger sons of smallholders who did not inherit the land but still remained part of the household. On the one hand, their maritime incomes could be important contributions to securing a property that was too small to feed the whole family or even to increasing the households' status and land holdings in the village. On the other hand, unemployed lascars could find some work in their home villages especially during the labour intensive seasons of the agricultural year, which is indicated by the fact that maritime labour supply in Bombay and Calcutta was less ample at these seasons than at other times.[96] Their households also covered most of the reproductive tasks of taking care of maimed, sick and aged seamen, but a lascar who stayed on in his village beyond a certain period ceased to be an esteemed contributor to his family's welfare and turned into a burden.[97] Yet steamship labour appears to have been considered even by households of traditionally non-seafaring communities rather more of an opportunity than a risk, rather a source of pride than of deprivation. Hence, it was reported in 1949 that photographs of steamships on which family members had worked were to be found in many village houses of maritime 'labour catchment areas'.[98] And it was for this reason that the 'serang', the recruiter and boatswain, was an important social figure not only in Calcutta's Kidderpore Docks area and around Bombay's Shipping Office but also in numerous distant villages. A rural community where more than one serang had its home was likely to be more prosperous, and Katy Gardner found in Talukpur, her fieldwork village in Sylhet, that even a generation after the link to seafaring had broken off, the home of an influential family was still known as 'sareng bari' – the serang's homestead.[99] This reflects the importance of the serang in constituting maritime labour networks spanning villages and colonial port cities. It is to the ways of meshing these networks that we turn now.

From village to ship: networks of recruitment

The numerous nodes of maritime labour networks were economically linked up with each other through a myriad of minor monetary transactions. Before a lascar could hope to join a steamship crew, various expenses occurred and numerous payments had to be discharged. This required some savings or access to credit, which accounts for the fact that Indian seamen were generally not recruited from the classes of the urban poor or landless agricultural labourers, but from the smallholding peasantry or even from more prosperous rural strata. In the pattern of payments that connected villages with ships in various ways, the institutions involved in the process of recruitment can be perceived.

When steamship crews were needed in the colonial recruitment ports, serangs were often contacted by recruitment agents in their home villages. Hence, the Royal Indian Marine was said to 'almost commandeer' maritime labour directly from certain villages of the Ratnagiri district for generations.[100] Mackinnon, Mackenzie & Co., the agents for the P&O Company, recruited deck crews and agvalas by sending messages to villages where one of their serangs or tindals (assistant foremen) stayed, informing him of the number of required ratings and the respective ship's date of arrival.[101] Similarly, Bombay's licensed shipping brokers, the Chichgars, sent out 'runners' even to remote areas of Northern Punjab for the recruitment of gangs of 'agvalas'.[102] The serangs were required to propose suitable men for employment and chances of employment were best for those who could approach a serang from their own or a neighbouring village – if he was not a close relative, this was the first instance when a monetary transaction became necessary.

Gaining the support and advice of a local serang was, however, also a worthwhile investment for the majority of intending seamen who had to travel to Bombay and Calcutta on their own as such assistance could facilitate their search of employment. These men also required some cash to pay for the cost of the journey. Having reached the port of recruitment, a wide range of further expenses occurred, which could usually not be covered by a lascar's savings but required credit. A loan could have been already obtained in the village from the local moneylender or, alternatively, from an urban 'Marwari' or 'Kabuli', but was often also provided by a lodging house owner or 'barivala', who was every so often a prosperous ship serang (active or retired), a ghat serang or a petty entrepreneur with no personal links to seafaring. Whatever their background, most lodging house owners preferred to accommodate and give credit to men from their own village or area, which facilitated the recovery of debts. It was not just accommodation and food that were expensive in the city, even getting a temporary job required payments to an intermediary. In Calcutta, for instance, the ghat serangs controlled not only the recruitment of lascars but also the distribution of jobs in the repair docks, which could only be had after ceding the best part of the wages to these intermediaries.[103] Fees were also demanded by clerks in the Shipping Office even before recruitment for providing a new 'nullie', as the 'Permanent Discharge Certificate' was called by the seamen – an important document that had to be produced before the 'articles' (the contract) was signed. Such new 'nullies' were necessary, for instance, if a lascar had failed to join his crew before the departure of the vessel, if he had jumped ship on a previous journey or if his old certificate contained unfavourable entries by one of his former shipmasters reducing his chances of employment.[104]

In order to be entered into a crew list, the intending lascar had to make a payment to the serang who then recommended him to the shipmaster or chief engineer as a member of the crew. If the lascar did not possess enough cash, as was frequently the case, he could also incur debt with the serang that had to be repaid with interest after receiving the advance on recruitment and/or after the payment of the full wages on being discharged at the end of a voyage.[105] Once again, the serang preferred kinsmen and fellow villagers if only because of the lower risk of being unable to recover his claims. If debts accumulated, there was also the possibility that the relationship between lascar and serang turned into one of long-term dependency or 'bondage'. The serang had, on his part, to 'bribe' various levels of intermediaries starting from the licensed shipping brokers, ghat serangs and their subordinates, continuing with the clerks of the shipping office and ending, in the case of the engine department, very frequently with the First Engineer, who was always a European.[106] The financial demands on serangs were considerable, and they tried to pass them on to their subordinates. There is evidence that, according to an informally determined scale, old hands had to pay less than newcomers. Hence, the Bombay Shipping Master was informed by a group of Indian seamen in 1913: 'We never give more than five rupees because we are senior men. Junior men pay more'.[107] Moreover, it is possible that relatives were charged less heavily, too.

After the contract had been concluded under the supervision of the Shipping Master, the seaman received the first monthly wage as an advance. This advance was, however, immediately appropriated by the subordinates of the shipping broker or ghat serang against receipt as a security against the lascar's desertion during the remaining days before the ship left port. Yet, as the seamen now urgently required cash, part of their advance was returned to them by the subordinates of the shipping broker/ghat serang or, to reduce the latter's risk, by further intermediaries (such as lodging house owners and other urban moneylenders) as a credit for which a high interest rate was demanded.[108] The lascar now paid the serang, discharged the bills of the lodging house and bought provisions for topping up the insufficient food rations on board.[109] The crew also purchased, individually or cooperatively, curios, parrots, coconuts and other foodstuffs with a view of improving their wages by way of hawking in ports outside South Asia – a customary practice of Indian Ocean sailors much condemned by shipmasters and port officials but apparently rather hard to suppress.[110]

In sum, access to the maritime labour market was far from being free to all having the required skills and the contract between employer and employee was merely one of many financial transactions through which steamship labour relations were established. Access to the maritime labour market was channelled through a system of financial transactions. Participation in this system (most importantly the access to credit) was restricted to a high degree to members of specific kinship groups, villages and areas. Throughout the period, under review officials of the colonial administration and of shipping companies explained the prevalence of this system of financial transactions in terms of civilizational backwardness – a view that was uncritically accepted by the ILO's James Mowat as late as in

1949.[111] The system was thus represented as a result of the Orientals' special propensity to corruption and bribery, as an articulation of the deeply ingrained custom of giving 'dasturi' (a commission) for any service received – a custom that could not be abolished as it was voluntarily conformed to by the lascars though it would eventually fade away with the progress of civilization.[112] This narrative is misleading not merely because colonial institutions were part and parcel of this system and British officers, especially the ship engineers, were deeply implicated in it.[113] If shipping companies, colonial chambers of commerce and most colonial administrators tenaciously defended this system against criticism on the part of trade unions and some state officials up to the 1930s, the reason was not their respect for 'native custom' but rather the substantial advantages the system offered to employers. For exactly this system of payments and dependencies decisively limited the lascar's 'freedom of contract' and turned him into the 'docile' and 'reliable' workman that shipmasters and companies celebrated in numerous eulogies throughout the period, into a labourer they deemed so much easier to handle than the notoriously 'insubordinate', 'ill disciplined', 'riotous' and 'permanently drunk' English 'Jack Tar' who had become a source of permanent complaint on the part of employers for decades.[114]

Consider for instance the role of the licensed shipping broker whose main function was, it was stated by employers time and again, to prevent lascars from absconding after receiving their advance.[115] They fulfilled this function by implicating the seamen in relationships of debt that could not be evaded easily as their immediate creditors (lodging house owners or serangs) relied, if necessary, on coercion and, even more importantly, originated often from the same or a neighbouring village. Therefore, they could hold the debtors' families responsible in case of default as effectively as a village moneylender. For the steamship companies, these relationships reduced not only recruitment costs but also the expensive time a steamship had to lie idle in port. This example may illustrate that the networks spanning village and port town were, in fact, 'networks of subordination' or, more precisely, infrastructures of subordinating labour. Yet they did not work all that smoothly, were ridden with contradictions and constantly subject to social conflict and renegotiation. Significantly, the most substantial conflicts arose concerning those nodes of maritime labour networks that were most unambiguously in the shipping companies' interest. There were in all likeliness numerous instances when lascars clashed with their serangs, though such incidents were recorded only occasionally.[116] The refusal or inability of a lascar to pay the previously agreed share of his wages to the serang could lead to extremely tense relations on board ship. Under the dual necessity of fulfilling his own financial obligations and of maintaining his authority, the serang could not afford to permit non-payment. In such cases of 'network disruption' conflicts appear to have not infrequently escalated to a point where lascars committed suicide by drowning themselves in the sea.[117] Yet the latter's ambivalent position as employer's foreman and moneylender on the one hand and kinsman, fellow villager, patron and spokesman on the other, appear to have individualized these conflicts and tended to prevent anything like a broad-based campaign against the serang. Lascars and serangs were, moreover, united in their opposition against the 'licensed shipping broker' or 'ghat serang', the very institution that was most valuable to shipping companies and colonial officials. The incomes of both serangs and lascars were considerably reduced by the establishment of this higher echelon of intermediaries who thus became the major focus of conflicts since the early twentieth century, and especially in the 1920s when seamen's trade unions established themselves more effectively. The internal power structure of seamen's unions arguably reflected this alliance of unequals as serangs tended to dominate them especially during their early years. While 'outsiders' (especially lawyers and politicians) frequently presided over these early unions and represented them in public, there is evidence that serangs were rather prominent among their cadre.[118] There were tensions between lascars and serangs within the seamen's unions, as became clear in Calcutta in 1933 when a faction broke away from the 'Bengal Mariners' Union' on the grounds that it was firmly controlled by a group of serangs who had even restricted the access of lascars to union membership to a certain quota.[119] As for the 'licensed shipping brokers', the unions only achieved their ultimate abolition in the 1930s after obdurate resistance on the part of employers and government officials despite moderate international pressure against such practices of maritime recruitment since the foundation of the ILO in 1919, and although a commission installed by the Government of India had recommended radical change of the recruitment system as early as in 1922.[120]

Fissures within the maritime recruitment networks did, however, not necessarily lead to open conflict. The character of the institutions constituting the nodes of these networks was to some extent open to negotiation and they could, therefore, acquire a wide variety of local forms. This is clearly borne out by the case of one of the core institutions of these networks, the seamen's lodging house. Here the Bombay case is of particular interest as the greater ethnic segmentation of the seamen recruited in this city was reflected by an organization of lodging houses on ethnic lines. Thus Punjabi agvalas lived under particularly poor conditions in so-called 'deras' while Kharwas, Konkanis and Muslims from other parts of India each had their own slightly better 'lattis' or lodging houses. As in Calcutta, many of these cheap and often small establishments were run on commercial lines and the owner was sometimes a former seaman.[121]

Yet the lodging houses of Goan Christians were different in more than one way. According to several reports, they were no commercial enterprises but rather cooperatives based on village communities and there were about three hundred of such so-called kurs (Konkani: 'room') in Bombay, most of them in Mazagaon and Dhobi Talao. The members of a 'kur' were always Catholics and usually belonged to the same village, were not necessarily seamen, but also men who sought work in Bombay as tailors or in various service occupations. Some 'kurs' were so large as to occupy spacious buildings, providing not only shelter to hundreds of men but also meals. The housing conditions were usually superior to those in lattis and deras. They were reportedly administered by elected councils, charged regular membership fees, which in some cases even had to be paid when the respective member was absent. 'Kurs' were often called 'clubs' and, in fact, many of them were far more than mere lodging houses. They were also cooperative societies providing benefit schemes in the case of death and loans at a modest rate of interest; they were cultural centres that served as chapels, contained shrines of local saints and celebrated the festivals of their respective villages; they were secret fraternities (in the literal sense as their membership was exclusively male) with rules of conduct and codes of punishment.[122]

In 1929, it was claimed that the institution of the 'kur' had existed for more than a century[123], and they may well have constituted the organizational foci from which the first seamen's unions emerged in Bombay from 1896, which accepted Goan stewards only as members well into the 1920s. In any case, the Bombay Seamen's Union expressly extended in 1926 the eligibility for union membership to 'the managers or procuradores of village clubs, where the seamen resided' and only managers of village clubs were eligible as members of the union's organizing committee. During the seamen's strike of 1938–39 'all Goan clubs [...] provided the wherewithal for the sustenance of the agitation, as well as men and material'.[124] Furthermore, more than half of all Goan seamen were reported to be organized in one of the two Bombay seamen's unions in the late 1920s – a proportion not nearly achieved in any other segment of the maritime labour force.[125] Links between trade unions and village clubs may have been complex, changing and deserve further enquiry. Consider the case of the village cluster of Assolna, Velim and Cuncolim in Southern Goa, which alone accounted for 21 'clubs' in 1927 who then merged into a 'federation'.[126] As late as in 2003, Joseph Mascarenhas, a retired Chief Steward, union member and third-generation seaman from Cuncolim stated that his village alone maintained seven clubs in Bombay and asserted that the total membership of all clubs of the three villages still exceeded 10,000. Mascarenhas denied any direct link between unions and 'clubs' but related with pride that 'the first' (actually one of five) representatives of Indian seamen at the 1920 ILO conference in Genoa hailed from his village (A. Mazarello who was then President of the newly founded 'Asiatic Seamen's Union').[127]

Further research may also confirm Baptista's findings in the 1950s that relations within the 'kurs' were less egalitarian than accounts from the period under review would have it, and that caste and class as well as family hierarchies of the village were reproduced in them.[128] Moreover, the new hierarchies of imperial shipping also left their mark on the internal structure of Goan seamen's clubs – the case of a P&O official who simultaneously acted as the president of three kurs and was also on the founding committee of a moderate, employer-friendly breakaway trade union of Goanese P&O stewards, is a telling case in point.[129] However, the case of the 'kurs' still demonstrates how an institution that was crucial for the subordination of labour could be renegotiated by communities of maritime workers, how a 'network of subordination' spanning village and port for purposes of recruitment and control could be appropriated to serve, under certain circumstances, as a 'network of the subordinated', too.

Conclusions and perspectives

The argument of this chapter has been that networks of steamship labour based on kinship and ethnicity can neither be understood as surviving elements of precapitalist societies and cultures nor solely as infrastructures of resistance against the incorporating forces of the capitalist world economy and imperialism. Rather, they were the concrete realizations of the abstract tendency towards incorporation into an imperial and, to some extent, global labour market. Both the spatial location of these networks and the social relations underlying them were shaped at every step by the exigencies of colonial capitalism: the centralization of steamship recruitment in two colonial port cities; the higher propensity of certain rural areas to develop into maritime 'labour catchment areas'; the segmentation of crews according to ethnicity; the imposition of institutions like the 'licensed shipping brokers' on these networks; the limitation of access to maritime employment through bureaucratic measures like the 'Continuous Discharge Certificate'; and the utilization and defence by both colonial capital and government of a system of so-called corruption, which restricted access to the maritime labour market to certain, often ethnically defined networks. Their acentric internal organization did not preclude their entanglement and even integration with the highly centralized institutions of imperial shipping and colonial state. Maritime labour networks served as networks of subordination under colonial capital, infrastructures of differential incorporation into the global maritime labour market that emerged in the nineteenth century. Yet these infrastructures were ridden with contradictions and could, therefore, also be used in ways sometimes clearly at odds with the interests of British shipowners and colonial government when groups of maritime labourers appropriated them to their own purposes. Hence, these networks competed not only with each other and tried to exclude 'outsiders' from their respective labour market segment, but could also be used as organizational foci of trade union development or for purposes of social welfare.

Though we have focused on those sections of maritime labour networks that lay within South Asia, they extended, of course, far beyond the subcontinent. The spatial reorganization of the maritime labour market, the emergence of a new labour 'seascape' is observable for the whole Indian Ocean region where colonial steam shipping induced the development of a new type of maritime centres and ports including Singapore, Rangoon, Colombo, Aden and Mombasa. Some ethnic groups were privileged above others and the ethnic composition of the Indian Ocean maritime workforce was partly reshaped under the influence of colonial capital. Thousands of Indian lascars were said, for instance, in 1913 to have annually been carried as 'passengers' mainly to ports on the Western shores of the Indian Ocean including Aden, Mombasa, Zanzibar and Cape Town during the preceding three decades to be hired there by British shipmasters in preference to local maritime labour.[130] Moreover, the spatial location and ethnic segmentation of these transoceanic labour networks as well as the social relations within them were to a high extent defined by both maritime and immigration legislation in the metropolises of world capitalism. Hence, the legal content of the word 'lascar' was repeatedly redefined in ethnic terms; Indian sailors were first excluded from voyages outside the Indian Ocean and Pacific and later from Northern Atlantic sea routes; non-South Asian seamen of the Indian Ocean region were partly marginalized but could also reserve or open up certain segments of the maritime labour market for themselves; the lascars' freedom of movement in ports outside South Asia was severely restricted by the British, Australian and US administrations and also by colonial authorities in Africa. Informal mechanisms, especially those of debt relations, were also used to restrict the mobility of a potentially highly mobile workforce.[131]

Despite all these limitations, Indian seamen found numerous ways to convert 'networks of subordination', at least partially and temporarily, into 'networks of the subordinated': infrastructures that had been created to reorganize social space in South Asia and beyond incorporated conflicting interests and turned out contradictory results. They produced, paradoxically as well as necessarily, not only 'spaces of order' but also what employers and state officials were likely to perceive as 'spaces of disorder'. These 'spaces of disorder' served Indian seamen from certain communities as islands of security, hope and sometimes even of social advancement. Yet they remained limited in extent and permanently in danger of being washed away by what appeared to be forces of a 'second nature': the seemingly eternal and actually inescapable violence of the labour market and of imperial domination.

Acknowledgements

Research for this essay was conducted on a fellowship at the Centre for Modern Oriental Studies (CMOS), Berlin, and funded by the German Research Council. A 'skeleton version' of this text was 'pre-published' in a volume of *CMOS* working papers: J.-G. Deutsch and B. Reinwald (eds), *Space on the Move. Transformations of an Indian Ocean Seascape in the Nineteenth and Early Twentieth Centuries*, Berlin: Klaus Schwarze Verlag, 2002, pp. 39–60. I am grateful to Joya Chatterjee, Markus Daechsel and

Willem van Schendel who readily shared their regional expertise and pointed out relevant literature to me. Critical comments by Gopalan Balachandran, Sabyasachi Bhattacharya, Jan-Georg Deutsch, Brigitte Reinwald and many other participants of seminars in Delhi and Heidelberg, where earlier versions were presented, helped to improve this paper, though they may not always approve of the outcome. Finally, I owe thanks to Christoph Gabler and Franziska Roy whose unfailing research assistance counterbalanced adverse effects of German academic short-terminism. Archival locations are indicated by the following abbreviations: ILO: Archives of the International Labor Organization, Geneva; NAI: National Archives of India, New Delhi; NMML: Nehru Memorial Library & Museum, New Delhi; OIOC: Oriental and India Office Collections of the British Library (now: Asia, Pacific and Africa Collections); PRO: Public Record Office (now: National Archives), London.

Notes

1 R. Visram, *Ayahs, Lascars and Princes. The Story of Indians in Britain, 1700–1947*, London: Pluto, 1986, p. 52; J. J. Ewald, 'Crossers of the Sea: Slaves, Freedmen, and Other Migrants in the Northwestern Indian Ocean, c. 1750–1914', *American Historical Review* 105, 1, 2000: 76–77.
2 *The Indian & Eastern Engineer. An Illustrated Weekly Journal for Engineers in India and the East* 24/439, 7 September 1895.
3 PRO, MT 9/1087 (1917): *Tables showing the Progress of Merchant Shipping in the United Kingdom and the Principal Maritime Countries (in continuation of Parliamentary Paper No. 167 of Session 1910)*. London: His Majesty's Stationary Office, 1912. See also: C. Dixon, 'Lascars: The Forgotten Seamen', in R. Ommer and G. Panting, *Working men who got wet*, Newfoundland: Memorial University of Newfoundland, 1980, p. 281.
4 W. H. Hood, *The Blight of Insubordination. The Lascar Question and Rights and Wrongs of the British Shipmaster*, London: Spottiswoode & Co., 1903, pp. 4–7.
5 The figures for Bombay refer to the administrative years 1920–21 to 1922–23, those for Calcutta to 1922–23 to 1926–27. OIOC, Bengal Marine Proceedings (hereafter BeMP) P/11178, A6 (November 1922); ibid. P/11312, A9 (September 1923); *Labour Gazette* 7,8 (1928), p. 668. For later figures see below.
6 G. Balachandran, 'Recruitment and Control of Indian Seamen: Calcutta, 1880–1935', *International Journal of Maritime History* 9, 1, 1997: 2; S. Küttner, *Farbige Seeleute im Kaiserreich. Asiaten und Afrikaner im Dienst der deutschen Handelsmarine*, Erfurt: Sutton Verlag, 2000, p. 10; Hood, *Blight of Insubordination*, p. 13; OIOC, Bombay Marine Proceedings (hereafter: BoMP) P/10793, A161: Bombay Shipping Master to Secretary to Government, Marine Department, 15 March 1920.
7 L. Tabili, *'We Ask for British Justice'. Workers and Racial Difference in Late Imperial Britain*, Ithaca, MY and London: Cornell University Press, 1994, p. 47.
8 S. G. Sturmey, *British Shipping and World Competition*, London: Athlone Press, 1962, p. 296.
9 One of the transformative effects of partition is that India's two main recruitment ports, Bombay and Calcutta, were separated from major areas of labour supply, now in Pakistan, by a contested international border. This is briefly discussed in my: 'Mobility and Containment. The Voyages of Indian Seamen, c. 1900–960', *International Review of Social History* 51, 2006, supplement: 111–41.

Some indication for subsequent shifts in occupational strategies is given in: C. Adams (ed.), *Across Seven Seas and Thirteen Rivers. Life Stories of Pioneer Sylheti Settlers in Britain*, London: Eastside, 1994 (first edn 1987), pp. 61–66. Air passenger traffic and container shipping had the combined effect that the British merchant fleet's labour force was reduced by half between 1951 and 1971 while the number of non-European seamen fell even more drastically from 48,000 to 20,000. R. Hope, *A New History of British Shipping*, London: John Murray, 1990, p. 436.

10 See e.g.: *Records of Fort St George, Diary and Consultation Books*, 1760, reprint, Madras: Madras Record Office, 1953, 4 March 1760, pp. 98, 101–2. See also: H. H. Wilson: *A Glossary of the Judicial and Revenue Terms, and of Useful Words Occurring in Official Documents Relating to the Administration of the Government of British India*, London: Allen, 1855, p. 310.

11 See e.g. the entries 'lascar' and 'sailor' in: G. Small, *A Laskari Dictionary or Anglo–Indian Vocabulary of Nautical Terms and Phrases in English and Hindustani. Chiefly in the Corrupt Jargon in use among Laskars or Indian Sailors* (originally compiled by Capt. Thomas Roebuck, revised and corrected by William Carmichael Smyth), London: W.H. Allen & Co., 1882. See also: Wilson, *Glossary of Judicial and Revenue Terms*, p. 274–75.

12 Some indication of how Indian seamen used these terms themselves is given in various translated deposits in: PRO, TS 34/8 'R.M.S. Egypt'.

13 Cf.: Tabili, *'We Ask for British Justice'*, p. 185; L. Barnes, *Evolution and Scope of Mercantile Marine Laws Relating to Seamen in India*, New Delhi: 1983, pp. 39, 343–45; G. Balachandran, 'Conflicts in the International Maritime Labour Market: British and Indian Seamen, Employers, and the State, 1890–1939', *Indian Economic and Social History Review* 39, 1, 2002: 80.

14 F. Broeze, 'Underdevelopment and Dependency: Maritime India during the Raj', *Modern Asian Studies* 18, 3, 1984: 435; M. Sherwood, 'Race, Nationality and Employment among Lascar Seamen, 1660 to 1945', *New Community* 17, 2, 1991: 230. For a summary of various reinterpretations of the legal term 'lascar' from 1888 to 1920 see: OIOC, BoMP P/10793, A345–46: Government of Bombay, Marine Department, Order 1900, 20 November 1920.

15 Sherwood 'Race, Nationality and Employment': 241.

16 *Reports from the Departmental Committee on Manning of Merchant Ships with Addenda and Statistical Tables*, London: Spottiswoode & Co., 1896, p. 15; D. D. Desai, *Maritime Labour in India*, Bombay: Servants of India Society, 1940, pp. 93–96; J. L. Mowat, *Seafarers' Conditions in India and Pakistan*, Geneva: ILO, 1949, p. 57; Hope, *A New History of British Shipping*, p. 441, 455; see also: Balachandran, 'Recruitment and Control', p. 2.

17 OIOC, BoMP P/5961, A3–4: Letter from Government of India, Finance and Commerce Department, to Bombay Marine Board, 15 January 1900; *Report of the Bombay Chamber of Commerce* (hereafter: *RBCC*) 1921, vol. 2, Bombay: Tutorial Press, 1922, pp. 884–85; Dixon, *Lascars: The Forgotten Seamen*, p. 278; F. Broeze, 'The Muscles of Empire – Indian Seamen and the Raj, 1919–39', *Indian Economic and Social History Review* 18, 1, 1981: p. 44, fn 3; Desai, *Maritime Labour in India*, p. 97.

18 OIOC, BoMP P/5961, A334: Bombay Chamber of Commerce to Government of Bombay, Marine Department, 28 February 1900. See also several related statements of British officials and Indian shipmasters: ibid., A335–54. The same argument could also be found in the contemporary Indian nationalist press. See e.g.: *Rast Goftar* (Bombay), 1 July 1900 (as quoted in Bombay Native Newspaper Report for the week ending 7 July 1900).

19 On occasion of a query by N.M. Joshi in the Indian Legislative Council on 12 February 1939, the Government of India's Commerce Member admitted that

Networks of subordination – networks of the subordinated 37

lascars' compensations for bad food were less because 'the ordinary dietary of European seamen costs more than that of Indian seamen' OIOC, India Office, E&O, Seamen L/E/9/973: Lascar Diet Scale, 1934–46. See also: OIOC, BoMP P/6705, A223–24 (August 1903); Dixon, *Lascars: The Forgotten Seamen*, p. 278; Broeze, 'Muscles of Empire', p. 44; Tabili, *'We Ask for British Justice'*, p. 45. For lascars' complaints concerning food see: OIOC, BoMP P/9083, A469: A. Challis to Board of Trade, 13 January 1911; OIOC, India Office, Commercial & Revenue Papers (hereafter: C&R) L/E/7/780, File 705 (1914–15).

20 Desai, *Maritime Labour in India*, pp. 102–4; see also: BoMP P/9083, A469: A. Challis to Board of Trade, 13 January 1911.

21 For problems in enforcing workman's compensation see: OIOC, India Office, C&R, L/E/7/1163, File 2886 (1923–31); Royal Commission on Labour in India (hereafter: RCLI), *Evidence*, London: His Majesty's Stationary Office, 1931, vol. V, pt. 2 (Bengal, oral evidence), pp. 9–10, 12; Desai, *Maritime Labour in India*, p. 177–78.

22 OIOC, BoMP P/10546, B15 (December 1919).

23 OIOC, BoMP P/8587, A205–8, A393–95; ibid., P/8838, A49–50 (February 1911): Despatch from Government of India to Secretary of State, 20 October 1910; ibid., A319–20 (July 1911); ibid., P/8587, A205–8 (May 1910); ibid., A393–95 (September 1910); ibid., P/11535, A35–36 (27 January 1926). The employment of Indian minors on British steamships and colonial arguments backing this practice were criticised by N. M. Joshi at the International Labour Conference in Geneva in 1921: 'what is the meaning of "earlier and more precocious development" which is said to take place in the case of youths in India and Japan[?] Is it meant that in India lads become full-grown men at the age of sixteen, while they become full-grown men at the age of eighteen in Europe? Is it meant that in India a lad of sixteen, when engaged as a trimmer or stoker in a steamer, will not suffer health, while a lad of sixteen in Europe, so engaged, will suffer in health? [...] I do not believe that the growth of youths in India stops at the age of sixteen. I believe if they are engaged in the engine room of a ship at the age of sixteen their growth will be checked to some extent'. Servant of India, 8 December 1921. See also: R.K. Das, *History of Indian Labour Legislation*, Calcutta: University of Calcutta, 1941, pp. 126–29.

24 OIOC, India Office, C&R L/E/7/853, file 7563; Tabili, *'We Ask for British Justice'*, p. 44.

25 See the various papers on 'lascar agreements' contained in: OIOC, India Office, E&O, Seamen L/E/7/977. See also: *Reports from the Departmental Committee on Manning of Merchant Ships with Addenda and Statistical Tables*, London: Spottiswoode & Co., 1896, p. 15.

26 OIOC, India Office, E&O, Seamen L/E/7/974; ibid., IOR/L/E/9/977, fol. 242.

27 Hood, *Blight of Insubordination*, p. 48.

28 Desai, *Maritime Labour in India*, pp. 204–8.

29 See: D. Hay and P. Craven (eds), *Masters, Servants, and Magistrates in Britain and the Empire, 1562–1955*, Chapel Hill, NC and London: University of North Carolina Press, 2004 (especially the editors' introduction, pp. 1–58).

30 Hood, *Blight of Insubordination*, pp. 48–49; *Reports from the Departmental Committee on Manning*, p. 15.

31 A.L. Valentini, *Lascari-Bât. A Collection of Sentences used in the Daily Routine of Modern Passenger Steamers, where Lascars are Carried as the Deck Crew*, London: Miller & Sons, 1896, p. 15.

32 OIOC, Government of India, Commerce Proceedings P/11247, A1: W.B. Brander, Secretary to Government of Burma, to Government of India, Department of Commerce, 28 March 1921.

33 See e.g. the Government of Bengal's comments concerning the application of the Genoa conventions of the ILO (1920) regarding maritime working hours

in: OIOC, Government of India, Commerce Proc. P/11247, A7–10: A. Marr, Secretary to Government of Bengal, to Government of India, Commerce Department, 23 June 1921. See also: *RBCC* 1921, vol. 1, Bombay: Tutorial Press, 1922, pp. 146f; ibid., vol. 2, 867–69; NMML, M.A. Master Papers, IV. Printed Material, file 39: Fakirjee Cowasjee, Report on the 13th International Labour (Maritime) Conference, Geneva, 10–26 October 1929; NMML, M.A. Master Papers, I. Subject Files, E. National Committees and Commissions, file 780: Replies to Questions Relating to Hours of Work ... [for International Labour Conference 1929]; NAI, Department of Commerce, Merchant Marine II, August 1929, file 465-M. I/29, s.nos. 1–27, part A, p. 97: Replies furnished by the Indian Merchants' Chamber, Bombay to Questions Relating to Hours of Work and Organization of Work on Board Ship; NMML, M.A. Master Papers, I. Subject Files, F. International Committees and Commissions, file 896: Memorandum on Regulation of Hours of Work of Indian Seamen (undated, probably 1944); Das, *History of Indian Labour Legislation*, pp. 129–30.

34 Hood, *Blight of Insubordination*, pp. 49–50; *Reports from the Departmental Committee on Manning*, p. 15.

35 For a detailed presentation of this argument see my 'Mobility and Containment'.

36 For debates on the definition of the term see: OIOC, BoMP P/9596, A17 (January 1915); ibid., P/10793, A345–48 (20 November 1920); ibid., P11008, A181–85 (15 June 1921); ibid., P/11188, A79–83 (22 March 1922); OIOC, Bengal Maritime Proceedings P/10315, A33–34 (February 1918); ibid., A3 (September 1918); ibid., P/11178, A36. For a more detailed account see my 'Mobility and Containment'. For the impact of British immigration policies on colonial maritime labour see: Tabili, *'We Ask for British Justice'*, passim.

37 Mowat, *Seafarers' Conditions in India and Pakistan*, p. 79; Balachandran, 'Recruitment and Control', pp. 9, 17; ibid., 'Searching for the Sardar', pp. 221–23.

38 K. Gardner, *Global Migrants, local lives: travel and transformation in rural Bangladesh*, second edn, Oxford: Clarendon Press, 2000, pp. 2, 269–81; see also: Adams, *Across Seven Seas*, passim.

39 The most influential exposition of this view is: D. Chakrabarty, *Rethinking Working-Class History. Bengal 1890–1940*, Princeton, NJ: PUP, 1989.

40 See e.g. Janaki Nair's discussion of the redefinition of *adidravida* identity in the gold mining town of Kolar in South India: J. Nair, *Miners and Millhands. Work, Culture and Politics in Princely Mysore*, New Delhi: Sage, 1998.

41 E.R. Wolf, *Europe and the People Without History*, Berkeley, Los Angeles, CA and London: University of California, 1997, p. 383.

42 Ibid., 'Incorporation and Identity in the Making of the Modern World', in ibid., *Pathways of Power. Building an Anthropology of the Modern World*, Berkeley/Los Angeles/London: University of California, 2001, p. 357.

43 J. Willis, *Mombasa, the Swahili, and the Making of the Mijikenda*, Oxford: Clarendon Press 1993.

44 This is rather different from Willis' more situational and short-term use of the concept as an 'action-set' (ibid., pp. 5–7). My attempt to conceive networks as modes of 'differential incorporation' is inspired by a presentation by Tim Harper, which I had the opportunity to hear in Cambridge in November 2001, though I do not wish to implicate him with my particular development of his idea.

45 This conceptualization assigns a far greater durability as well as adaptability to networks than the influential rendering of this term by Manuel Castells. Cf.: M. Castells, 'Materials for an Exploratory Theory of the Network Society', *British Journal of Sociology*, 51, 1, 2000: 15–16.

46 H. Yule and A.C. Burnell, *Hobson-Jobson. A Glossary of Colloquial Anglo-Indian Words and Phrases*, New Delhi: Munshiram Manoharlal, 1984 (first edn 1903), pp. 812–13.
47 For the role of butlers and serangs in the early history of Calcutta seamen's unions see the account of the Government of Bengal's Department of Industries in: OIOC, Government of India, Commerce Proc. P/11247, 41–45: A. Marr, Government of Bengal, to Government of India, Department of Industries, 27 September 1921. See also: T.G. Mazarello, *Maritime Labour in India*, Bombay: Maritime Union of India, 1961, p. 66; G. Balachandran, 'Searching for the Sardar: The State, Pre-capitalist Institutions and Human Agency in the Maritime Labour Market, Calcutta, 1880–1935', in B. Stein and S. Subrahmanyam (eds), *Institutions and Economic Change in South Asia*, Delhi: OUP, 1996, p. 222.
48 The concept of 'seascape' has been introduced as a heuristic tool for understanding changing patterns of social and cultural exchange in the Indian Ocean region by the Indian Ocean History Group of the Centre of Modern Oriental Studies (Berlin). For an explanation of the concept see: B. Reinwald, 'Space on the Move. Perspectives on the Making of an Indian Ocean Seascape', in J.-G. Deutsch and B. Reinwald (eds), *Space on the Move. Transformations of an Indian Ocean Seascape in the Nineteenth and Early Twentieth Centuries*, Berlin: Klaus Schwarze Verlag, 2002, pp. 9–20.
49 For the sections of these networks extending beyond South Asia see my 'Mobility and Containment', which is a 'sequel' to this chapter and also develops its argument further.
50 D.E. Sopher, 'The Geographical Patterning of Culture in India', in ibid. (ed.), *An Exploration of India: Geographical Perspectives on Society and Culture*, London: Longman, 1980, pp. 289–326.
51 Hood, *Blight of Insubordination*, p. 13.
52 A. Pope, 'British Steamshipping and the Indian Coastal Trade, 1870–1915', in *Indian Economic and Social History Review* 32, 1, 1995, pp. 14–15.
53 OIOC, India Office, E&O, L/E/9/957, 3256 (1926), p. 3: Brief for the International Labour Conference on Seamen's Articles of Agreement; K.B. Vaidya, *The Sailing Vessel Traffic on the West Coast of India and its Future*, Bombay: Popular Book Depot, 1945, pp. 15f; Broeze, 'Underdevelopment and Dependency', p. 454.
54 Cf.: Broeze, 'Underdevelopment and Dependency'; F. Harcourt, 'British Oceanic Mail Contracts in the Age of Steam, 1838–1914', *Journal of Transport History* 9, 2, 1988: 1–18.
55 F. Broeze, P. Reeves and K. McPherson, 'Imperial Ports and the Modern World. The Case of the Indian Ocean', in *Journal of Transport History* 7, 2, 1986: 1–20.
56 RCLI, *Report*, Calcutta: Government of India Central Publication Branch, 1931, p. 173.
57 RCLI, *Evidence*, vol. I, pt. I (Bombay Presidency, including Sind; written evidence), p. 232, 290; ibid., vol. V, pt. I (Bengal, excluding Coalfields and the Dooars), p. 242. The numbers for Karachi appear to be a mere 'guesstimate' and may be exaggerated. See also: Desai, *Maritime Labour in India*, p. 40.
58 OIOC, BoMP P/6705, A223–24 (August 1903); OIOC, BeMP P/11312, A41: Reply to the Report of the Seamen's Recruitment Committee (Clow Committee), August 1923, pp. 58, 66–67; RCLI, *Evidence*, vol. V, pt. II, p. 278.
59 Harcourt, 'British Oceanic Mail Contracts'; Broeze, 'Underdevelopment and Dependency', pp. 443–46; Munro J. Forbes, 'Shipping Subsidies and Railway Guarantees: William Mackinnon, Eastern Africa and the Indian Ocean, 1860–93', *Journal of African History* 28, 2, 1987: 209–30, M. Pearson, *The Indian Ocean*, London/New York: Routledge, 2003, pp. 203–5.

60 See e.g.: OIOC, BoMP P/7461, A567 (December 1906).
61 OIOC, BoMP P/11008, A211: Letter from Shipping Master Bombay to Marine Board, 23 March 1921. See also: OIOC, BoMP P/6705, A315 (November 1903).
62 See the detailed analyses of the Calcutta recruitment system in Balachandran, 'Recruitment and Control' and ibid. 'Searching for the Sardar'.
63 OIOC, BeMP IOR/P/11312, A41, p. 58, 65, 68: A. Marr, Secretary to Government of Bengal, to Government of India, Commerce Department (reply to the report of the Seamen's Recruitment Committee [Clow Committee]), 15 August 1923; Mowat, *Seafarers' Conditions in India and Pakistan*, pp. 19–20, 23.
64 See, for instance, the lists of the lascar crews that were captured at the beginning of the First World War and detained in German camps. Here the majority of the firemen were identified as Sylhetis and, moreover, certain subdivisions and localities of this district were particularly prominent in each of the crews: OIOC, L/MIL/7/18547. The ability of recruiters to achieve ethnic homogeneity should, however, not be exaggerated. This ability was particularly limited in periods of labour scarcity (e.g. during the two world wars), when the composition of crews became significantly more heterogeneous. Cf. T. Lane, *The Merchant Seamen's War*, Manchester: Manchester University Press, 1990, p. 157.
65 Hood, *Blight of Insubordination*, pp. 51–53; PRO TS 34/10: 'RMS Egypt – Transcript of proceedings', 24 July 1922, p. 75.
66 OIOC, BoMP P/9083, A347 (September 1912); PRO MT 9/531 M. 3965 (1895): Letter to Manning Committee.
67 For seamen from the Maldive and Lakhadive islands recruited from Calcutta see: Hood, *Blight of Insubordination*, p. 10; OIOC, BeMP P/11312, A41: Reply to the Report of the Seamen's Recruitment Committee (Clow Committee), August 1923, p. 58, 65.
68 RCLI, *Evidence*, vol. V, part I (Bengal, written evidence), p. 242: Memorandum of the Indian Seamen's Union; Mowat, *Seafarers' Conditions in India and Pakistan*, p. 6.
69 OIOC, BoMP P/9083, A347 (September 1912); ibid., P/10793, A160: Shipping Master Bombay to Bombay Marine Department, 10 March 1920; NAI: Department of Commerce and Industry, Lascar Seamen, July 1918, s.nos. 4–19, filed; P. G. Kanekar, *Seamen in Bombay. Report of an Enquiry into the Conditions of their Life and Work*, Bombay: Servants of India Society, 1928, 10–14. Proceedings concerning war compensation for the families of lascars deceased during the First World War give some details about their home districts. Of a sample of 45 cases that were considered by the Bombay Marine Board in 1919 and for whom details of their circumstances were recorded the distribution of home districts was as follows: Goa 15, Ratnagiri 14, Bombay 6, Kolaba 5, Daman, Sindh and Kanara one each. OIOC, BoMP P/10546 (1919), *passim*.
70 R.E. Enthoven, *The Tribes and Castes of Bombay*, vol. 3, Bombay: Government Central Press, 1922, pp. 103, 106.
71 G. Yarmin, 'The Character and Origins of Labour Migration from Ratnagiri District, 1840–1920', *South Asia Research* 9, 1, 1989, p. 36.
72 See Enthoven, *Tribes and Castes of Bombay*, vol. 3, pp. 103, 106. However, the Bombay Shipping Master asserted in 1920 that 'Ratnagiri and local Mahomedans do not as a rule work on the land'. OIOC, BoMP P/10793, A160.
73 S. Mascarenhas-Keyes, 'Death Notices and Dispersal: International Migration among Catholic Goans', in J. Eades (ed.), *Migrants, Workers, and the Social Order*, New York and London: Tavistock, 1987, pp. 86–87; O.E. Baptista, *The 'Coor' System – A Study of Goan Club Life*, unpublished M.A. thesis, University of Bombay, 1958, p. 91.

74 Baptista, *The 'Coor' System*, p. 89.
75 Hood, *Blight of Insubordination*, p. 52.
76 RCLI, *Evidence*, vol. I, pt. I, p. 149.
77 These are the only groups of permanent townspeople mentioned in the context of steamship labour, but I have not been able as yet to find more precise information on their social and cultural background. OIOC, BeMP P/11312, A9: Annual Administration Report of the Calcutta Shipping Office for 1922–23, p. 22; Mowat, *Seafarers' Conditions in India and Pakistan*, p. 6.
78 OIOC, C&R L/E/7/696, F. 405: W. A. Cosgrave, Off. Deputy Commissioner Sylhet, to Commissioner Surma Valley and Hill Districts, 21 August 1913. The same letter mentions that some of the lascars Cosgrave had dealt with belonged to Muslim communities covered by the Criminal Tribes Act.
79 Gardner, *Global Migrants, Local Lives*, pp. 37–40; Adams, *Across Seven Seas*, pp. 12–13. See also: Y. Choudhury, *The Roots and Tales of the Bangladeshi Settlers*, Birmingham: Sylheti Social History Group, 1993, pp. 58f.
80 Adams, *Across Seven Seas*, p. 179.
81 Hood, *Blight of Insubordination*, p. 11; see also: Hope, *A New History of British Shipping*, p. 324.
82 Ewald, 'Crossers of the Sea', p. 84; Kanekar, *Seamen in Bombay*, p. 14–15; R.P. Cholia, *Dock Labourers in Bombay*, Bombay: Longmans, Green & Co., 1941, p. 158. However, the presence of 'Somalli' and 'Shidi' seaman was still reported in the port of Karachi in the late 1920s: RCLI, *Evidence*, vol. I, pt. I, p. 232.
83 OIOC, BoMP P/10326, B19 (October 1918); RCLI, *Evidence*, vol. I, pt. I, p. 544; Kanekar, *Seamen in Bombay*, p. 17; see also: D. Omissi, *The Sepoy and the Raj. The Indian Army, 1860–1940*, Basingstoke and London: Macmillan, 1994, pp. 49–50.
84 R. Ballard, 'The Context and Consequences of Migration: Jullunder and Mirpur Compared', *New Community* 11, 1–2, 1983, p. 125. The following districts were recorded as recruiting ground for 'firemen' in 1918: 'Gujrat, Jalandar, Peshawar, Rawalpindi, Campellpur, Ferozepur, Amritsar, Kamalpur, Multan, Mirpur, Jhelum, Lahore, Ludhiana and Hazara'. OIOC, BoMP P/10326, B8 (February 1918): Shipping Master, Bombay, to Marine Board, 15 January 1918.
85 Olga Baptista's evidence suggests that Goan migrant networks (which included many seamen) established themselves in Bombay not later than in the 1850s. Baptista, *The 'Coor' System*, pp. 20f, 43, 48.
86 Cf.: R. Das Gupta, *Labour and Working Class in Eastern India: Studies in Colonial History*, Calcutta: K.P. Bagchi, 1994, pp. 236–37; P. Ghosh, *Colonialism, Class and a History of the Calcutta Jute Millhands 1880–1930*, London: Sangam Books, 2000, pp. 11–14.
87 See e.g. the report on the deliberations of the Legislative Assembly on 26 September 1921 concerning the resolutions and conventions of the International Labour Conference in Genoa in: *Labour Gazette* 1, 4, 1921, p. 22.
88 The earliest published account of Indian seamen's living conditions and labour relations was commissioned by the Servants of India Society in 1928: Kanekar, *Seamen in Bombay*. See also: Balachandran, 'Searching for the Sardar', p. 220.
89 RCLI, *Evidence*, vol. I, pt. I, p. 290. See also the interesting account by S.V. Parulekar of the Servants of India Society on working conditions on coastal steamers of Bombay Steam Navigation Company as summarised in: ILO, Indian Branch, Report for July 1931, p. 85.
90 Ibid., vol. V, pt. II, p. 279; Mowat, *Seafarers' Conditions in India and Pakistan*, pp. 8–9.
91 Desai, *Maritime Labour in India*, p. 172.
92 Balachandran, 'Searching for the Sardar', p. 236.
93 RCLI, *Evidence*, vol. I, pt. II (Bombay Presidency, including Sind, oral evidence), p. 223–24.

94 RCLI, *Evidence*, vol V, pt. II, p. 80–81, 273.
95 Even the Indian Seamen's Union who was intent to stress the proletarian character of the seamen admitted that they 'very rarely live with their families' whom they 'kept' 'in their native villages'. RCLI, *Evidence,* vol. I, pt. I, p. 291.
96 In Bombay, less sailors seem to have looked for engagement during the monsoon months (June to September): OIOC, BoMP P/10793, A160: Bombay Shipping Master to Secretary to Government, Marine Department, 10 March 1920. In Calcutta, there were reportedly moderate and temporary shortages during the sowing seasons of the agricultural year. RCLI, *Evidence,* vol. V, pt. II, p. 277.
97 See e.g. the cases of Punjabi agvalas referred to in: Kanekar, *Seamen in Bombay*, pp. 16–17.
98 Mowat, *Seafarers' Conditions in India and Pakistan*, p. 6.
99 Gardner, *Global Migrants, Local Lives*, p. 53.
100 Hood, *Blight of Insubordination*, p. 9; OIOC, BoMP P/8306, A555 (November 1909); RCLI, *Evidence,* vol. I, pt. I, p. 218.
101 RCLI, *Evidence,* vol. I, pt. I, p. 544. See also: BoMP P/11324, A48: Shipping Master Bombay to Bombay Marine Department, 26 August 1922; PRO, TS 34/10: 'RMS Egypt – Transcript of proceedings', 28 July 1922, p. 76.
102 BoMP P/10133 B15 (December 1917).
103 Kanekar, *Seamen in Bombay*, pp. 11–18; Desai, *Maritime Labour in India*, pp. 34, 44–48, 91; Mowat, *Seafarers' Conditions in India and Pakistan*, p. 21; Adams, *Across Seven Seas*, pp.26–27.
104 OIOC, BoMP P/8306, A329–37, Juni 1909; NAI, Department of Commerce and Industry, Lascar Seamen, February 1920, s.nos. A1–18; NAI, Department of Commerce, Lascar Seamen, August 1922, s.nos. A1–7: Seamen's Recruitment Committee, Report (1922), S. 14; NAI, Department of Commerce, Mercantile Marine I, July 1929, F. No. 451-M. I./29, s.nos. B1–3.
105 RCLI, *Evidence,* vol. I, pt. II, p. 215.
106 OIOC, BoMP P/9083, A468: A. Challis to Board of Trade, 13 January 1911; see also the statements of officers of various Mercantile Marine Offices in Britain and other relevant letters: ibid., A470–76; ibid., P/9342, A215: A. Challis to Board of Trade, 22 February 1913; ibid., A216: A. Challis to Under Secretary of State for India, Revenue Department, 15 March 1913.
107 OIOC, BoMP P/9342, A213–14: R.H.H. Hopkins, Shipping Master Bombay, to Marine Department, 29 March 1913.
108 These transactions have already been minutely analysed in: Balachandran, 'Searching for the Sardar'.
109 OIOC, BoMB P/6705, A223–24 (August 1903).
110 OIOC, BoMP P/4257, A193 (15 July 1892); ibid., P/5961, A339.1: Statement of F. E. Hardcastle, Marine Surveyor [Bombay, on lascar accommodation, 1900]; ibid., A348 [statement of J. Robinson, Commander of BISN steamer Kola, 25 June 1900], Ewald, 'Crossers of the Sea', p. 72; Balachandran, 'Searching for the Sardar', p. 218.
111 Mowat, *Seafarers' Conditions in India and Pakistan*, p. 5–6.
112 See e.g.: Hood, *Blight of Insubordination*, pp. 50–51; OIOC, BoMP P/7191, A222: Memo of the Commissioner of Sind, 29 May 1905; ibid., A230: W. Aves, Port Officer, Karachi, to Commissioner of Sind, 24 May 1905; OIOC, India Office, C&R L/E/7/696, file 405: Government of India, Department of Commerce & Industry, to Secretary of State for India, 12 March 1914, p. 2.
113 OIOC, BoMP P/9083, A468–69: A. Challis to Board of Trade, 13 January 1911; ibid., A476, A. Challis to India Office, 19 October 1912; see also related papers in ibid., A467–76; ibid, P/9342, A211: R.H.H. Hopkins, Shipping Master Bombay, to Bombay Marine Department, 23 January 1913; ibid., A217: J. L.

Rieu, Bombay Marine Department, to Government of India, Department of Commerce and Industry, 22 May 1913; RCLI, *Evidence,* vol. I, pt. II, p. 225.
114 For expositions of such clichés by British shipmasters see e.g. the statement of Alfred Symmons, commander of the P&O ship Paramatta in: BoMP P/5961, A346–47 (September 1900). See also: Hood, *Blight of Insubordination,* pp. 17–18, 62–63 and 72.
115 NAI, Department of Commerce, Lascar Seamen, August 1922, s.nos.1–7, part A, pp. 37–38: Report of the Seamen's Recruitment Committee (Clow Committee), Appendix B: Report on the Preliminary Inquiry in Calcutta; NAI, Department of Commerce, Shipping, 1927, F.No.104-S.(4)-s.nos.1–6-Part A: confidential Letter from H.F. Darvall, Shipping Master Calcutta, to Government of Bengal, Marine Department, 17 March 1925.
116 For conflicts between serangs and lascars see: OIOC, BoMP P/9342, A213–14: R.H.H. Hopkins, Shipping Master Bombay, to Marine Department, 29 March 1913; ibid., P/11008, B181 (June 1921); RCLI, *Evidence,* vol. V, part II, p. 267–68: Oral Testimony by H.F. Darvall, Shipping Master Calcutta; ibid., vol. V, part II (Bengal, oral evidence), p. 279: Oral Testimony by R. Liddle, Marine Superintendent, British Indian Steam Navigation Company, Calcutta; NAI, Department of Commerce, Lascar Seamen, May 1921, s.nos. 156–57, filed; OIOC, BoMP, IOR/P/9342, A212: F.S. Purnett, Chief Collector of Customs in Sind and Shipping Master Karachi, to Commissioner of Sind, 21 February 1913; ibid., A213–14: R.H.H. Hopkins, Shipping Master Bombay, to Secretary to Government of Bombay, Marine Department, 29 March 1913; NMML, M.A. Master Papers, I. Subject Files, A. Scindia Steam Navigation Company, file 150: Indian Seamen's Union, Resolution on the Pending Grievances of the Indian Seamen, 31 August 1943. For further discussions of the debt problem see also my essays 'Mobility and Containment' and 'Die Lenksamkeit des Lascars'.
117 OIOC, BoMP, P/7191, A228: W. H. Howell, Board of Trade, Marine Department, to Under Secretary of State for India, 12 December 1904; ibid., A229: D. A. Cameron, British Consul in Port Said, to Board of Trade, Marine Department, 3 November 1904. Cameron stated that 15 suicides of lascars had been reported to him in Port Said within the last two years. See also: RCLI, *Evidence,* vol. V, part II (Bengal, oral evidence), p. 279: Oral Testimony by H.F. Darvall, Shipping Master Calcutta. Suicides (and unnatural deaths in general) of lascars were so frequent as to set off official enquiries from 'British–Indian' and even German authorities: NAI, Department of Commerce, Merchant Marine II, January 1932, F. No. 54-M. II/31, s. nos. 1–42, part B; H. Rübner, 'Lebens-, Arbeits-und gewerkschaftliche Organizations bedingungen chinesischer Seeleute in der deutschen Handelsflotte. Der maritime Aspekt der Ausländerbeschäftigung vom Kaiserreich bis in den NS-Staat', *Internationale wissenschaftliche Korrespondenz zur Geschichte der deutschen Arbeiterbewegung* 4, 1, 1997: 1–41, 19.
118 When names of trade union militants were recorded at all, e.g. the signatories of petitions or in obituaries in trade union reports, suffixes like 'butler' or 'serang' are remarkably frequent. See: NAI, Department of Commerce and Industry, Lascar Seamen, November 1918, s.nos. 3–6, filed: 'The humble Petition of the native seamen of Calcutta', 11 December 1917'; NAI, Department of Commerce, Shipping, June 1927, F.No.61-S.(52)-s.nos.1–2-part B: 'The Indian Seamen's Union. Report for the Years 1925–26.' The most prominent case is surely that of the trade union dynasty founded by 'Khan Saheb' Mohammed Ebrahim Serang. A seaman from Calicut, he became one of the major trade union leaders of the Bombay seamen in the interwar period – a position inherited by his son 'Bachu' Abdul K. Serang in the 1940s. The present General Secretary of the National

Union of Seafarers of India, Abdulgani Y. Serang, is his great-grandson. A.K. Aurora, *Voyage. Chronicle of Seafarers' Movement in India*, Bombay: National Union of Seafarers, 1996; Interview with Abdulgani Y. Serang, 10 March 2003. A petition of Bengali seamen recorded in the context of the 'Irrawaddy Flotilla Strike' of 1920 is particularly interesting in this context as the demands aim to a considerable extent at the removal of grievances of the serangs: NAI, Department of Commerce, Lascar Seamen, January 1921, s.nos. 12–13, filed.

119 ILO, India Branch, Monthly Report for January 1933. A selection of official BMU papers from 1926/27 preserved in the ILO office in Geneva also clearly indicate the serangs' control of the union: ILO, MA 40/13/2. A confidential report of the Calcutta Shipping Master on seamen's union in 1938 suggests a differentiation according to rank between the five registered maritime seafarers' unions of that city: three of them were, according to this colonial official, mainly supported by 'senior ratings'. NAI, Department of Commerce, Merchant Marine II, 1938, F.No.21-MII(3)/37-s.nos.1–3-part B.
120 For detailed accounts see: Broeze, 'Muscles of Empire', pp. 43–67; Balachandran, 'Searching for the Sardar'.
121 Kanekar, *Seamen in Bombay*, pp. 10–17; Desai, *Maritime Labour in India*, pp. 126–28; for Calcutta lodging houses see: ibid., p. 133; Adams, *Across Seven Seas*, pp. 26–27, 146.
122 Baptista, *The 'Coor' System, passim*; Kanekar, *Seamen in Bombay*, pp. 5–8; Desai, *Maritime Labour in India*, pp. 121–26; RCLI, *Evidence*, vol. I, pt. I (Bombay Presidency, including Sind), p. 545; Mowat, *Seafarers' Conditions in India and Pakistan*, p. 65.
123 RCLI, *Evidence*, vol. I, pt. II, p. 230 See also Baptista, *The 'Coor' System*, pp. 20f, 43, 48.
124 A. Colaco (ed.), *A History of the Seamen's Union Bombay*, Bombay: Pacoal Vaz, 1955, pp. 20, 70–71; RCLI, *Evidence*, vol. I, pt. II, pp. 231–32.
125 RCLI, *Evidence*, vol. I, pt. I, p. 182. The proportion of Indian seamen organized in trade unions amounted to about 15 per cent by the end of the colonial period. Cf. Broeze, 'Muscles of Empire', p. 66.
126 Baptista, *The 'Coor' System*, p. 175.
127 Interview with Joseph Mascarenhas, 13 March 2003; OIOC, BoMP P/10793, A 167–71: Various papers regarding the preparation of the ILO conference in Genoa (July 1920).
128 Baptista, *The 'Coor' System*, pp. 42, 60f, 67, 71f, 84f.
129 RCLI, *Evidence*, vol. I, pt. II, pp. 231–32.
130 OIOC, BoMP P/9596, A309: R.H.H. Hopkins, Shipping Master Bombay, to Bombay Marine Department, 2 December 1913. See also: ibid., P/11008, A 207: Report by the Shipping Master Calcutta, 17 August 1918.
131 Transoceanic extensions of Indian maritime networks are discussed in greater detail in my 'Mobility and Containment'.

Bibliography

Manuscript sources

British Library, Oriental and India Office Collection (OIOC, now: Asia, Pacific and Africa Collections)
Government of Bengal, Bengal Marine Proceedings (BeMP), 1918–23.
Government of Bombay, Bombay Marine Proceedings (BoMP), 1892–1926.
Government of India, Commerce Proceedings, 1921.

India Office, Commercial & Revenue Papers (C&R), 1913–31.
India Office, Economic & Overseas Department (E&O), 1926–46.
Archives of the International Labor Organization, Geneva (ILO)
India Branch, Monthly Reports, 1931–33.
Various Files, 1926–27 files.
National Archives of India, New Delhi (NAI)
Department of Commerce, 1918–38.
Nehru Memorial Library & Museum, New Delhi (NMML)
M.A. Master Papers, 1929–44.
Public Record Office (PRO, now: National Archives), London.
MT (Records created or inherited by the Transport Departments and of related bodies), 1895–1917.
TS (Records created or inherited by the Treasury Solicitor and HM Procurator General's Department), 1922.

Published material

Adams, C. (ed.), *Across Seven Seas and Thirteen Rivers. Life Stories of Pioneer Sylhetti Settlers in Britain*, London: Eastside, 1994 (First edn 1987).
Ahuja, R., 'Mobility and Containment. The Voyages of Indian Seamen, c. 1900–960', *International Review of Social History* 51, 2006, supplement: 111–41.
Aurora, A.K., *Voyage. Chronicle of Seafarers' Movement in India*, Bombay: National Union of Seafarers, 1996
Balachandran, G., 'Conflicts in the International Maritime Labour Market: British and Indian Seamen, Employers, and the State, 1890–1939', *Indian Economic and Social History Review* 39, 1, 2002: 71–101.
——, 'Recruitment and Control of Indian Seamen: Calcutta, 1880–1935', *International Journal of Maritime History* 9, 1, 1997: 1–18.
——, 'Searching for the Sardar: The State, Pre-capitalist Institutions and Human Agency in the Maritime Labour Market, Calcutta, 1880–1935', in Stein, B. and Subrahmanyam, S. (eds), *Institutions and Economic Change in South Asia*, Delhi: OUP, 1996.
Ballard, R., 'The Context and Consequences of Migration: Jullunder and Mirpur Compared', *New Community* 11, 1–2, 1983: 117–37.
Baptista, O.E., *The 'Coor' System – A Study of Goan Club Life*, unpublished M.A. thesis, University of Bombay, 1958.
Barnes, L., *Evolution and Scope of Mercantile Marine Laws Relating to Seamen in India*, New Delhi: Maritime Law Association of India, 1983.
Broeze, F., 'Underdevelopment and Dependency: Maritime India during the Raj', *Modern Asian Studies* 18, 3, 1984: 429–58.
——, 'The Muscles of Empire – Indian Seamen and the Raj, 1919–39', *Indian Economic and Social History Review* 18, 1, 1981: 43–67.
Broeze, F., Reeves, P. and McPherson, K., 'Imperial Ports and the Modern World. The Case of the Indian Ocean', *Journal of Transport History* 7, 2 1986: 1–20.
Castells, M., 'Materials for an Exploratory Theory of the Network Society', *British Journal of Sociology*, 51, 1, 2000: 5–24.
Chakrabarty, D., *Rethinking Working-Class History. Bengal 1890–1940*, Princeton, NJ: PUP, 1989.
Cholia, R.P., *Dock Labourers in Bombay*, Bombay: Longmans, Green & Co, 1941.

Choudhury, Y., *The Roots and Tales of the Bangladeshi Settlers*, Birmingham: Sylheti Social History Group, 1993.

Colaco, A. (ed.), *A History of the Seamen's Union Bombay*, Bombay: Pacoal Vaz, 1955.

Das, R. K., History *of Indian Labour Legislation*, Calcutta: University of Calcutta, 1941.

Das Gupta, R., *Labour and Working Class in Eastern India: Studies in Colonial History*, Calcutta: K. P. Bagchi, 1994.

Desai, D. D., *Maritime Labour in India*, Bombay: Servants of India Society, 1940.

Dixon, C., 'Lascars: The Forgotten Seamen', in Ommer, R. and Panting, G., *Working men who got wet*, Newfoundland: Memorial University of Newfoundland, 1980.

Enthoven, R.E., *The Tribes and Castes of Bombay*, vol. 3, Bombay: Government Central Press, 1922.

Ewald, J. J., 'Crossers of the Sea: Slaves, Freedmen, and Other Migrants in the Northwestern Indian Ocean, c. 1750–1914', *American Historical Review* 105, 1, 2000: 69–92.

Gardner, K., *Global Migrants, Local Lives: Travel and Transformation in Rural Bangladesh*, 2nd edn, Oxford: Clarendon Press, 2000.

Ghosh, P., *Colonialism, Class and a History of the Calcutta Jute Millhands 1880–1930*, London: Sangam Books, 2000.

Government of Bombay, *Native Newspaper Report for the Week Ending 7 July 1900*.

Harcourt, F., 'British Oceanic Mail Contracts in the Age of Steam, 1838–1914', *Journal of Transport History* 9, 2, 1988: 1–18.

Hay, D. and Craven, P. (eds), *Masters, Servants, and Magistrates in Britain and the Empire, 1562–1955*, Chapel Hill, NC and London: University of North Carolina Press, 2004.

Hood, W. H., *The Blight of Insubordination. The Lascar Question and Rights and Wrongs of the British Shipmaster*, London: Spottiswoode & Co, 1903.

Hope, R., *A New History of British Shipping*, London: John Murray, 1990.

Kanekar, P. G., *Seamen in Bombay. Report of an Enquiry into the Conditions of their Life and Work*, Bombay: Servants of India Society, 1928.

Küttner, S., *Farbige Seeleute im Kaiserreich. Asiaten und Afrikaner im Dienst der deutschen Handelsmarine*, Erfurt: Sutton Verlag, 2000.

Labour Gazette: The Journal of the Labour Department of the Board of Trade (London) 1921–28.

Lane, T., *The Merchant Seamen's War*, Manchester: Manchester University Press, 1990.

Mascarenhas-Keyes, S., 'Death Notices and Dispersal: International Migration among Catholic Goans', in Eades, J. (ed.), *Migrants, Workers, and the Social Order*, New York/London: Tavistock, 1987, pp. 82–98.

Mazarello, T. G., *Maritime Labour in India*, Bombay: Maritime Union of India, 1961.

Mowat, J. L., Seafarers' Conditions in India and Pakistan, Geneva: ILO, 1949.

Munro, J. F., 'Shipping Subsidies and Railway Guarantees: William Mackinnon, Eastern Africa and the Indian Ocean, 1860–93', *Journal of African History* 28, 2, 1987: 209–30.

Nair, J., *Miners and Millhands. Work, Culture and Politics in Princely Mysore*, New Delhi: Sage, 1998.

Omissi, D., *The Sepoy and the Raj. The Indian Army, 1860–1940*, Basingstoke/London: Macmillan, 1994.

Pearson, M., *The Indian Ocean*, London and New York: Routledge, 2003.
Pope, A., 'British Steamshipping and the Indian Coastal Trade, 1870–1915', *Indian Economic and Social History Review* 32, 1, 1995: 1–22.
Records of Fort St George, Diary and Consultation Books, 1760, reprint, Madras: Madras Record Office, 1953.
Reports from the Departmental Committee on Manning of Merchant Ships with Addenda and Statistical Tables, London: Spottiswoode & Co, 1896.
Reinwald, B., 'Space on the Move. Perspectives on the Making of an Indian Ocean Seascape', in Deutsch, J.-G. and Reinwald, B. (eds), *Space on the Move. Transformations of an Indian Ocean Seascape in the Nineteenth and Early Twentieth Centuries*, Berlin: Klaus Schwarze Verlag, 2002, pp. 9–20.
Royal Commission on Labour in India (RCLI), *Evidence*, London: His Majesty's Stationary Office, 1931,
——vol. I, part I (Bombay Presidency, including Sind; written evidence).
——vol. I, part II (Bombay Presidency, including Sind, oral evidence).
——vol. V, part I (Bengal, written evidence).
——vol. V, part 2 (Bengal, oral evidence).
Rübner, H., 'Lebens-, Arbeits-und gewerkschaftliche Organisationsbedingungen chinesischer Seeleute in der deutschen Handelsflotte. Der maritime Aspekt der Ausländersbeschäftigung vom Kaiserreich bis in den NS-Staat', *Internationale wissenschaftliche Korrespondenz zur Geschichte der deutschen Arbeiterbewegung* 4, 1, 1997: 1–41.
Servant of India (Poona), 1921.
Sherwood, M., 'Race, Nationality and Employment among Lascar Seamen, 1660 to 1945', *New Community* 17, 2, 1991: 229–44.
Small, G. *A Laskari Dictionary or Anglo–Indian Vocabulary of Nautical Terms and Phrases in English and Hindustani. Chiefly in the Corrupt Jargon in use among Laskars or Indian Sailors* (originally compiled by Capt. Thomas Roebuck, revised and corrected by William Carmichael Smyth), London: W. H. Allen & Co, 1882.
Sopher, D.E., 'The Geographical Patterning of Culture in India', in idem (ed.), *An Exploration of India: Geographical Perspectives on Society and Culture*, London: Longman, 1980, pp. 289–326.
Sturmey, S. G., *British Shipping and World Competition*, London: Athlone Press, 1962.
Tabili, L., *'We Ask for British Justice'. Workers and Racial Difference in Late Imperial Britain*, Ithaca, NY and London: Cornell University Press, 1994.
The Indian & Eastern Engineer. An Illustrated Weekly Journal for Engineers in India and the East (Calcutta), new series, 1895.
Vaidya, K.B., *The Sailing Vessel Traffic on the West Coast of India and its Future*, Bombay: Popular Book Depot, 1945.
Valentini, A.L., *Lascari-Bât. A Collection of Sentences used in the Daily Routine of Modern Passenger Steamers, where Lascars are Carried as the Deck Crew*, London: Miller & Sons, 1896.
Visram, Rozina, *Ayahs, Lascars and Princes. The Story of Indians in Britain, 1700–1947*, London: Pluto, 1986.
Willis, J., *Mombasa, the Swahili, and the Making of the Mijikenda*, Oxford: Clarendon Press, 1993.
Wilson, H.H., *A Glossary of the Judicial and Revenue Terms, and of Useful Words Occurring in Official Documents Relating to the Administration of the Government of British India*, London: Allen, 1855.

Wolf, E.R., 'Incorporation and Identity in the Making of the Modern World', in idem, *Pathways of Power. Building an Anthropology of the Modern World*, Berkeley, Los Angeles, CA and London: University of California, 2001, pp. 353–69.
——, *Europe and the People Without History*, Berkeley, Los Angeles, CA and London: University of California, 1997.
Yarmin, G., 'The Character and Origins of Labour Migration from Ratnagiri District, 1840–1920', *South Asia Research* 9, 1, 1989: 33–53.
Yule, H. and Burnell, A.C., *Hobson-Jobson. A Glossary of Colloquial Anglo-Indian Words and Phrases* ... , new fourth edn, New Delhi: Munshiram Manoharlal, 1984 (first edn 1903).

2 Passport, ticket, and india-rubber stamp

'The problem of the pauper pilgrim' in colonial India *c*. 1882–1925

Radhika Singha

Introduction

The explorer Richard Burton encountered four destitute Indians at Mecca, working as servants, hoping to complete their pilgrimage by begging their way to Medina. He feared they would not survive their desert ordeal:

> Such, I believe, is too often the history of those wretches whom a fit of religious enthusiasm, likest to insanity, hurries away to the Holy Land. I strongly recommend the subject to ... our Indian Government as one that calls loudly for their interference. No Eastern ruler parts, as we do, with his subjects; all object to lose productive power. To an 'Empire of Opinion' this emigration is fraught with evils. It sends forth a horde of malcontents that ripen into bigots; it teaches foreign nations to despise our rule; and it unveils the present nakedness of once wealthy India.[1]

For Burton it was the spectacle of naked want that was most disconcerting. It suggested that India's riches, still proverbial in the Hijaz, had dissolved under British rule. His solution was a compulsory passport system based on proof of solvency.[2] Passport controls, he conceded, were dying out in Europe, but the Pasha of Egypt had re-invigorated them 'to act as a clog' upon dangerous emigrants from Europe and to confine his subjects to 'the habit of paying taxes'.[3] To paraphrase, when Britannia donned the turban of an Eastern ruler, she too could veer away from liberty of movement.

With the opening of the Suez Canal in 1869, the Ottoman Sultan began to tighten his hold over the Hijaz and Britain pressed to expand her influence along the Red Sea.[4] The figure of 'the Hindi' in Ottoman domains, the pilgrim, sojourner or settler from the Indian subcontinent began to transmute into the figure of the 'Mohammedan British Indian subject'.[5] But the embarrassing figure of the *miskeen*, the beggar-pilgrim, also had to be accepted as a part of this constituency.[6]

In a parallel development, the Sultan acquired reasons to pull influential and wealthy Hindis into the circumference of Ottoman nationality and to press for the speedier return of the poor.[7] The fiscal resources of the Hijaz were extremely limited, and food and monetary subsidies were sent annually from Istanbul.[8] If the British consulate was going to claim poor pilgrims as British subjects, then there was both a ground on which to ask for their speedy repatriation and a strong reason to do so.[9]

At international sanitary conferences the pilgrim stream into the Hijaz also began to be characterized as a deadly conduit of cholera, which had to be prevented from curling into Europe. Indigent pilgrims were characterized as a special threat because of their supposedly 'reckless' reliance on 'chance charity' to make an arduous journey. Enfeebled by deprivation, unable to provide for their return, their bodies, both in their manner of travelling and their way of dying were described as a pathogenic danger. States were called upon to correct this lack of forethought.[10]

The French in Algeria, the Netherlands regime in Java, and Russia in its Muslim provinces all adopted some form of compulsory passport or deposit system to regulate Hajj mobility.[11] Later Russia, the Netherlands and France, adopted a compulsory return ticket, so too, from the fold of British Empire, Egypt and the Straits Settlement.[12] Yet till the First World War, the Government of India hung back from all these options. From 1882 it issued a pilgrim passport, but it did so 'unconditionally' – that is, without making it compulsory or linking it to a fee, a deposit or a pre-paid return ticket.[13]

Historians assessing European interventions in the Hajj have focused on sanitation and subversion, geo-political rivalries and business practices.[14] They have shown how images of poverty and disease fused in international forums to justify sanitary measures of special stringency for the pilgrim traffic. However, indigence itself is usually taken as a given.[15] I want to prise these two images apart and examine 'pauperization' as the product of an institutional and discursive process, one by which resources were stripped away from undoubtedly poor pilgrims and stigma and incapacity tagged to them. 'Modern' states began to treat begging one's way to Mecca and back as a species of 'professional' mendicancy and an anachronism in a modern regime of international travel. 'Enlightened' Muslims were invited to declare that this was a violation of the Islamic injunction that the pilgrim must 'be able' to perform the Hajj.[16] Yet for reasons related to geo-politics, commerce and legitimacy of rule, the Government of India too could not entirely subsume 'the problem of the pauper pilgrim' into 'the problem of the diseased pilgrim'. Sections of the Muslim intelligentsia also refused to let it do so.[17]

This article examines the career of the pilgrim passport to understand the contradictory drives shaping the Government of India's interventions in Hajj mobility. My argument is that this document played a symbolic rather than instrumental role in colonial border management till 1916, during the Great War, when it was deployed to attach the pilgrim to a pre-paid return ticket or deposit. An amendment to the Indian Merchant Shipping Act in 1925 formalized this arrangement, and the pilgrim pass linked to the ship ticket came to constitute a composite artefact of colonial governmentality designed to ensure that poor pilgrims returned to India at their own expense.[18]

Debates about the pilgrim passport expose the issues at stake when modern documentary regimes had to be devised for populations understood to be poor and illiterate. Pilgrims were characterized as unable to appreciate the need for travel documents, incapable of holding onto them, or of distinguishing between their papers and those of others. The suturing of return-ticket to pilgrim passport illustrates the crucial role of business firms and the drives of cartelization in the institution of international travel and identity documentation. Yet the forms in which pilgrims, petty ticket-brokers and guides shaped the Hajj, also left their mark on colonial governmentality.

The 'reckless' pilgrim and 'chance' charity: or how the poor devised a Hajj

The poor counted on the stream of charity, which flowed seasonally towards Mecca and Medina and pooled there, but they also counted on a particular way of patching together a Hajj. With the opening of the Suez Canal the number of steamships touching at Jidda rose sharply, and there was a rapid expansion of imports in cotton-piece goods, wheat and rice from India.[19] Indian brokers and merchants who sent cargo ships to Jidda and the Persian Gulf diversified into pilgrim shipping. They also began to compete with the landed elite in pious assistance to poor pilgrims.[20]

However, in contrast to steamers from Java and Singapore that touched at Jidda on their way to Europe, a regular passenger service was not profitable on the Bombay–Jidda route.[21] Hence, pilgrim shipping from India did not operate on a fixed timetable, but picked up pace over the Hajj season. Seasonality, and an ability to cut costs for a low-end clientele created a niche for Muslim businessmen in Bombay, allowing them to hold out against British shipping cartels till the First World War and to retain a small slice of the business thereafter.[22] Speculators in Bombay sometimes pooled their capital to charter a ship for the season, or refurbished an old steamship to get it licensed for pilgrim traffic.[23] An 1886 report describes pilgrim steamers as 'chiefly colliers or worn-out old passenger vessels'.[24] Shipowners depended on petty brokers, at one estimate about 300 to 400 in Bombay, to sell passage for a commission. Brokers were often blamed for encouraging pilgrims to accumulate at Bombay with the promise of cheap fares, then delaying embarkation and raising fares as the Hajj drew closer.[25] M. Edwardes, Commissioner of Police, Bombay, wrote of 'shoals of pilgrims' creating an uproar to press for embarkation, and warned darkly of the Muslim quarters of the city being exposed to spasmodic disturbances.[26] Such complaints about 'disorder' give us a sense of the ways in which pilgrims tried to shape the terms of their mobility.[27]

Hijazi *mutawwifs*, would send deputy guides to India who would fan out into the interior, contacting *maulvis*, clerics, and inspiring people to make the Hajj by drawing upon genealogical knowledge about relatives who had done so.[28] Brokers in Bombay and Calcutta were one of the links in this circuit between India and the Hijaz. Some did dupe their customers, but they also connived with shipowners to pack in more than the legally permitted number, on lower fares with a few free fares for guides. We find even the lordly travel firm Thomas Cook and Son offering some free fares for business goodwill.[29] The Bombay Act II of 1887, which obliged every broker to get a licence from the Police Commissioner, gave the Bombay Pilgrim Department a means to tap this broker network. The Muslim Protector of Pilgrims, managing this department under the supervision of the Bombay Police Commissioner was always seriously short-staffed. He had to rely extensively upon brokers to distribute passports, get pilgrims vaccinated and to assist the police in embarkation.[30]

The bulk of the traffic was made up of pilgrims travelling in 'the lowest class', that is those who had no demarcated space on board ship. The price of the ticket varied with the date of the Hajj and location on deck. From a nostalgic account of the Khandwanis, a Muslim business family of Bombay, I came across this imaginative reconciliation of business practice and piety:

> From 1914 onwards, the Khandwani Steam Navigation Company embarked upon ferrying the pilgrims during the Haj season and cargo, mainly food grain, for rest of the year, for the Hejaz region. Fares would peak up to Rs. 210 and ebb down to Rs. 10 for passengers, who could not spare more. But booking manager had instructions to insist on people paying according to their status, more in line with the spirit of the Haj.[31]

Disorderly embarkation allowed brokers to load on excess numbers, and stowaways to escape detection. Lower fares were negotiated once it was clear that eviction would be impossible. 'A gentleman engaged in the pilgrim trade' said that if some stowaways were troublesome, 'the police conclude that we had better let them stop … there is not enough force on board to keep order'.[32] One British consul carped about the prevailing idea that it would offend religious feeling to send stowaways back without allowing them to land at Jidda.[33]

In the rush to the deck the strong and the well-to-do would spread their mats over the better places while the rest overflowed onto the stairs and along the corridors, or huddled on top of the latrines.[34] A Parsi doctor said prosperous pilgrims would rig up a tent on deck, making it very difficult to detect disease.[35] For the poor, travelling in a band was economical, and made it possible for women, children, the elderly and the ill to go on the Hajj. If the space on deck was 'not very scientifically disposed of' commented L. Moncrief, British consul at Jidda, it was because the captains believed it was 'best to leave pilgrims to follow their own ideas'.[36]

Poor pilgrims needed a flexible timetable, setting out early to secure a cheap fare, and generating resources along the way through labour, begging or petty retailing.[37] Describing the miscellaneous nature of pilgrim baggage, the Police Commissioner Bombay wrote of 'bags, sacks, *ghi* tins, stoves and even implements, such as knife-grinding machines etc., used to or to be used as a means of livelihood'.[38] The Health Officer Bombay said pilgrims refused to be parted from their luggage, which could occupy '20 cubic feet, or about the size of two cotton bales' per person.[39] *Mutawwifs* would persuade clients to carry their merchandise so they could save on freight charges and evade customs duty.[40] Despite pilgrim ship rules, the line between passenger and cargo shipping was probably blurred for quite some time.[41]

At Qamaran, when the pilgrims were counted off the ship for a five- or ten-day quarantine, the number was always more than the total derived from ship-lists compiled at Bombay.[42] Then came the haggling. One Hajji, Alim Uddin, described the scene in 1887 when, out of the 980 pilgrims who alighted, 320 insisted they had no money for quarantine charges:

> The unpaid male persons were verbally threatened, and after taking an oath, arrested in a separate shed in the next camp, but after a while, i.e. at the end of the fee receiving business, all were released.[43]

The percentage of pilgrims from Indian ports who got off by pleading an inability to pay was sometimes 25–45 per cent of the total, but the figure was even higher from some other areas.[44] Once at Jidda, the indigent might beg a camel-ride to Mecca, hoping to cover the next lap to Medina on foot. In 1923, when the Sharif of Mecca prohibited pilgrims from walking to Medina, there were protests in India that this was a meritorious act.[45]

On the return journey the better-off would pay a premium to get away early, and the poor would wait it out till fares dipped. Rough cargo ships sent by Bombay merchants to the Red Sea and the Yemen coast competed surreptitiously for the return pilgrim traffic.[46] Having creamed off the solvent customers, shipping agents would give reduced or free return passage at the very end of the season. This made business sense – it maintained goodwill and the shipper's reputation for piety, and encouraged pilgrims to come out again.[47] The poor therefore needed to tarry.[48]

The 'pauperization' of the poor pilgrim

Officials in India cast poor pilgrims as ignorant rustics, lured out by wily guides, with no idea about what lay ahead and with no forethought about the means of return. Even if not destitute at the outset, they would be reduced to this state by touts, marauding Bedouins, and extortionate Ottoman or Sharifian officials. The narrative usually concluded with a description of famished and dying pilgrims, stranded at Jidda clamouring at the British consulate for a free passage home:

> As a warning to pilgrims on passports issued to them from India, it is printed that the British Government does not undertake to bring back

pauper pilgrims from the Hedjaz. This warning falls on deaf ears ... and every year there are, 1,000 to 1,500 or even more destitute pilgrims who surround this consulate ... and ask for repatriation, and hundreds of them die here.[49]

The consulate's annual Hajj reports give a sense of the suffering that befell the poor, but also glimpses of a figure who was knowledgeable and resolute and tried to make a little go a long way. One consul pronounced that if Indian pilgrims were charged less at every point than the Malay and Javanese it was not only because they had less money, but also because they were more familiar with the rules of pilgrimage, and resisted extortion.[50]

Government blamed the 'casual' nature of charity in India for encouraging pilgrim 'recklessness' and called upon princely states to set an example by arranging for the return journey.[51] The Begum of Bhopal said she had deputed a city magistrate to quiz pilgrims about their resources, and peevishly accused her competitors in piety, 'the Memons and other shipowning classes of Bombay' of irresponsible charity.[52]

The British consulate at Jidda contended that it was under no international obligation to repatriate the destitute but would use its 'good offices'.[53] In fact, its efforts to direct charity towards the return journey gave it a niche within the commercial, civic and pious activity sustained by Indian merchants, shippers and notables in the Hijaz.[54] For all its laments about the headache and expense of repatriating 'stranded' pilgrims the Government of India's own spending was very modest till 1912–13.[55] So long as there was competition for the return traffic, the consulate could rely on shipping agents to rally around with reduced and free passage at the very end of the season.

On the other hand, every round of official hand-wringing about the suffering of poor pilgrims was usually followed by enactments to 'improve the journey', which raised the cost of the fare and eliminated smaller craft. For instance, to protect the 'ignorant and poor' against rapacious touts the Pilgrim Protection Act (Bombay Act II of 1883) made brokers get a license from the Bombay Police Commissioner. However, this also limited the number of pilgrims who could be loaded onto any one ship. The Native Passenger Ships Act (Act X of 1887) declared that passenger ships to any Red Sea port had to be steam-propelled, and carry a medical officer if the passengers exceeded a hundred.[56] The only permitted ports for pilgrim traffic were Bombay, Karachi and Calcutta, and for the period 1903–12 the pilgrim port was principally Bombay. From the late 1890s, as pilgrim-ship regulations were enforced more rigorously, cargo ships began to be excluded from the return traffic. In consequence, brokers and shipping agents in the Hijaz could combine more easily to raise the return fare and keep it higher. Pilgrims forced to wait longer for fares to drop became destitute.[57] Given the epidemiological anxieties expressed at international sanitary conferences, such 'starving and importunate' pilgrim clusters began to be termed a 'public nuisance' and a microbe-generating hazard.[58]

The sanitary and fiscal re-shaping of the Hajj not only pressed hard upon the poor, but also generated documents and statistics, which lent a seeming concreteness to complaints about 'the beggar influx'. From 1882 the Ottoman government took fees for ten-day quarantine at Qamaran, and eight piastres at Jidda for the *tezkirah marur*, a permit for the journey to Mecca.[59] At Qamaran the percentage of pilgrims who took an oath that they did not have the money to pay these fees was recorded as the figure for those who sailed 'destitute at the very outset'.[60] In 1911, when the Sultan insisted once again on a compulsory passport for pilgrims from India, he waived the visa fee for 10 per cent of the number.[61] If the pilgrim produced a certificate of indigence, the Turkish consul stamped the word *miskeen* on his or her passport.[62] And from 1925, ships kept a list of 'Government destitutes', that is of pilgrims repatriated at official expense, to deter them from setting out again.[63]

The pilgrim passport: a failure of colonial governmentality?

However, what is also remarkable is the Government of India's persistent refusal to take direct measures to stem the 'pauper' outflow. From the 1860s, consular officials, British and Indian, pressed for a compulsory passport linked to a means test or pre-paid deposit. To press their case they outlined the other potential benefits – a compulsory passport they said, would provide documentary proof of 'British nationality', a statistical tally to detect the overloading of pilgrim ships, and an instrument of political surveillance.[64]

For instance, in July 1880 when the Ottoman authorities demanded a passport, Zohrab, the British consul attempted to make each pilgrim deposit Rs. 40 for the return journey. The Turks, he reasoned, 'will now insist on the destitute pilgrims, now recognized as accredited British subjects, being taken off Turkish soil'.[65] Compulsory passports, he added, would permit foreign consuls, barred from travelling to Mecca and Medina, to penetrate the 'barrier of fanaticism' and track the fate of their pilgrim contingents.[66] Surgeon Abdur Razzack, the first and perhaps most remarkable of the Indian Vice-consuls appointed at Jidda, also had detailed suggestions for expanding upon the Ottoman order.[67] If shipowners issued a ticket only on the production of a passport and the passport number was added to the ticket, it would put government in a position:

> To know with something like exactness how many of its Muhammadan subjects leave India every year, how many return and the number of those who do not; besides which Government will be able to keep a check on the movements of those who are suspected or disaffected.[68]

Razzack, like Zohrab, felt pilgrim passports could also be deployed to extend the extra-territorial jurisdiction of the British consulate.[69] Under the regime of capitulations forced on the Ottomans, 'British born', that is European British subjects, were tried in separate criminal courts constituted by the British consul and could ask for his presence in civil cases.[70] However, British Indians who stayed on beyond a month could claim extra-territorial privileges only if they registered themselves annually at the British consulate, paying 5 shillings (Rs. 3–2 annas) every time.[71] Razzack stressed this was a high fee for most Indians, and claimed that many did not realize that a prolonged stay brought them under Turkish jurisdiction.[72] If pilgrims had a passport they could seek protection as British subjects if local officials mistreated them.[73]

However the next consul, Moncrief, veered away from these ambitious projects. He suggested that the Government of India issue pilgrim passports freely and without any fee or deposit, because of 'the advantage to be gained by casting the entire odium of passport regulations on the Turks'.[74] The Government of India chose this as its public stance, namely that it was the Sultan who had insisted on passports, and that:

> to render these Turkish regulations as little irksome as possible ... the Government of India ... resolved to establish a system under which passports should be *unconditionally* given.[75]

As it happened, just a year later, the Ottoman authorities stopped inspecting to see if pilgrims had a passport, and those who came without one were not turned away.[76] In 1880, the Sultan may have wanted to underline his territorial sovereignty over the Hijaz.[77] But with European powers making harassing claims to extra-territorial jurisdiction, passports could turn into a double-edged weapon. Moncrief felt Turkey would not allude again to passports as 'they will give increased sanction for protection of their subjects by the foreign states issuing them'.[78] The bottom line was that the Sultan's status as Caliph, protector of the faithful and patron of Mecca and Medina, made it difficult for him to turn pilgrims away once they had landed.[79] As Razzack put it,

> Even the Turks themselves admit that it is impossible to repulse a person simply for not having a passport when he is dressed in the pilgrim's garb and sings out 'Allah hooma labaik'.[80]

In a strange parallax, therefore, the Ottoman government stopped checking for pilgrim passports but the Government of India went on issuing them. Pilgrims were encouraged to take a passport but not prevented from leaving without one. A peculiar phrase in the Government of India's Pilgrim Manual captures this position, 'pilgrims are *warned* that it is *desirable* to supply themselves with a passport', but they were also informed that a passport was not compulsory.[81]

The pilgrim passport was meant for all travellers who embarked on a ship licensed for the Red Sea pilgrim traffic even if they were setting out for some other purpose.[82] The Government of India decided its Home Department would issue this document, not the Foreign Department which issued the 'regular' British Indian passport and took a fee of Rs. 1 for it. Its explanation for using a 'Department of the Interior' was that, unlike the regular passport, the pilgrim passport could be issued from any district office, and that the traffic involved sanitation, medical inspection and orderly embarkation.[83] The documentation of such a humble body of travellers may have also been deemed unworthy of the Foreign Department.[84] Nevertheless, the decision indicates that when it came to the Hajj the Government of India's gaze ranged anxiously inwards before it turned outwards.

The pilgrim passport certainly didn't measure up to the ambitious schemes conceptualized around it. Its value as a statistical instrument was dubious because it was not compulsory. Pilgrims themselves had virtually no incentive to take a passport, and over one-tenth left without one.[85] Many did not register their passport with the British consulate, or retain it thereafter.[86] It was not the passport count, but the ship-list that provided the more reliable tally and even then the count at Qamaran always revealed excess numbers.[87]

Sugata Bose's sensitive account of the play between pilgrim spirituality and colonial rationality may overestimate the latter.[88] In 1905, the Protector of Pilgrims reported that to evade a segregation camp at Bombay, nearly a thousand pilgrims set out earlier for Aden, then took sailing boats to Jidda.[89] As fares on licenced pilgrim ships increased, some pilgrims took a cargo ship to the Persian Gulf and then the overland route to Medina.[90]

The statistical grasp over pilgrim traffic from India improved but it remained loose for the return traffic. In 1894, a Health Officer of Bombay port confessed despondently, 'the causes which lead to the 33 per cent discrepancy between the number of outgoing and returning pilgrims to Bombay are still unknown'.[91] The 'missing' pilgrims were important to debates about the management of the Hajj. The Government of India contended that pilgrims did not carry cholera from India but contracted it at Qamaran or in the Hijaz because of Ottoman mismanagement. The Jidda consulate attributed the difference to the high mortality of destitute pilgrims, an argument for not allowing them to leave.[92] Muslim associations said it proved that many settled down in the Hijaz, or returned by uncertified ships or overland routes, so pre-paid return tickets would involve a financial loss.[93]

The pilgrim passport was also of limited value for political surveillance. The bulk of pilgrim passports were issued, not at the district headquarters, but in a great rush at Bombay, by the Protector of Pilgrims, working under the Commissioner of Police, and with no great concern for verification.[94] No fee was taken for pilgrim passports, so the Protector was understaffed and heavily dependent on broker assistance.[95] He sometimes recorded the social position of notables in the passport's column for 'General Remarks',[96] and, at the other end, in Jidda, Indian vice-consuls were invaluable to information-gathering. However, the surveillance of individual malcontents became significant only with the declaration of war with Turkey in November 1914, and with the emergence of the Khilafat movement to defend the Sultan-Caliph's sovereignty over the holy places of Islam.[97] From the 1920s, pilgrims were repeatedly advised to get their passport made out in their own district.[98] Yet I have not come across any case where a Hajj passport was refused, citing political reasons.[99] The Government of India's greater concern was to prevent pan-Islamic spokesmen from entering India, and to black-list recalcitrant guides.[100]

The surveillance value of the pilgrim passport was also compromised by the fact that it was a collective document, one on which the holder included, not only spouse and children but also other relatives and domestic servants.[101] Women and children were not even entered by name on the passport, only by the number in the party.[102] Ottoman authorities accepted this arrangement, and in 1911 when they introduced visa fees, they exempted wives, children and domestic servants entered on the one passport.[103] The thinness of bureaucratic infrastructure meant that the networks that mobilized the pilgrim band had to be inducted into the forms of colonial governmentality. A document that recognized parties held together by some affiliation offered tangible administrative conveniences.[104]

If the pilgrim passport was not a very effective instrument for census or surveillance, it was also not a very definitive document of British nationality. First, it was always difficult to make out which side of India's frontier a pilgrim had travelled from. Pilgrims thought 'within borders' when they debated the condition of Muslims under different regimes, but they could treat nationality labels as a matter of making the best of circumstances[105] Second, when pilgrims came to petition the British consul they did not always have a passport to proffer.[106] This nebulous situation had advantages for the British consul, allowing him to choose the issues he wanted to raise with Ottoman and Sharifian officials while avoiding fiscal responsibility for each and every poor sojourner.[107]

In contrast, the Sharif of Mecca and the Ottoman governor wanted to sharpen the line of nationality in relation to key offices in the Hijaz and to obstruct wealthy Indians from assuming too conspicuous a civic role.[108] The Sharif refused to re-confirm Indian *Mutawwifs* and their vakils, agents, unless they registered themselves as Ottoman subjects. At one time, wrote Alban, the British consul:

> [T]here were ... among the Motuwwafs of the Indian pilgrims some registered British subjects, and certainly at least five of the Wakeels ... were registered in this consulate. Since the last year or two, however the Grand Shereef has gradually excluded all registered British subjects by declining to re-appoint them unless they become Turkish subjects.[109]

For Thomas Cook and Son the discovery that in India pilgrim passports were not compulsory was a disappointment. This firm had expected to batten onto official infrastructures to take a dominant share of the pilgrim traffic. The Government of India subsidised it against losses for a full six years (1887–93), hoping it would eliminate the problem of 'stranded paupers' by re-shaping the Hajj as a round-trip journey.[110] It instructed the Police Commissioner to distribute all pilgrim passports through the Bombay agent for Thomas Cook. However, the firm complained that an increasing percentage of pilgrims were leaving without passports.[111] The real problem was that Thomas Cook did not have its own pilgrim ships. It had to book with Muslim shipowners of Bombay, so it could not guarantee the space and facilities it promised. It was also unresponsive to requests to provide comfort and privacy for 'respectable' women, and relied too much on official support to capture business.[112] On the other hand, Muslim shipowners and brokers had a better network in the districts, could operate more cheaply and fought effectively to re-capture customers.[113]

The necessity of mixed messages: protecting and excluding

> The Government of India have for years deemed it a matter of high political importance to cheapen and facilitate the journey to Mecca.[114]

My surmise is that, till the First World War, the pilgrim passport served two rather conflicting ideological imperatives. It was part of a package of measures meant to demonstrate in international forums that the Government of India was a modernizing regime, capable of counting and documenting pilgrims and monitoring them for contagious disease. However, in relation to Muslim populations the 'unconditional' issue of the pilgrim passport was supposed to communicate a different kind of message, not one about regulation, but about protection, assistance and religious liberty. These rather different positions drove one British consul, Avalon Shipley, to burst out in exasperation:

> I do not pretend to know from what point of view the Government of India regards the question of the Pilgrimage, whether it considers it advisable to obtain the cheapest possible terms for the pilgrims or only the best. The two are evidently not compatible.[115]

'Better' conflicted with 'cheaper', but the Government of India clung grimly to a position from which it could emit mixed messages.

The alien pass: routing the frontier Hajji through, and back

Pilgrim travel was supposed to symbolize religious liberty not only for Muslims within India, but also for those across its borders. Railway lines laid to rush troops from Bombay to the North West Frontier, began to bring pilgrims down from Afghanistan and Chinese and Russian Turkestan. In 1882 when the Government of India inaugurated its pilgrim passport, it also authorized the Bombay Commissioner of Police to issue informal passes to 'alien' pilgrims stating that they were 'quiet and orderly' in their passage through British territory so they could be helped to embark.[116]

This was an interesting description. After the 1878–79 Afghan war, as the boundaries of British India pressed outwards along the North West Frontier, images of the aggressive Kabuli, the Pathan bully, and the fanatic frontier *maulvi* populated the colonial imagination.[117] Peripatetic bands wandering over the North West Frontier were cast as unruly elements who had to be prevented from intimidating 'non-martial' populations in the interior and setting up dangerous migrant clusters in Muslim princely states such as Hyderabad.[118] In the large cities, the colonial police began to treat trans-frontier sojourners as a turbulent component of the urban lower classes. In this instance, however, the Foreign Department weighed the advantages of 'interchange of information and free intercourse' against the danger of admitting 'fanatics, spies and sedition mongers' and decided it would be 'more in accordance with English habits and principles' to give this facility to foreign pilgrims.[119]

The intention perhaps was to impress trans-frontier Hajjis with the contrast between their 'backward' polities, and a government capable of providing the documentation, medical inspection and licensed pilgrim ships they now needed.[120] Rivalry with Russia over Central Asian trade routes and the British mantra of 'free trade' in forcing open Chinese markets also shaped the Government of India's decision to allow pilgrims to cross over from Yarkand and Kashgar and make their way down to Bombay.[121] In international forums, British spokesmen invoked 'liberty of travel' to critique continental rivals for wanting to impose sanitary cordons on commerce and movement. When a fee of Rs. 2 seemed to discourage applications for the alien pass, it was withdrawn.[122] However, to discourage trans-frontier travellers from loitering about in the interior, the alien pass was issued only at Bombay.

Geo-politics, 'liberty' and a niche for the poor pilgrim

Sending their subjects to the Hijaz with papers that distinguished them as 'British subjects, residents of India' put the Government of India in a strange predicament. Within India it was very reluctant to acknowledge any obligation for poor relief except in dire famine. Now outside its territorial borders, it found itself under pressure to arrange for the repatriation of pauper pilgrims.

The Ottoman government complained to British consular officials about 'l'affluence des vagabonds et des gens sans aveu'.[123] They, in turn, complained to the Foreign Office that the Government of India was allowing the 'scourge of mendicancy' to overflow into Ottoman domains where European empires were measuring up to each other. In 1912, the Indian vice-consul urged the need to check the arrival of Indians:

in such circumstances and under such conditions as are a disgrace to Islam as well as to the British community ... It is a disgrace also to the fair name of the British Government, that long after the Javanese and other pilgrims have left this country, British Indians may be seen mere disease-stricken skeletons, lying about in the streets of Jeddah, begging their bread and filling the town with their ordure and their microbes, and Governor should have occasion to write to the consulate to ask it to remove its outcasts.[124]

One could line up a variety of such discourses and conclude that they add up to a familiar episteme in which colonial rule is confirmed as a civilizing dispensation, struggling to coax 'bigoted and backward' subjects into the modern era of international travel.[125] The story is, in fact, one of conflicting objectives, because the trek of the poor pilgrims into Ottoman Arabia was not merely a problem for empire but also a resource. At the 1892 Venice sanitary conference Britain could resist proposals for maritime quarantine, by invoking the principle of commercial liberty, but also the right of her Muslim subjects to travel for the Hajj.[126] The outward journey of British and Indian cargo ships from India was balanced by the return pilgrim traffic.[127] As one Health Officer at Bombay complained, he was sometimes told to enforce pilgrim ships rules very strictly, at other times he was expected to aid commerce, which meant bending the rules.[128] Third, the pilgrim trek from India allowed the British Empire to claim a say over access routes into Ottoman territory and order and civic management in Arabia. The Indian vice-consuls set themselves up as mediators on behalf of Indian merchants and other Indian sojourners, and the consulate's charitable projects acquired imperial titles such as the 'Jubilee Indian Pilgrims Relief Fund'.[129]

Finally, as 'Protector of the faithful' the Ottoman Sultan could not publicly debar the *miskeen*, but neither could the Government of India, vying with him for prestige with Muslim populations. This strange brinkmanship kept the poor pilgrim moving along this stretch of the 'naval high street of empire'. At the 1894 Paris Sanitary conference, both British and Turkish delegates rejected a proposal to institute a means test for pilgrims. Dr Cuningham declared that the Government of India would introduce this only if the Sultan pronounced that Muslim religious law prohibited paupers from the Hajj and enforced this rule in his own domains. The Government of India declared that 'even in such circumstances' it would not agree.[130]

In international forums the Sultan's position was that each Muslim was free to decide on his or her ability to perform the Hajj.[131] However, since the Ottoman regime had to generate taxes for sanitary improvements, it was easier for Britain to assume the moral high-ground and declare that pilgrimage should not be made a source of revenue. In private, the Government of India acknowledged a contradiction between its own efforts to prevent pauper Asians and Africans from landing at the British garrison of Aden and its refusal to prevent indigent pilgrims from leaving for Jidda.[132]

The compulsory return ticket, the 'the Hajj question' and a Muslim public sphere

At the 1894 Paris International Sanitary Conference, Britain signed a convention agreeing to higher standards for pilgrim ships.[133] The Government of India protested vehemently that these norms were formulated too much from a European perspective, ignoring its own experience with 'Asiatic passenger traffic' and its political compulsions in India.[134] However, under pressure from the India Office it was obliged to draft a distinct Pilgrim Shipping Bill to meet the new standards set by the convention, as for instance, the prescription of 21 superficial feet per pilgrim on board ship, instead of the previous criteria of 9 superficial feet.[135] The convention also stated that in calculating per capita space children below twelve were to be counted as one adult, instead of as a 'half'. In defending this clause Alexander Mackenzie, the official steering the bill, exposed its slant against the poor. He said it was 'the promiscuous way in which Indian families go on pilgrimage that causes much of the distress and mortality'.[136] Sanitary fees were now included in the cost of the ticket, which meant that exemptions could not be negotiated at Qamaran.[137]

There were sharp protests in India that a price barrier was being erected against the Hajj, and that medical examination might be used to disqualify the very infirm, not just those detected with contagious disease.[138] However, the formulation of a distinct Pilgrim ships bill, an index of the special anxieties aroused by this traffic, also created a context in which Muslim spokesmen could demand a more pious journey.[139] They suggested that only Muslims be appointed as doctors, or cooks and that only a woman doctor scrutinise female pilgrims at embarkation.[140] Yet Dr J. Crimmin, a Bombay Health Officer, contended that *pardah*, the norm of veiling and seclusion for respectable women, did not pose a great problem, because female pilgrims from India, unlike those from Central Asia, did not cover their faces.[141] Piety was therefore not the only point at issue. A distinct figure was separating out from the pilgrim 'mass' – that of the solvent consumer demanding value for money, and procedural distinctions to ensure that respectability was not compromised. Some Muslim spokesmen said shipowners should be made to put in fittings, not only to improve cleanliness and comfort, but also to maintain orderly demarcations of space.[142] Haji Muhammad Ismail Khan, a member of the North Western Provinces Legislative Council, compared the comfort of P&O, or Lloyds, with pilgrim ships where the saloon was crammed with passengers instead of being kept free for the cabin class. The Prophet, he pronounced, had declared that no-one should trouble others, so the poor, and the diseased 'ought not to endanger the health of others'.[143]

However, this kind of voice was undercut by others who insisted that the Hajj should not be put beyond the reach of the poor.[144] These swelled in volume as the Turko–Italian and Turko–Balkan wars of 1911–13 created an intense anxiety in India about the weakening power of the Sultan-Caliph. The trek of poor pilgrims seemed to sustain a line of defence around the sacred sites of Islam and their sufferings upheld an ideal of sacrifice in the cause of religion. Even prominent Muslims, who invoked the Islamic tenet that a man had 'to be able to' perform the Hajj, could not entirely disavow the zeal of the poor.[145]

War clouds over the Red Sea had made Indian merchants reluctant to send cargo ships, creating an acute shortage of return shipping. In 1913, for the first time, the Government of India made a substantial payment, Rs. 17,000, to repatriate destitute pilgrims.[146] The plague panic of the 1890s may have made it particularly sensitive to international opinion. However, S.H. Butler, of the Indian Department of Education, also raised, if rather uncertainly, the idea that a welfare norm might be at stake: 'It is outside India but they are British subjects and we have elaborate famine measures to prevent British subjects dying'.[147] The very possibility that the poor pilgrim might emerge as a legitimate object of state welfare, with a claim on tax revenues, generated a new anxiety. Would shipping companies begin to retract their own charity and refuse to reduce their rates, expecting that government would eventually pay?[148]

In March 1913, in another significant development, Turner Morrison and Company, a British managing agency, took over the Bombay Persia Steam Navigation Co. and offered to introduce compulsory return tickets if it was given a monopoly of the Hajj traffic.[149] Compulsory return tickets had been discussed once before, in 1906–7, when pilgrim numbers were picking up, and the spectre of 'stranded paupers' loomed again. At that conjuncture, the key Bombay officials had declared flatly that pre-paid return fares would mean a financial loss for pilgrims because:

> many of them obtain return passages at nominal rates, or for nothing. If the return rates were fixed in Bombay they would certainly be substantial. Many more do not return to Bombay at all, or at any rate do not return in pilgrim ships; and all these would get no value for their return tickets.[150]

Yet in 1913 the same Bombay Government now pressed the Government of India to accept Turner Morrison's offer.[151] It did so even though the experience of the Straits Settlement with the compulsory return ticket had shown that it led to a sharp increase in fare.[152]

Muslim shipowners and brokers realized that with or without official monopoly, compulsory return tickets would edge them out. Turner Morrison had the largest number of ships so it could guarantee the return journey. With the total fare fixed at the outset, it would also be protected against rate wars on the homeward run. As long as smaller companies, however short-lived, had the opportunity to enter the Hajj traffic, tickets were still priced down at the end of the season.[153] Rate wars meant poor pilgrims could pay their own way home, but consulate officials complained that they also tempted the indigent to come out in larger number.[154] For poor pilgrims, compulsory return tickets would mean a higher overall fare and having to find it all at once.

Nervous about a rapprochement between the Muslim League and the National Congress, the Government of India insisted on a wider consultation with Muslim public opinion.[155] Educated Muslims found a leadership role and a common ground with the ulama, the clergy, in opposing this move to price out the poor pilgrim. In the *Bombay Chronicle*, Shaukat Ali, charismatic leader of the Muslim League, accused government of wanting to divest itself of all responsibility for pilgrims by gifting a British firm with monopoly. Forty years ago he said, when there was a good deal of shipping owned by Muslims, '[T]he question of destitute Hajis was always there, but it never caused any trouble'.[156] Towards the end of the season, Muslim shipowners would bring the destitute back as an act of charity. The growing influence of Turner Morrison, he said, had eliminated competition, leading to an escalation in fares. A compulsory return ticket would exclude all Muslim shipowners because they did not have sufficient ships to guarantee a return passage.[157]

Oishi Takashi has given an excellent account of the link between pan-Islamic support in Western India for the Ottoman Empire and the defence of Muslim business and shipping networks with Arabia and the Persian Gulf.[158] The public protest against a monopoly for Turner Morrison is an unexplored dimension of the defence of indigenous entrepreneurship.[159] Critics such as M. Rafiuddin Ahmed, secretary of the Anjuman-i-Islam, Bombay, drew freely upon imperial rhetoric about liberty of commerce and freedom of religion. Britain, 'the greatest Moslem Power upon earth' and the greatest carrier of the world, had nothing to learn, he declared, from France, whose Arab subjects had revolted no less than 18 times in 60 years, or from the Netherlands.[160] 'It is the pride of the Indian Muslims alone that they are contented and happy under a christian Government.'[161] Others said the rigidity of schedule imposed by the compulsory return ticket would disorient the state of mind appropriate to the Hajj, discouraging the pilgrim who might feel spiritually inspired to stay on for the next Hajj or journey to other holy sites.[162] What was being resisted was the erosion of a claim to linger at length, and even perhaps forever, on the routes and sites of Islamic pilgrimage.

In May 1913, Shaukat Ali and Maulana Abdul Bari founded the Anjuman-i-Khuddam-i Kaba, a society to maintain the sanctity of Mecca, Medina and Jerusalem, which captured the public imagination.[163] Shaukat Ali actually took out a licence as a pilgrim broker to help the poor secure passage, and his brother described the transformation:

> From a smart, half-Europeanised, fashionably dressed officer of Government ... he became a ... shabbily-dressed Bombaywallah ... On the erstwhile smooth cheeks and chin was now to be seen a shaggy beard,

which ... was his fiercest protest against Europe and Christendom. In Bhendi Bazaar and its noisome purlieu he soon became a familiar sight trudging ... to overcrowded 'Pilgrim Shelters'.[164]

Some Muslim spokesmen challenged the characterization of their community as helpless or indifferent and rejected all official regulations as an encroachment on religious liberty. The poor chose to suffer rather than to forgo the Hajj and they should be allowed the choice.[165] However, another approach also began to crystallize – one in which the state was called upon to take responsibility for the cultural needs of poor Hajjis. The argument was that since public revenues were tapped to improve sanitation at Hindu pilgrim sites, and special trains scheduled for Hindu pilgrims, then, government should also assist poor Muslims to make the Hajj, not just hold them back.[166] It could legislate for fixed and moderate passage, or subside the fare for the poor, or generate some revenue to repatriate the indigent.[167] The Surat Anjuman-i-Islam suggested a capitation tax of Rs. 1 per pilgrim to pay the return fare for the indigent.[168] Rafiuddin Ahmed suggested a 5 per cent brokerage fee on shipowners for a repatriation fund.[169] However, such proposals only underscored official worries that the indigent would come to expect free return tickets 'as a matter of right' and set out in increasing numbers.[170] However, in the face of widespread opposition to the return-ticket scheme, the Government of India dropped it and fell back on a familiar strategy – on the one hand, raising the bar for pilgrim ships, on the other, trying to systematize charity and gather it under an official umbrella.[171] In the turmoil of the Great War it did finally introduce pre-paid return tickets, but initially through informal negotiation with shipping companies, not by legislation.

A conditional mobility for 'a pilgrim of the lowest class'

> A 'pilgrim of the lowest class' is a pilgrim for whom no separate accommodation in any cabin, state-room or saloon is reserved.[172]

With the declaration of war with Turkey, the Viceroy of India announced that the holy places of Arabia would be 'immune from attack ... so long as there is no interference with pilgrims from India'.[173] The British navy was blockading Ottoman ports, but the Government of India did not prevent the 2,400-odd pilgrims at Bombay from leaving for the Hajj.[174] In June 1916, the Sharif of Mecca, with British backing, declared his independence from Ottoman rule. The Government of India felt it was imperative now to demonstrate that change of regime would not affect access to the Hijaz. It negotiated with Turner Morrison, now managing agent for the Mogul Line, to resume the pilgrim traffic. The firm seized this opening to get its steamships released from war-use and to carry valuable foodstuffs to Jidda.[175] Shustary and Co., a Bombay Muslim firm managing the Persian Gulf Steam Navigation Co. was the only other company in the picture during the war.[176]

Pre-paid return tickets became virtually compulsory because the Mogul Line refused to issue single-journey tickets.[177] However, to mollify critics, the Government of India gave a subsidy to keep the round-trip fare at Rs. 125.[178] Its major anxiety now was to keep pilgrims attached to the return tickets, which were meant to loop them back.[179] Officials complained that pilgrims and *mutawwifs* were treating return tickets or deposit-stamped passports as a species of negotiable currency, selling them at a premium, and then clamouring once again for help in getting home.[180] The pilgrim passport assumed a new importance as a record of individual particulars, which would help to detect the illegal re-sale of return tickets, and deter misuse of the original ticket if lost or stolen.[181]

However, pilgrim or *mutawwif* deviousness was not the only factor re-creating the problem of 'stranded pilgrims'. Having secured their return customers, shipping agents began to keep pilgrims waiting at Jidda while they explored other deals, or gave out-of-turn embarkation to new clients.[182] Critics of the pre-paid ticket had warned of customer neglect.[183] To give pilgrims some leverage, the Government of India persuaded shippers to experiment with pre-paid deposits that could be used to return on any line. As the Khilafat movement ebbed away, it was able to convince some Muslim legislators in the Imperial Legislative Assembly to support an amendment to the Indian Merchant Shipping Act which regularized the new arrangements.[184]

In February 1924, introducing the amending Bill, S. H. Butler, Secretary Education, Health and Lands, declared that India was 'now a nation among nations'.[185] The implication was that putatively sovereign entities did not let their beggars wander over borders.[186] Invoking the theme of welfare, Butler said the destitute compromised the comfort of other pilgrims. Yet in the same breath, he also warned of controversy if public revenues were tapped to repatriate pilgrims of one religious community.[187] Muhammad Yaqub and S. A. K. Jeelani explained that they supported the Bill because it targeted only the 'professional mendicant' not the 'bona fide Hajji'.[188] However, Muslim legislators also modified the measure in significant ways.[189] Section 205-A of the Bill had empowered local governments to lay down a period during which the carriage of pilgrims would be illegal. The vague explanation was that when ships set out too late pilgrims missed the Hajj.[190] However, the clause was widely understood and condemned as a bid to compress access to the Hijaz and it was dropped.[191] Second, Muslim legislators insisted on a status distinction – only pilgrims travelling 'in the lowest class' had to produce a return ticket or a deposit-stamped passport to get an embarkation ticket, not those travelling in first or second class.[192] They also formulated a provision (section 208-A of Act XI of 1925) by which pilgrims could be permitted to embark with a single ticket if they gave an oath or a declaration that they intended to stay for three years or more in the Hijaz.[193]

The rules framed under Act XI of 1925 made the pilgrim pass virtually compulsory.[194] The endeavour to link each pilgrim to a return ticket or deposit coupon also resulted in a greater 'individualization' of this document.[195] However, pilgrims who went in a party could still travel on a collective pass. The new rules substituted the phrase 'pilgrim pass' for 'pilgrim passport' – the difference in nomenclature seems to underline the limited arc of transnational circulation permitted to the poor. Yet even Act XI of 1925 did not impose any conditions on the issue of a *pilgrim pass*. It imposed a condition on the issue of an *embarkation ticket* to a pilgrim 'travelling in the lowest class'.

The 'anachronisms' of colonial pilgrim management

Colonial and 'international' identity protocols

The continuous stress placed on the free and 'unconditional' issue of the pilgrim passport seems to explain why it was not integrated to the regular British Indian passport.[196] The Government of India thought of doing so in 1911 when the Ottoman Government made the pilgrim passport compulsory, but decided not to.[197] Around the same time, it began to 'improve' the descriptive roll on the regular British Indian passport, for two rather different reasons.[198] With British power coursing strongly around the land and sea frontiers of India, the British Indian passport had come to acquire some value in the neighbourhood, and there were reports of trafficking in this document from Russia.[199] However, further away in British colonies of white settlement such as Canada and Australia, Indians were being refused entry. Here the problem was the potential devaluation of the British Indian passport. Officials were instructed to restrict its issue to Indians of 'means and respectability', and a detailed descriptive roll was introduced.[200] A comparison *c.* 1913 indicates that, in contrast to the general passport, there was no great anxiety about trafficking in the pilgrim passport (Table 2.1).

The pilgrim passport does not attempt a 'portrait parle', and there is no designated column for signature or thumbprint. The special column for the 'names and places of residence of nearest relatives in India', signals the Government of India's effort to claw back the property of deceased pilgrims, which might otherwise trickle away to *mutawwifs* or the Sharif of Mecca.[201] The Jidda consulate tried to re-claim these assets, among them the unused ticket, to swell its pilgrim repatriation fund, or to send back to India through returning relatives. The pilgrim ship rules of 1911, required the shipowner to note the buyer's name, father's name and place of residence on the ticket and stated that the ticket was not transferable.[202] These specifications were meant to discourage stowaways, to detect overloading, and to ensure that stamp duty was paid on higher-value tickets. However, the overlap of details between ticket and passport was also meant to underline property ownership, to check a loss or theft that might mean pilgrim destitution, and to discourage the 'expatriation' of assets.[203]

Table 2.1 The British Indian and pilgrim passports

The British Indian passport	The pilgrim passport
Name	Name
Father's name	Father's name
Signature	
Thumb impression	
Height	
Colour of eyes	
Hair	
Residence	Residence
Profession	Occupation
Age	Age
'Any real distinctive marks'	Distinctive marks
	Names and places of residence of nearest relatives in India
Payment Rs. 1	No payment

The Great War provided the backdrop to the next discussion about standardizing the pilgrim passport to the general passport. Over 1915–16, the template for the 'international form' of the passport was worked out both in metropolis and colony. This was the book form of the passport with its special paper, compulsory photograph, detailed descriptive roll, and signature. In March 1917 this re-modelled British Indian passport was made compulsory for entry and exit into India by sea, but pilgrims travelling to Basra or to the Hijaz were specifically exempted.[204] What the Government of India issued instead was the usual pilgrim passport, stripping it first of all reference to Turkish authorities and regulations.[205] The introduction simultaneously of pre-paid and subsidized return tickets, indicated a more instrumental role for the pilgrim passport, as an identity document that would suture the pilgrim to the return ticket. In April 1919, the Bombay Government convened a committee to consider changes in the pilgrim passport. Some members, for instance Ibrahim Rahimtoolah, a prominent Bombay Khoja Muslim, said Muslims might object to carrying a representation of the human form on a religious journey, so the committee decided not to prescribe a compulsory photograph.[206] Thumbprints were also rejected as an alternative, lest Hajis complain that they were being treated 'like convicts'.[207]

Yet in colonial India the thumbprint was an identity technique that had proliferated at a variety of institutional sites, not only in criminal records.[208] From 1903, fingerprint identification had also come to be associated with the 'criminalization' of Indian migration to South Africa and civic discrimination against Indian settlers there.[209] Educated and 'respectable' Indians had developed a special sensitivity therefore to identity techniques on the 'international' passport, insisting that when a signature could be given a thumbprint should not be taken.[210] Curiously enough, tracking the pilgrim passport up to 1925, I could not find a designated column for a signature. The discussion on improving the pilgrim passport seems to move only between photograph and thumbprint, suggesting that 'indexical' technologies alone were considered of any use to the management of a passenger traffic characterized as poor and ignorant. To buttress their case for a photograph officials sometimes said it would enable 'illiterate' pilgrims to distinguish their documents from those of others.[211] But their overriding concern was not so much to assist the unlettered by providing a visual aid, as to curtail the traffic in return tickets. The photograph would provide a *ready* if rough way of checking whether the person named in the passport was the one holding the ticket.[212] Pressing for thumbprints, Curtis, a Bombay official on the pilgrim passport committee said there was another reason why the Government of India should improve the identifying capacities of the pilgrim passport:

> we are sending the pilgrims for the first time to a country under a more or less civilised Government. It is absolutely necessary that *we should provide both ourselves and that government with means of identifying individual members of this horde of strangers.*[213]

However, feeling under siege because of the Khilafat and Rowlatt agitations, the Government of India set its face against innovations 'which would wear any appearance of oppression to the Hajis'.[214]

The pilgrim pass: antiquated and obsolete?

The complaint that the pilgrim pass lagged behind 'international' standards of travel and identity documentation persisted into the 1920s. In 1926, the British consul at Jidda criticized the pilgrim pass as 'antiquated and obsolete' because of the 'nervous refusal' of the Government of India to use a photograph or thumbprint.[215] The photograph, he wrote, would permit a quick correlation between the passport and the ticket-holder, to detect the theft or illegal sale of pre-paid return tickets and deposit-stamped passports.[216] He felt the return ticket option should be withdrawn, because it was easier to transfer than the deposit-stamped passport.[217] The consul also wanted section 208-A to be dropped, alleging that some pilgrims, abetted by *mutawwifs*, would declare that they were *Hijazis*, embark with single tickets, then clamour for repatriation as destitute British subjects.[218]

In a post-war world of more sharply delineated national affiliation, the Government of India's 'alien' pilgrim pass also seemed to constitute an anomaly. Afghanistan and Persia began to insist that their subjects should proffer their national passports when they embarked for the Hajj from some Indian port, instead of travelling on the 'alien pass'. However, the alien pass, like the pilgrim pass, underpinned the return ticket or deposit system, so the Government of India wanted to retain it. Nor did it want the onus of turning away foreign Hajjis who landed up without passports.[219] One option was to prune away the 'quasi-passport' character of the pilgrim pass, by scoring out the 'writ of assistance and protection' inscribed on it, and declaring it was merely a deposit certificate, an extension of the return ticket.[220] However, the 'quasi-passport' invocation of sovereignty and care was something the Government of India wanted to communicate to its own Hajjis, so the writ was retained for British Indians but scored out for 'aliens'.[221]

The ' stamp of the beast'

For Muslim legislators and the vernacular press, the point of anachronism was the retention of 'obsolete' quarantines for pilgrim shipping, which were not prescribed for liners going along the same route to Europe.[222] They also objected to embarkation procedures which treated pilgrims 'like cattle', especially when no distinction was made between first class and deck traffic.[223] And, indeed, officials did not trust to documentary inspection alone to ensure that the pilgrim's body had been processed as one safe for travel. In 1913, A. K. Ghuznavi, a member of the Viceroy's Legislative Council, described how medical officers went down the line of pilgrims feeling the forehead and the body for temperature.

> Pilgrims that are passed have the backs of their hands and their breasts stamped with an india-rubber stamp. This I consider to be highly objectionable. After all they are human beings and not animals.[224]

The practice continued into the 1920s.[225] In 1926, the Calcutta Pilgrim Department stated that the body-stamp had been replaced by a stamp on the passage ticket and that the new method was 'satisfactory and expeditious'.[226] However, the Bombay Pilgrim Department stated that its attempt to use a police cordon to distinguish pilgrims who had been put through medical inspection and disinfection had collapsed.[227] Given that 882 pilgrims had embarked from Calcutta and 14,501 from Bombay, the real issue, I suspect, was not the incorrigibility of the pilgrim mass but official reluctance to spend on sufficient agency, and a perception that it was unnecessary to do so. At the other end, the British Agency in Jidda, struggling to handle the documentary complexity created by this new regime of conditional mobility, fell back upon the *mutawwifs* to collect and re-distribute deposit-stamped pilgrim passes and return tickets, despite complaints that they misused this mediation.[228]

Conclusion

As the Government of India began to be called upon to ensure that pilgrims did not just drift across on overcrowded sailing ships, but were counted, medically inspected, and put onto licenced steam-ships, discourses about the *miskeen* took on a particular resonance. Here was a figure that seemed to undermine all these procedures, to compromise the ability of the authorities in India to meet the standards of 'civilized' travel being formulated at international conferences.

The characterization of the poor pilgrim as unable to deal with tickets and travel documents was an image invoked for different agendas. In 1896, calling upon the Sublime Porte to withdraw his demand for a passport, the British ambassador described Indian pilgrims as 'simple folk unaccustomed to travel', who would lose these papers.[229] When educated Muslims opposed compulsory return tickets they declared that 'illiterate Bokharis and Bengalis' would lose them.[230] In 1924, Haji Wahiuddin, speaking on the shipping Bill, attributed pilgrim destitution to the demands of spirituality – in the state of *Ihram* when they wore only two unstitched pieces of cloth, they lost currency drafts and return tickets.[231] Pilgrims were often quite willing to characterize themselves as ignorant and easily duped to explain why they were 'stranded', why they had 'lost' their pre-paid return tickets, or were detected with someone else's deposit-stamped passport.[232]

The pilgrim traffic was one stigmatized for its associations with disease and poverty but it was a mobility which could be circumscribed but not closed off. The surveillance and regulatory capacities of the pilgrim passport always seemed to lag behind those accruing to the 'international' form of the British Indian passport, and the former was used sometimes to evade postwar immigration controls in the Middle East. The salience of this 'lesser standard' can be understood if one examines the pilgrim passport against a backdrop of contending geographies. One was a cultural landscape constituted by networks of commerce, shipping and pilgrimage, access to which was strongly defended by various strands of Muslim public opinion in India.[233] The other was an 'international sphere' strongly shaped by imperialist rivalry around the Ottoman Empire. Finally we have the British Empire, projecting itself from the hub of India as the 'largest Muhammadan empire' in the world. Its contest for legitimacy with the Sultan-Caliph meant that in the sphere of 'high politics' a very unlikely protagonist kept coming into sight – the disorderly, suffering and resourceful *miskeen*.[234]

Acknowledgements

I am very grateful to James C. Scott and Kay Mansfield at the Agrarian Studies Program, Yale University for a wonderful research break and Chris Bayly and Jane Caplan for their support. William Ochsenwald and Ravi Vasudevan gave this paper a careful and helpful review. I am indebted to the research staff of the National Archives of India, Delhi, and the canteen workers there for years of friendly assistance. All manuscript references are from this archive unless otherwise stated.

Notes

1 I. Burton (ed.), *Personal narrative of a pilgrimage to al-Medina and Meccah, by Captain Sir Richard F. Burton*, 1855, Vol. II, London, G. Bell and Sons, 1913, pp. 184–85.
2 Ibid. p. 185.
3 Ibid. Vol. I, p. 18 and n. 1.
4 W. Ochsenwald, *Religion, society and the state in Arabia, the Hijaz under Ottoman control, 1840–1908*, Columbus, OH: Ohio State University, 1984; S. Deringil, *The well-protected domains: ideology and legitimation of power in the Ottoman empire, 1876–1909*, New York: I. T. Taurus, 1998.
5 V. P. Burrell, acting British Consul emphasized the growing number of British Indians residing in the Hijaz, holding large properties as *wakfs*, and taking an interest in water-supply, railways, quays, and piers. Report, 14 Oct 1880, *Parliamentary Papers*, (henceforth *PP*) 1881, Vol. C. 797, paper no. C.3008, pp. 40–41.
6 For J. F. Keane, another 'Englishman professing Mahommedanism' all Hindis in the Hijaz – artisans, officials, jurists, tradesmen – dissolved into the beggar. Once an overseer on a West Indian sugar plantation, Keene probably associated labour migration from India with the abolition of slavery, a development he critiqued for de-stabilizing 'the Negro' as a docile worker. J. F. Keane, *Six months in Mecca: An account of the Mohammedan pilgrimage to Mecca*, 1881, in *Records of the Hajj. A documentary history of the pilgrimage to Mecca* (henceforth *ROH*), 3, (1814–87), Archives Editions, pp. 422–25.
7 *The well-protected domains*, p.58.
8 *Religion, society and the state in Arabia*, pp.169–83.
9 A petition from one 'Moonerod deen and other natives' indicates that Ottoman officials began to sweep beggars out of Mecca after the Hajj. Bombay Government to British Consul Jidda (henceforth *BCJ*), 8 Sept 1866, *ROH* 3, pp.335–37.
10 J. Netten Radcliffe, 'Memorandum on quarantine in the Red Sea and on the sanitary regulation of the pilgrimage to Mecca', *PP*, C.2905, 1881, p.161. 'Correspondence respecting the International Sanitary Conference at Rome', *PP*, Commercial No. 27, 1885, p. 32.
11 A. Reid, 'Nineteenth century Pan-Islam in Indonesia and Malaysia', *Journal of Asian Studies*, 2, 1967: 267–83. D. Brewer, 'Russian roads to Mecca: Religious tolerance and Muslim pilgrimage in the Russian empire', *Slavic Review*, Vol. 555, No. 3, 1996: 567–84. Both historians point out that actual ability to prevent exit was limited.
12 Home, Sanitary, A, September 1901, 18–19; Home, Sanitary, A, September 1907, 260–63.
13 Once before, in 1847, the Sultan had demanded a passport from Indian pilgrims, but the British Foreign Office persuaded him to withdraw the order. Foreign, Political, 2 September 1848, No. 27.
14 For important accounts: W. Roff, 'Sanitation and security: The imperial powers and the nineteenth century Hajj', *Arabian Studies*, 6, 1982: 143–60; M. Harrison, 'Quarantine, pilgrimage, and colonial trade, India 1866–1900', *Indian Economic and Social History Review*, 29, 1994: 117–38; M. Miller, 'Pilgrim's progress: the

business of the Hajj', *Past and Present*, 191, May 2006: 189–228. Miller argues that European shipping companies brought regularity and predictability to Hajj travel, but he overlooks the progressive exclusion of the poor.
15 As in two otherwise very suggestive articles: O. Takashi 'Friction and rivalry over pious mobility: British colonial management of the hajj and reaction to it by Indian Muslims', in K. Hidemitsu (ed.), *The influence of human mobility in Muslim societies*, London: Kegan Paul, 2003, pp.151–75, 155, 163; and M. C. Low 'The 'twin infection': pilgrims, plagues, and pan-Islam under British surveillance, 1865–1924', http://harrimaninstitute.org/Media/00415.pdf, 10 March 2006. Complaints that beggar pilgrims compromised British prestige seem to antedate complaints that they brought contagion in their trail.
16 In 1886 the Government of India (henceforth GOI) circulated an Ottoman dispatch complaining about Indians who came 'not from religious motives' but to subsist on public charity. The Central National Mohammedan Association accepted that the indigent might have such 'worldly motives'. However, the Commissioner of Police, Bombay (henceforth CPB) insisted that the indigent could do better begging in India, and that they were drawn to the Hijaz by a desire to die in its sanctity. *ROH* 3, p. 615.
17 Harrison may posit too stark a divide between poor pilgrims as opposed to all colonial interventions in sanitation and pilgrim shipping, and affluent Muslims as supportive. 'Quarantine, pilgrimage and colonial trade.'
18 Indian Merchant Shipping Act of 1923 as amended by Act XI of 1925.
19 W. Ochsenwald, 'The commercial history of the Hijaz Vilayet, 1840–1908', *Arabian Studies*, VI, London, pp. 57–76.
20 Wealthy pilgrims took bills of exchange, on the strength of this network. Indian merchants at Jidda and Mecca assisted poor pilgrims to return. *ROH* 4, (1888–1915), p. 784; Home, Sanitary, A, Sept 1907, 260–63.
21 BCJ to British ambassador, Constantinople, 19 July 1912, Foreign, Internal, A, October 1912, 1.
22 'Friction and rivalry', pp. 163, 175.
23 Ibid. p. 172; *Bombay Legislative Council Proceedings*, Vol. XXIV, 1887, p. 34; Foreign, Internal, A, October 1912, 1.
24 Secy, Bombay Government to GOI, 21 Jan 1886, *ROH* 3, p. 611. A. K. Ghuznavi, *Note on the pilgrim traffic to the Hedjaz and Palestine*, Calcutta, 1915, Pt I. An internet search reveals that steam-ships entered the pilgrim business late in their life cycle. The 'Duart Castle', 1878, sold in the 1920s to Khandwani and Co. of Bombay, and scrapped in 1925. 'The Mirzapore', 1871, P&O, sold to Haji Casssum Jossub for the pilgrim trade in 1898 and scrapped the following year. 'The Clan Sinclair', 1882, sold in 1905 to the Bombay Persia Steam Navigation Company and renamed the 'Rahmani' for the pilgrim traffic, 1912–14.
25 *Bombay Legislative Council Proceedings*, Vol. XXIV, 1887, p. 34.
26 CPB to Bombay Government, 14 Dec 1909, in Bombay, General Department, 1915, No. 768, Maharashtra State Archives, Mumbai (henceforth General, MSA).
27 In 1894 pilgrims on a ship from Bombay mutinied against a quarantine that would have made them miss the Hajj. Legislative Department, (henceforth Leg) October 1895, 13–95.
28 *Report of the Haj Inquiry Committee*, Calcutta, Government of India, 1931, p. 25 (henceforth *RHIC*). The Indian Vice-Consul said pilgrims believed that their guides were Arabs, but he categorized most who went to Bengal as 'Indians'. Home, Sanitary, A, April 1898, 779–83. *Mutawwifs/muallims*: pilgrim guides
29 GOI threatened to withdraw the subsidy it was giving to this firm to 'improve' pilgrim carriage. Secy, Home, to F. H. Cook, 26 Feb 1887, *ROH* 3, p. 625.
30 *Note on the pilgrim traffic*, I, p.9; also Miller, 'Pilgrim's progress'.

31 M. A. Siraj, 'A peep into the past. From riches to rags'. http://www.radianceweekly.com/ archives/issue18/articl10.htm
32 Extract, *Times of India*, 9 November 1885 in 'Papers relating to the arrangements made with Messrs. Cook and Son for the conduct of the pilgrim traffic to and from the Red Sea during the years 1884–95', *Selections from the Records of the Government of India*, Home Department, CCCXXX, 16, (henceforth *SRGOI*). Sometimes other pilgrims paid their fare.
33 BCJ, 27 Feb 1927, *ROH* 6, p. 591.
34 This account is put together from: *SRGOI*, CCCXXX, No. 16; Foreign, Internal, A, Oct 1912, 1; General, 1914, No.748, MSA; *RHIC*, p. 28.
35 Leg, October 1895, 13–95, Appendix T.
36 BCJ to Foreign Dept., GOI, 30 June 1883, in Foreign Dept. A, Political, E, March 1884, 115–48.
37 In 1878 Indian pilgrims and Bedouins were employed to restore the water system of Mecca. *Religion, society and the state in Arabia*, p. 176. The presence of African labour, slave and free, and a wariness about enslaving British Indians may have obscured the Indian component of the labour and service pool in the Hijaz.
38 General, 1912, Vol.132, MSA; *ROH* 3, p. 614.
39 *Report of the Native Passenger Ships Commission appointed in November 1890*, appendix IV.
40 Ibid.
41 Indian shippers went on combining pilgrims and cargo on routes to the Persian Gulf, where pilgrim ships rules did not apply till 1912. Fares were, therefore, cheaper than on the Bombay–Jidda route. Pilgrims would disembark at Baghdad and follow the overland route to Medina, or take another ship for the Hijaz. General, 1914, No. 993, Pt. II.
42 *ROH* 3, p. 587.
43 24 June 1887, *SRGOI*, CCCXXX, No. 16, p. 46.
44 Home, Sanitary, A, October 1905, 344. The percentage of pilgrims between 1887–1902 who got an indigent pass at Qamaran is: 20.88 per cent for Indians and Afghans, 91.47 per cent for the Hadramaut and Muscat, 41.21 per cent for Somalis, 53.28 per cent for Sudanese, and 44.71 per cent for Ottoman subjects. Dr Duguet, *Le Pelerinage de la Mecque*, Paris: Rieder, 1932, pp 34–35.
45 GOI asked the Secretary of State for India (henceforth SOS) to intervene. F&P, External, Secret, File 29/1924, 1–50.
46 The Ocean Steam Ship Company, competing for the pilgrim business complained about this practice. Leg, October 1895, 13–95.
47 Note by H. Luson, 31 Dec 1893, ibid.
48 The more destitute and debilitated would sleep in the streets and mosques, and eat at almshouses. Isabel Burton describes returning Bengali pilgrims as subsisting on sun-dried meat from the ritual sacrifice of animals at Mina. I. Burton, *Arabia Egypt India, A narrative of travel*, London: W. Mullan and Son, 1879, p. 101.
49 Actg BCJ to British Ambassador, 15 May 1912, General, 1914, No. 993–1, MSA.
50 BCJ to Earl of Salisbury, 20 December 1895, *ROH* 4 (1888–1915), pp. 238–41.
51 The Nawab of Hyderabad began to arrange a return fare. Home, Sanitary, A, September 1903, 60–81.
52 Foreign, External, B, September 1908, 77–78.
53 Home, Sanitary, A, 1882, 84–220; Education, Sanitary, B, November 1912, 1–3.
54 Ibid.
55 Education Health and Lands (henceforth EHL), Health, B, February 1925.
56 Shipping acts and rules with even more demanding specifications followed in 1895, 1915, 1923 and 1925.
57 See Indian Vice-Consul Jidda (henceforth VCJ) to BCJ, 20 May 1901, Home, Sanitary, A, September 1901, 18–19.

58 The Ottoman governor and the Sharif of Mecca tried to prohibit pilgrims from sleeping in the streets and mosques. Education, Sanitary, A, June 1913, 5–49; *ROH* 5 (1916–25), p.58.
59 Home, Sanitary, A, April 1898, 779–83.
60 *Le Pelerinage*, p. 34. Red paper passes were issued to those exempted from fees at Qamaran and Jidda. Leg, October 1895, 13–95, Appendix T.
61 General, 1912, No.134, MSA.
62 Ibid.
63 F&P, Near East, File 216-N/1929, 1–12.
64 Home, Public, A, 21 November 1861, 26–34; BCJ to Bombay Government, 30 April 1875, *ROH* 3, pp. 363–67.
65 Home, Sanitary, A July 1882, 84–220. The SOS for India hinted that the Ottomans expected a means test to be linked to the passport. SOS to GOI, 26 October 1882. Ibid.
66 BCJ, 4 May 1881, in Home, Sanitary, B, August 1881, 6.
67 In 1878, Razzack had suggested that pilgrims deposit a sum of money for the return journey, the receipt to serve as a passport. Medico-Sanitary Report, 1878, *PP*, C.2905, 1881, p. 239.
68 VCJ to BCJ, 17 April 1883, in Foreign, A, Political, E, March 1884, 115–48.
69 Ibid.
70 N. Sousa, *Capitulatory regime of Turkey*, Baltimore, Johns Hopkins, 1933.
71 VCJ, to BCJ, 17 April 1883, Foreign, A, Political, E, March 1884, 115–48. There was a much lower fee for registering as an Ottoman subject.
72 VCJ to BCJ, 10 November 1883, ibid.
73 Ibid.
74 Home Dept Note, 14 September 1881, in Home, Sanitary, A July 1882, 84–220. Moncrief said the Dutch attempt to use the pilgrim passport for surveillance had not been very successful. Moncrief to Foreign Dept, 13 May 1883, Foreign, A Political, E, March 1884, 115–48.
75 Resolution, Home, Sanitary, 21 January 1886, in *SRGOI*, CCCXXX. No.16, p. 8.
76 Abdur Razzack to BCJ, 13 May 1883, Foreign A, Political, E, March 1884, 115–48.
77 The Ottoman Sultan suspected that the late Emir of Mecca (1877–80) had been conspiring with the British consul to challenge his claim to the Caliphate and to establish an independent Arab government. S. T. Buzpinar, 'Vying for power and influence in the Hijaz: Ottoman rule, the last emirate of Abdulmuttalib and the British (1880–82)', *The Muslim World*, Vol. 95, 1, January 2005.
78 BCJ to Foreign Dept, GOI, 13 May 1883, Foreign, A, Political, E, March 1884, 115–48. The consulate also thwarted an Ottoman attempt to use the pilgrim passport as a fiscal device. BCJ to H. M's Charge D'Affaires, Constantinople, 22 May 1885, *ROH* 3, pp. 599–600.
79 The position of Caliph became ever more important to the Ottoman Sultan as he re-worked the terms of legitimacy and allegiance within the shrinking frontiers of his empire (*The well protected domains*).
80 VCJ to BCJ, 17 April 1883, Foreign, A, Political, E, March 1884, 115–48.
81 *General instructions for Pilgrims to the Hedjaz and a manual for the guidance of officers and others concerned in the Red Sea Pilgrim Traffic*, Calcutta, 1904, p. 1 (Henceforth, *Manual*). Emphasis added.
82 This blanket designation was systematized by section 5(1) of the Pilgrim Ships Act (Act XIV of 1895) which stated: '"pilgrim" means a Muhammadan passenger going to, or returning from, the Hedjaz.'
83 Home, Sanitary, A, July 1882, 84–220.
84 Ibid.

85 In 1889, out of 11,544 who embarked from Bombay, 2,000 were without passports, in 1890, 1,141 out of 9,953, and in 1891, 2,967 out of 12,032. *SRGOI*, pp. 105, 117, 128.
86 VCJ to BCJ, 23 March 1887, *ROH* 3, pp. 741–42; Home, Sanitary, A, April 1898, 779–83.
87 *ROH* 3, p. 587.
88 S. Bose, *A hundred horizons. The Indian Ocean in the age of global empire*, Harvard University Press, 2006, p. 203.
89 Protector of Pilgrims (henceforth POP), Bombay to CPB, 27 May 1905, Home, Sanitary, (Plague), A, October 1904, 199–201.
90 POP, Karachi, to Collector Karachi, 17 May 1913, General 1914, No.993 II, MSA.
91 6 October 1894, Home, Sanitary, May 1895, 50–55.
92 Home, Sanitary, A September 1907, 260–63.
93 Secretary, Anjuman–I – Islam, Bombay to CPB, 29 Jan 1906, General, 1912, No.132, MSA.
94 Of the 51,302 pilgrim passports issued between 1892–93 and 1896–97, only 1,079 were issued by local authorities. The rest were issued at Bombay (Bombay, Judicial Dept., 1898, No.162, MSA). Problems had emerged when pilgrims from the eastern Bengal districts were asked to vouch for their identity at Calcutta, so local governments were instructed not to harass pilgrims about verifying particulars. Foreign, A, Political, E, March 1884, 115–48.
95 When Turner Morrison and Co. replaced brokers with paid employees the Commissioner of Police, Bombay, experiencing a loss of control, complained that 'poor and ignorant pilgrims' should not be left to the mercy of a private company. F. A. M. Vincent, 10 October 1917, in General, 1917–18, No. 992, MSA. See also Miller, 'Pilgrim's progress'.
96 GOI, Resolution, 12 July 1882 in *SRGOI*, No.CCCXXX, p.4
97 F&P, Secret, War, May 1918, 159–60; Note, General Dept, 13 May 1925, General File No. 5692, 1924–27, MSA.
98 *Manual* 1922; *RHIC*, 1931, p. 32.
99 M. A. Khan, a Khilafat leader, was denied a passport for Iraq or Persia but given a pilgrim pass for the Hijaz. F&P, Near East Branch, File, 292-N/1924, 1–3. After Act XI of 1925, ten persons were refused a pilgrim pass in 1926 on the grounds that they were 'likely to fall into destitution'. F&P, Near East, File 295-N/1924–27, p.78.
100 F&P, Near East, File 216-N/1929, 1–12; *ROH* 6, pp. 39, 139.
101 General, 1912, No. 134, MSA. However, till 1914 the holder of the regular British Indian passport also quite often entered the names of servants on it.
102 Leg, October 1895, 13–120. However, there are instances in which women led a party and the pilgrim passport was issued in their name.
103 Education, Sanitary, B, March 1913, 52–59.
104 If one person was detected with infectious disease, the whole party could be held back. Leg, October 1895, 13–95. In the 1920s, to cope with the rush at return, the consulate would issue return tickets and deposit-stamped passports in bundles to guides or leaders of parties. *ROH* 5, p. 456.
105 In 1927–28, when Persia prohibited its subjects from going on the Hajj, Persian pilgrims set off from Bombay as Indians. File No. 87-N/1928 (Secret).
106 BCJ to Secy, Foreign Dept., 21 January 1885, *ROH* 3, p. 585.
107 For instance, Moncrief turned down Abdur Razzack's proposal to extend the consulate's influence in Mecca by setting up a pilgrim hospital, saying it might 'degenerate' into a poor house. BCJ to Foreign Dept, 23 May 1883, in Foreign Dept., A, Political, E, March 1884, 115–48.
108 *The well protected domains*, pp. 56–57

109 20 December 1895, *ROH* 4, p. 222; Home, Sanitary, A, April 1898, 779–83.
110 *SRGOI*, CCCXXX, No.16.
111 The underlying allegation was that brokers were keeping clients out of reach and overloading ships with undocumented pilgrims (ibid. pp. 105, 117, 128, 137).
112 Ibid. pp. 45–46, 77–78, 93–94, 97.
113 Ibid. pp. 83–85, 151.The firm's share of bookings fell from 42 per cent in 1890 to 9.5 per cent in 1893. Ibid. pp. 131, 157.
114 GOI to SOS 11 September 1895, Leg, October 1895, 13–95.
115 BCJ to British Ambassador, 19 July 1912, Foreign, Internal, A, Oct 1912, 1.
116 Home, Sanitary, A, July 1882, 84–200.
117 Bombay, Judicial Dept, 1879, No.83, MSA. Also 'Vagrant bands of foreigners', *SRGOI*, Home, No. CLVII, Calcutta, 1879.
118 Ibid. Home, Police, A Dec 1879, 610–18 Foreign, Internal, A Feb 1896, 1–2. However *powindas* (graziers), were permitted if they kept to the border provinces of Punjab and Sindh and substantial merchants were welcomed.
119 Note, Secy, Foreign Dept, 25 September 1881, Home Sanitary, A, July 1882, 84–220.
120 Until the 1920s the British consulate involved itself with the repatriation of destitute pilgrims from Afghanistan, Bokhara and Chinese Turkestan, as much as with those from India.
121 A British trade delegation went to Kashgar in 1890, and in 1908 a consulate was installed. In 1914 the British resident in Kashmir wanted to block the entry of indigent pilgrims from Chinese Turkestan but GOI would not agree. F&P, General, A, August 1914, 32–37. In 1930, the authorities in Chinese Turkestan discouraged the exit of Hajjis but GOI assisted them despite anxieties about Soviet infiltration. F&P, External, 353/X/1930, 1–20.
122 Foreign, A, Political, E, March 1884, 115–48.
123 SOS to GOI, 26 Oct 1882, ibid.
124 Hajj report, 1911–12, General, 1914, No. 993–1, MSA.
125 In fact, the civilizing ambition can also be detected in certain aristocratic or educated Indian Muslims demanding political room to re-shape the Hajj experience in the Hijaz as a comfortable and sanitary one. In 1919 one Captain Agub Khan of the Indian Army, describing the Sharif's government as 'well-meaning but backward', declared, 'As we are the greatest Moslem ruling power in the world, our share of protecting the interests of our Moslem fellow-subjects at their holy places is equally greater' 15 October 1919, in General Dept, 1920, No.946, MSA.
126 W. R. Roff 'Sanitation and security'. GOI criticized the Paris Sanitary Conference for imposing 'useless restrictions on trade and upon the great Muhammadan population of India', GOI to SOS, 11 September 1895, Leg, October 1895, 13–95.
127 For a sea-saga about an English captain who contracts with a Parsi shipowner at Bombay to carry corn, cotton cloth and earthenware to Jidda, then surreptitiously carries African pilgrims on his return, see C. J. Cutcliffe Hyne, *Adventures of Captain Kettle*, 1898, http://gaslight.mtroyal.ab.ca/Gaslight/ketleX04.htm.
128 Memo, 9 October 1894, Leg, October 1895, 13–95.
129 *ROH* 4 (1888–1915), p. 330. In 1913 the Turkish consul in Bombay complained about a proposal to inaugurate a 'King George V Hospital' at Jidda. A. K. Ghuznavi, *Note on the pilgrim traffic*, Part I, pp. 16–17.
130 GOI despatch No.2, 27 January 1892, Leg, October 1895, 13–95.
131 N. M. Goodman, *International Health Organisations and their work*, London: Longman, 1971, p. 68.
132 Leg, September 1887, 1–18. In 1886 an ordinance also penalized persons landing vagrant and destitute people at Hong Kong. Home, Public, A, May 1888, 27–29.

133 SOS to GOI, 29 November 1894, Leg Dept, October 1895, 13–95.
134 GOI to SOS, 11 Sept 1895, ibid. In the 1890s a widespread 'cow-protection movement' had made GOI apprehensive about 'outbursts of religious fanaticism'. Modern associational politics, aided by a contentious vernacular press, were gaining strength, and official spokesmen had to make a case for new bills in the Imperial Legislative Council.
135 The Managing Agent of the Bombay Persia Steam Navigation Co. pointed out that the norm was 10 square feet for British troop ships, 12 for merchant seamen and 6 for lascars. Leg, October 1895, 13–95, Appendix A3, Appendix T. Rules under the Indian Pilgrim shipping act of 1895 raised the norm, but to 16 superficial feet, not to 21. Notification 17 September 1897.
136 Leg, October 1895, 13–95, Appendix A3. The Central Muhammadan Association, Madras, declared that this provision was 'without a precedent on any line of traffic by land or sea in any civilized country' ibid. However, the Pilgrim Ships Act of 1895, Section 5 (i) continued to count two children between one and twelve years of age as one pilgrim.
137 Ibid.
138 Memorial from two *kazis* and other inhabitants of Bombay, 31 July 1895, ibid.
139 Under pressure from the India Office, the Government of India did not wait to amend the general Indian Merchants Shipping Act, but rushed through a separate Pilgrim Ships Bill. Leg, October 1895, 13–95.
140 Ibid.
141 9 October 1894, in Leg, October 1895, 13–95.
142 Prince Sir Jahan Kadr, member Imperial Legislative Council, ibid. Appendix A-3.
143 7 August 1895, Leg, October 1895, 13–95, appendix O. The Muslim Association of Rangoon welcomed the enactment in the same terms. Ibid. Appendix R.
144 Representation from Mohammadan Literary Society, Calcutta, 14 August 1895, and from Kazi Mahomed Saleh and others of Bombay, 31 July 1895 in Leg, October 1895, Appendix S, Appendix T.
145 General, 1914, No. 993, Pt II, MSA.
146 In early 1912, an Italian blockade along the Yemen coast created a scare leading to a shortage of shipping from India. Education, Sanitary, A June 1913, 5–49.
147 7 January 1913, ibid.
148 Note, Maharaj Singh, 18 February 1913, ibid.
149 General, 1914, No. 993–1, MSA. BCJ Avalon Shipley made it clear that he wanted a British firm to supplant the Bombay Persia Steam Navigation Co., an Indian firm, whose agents at Jidda he described as 'a gang of Arabs whose chief source of profit is the carrying of excess pilgrims'. It was 'intolerable' that natives should control 'so important and remunerative a concern as the Indian pilgrim traffic' BCJ to Secretary of State for Foreign Affairs, 2 September 1912, General, 1912, No. 129, MSA. Turner Morrison entered the pilgrim business in 1913 with six steamers, none specially built for this traffic. By 1929 it had eight pilgrim steamers, which it diverted to cargo in the off-season. Its competitors in the pilgrim business were Shustary and Co., with only one ship, and the Nemazee line with two. *RIHC*, para. 119.
150 Commissioner Customs, CPB, and Health Officer, Bombay Port to Secy, Bombay Government, 22 March 1906, General, 1912, No. 132, MSA.
151 Education, Sanitary, A, June 1913, 54–59. The plague crisis of 1897–98 had made urban re-construction in Bombay a priority, and the clearing operations of the Port Trust had reduced pilgrim accommodation around the docks. The Bombay Government wanted to ease harbour congestion in the pilgrim season, and to discourage returning 'paupers' from adding to the indigent of the city. Home, Sanitary, June 1904, 199–209; *RIHC*, p.11.

152 Colonial Secretary, Straits Settlement to Bombay government, 21 November 1911, General, 1912, Vol. 132, MSA
153 In 1905, competition between the Bombay and Persia Steam Navigation Company and Essaji Tajbhoy, brought the return fare down from Rs. 20 to Rs. 2. Home, Sanitary, A, October 1905, 344. In 1922, competition brought the return fare down to Rs. 35. EHL, Sanitary B, April 1923, 67–68. When a pre-paid deposit was introduced the following season, the return fare shot up to Rs. 60. *ROH* 5 (1916–25), p. 530.
154 Report on the Hajj of 1922, *ROH* 5, p. 379.
155 Education, Sanitary, A June 1913, 5–49.
156 'The Haj Pilgrimage, The proposed monopoly', *Bombay Chronicle*, 19 July 1914, press clipping, in General, 1914, No. 993, Pt. III, MSA.
157 Ibid.
158 O. Takashi, 'Muslim merchant capital and the relief movement for the Ottoman empire in India, 1876–1924', *Journal of the Japan Association for South Asian Studies*, 11, 1999: 71–103.
159 For a brief discussion, A. Mehta, *Indian shipping, a case study of the working of imperialism*, Bombay 1944, pp. 55–56.
160 M. Rafiuddin Ahmed to Acting CPB, 29 Jan 1906, General, 1912, No. 132, MSA.
161 Ibid.
162 For complaints in this vein in 1906–7 and in 1913, see General, 1912, No. 132, and General, 1914, No. 993, Pt-II, MSA.
163 A. Ozcan, *Pan-Islamism: Indian Muslim, the Ottomans and Britain (1877–1924)*, Leiden, E.J. Brill, 1997, pp. 54–61; O. Takashi, 'Muslim merchant capital'.
164 Mohammed Ali, *My Life*, pp. 48–49.
165 M. Rafiuddin Ahmed, 29 January 1906, General, 1912, No.132, MSA; F&P, General, A, August 1914, 32–37.
166 Fuzul Currimbhoy Ebrahim, in the Imperial Legislative Council, 20 March 1913, General, 1913, No.140, MSA.
167 There were precedents for such suggestions. The Egyptian Sultan and the Shah of Persia made returning pilgrim ships take a certain percentage of destitutes. VCJ to BCJ 20 May 1901, Home, Sanitary, A, September 1901, 18–19. The Anjuman-i-Moinul-Islam, Bhiwandi, compared GOI's position with that of the Ottoman sultan, said to sympathize with his destitute pilgrims and to pay for their return. March 1906, in General 1912, Vol.132, MSA.
168 District Magistrate Surat, 16/17 March 1906, General, 1912, No.132, MSA.
169 13 May 1913, General, 1914, No.993-II, MSA.
170 District Magistrate Surat, 16/17 March 1906, General, 1912, No.132, MSA; J. L. Rieu, Secretary, General Department, Bombay, remarks on Rafiuddin Ahmed's proposal, 13 May 1913, General, 1914, No.993-II, MSA.
171 'The pilgrim traffic', press note, Bombay, General Department, 1 August 1914, General, 1914, No.768, MSA.
172 The Pilgrim Ships Act (Act XIV of 1895)
173 *Legislation and orders relating to the war*, 1915, p. 105.
174 General, 1916, No. 946, MSA.
175 Ibid. also *RHIC*, 1931, p.9
176 In the meantime, Turner Morrison had taken over another Indian Muslim firm, 'Arab Steamers Ltd'.
177 F&P, Secret, War, May 1918, No. 159–60
178 The subsidy was eleven lakhs (Rs. 11,00,000) for the 1916–17 Hajj, eight lakhs for the 1917–18 Hajj, and a combined total of ten lakhs for 1918–19 and 1919–20 Hajj. In 1920, Shustary and Co. reverted to single tickets, because the Mogul Line was edging it out by refusing to allow ticket interchange on the return run. The official subsidy was stopped (General, 1921, No.518, MSA).

179 Ibid.
180 Report on the Haj of 1917 by an Indian police officer, *ROH* 5, p.72.
181 CPB 18 July 1916, General, 1916, No. 946, MSA.
182 British Agent, Jidda, 1 December 1919, and GOI to SOS 29 April 1920, in *ROH* 5, pp. 162–66; Haj report 1927, in *ROH* 6 (1926–35), pp. 137, 237.
183 See General, 1912, No.132, MSA.
184 Act XI of 1925, Leg, File 110–11/1924.
185 6 Feb 1924, ibid.
186 Ibid.
187 Ibid.
188 Ibid. However, Muhammad Shafee insisted that pilgrim destitution was the product of specific interventions – the special burdens imposed on pilgrim shipping and the privileged position given to Turner Morrison, both of which had hiked up fares. Ibid.
189 There were six Muslims on the ten-member Select Committee, among them, M. A. Jinnah, who supported the enactment. Ibid.
190 S. D. Butler, 6 February 1924, Leg File 110-I/1924.
191 Leg File 110-I/1924.
192 Muslim legislators also insisted that pilgrims retain the right to choose between pre-paid tickets or deposits. EHL, Health, A, January 1927, 1–9.
193 Those who declared that they were Hijazis, that is subjects of the Sharif of Mecca, were also allowed this option.
194 'Every intending pilgrim shall obtain ... a pilgrim pass and present it for registration to the authorities appointed by the local Governments at the port of embarkation. No ticket shall be issued to a pilgrim who does not produce his Pilgrim Pass duly registered.'
Notification 15 December 1926, EHL, Health, A, January 1927, 1–9.
195 F&P, Near East, File 431-N/1926. In 1926, 14,428 passes were issued to 14,501 pilgrims. Separate passes were not issued to 83 babies. To travel to other places in the Middle East pilgrims had to acquire the regular 'international' passport. Ibid.
196 Political loyalty came to constitute a component of 'respectability'.
197 F&P, Internal, B, December 1911, 89–91.
198 Education, Sanitary, B, March 1913, 52–59; Education, General, B, March 1913, No. 10.
199 Foreign, General, B, May 1913, 177–83.
200 Ibid; General, 1912, Vol.56, MSA.
201 Education, Sanitary, A September 1913, 26–28. The column for dependents was also inserted into the alien pass citing the 'difficulty of tracing the whereabouts of pilgrims who die intestate'. Ibid.
202 General, 1912, No.132, MSA.
203 For complaints about evasion of ticket rules, Legal Dept 1915, No.6 MSA.
204 F&P, General B, March 1917, 18. See Radhika Singha, 'Exceptions to the law and exceptional laws: a 'proper' passport for colonial India, 1914–20', www.cishsydney2005.
205 F&P, War, B (Secret). February 1917, 66–67.
206 General, 1919, No. 946. The cost of a photograph was taken into account for the pilgrim passport, but ignored in the case of the general passport. Note, M. I. Huk, 23 February 1926, in F&P, File 431/N/1926. In October 1918 Hindu and Muslim pardah women had been exempted from a photograph for the general passport, but had to give their thumbprint instead 'Exceptions to the law'.
207 General, 1919, No. 946.
208 Thumbprints were deployed in the registration and pension departments in India and were also used by money-lenders and employers of labour to

reinforce the judicial authority of contract. See Radhika Singha 'Settle, mobilize, verify: identification practices in colonial India', *Studies in History*, 2000, 16, 2: 151–98.
209 Ibid.
210 Foreign, General, B, May 1913, 177–83.
211 'Report of the Pilgrim Department, Bengal' in F&P, Near East, File 295-N/1924–27.
212 General, 1919, No.946, MSA. Discussing the advantages of a photograph, the Indian Hajj Committee of 1931 hinted darkly that in the past, guides had even done away with pilgrims to appropriate their passes and tickets! *RHIC*, p.51.
213 April 1919, in General Dept, 1921, No. 413, MSA. Emphasis added.
214 Ibid. However the Protector at Karachi reported that he took a thumbprint 'voluntarily' from male pilgrims. F&P, External, B, September 1922, 8–19.
215 4 August 1926, in F&P, File No.855-N of 1927. He pointed out that even the orthodox Wahhabi regime issued Hijazi passports with a photograph, though women were exempted. Ibid. The CPB held that the pilgrim pass was of 'little practical value' for identification. 14 August 1926, EHL, Health, A, January 1927, 1–9.
216 F&P, File No.858-N of 1927.
217 Ibid. Shipping companies tried to popularize pre-paid return tickets to retain their clients. See *RHIC*, 1931, p.55.
218 F&P, File No.855-N of 1927.
219 F&P, File No.87-N/1928. The Foreign and Political Department in India observed that assistance to Central Asian pilgrims was 'the soundest form of propaganda.' Note, 22 June 1928, ibid.
220 F&P, File No. 87-N/1928.
221 Ibid.
222 The *Roznama-i-Khilafat* protested against a double pilgrim quarantine, one at Qamaran and another at Jidda, whereas there was no quarantine for passengers going to England. *Report on Indian newspapers*, Bombay Presidency, No. 13 of 1926 and No. 5 of 1927.
223 *Report on Indian newspapers*, Bombay Presidency, No. 6 of 1926; *ROH* 5, p. 564.
224 A. K. Ghuznavi, *Note on the pilgrim traffic*, Part I, p. 12 Ghuznavi declared this was akin to putting a 'stamp of the beast'. Ibid.
225 *ROH* 5, p. 564.
226 F&P, Near East, File 295-N/1924–27.
227 POP to CPB, 23 December 1926, ibid.
228 Report of the Hajj, 1923, *ROH* 5, pp. 456–57; *ROH* 6 (1926–30), pp. 126–30, 135; F&P, Near East, File 216/N/1929, 1–12. *Mutawwifs* used their grip over return tickets and passes to ensure that pilgrims did not return without paying their dues. F&P, File 157-N, 1931.
229 Foreign, External, A, May 1896, 1–21.
230 H. S. Abdool Wahed, Bombay Hajj Committee, 19 May 1913, in General, 1914, No. 993, Part II, MSA.
231 18 March 1924, in Leg, File 110-I/1924.
232 Petition from certain Hajjis, 24 Nov 1919, *ROH* 5, pp. 166–73.
233 O. Takashi and S. Bose invoke this landscape very imaginatively. See 'Friction and rivalry'; and *A Hundred Horizons*.
234 Randall Baker attributed King Husain's 'low opinion' of the Government of India to this figure. R. Baker, *King Husain and the Kingdom of the Hejaz*, Cambridge, 1979, pp. 122–23. The development of motor transport in the 1920s gave pilgrims a new combination of routes to elude barriers.

Bibliography

Archival material

1. Maharashtra State Archives, Mumbai (formerly Bombay), India.
General Department Proceedings
Judicial Department Proceedings
Legal Department Proceedings
2. National Archives of India, New Delhi, India
Home Department Proceedings
Foreign Department Proceedings
Education Proceedings
Education, Health and Lands Proceedings
Legislative Department Proceedings

Published material

Baker, R., *King Husain and the Kingdom of the Hejaz*, Cambridge: The Oleander Press, 1979.
Bose, S., *A Hundred Horizons. The Indian Ocean in the age of global empire*, Cambridge, MA: Harvard University Press, 2006.
Brewer, D., 'Russian roads to Mecca: Religious tolerance and Muslim pilgrimage in the Russian empire', *Slavic Review* 55, 3, 1996: 567–84.
Burton, I., *Arabia Egypt India, A narrative of travel,* London, W. Mullan and Son, 1879.
——, *Personal narrative of a pilgrimage to al-Medina and Meccah, by Captain Sir Richard F. Burton*, Vol. I, Vol. II, London: G. Bell and Sons, 1913, [1855].
Buzpinar, S. T., 'Vying for power and influence in the Hijaz: Ottoman rule, the last emirate of Abdulmuttalib and the British (1880–82)', *The Muslim World* 95, 1, 2005: 1–22.
Cutcliffe Hyne, C. J., *Adventures of Captain Kettle*, 1898, http://gaslight.mtroyal.ab.ca/kettmenu.htm, accessed 23 May 2007.
Deringil, S., *The well-protected domains: ideology and legitimisation of power in the Ottoman empire, 1876–1909*, New York: I. T. Taurus, 1998.
Duguet, F., *Le Pelerinage de la Mecque*, Paris, Rieder, 1932.
General instructions for Pilgrims to the Hedjaz and a manual for the guidance of officers and others concerned in the Red Sea Pilgrim Traffic, Calcutta: Government of India, 1904.
Ghuznavi, A. K., *Note on the pilgrim traffic to the Hedjaz and Palestine*, Calcutta, unknown publisher, 1915.
Goodman, N. M., *International Health Organisations and their work*, London: Longman, 1971.
Harrison, M., 'Quarantine, pilgrimage, and colonial trade, India 1866–1900', *Indian Economic and Social History Review* 29, 2, 1994: 117–44.
Keane, J. F. *Six months in Mecca: An account of the Mohammedan pilgrimage to Mecca*, 1881, in *Records of the Hajj. A documentary history of the pilgrimage to Mecca*, 3, (1814–87), Archives Editions.
Low, M. C., *The 'twin infection': pilgrims, plagues, and pan-Islam under British surveillance, 1865–1924*, http://harrimaninstitute.org/Media/00415.pdf, accessed 10 March 2006.

Mehta, A., *Indian shipping, a case study of the working of imperialism*, Bombay: N. T. Shroff, 1944.
Miller, M., 'Pilgrim's progress: the business of the Hajj', *Past and Present* 191, 1, 2006: 189–228.
Mohamed, A., *My Life, a fragment: an autobiographical sketch of Maulana Mohamed Ali*, New Delhi: Manohar, 1999.
Ochsenwald, W., 'The commercial history of the Hijaz Vilayet, 1840–1908', *Arabian Studies* 6, 1982, 57–76.
Ochsenwald, W., *Religion, society and the state in Arabia, the Hijaz under Ottoman control, 1840–1908*, Columbus, OH: Ohio State University, 1984.
Ozcan, A., *Pan-Islamism: Indian Muslim, the Ottomans and Britain (1877–1924)*, Leiden, E. J. Brill, 1997.
Parliamentary Papers (House of Commons), 1881–82.
Reid, A., 'Nineteenth century Pan-Islam in Indonesia and Malaysia', *Journal of Asian Studies* 26, 2, 1967: 267–83.
Report of the Haj Inquiry Committee, Calcutta, Government of India, 1931.
Report on Indian Newspapers, published in Bombay Presidency, 1926–27
Roff, W., 'Sanitatation and security: The imperial powers and the nineteenth century Hajj', *Arabian Studies* 6, 1982:143–60.
Selections from the Records of the Government of India, Home Department, CCCXXX, 16.
Singha, R., *Exceptions to the law and exceptional laws: a 'proper' passport for colonial India, 1914–20*, accessed through: www.cishsydney2005.
——, 'Settle, mobilize, verify: identification practices in colonial India', *Studies in History* 16, 2, 2000: 151–98.
Siraj, M. A., *A peep into the past. From riches to Rrags* through: http://www.radianceweekly. com/archives/issue18/articl10.htm, accessed 11 June 2007.
Sousa, N., *Capitulatory regime of Turkey*, Baltimore, MD: Johns Hopkins Press, 1933.
Takashi, O., 'Friction and rivalry over pious mobility: British colonial management of the hajj and reaction to it by Indian Muslims', in K. Hidemitsu (ed.), *The influence of human mobility in Muslim societies*, London: Kegan Paul, 2003, pp. 151–75.
——, 'Muslim merchant capital and the relief movement for the Ottoman empire in India, 1876–1924', *Journal of the Japan Association for South Asian Studies* 11, 1999: 71–103.

3 Do not destroy our honour

Wartime propaganda directed at East African soldiers in Ceylon (1943–44)

Katrin Bromber

Introduction

Following the outbreak of hostilities in Europe, Britain's Colonial Office public relations department came to realise the weaknesses of an improvised 'win the war' propaganda for their colonial possessions.[1] The truth of this observation became especially apparent, when the deployment of East African soldiers of *The King's African Rifles* (KAR) shifted primarily to territories outside East Africa. In a sign of their resistance, some of the contingent, which were stationed in Ethiopia and British Somaliland, refused to be immediately transferred to theatres of war abroad.[2] At the same time, however, other KAR units were already under way for operations in Madagascar, the Middle East, North Africa and South Asia. Simultaneously, special propaganda measures for the East African services started to work for a legitimization of their deployment outside the African continent.

The massive transfer of East African soldiers to South Asia was a response to the threat of a Japanese invasion of Eastern India in 1942 and the growing reluctance of the Indian troops and people to fight alongside the British. The War Office demanded three KAR infantry brigades to be deployed in Asia. General Sir William Platt, head of the East Africa Command, however, convinced London to raise an entire East African Division, later known as the 11th (EA) Division, including specialists and support units.[3] In 1943, approximately 35,000 *askaris*, as African soldiers are called in Swahili, were sent to Ceylon (today's Sri Lanka) for garrison duties and special training. They released Indian contingents for other military purposes and to, at a later stage, reinforce the Empire troops in Burma.[4]

Scholarly works and personal accounts by British officers emphasize that most soldiers were willing to fight in Asia. However, they were not immediately transferred to the Burma front, but had to await active service until summer 1944. This waiting stare caused a major problem for British military officers and the East African ranks alike and required patience on both sides. During the 'hardening period', as the time between 1943 and 1944 was called, the soldiers faced a demanding physical training programme, long-term separation from their families and a dwindling chance of being rewarded for active combat. Hence, a cleverly designed propaganda was required to keep them motivated and disciplined.

Heshima, the army weekly of the 11th (East African) Division and the focus of this chapter, played a decisive role in this respect. I argue that this army publication went far beyond the countering of inactivity and boredom. It was one of a bundle of measures that had been introduced to secure the individual and collective discipline of the *askaris* and to structure their war experiences in line with the Imperial project. I will show that both the content and the discursive strategies applied in *Heshima* served one overwhelming aim: the transformation of the Division into a 'highly skilled, self-reliant and disciplined fighting machine'.[5]

Heshima and the propaganda scheme for East African troops in Ceylon

The propaganda directed at East African units in Ceylon was primarily the responsibility of the East Africa Command.[6] The Principal Information Officer in Nairobi had to maintain a close liaison between the military authorities and the information officers under his authority[7] in all the activities that concerned them both. He had to assist the military as far as possible in publicity and propaganda matters vis-à-vis the Army, especially African troops, and prisoners of war.[8] This was achieved through weekly meetings attended by military intelligence, the Navy, the Royal Air Force, the East African Intelligence Centre, and Kenya Security.[9] Army representatives, regardless of the central organization they belonged to, were responsible for dealing with information and propaganda activities directed at all troops within the Command, as well as the East African troops serving outside it. Evidence that this liaison was somewhat problematic is revealed in the correspondence between the PIO in Nairobi and the authorities in the Ministry of Information (MOI) in London, to whom the former was responsible:

> We are not quite clear here to what extent the military view this as their exclusive function, or whether there is indeed close liaison between the military and the civilian authorities in respect to these troops. After all, these men will be returning to civilian life in East Africa, and the whole number of social problems are being created for which the civilian authorities would be more competent to deal than the military, and for this reason should have a considerable say in what type of propaganda is put across to them while they are actually in the Forces. If this is agreed, and a propaganda scheme is being prepared, the next question is finance. Naturally, if the military are providing the money they may very well wish to call the tune. On the other hand, if all or a part of the money is to be found from a non-military source, the type of propaganda suitable

for these troops can be more readily controlled by those who will be subsequently responsible for their welfare.[10]

Finance seems to have been a major problem between the civilian and military authorities in the East Africa Command, including the MOI policy on the provision of propaganda material to the East and West African Forces outside their home territories. Even the provision of two crystals to service broadcasts from African troops in Ceylon to their homes in East and West Africa began to cause headaches when the Governor of Ceylon raised the question as to who was going to pay for them.[11]

Despite cooperation between civilian and military authorities on disseminating propaganda aimed at the troops in out-of-area employments, its content lay exclusively with the military, or to be more precise, in the hands of the respective intelligence branches.[12] This also holds true for the production of *Heshima*.

The birth of this army weekly reads as follows: on 3 May 1943, Lieut. R.W. Circus took command of the 11th (EA) Division Intelligence Section. The unit began to operate in Moshi (Tanganyika Territory), where Sgt. De Woronin, a photographer, Sgt. Ryan and Sgt. Turner were employed in the Intelligence Section. Captain Crawford and 'two Africans' were also posted there at a later date. The unit disembarked at Colombo on 27 June 1943 and continued to Peradeniya, where the headquarters of the 11th (EA) Division SEAC were camping in the Royal Botanic Gardens.[13] On 3 July 1943, Capt. Crawford was ordered from Peradeniya to Colombo, PR Directorate Ceylon Army Command. Two weeks later Crawford and De Woronin began preparing the first issue of *Heshima*. Written in Kiswahili, Chinyanja and English, it finally appeared on Friday, 4 August 1943. Crawford, who seems to have been the editor of the weekly, was assisted by an African sergeant. Archival documents suggest he was Sgt. Mfaume Omari. According to the Division's Progress Report, *Heshima* appears to have been rather successful. The African ranks showed great appreciation of their army weekly, and the editor faced increasing 'fan' mail.[14] However, Mfaume Omari commented that some units were reluctant to subscribe to the newspaper and that measures had to be taken to ensure that the 2,500 copies did not prove a waste of effort and paper. Nevertheless, he stressed the enormous educational value of the army weekly, which made the disbursement of a certain amount of regimental funds worthwhile.[15]

However, announcements such as 'All issues have been sold out. It makes no sense to order them now', and a change of publishing house, which could have been responsible for the improvement in quality, speak for a positive reception by the readership and greater attention to detail by army officials, especially within the Ceylon Command.[16] Admiral Sir Geoffrey Layton, Commander-in-Chief, took a keen interest in high quality publications for the troops.[17] In 1945, *Heshima* not only saw an opportunity for a change of the publishing house but also for the removal of the Chinyanja-speaking section of the paper.[18]

While *Heshima* served the East African troops, the field newspaper *Rhino* was primarily produced for the British ranks, although a news section – *Habari ya Swahili* (News in Swahili) – was included.[19] Furthermore, headquarters distributed the weekly bulletin *Second Echolon* to the East African troops in Ceylon.[20]

Apart from print material, propaganda directed at the services also included films, information rooms, broadcasting and, of course, individual talks. Film shows for East African units in Ceylon were reported to have had a poor reputation. Compared with those in British Somaliland and Ethiopia, they were few and the films were mostly 'unsuitable' for showing to African ranks.[21] Apart from choosing the 'right' films for the African combatants, an undisturbed performance had to be secured for British officers. Consequently, orders were given that African ranks had to stay at least 100 yards away from film shows intended exclusively for British personnel. This order caused a newspaper debate in *Heshima*, which ended with the remark that there were many Africans who do not like European films and that they should be kept away, because they would only giggle.[22]

Compared with film and the press, information rooms and broadcasting seem to have been more effective methods of propaganda. The information room was seen as combining the work of the Unit Education Officers and Information Officers. It was used as the unit schoolroom, but also as a recreation room, library, newsroom and letter-writing centre for the *askaris*. Set up as a kind of showroom, it was to be both functional and attractive.[23]

Broadcasting was the medium with the best reception among the African rank-and-file. The Kenya Information Office handled broadcasting in Kiswahili and Chinyanja to East African troops away from home. The Principal Information Officer in Nairobi had to finance this service in part.[24] Broadcasts from Nairobi or Colombo could be heard twice a week. According to official reports, local topics were enthusiastically received. The fact that several soldiers heard their relatives caused great excitement. All this called for a continuance of the two-way broadcasts.[25] Wireless sets were distributed but initially used more by officers. This led to the following critical comment:

> Welfare wireless sets should be used to broadcast special troops' programmes and not allotted for the sole use of officers and BNOCs messes. An officer will be made responsible for making the necessary arrangements for broadcasts to the troops. It is often the case that the *askaris* do not hear the broadcasts owing to lack of interest in making arrangements for them.[26]

Referring to the responsibilities of Unit Educational Officers, the document continues to say that a raise in the academic standard of a unit would result in more appreciation to sound and reasonable propaganda and information. As early as 1940, the newly established public relations department of the

Colonial Office, which was obliged to coordinate its work with the Empire Division of the MOI and the War Office, had dissociated itself from short-sighted 'win the war' propaganda, and derived it as a by-product of education, based on the principles of truth, mutual tolerance and respect.[27]

The content of the propaganda was deduced from three sources. First of all, material provided by the MOI and the military, second information given by the Chiefs in their monthly letters on the situation in the home areas and third, the unit censorship board. The latter is particularly reminiscent of activities described by Sanjoy Bhattacharya for propaganda directed at Indian troops in East India (1939–45). However, while Bhattacharya explained that the examination of the Indian soldiers' personal correspondence was done secretly, as it allowed more valuable information be collected, East African soldiers stationed in Ceylon were made fully aware that every single letter would be censored.[28] Apart from lecturing on the need for censorship, *Heshima* published a two-page article about the work of the Division Command censorship board. It explained in detail the type of information that should not be written home about and promised immediate postage of censored letters.[29]

The issue of literacy is of crucial importance to the study of army newspapers for East African military personnel and their potential effect on the readership. Who was in a position to actually read newspapers, given the fact that the literacy rate among East Africans was still fairly low at the time? While the KAR contingent of educated soldiers amounted to no more than a hundred drivers and signallers in the 1930s, the number of trained and, therefore, literate *askaris* rose to tens of thousands during the course of the Second World War. Approximately 600 African teachers from the East African Army Education Corps trained African soldiers from all ranks to read in their own vernaculars. A substantial number became literate in Kiswahili in the same period, while English language education was particularly in demand.[30] To give an example: the British journalist Gerald Hanley observed that almost 85 per cent of an artillery battery in Burma had to learn to read and write in just six months. This development was brought about by the fact that the British Army needed inexpensive African specialists to function and that British officers had no alternative but to produce their own educated *askaris*. Rank and file African soldiers enthusiastically embraced the new educational opportunities provided by the military. In his book *Monsoon Victory*, Hanley described the situation as follows:

> The passion for writing and reading had gripped them and every man had learned even a few words. In their spare moments they sat down with stubs of pencil, pushed out their tongues, and with much labour wrote a letter to Africa. [...] Soon the output of letters to Africa increased [and] became vast.[31]

Some of the soldiers even advised their relatives to attend adult classes whenever possible,[32] and in an attempt to provide them with reading material, even sent their army newspapers home. Although the scope of this chapter does not allow for a detailed discussion, it can at least be stated that apart from government and missionary education, the army played a major role in making a substantial section of the East African population literate, especially during the Second World War. Furthermore, the KAR language policy forced both African and British soldiers to learn Kiswahili or Chinyanja, thus broadening the opportunities for African rank-and-file soldiers in postwar civilian employment. Furthermore, English lessons were in great demand from the soldiers. In an attempt to encourage them to improve their English, *Heshima* hinted at the fact that English was the most widely spoken language and spoken by many Ceylonese. Knowledge of English was a way to make friends in foreign countries.[33] In the initial phase, English texts were occasionally accompanied by a Kiswahili translation. Occasionally, the letter box (*Barua za Askari*) even published *askaris*' questions and the editor's answers in English. In mid-1944, however, English texts gradually began to disappear and by 1945 had petered out completely.

Structure and aim of *Heshima*

'This is the first issue of "Heshima", a newspaper designed to help East African soldiers in Ceylon.'[34] In the opening sentence of his editorial statement to the readership, Major-General Fowkes, Commander of the East African troops in Ceylon, makes the general intent of the army weekly quite clear: to help. What exactly did this mean? In the first place it meant to provide the troops with news from home and information on the various theatres of war. Home news was not merely to remind them of those left behind, but also to clarify that their transfer to Ceylon was vitally linked to the security of their families.[35] Second, he encourages the readership to personally take part in the selection of news and information. Interestingly, the discussion was to be conducted within the units, and criticism not addressed primarily to the editor. This message was repeated in December 1943, when the editorial board was faced with almost 200 letters per week. In an editorial note, the *askaris* were urged to consult their '[...] officers, clerks, teachers and post orderlies, who are responsible for your needs, especially pay, promotion, leave, and mail'.[36] However, a second letter contest initiated in edition No. 8 invites the readership to openly criticize the contents of the newspaper. Frankness was marked explicitly as the 'most agreeable feature' of the first letter competition, which had requested soldiers to write about their situation in Ceylon.[37]

By drawing attention to broadcasts in Kiswahili and Chinyanja on Radio Colombo, the first editorial places the newspaper within a larger propaganda context. According to the editor, *Heshima* would not only advertise the scheduled vernacular programmes, but also give space to pro and contra opinions on the respective content. Arguably, *Heshima* was part of a major propaganda concept, one of whose aims was to establish a culture of discussion between soldiers and their officers. With reference to the original question posed above, the aim of *Heshima* was to help soldiers channel their criticism effectively, in turn providing the Command with an ideal basis for control and subsequent countermeasures.

So far, nothing is known about the choice of the name. *Heshima*, which means honour, respect or good reputation, refers to the key concept of respectable behaviour as cultivated in the East African (coastal) cultural context. While the Kiswahili version of the editorial places *heshima* in this wider (civilian) context by linking it to 'us the people of East Africa', the English version as well as other articles narrows its scope to military honour: 'The name chosen for this paper is "HESHIMA" because the *heshima* of our E.A-Army is high. As strangers in Ceylon, let us be careful not to spoil our good name'.[38]

Although the structure of the weekly newspaper changed slightly when vital information needed front positioning, most issues were composed of separate sections in the following order: *Kwa Wasomaji* (Editorial) introduced the main topic of the issue and was often visually backed up by a suitable front-page photograph. *Habari za vita* (War News) provided the *askaris* with brief information on the movements of the Allied Forces. *Habari za Nchi* (Home News), which according to a letter competition was the most popular section of the newspaper, was published in two languages – Kiswahili for information from Tanganyika, Kenya and Uganda, and Chinyanja in the case of Nyasaland and Northern Rhodesia. This news became increasingly personalized or, to be more precise, authorized by letters from African Chiefs. *Mazungumzo ya Bwana Kiko* (Talks of the Officer with the pipe)[39] – fictitious dialogues between a British officer and his soldiers – seems to have enjoyed equal popularity. It served mainly to address difficult issues of army life, such as finances, homesickness, declining morale, and leave.[40] As the editors believed story-telling to be a must in an African newspaper, it reserved space for a *Hadithi* section. However, the letter competition clearly voiced a declining interest in *hadithi* (story), so that this section was soon dropped altogether. A similar dislike was expressed for crossword puzzles. Articles on technical equipment and the latest weapons were often accompanied by photographs showing African instructors in action. Both text and pictures depicted African soldiers as educated military elite, fit for jungle fighting and wholly prepared for the action ahead of them. The final section of the newspaper was reserved for the voice of the troops. It appeared in the form of letters to the editor, fictitious dialogues and educational comments by senior soldiers to their young comrades, or short poems.

Apart from the very first issue of the paper, which gave information on the topographic position, ethnographic peculiarities, and the animals to be found in Ceylon, no local news was published. Ceylon and the Singhalese were mentioned in concrete interaction with East African soldiers only, as in the case of Islamic holidays or car accidents. All in all, the newspaper was army-referential. Interestingly, similar blanks exist for the *adui* (enemy) – the

Japanese Army – which is described in detail only once by a Chinese soldier.[41]

Visual back-up for textual information was provided in the form of photographs, cartoons and maps. As war geography and map-reading was part and parcel of elementary army education, most of the news on different areas of operation were accompanied by maps, to which the readership responded very positively. Furthermore, it can be said that army newspapers especially introduced cartoons to the Kiswahili press.[42] By mid-1945 it even began to print photographs of African women, allegedly copying the British army newspaper style. As part of information on the people involved in media work, *Heshima* also published an extensive article about war-time photographers. Apart from factual information on the nature of their work in the war zones, the readership learned of the two British photographers who belonged to the 11th (EA) Division. 'The two Europeans, whose duty it is to take pictures of our soldiers while route taking or training, will accompany us later when we go to war.'[43]

Although the editors attempted to create a discursive atmosphere that would give African ranks a voice and permit a certain amount of candour, the army weekly pursued the general propaganda line to the services. This served the purpose of maintaining a motivated fighting force and, when demobilization became a topic, of educating the *askaris* to become good citizens. Or to put it in another way, minds were disciplined for times of war and peace.

Discursive strategies to keep the African soldiery disciplined

The 1943 and 1944 issues of *Heshima* reveal four main topics that served to maintain discipline in the 11th (EA) Division. Most important of all was discipline within the units, as strict adherence to military regulations on and off duty, at least in the eyes of the commanding officers, constituted a sound preparation of the *askaris* for the military action that lay ahead of them. It goes without saying that this included unquestioned observance of orders along the lines of the military hierarchy – with King George at the top. This theme formed a second focus around which disciplinary discourse revolved. The fact that the soldiers were deployed outside East Africa and tension with the local population could lead to a moral decline on both sides, decent behaviour was demanded of the KAR soldiers. Thus, self-control and control of (uncertain) situations, especially off duty, was a third aspect highlighted by *Heshima*. Last but not least, the KAR units were in close contact with units from other command areas, especially the South East Asia Command. Discipline, therefore, included cooperation when necessary. In this respect, *Heshima* responded to the growing sense of egalitarianism that had permeated the Forces.

According to the relevant documents of the War Office, the prior aim of the KAR stay in Ceylon was to prepare the *askaris* for the 'jungle war' that awaited them in Burma. In the words of Major-General Fowkes, 'fitness does not only imply mighty muscles but also a sound mental and physical stamina able to support anxiety and hardship with unimpaired efficiency'.[44] This 'hardening period' included in the first instance *ruteki* (route marches) and physical training in a natural terrain similar to that of their future operational service. Arguing that Ceylon was halfway to East Africa and that the 1942 Japanese air raids had clearly indicated its strategic importance, *Heshima* pointed out the natural conditions.[45] Soldiers would be trained in 'jungle war' methods and, no less important, in patience, so as to 'finally drive the Japanese devils out from their hiding place in the bush'.[46] For the soldiers, however, it was completely new to march long periods of the route barefoot, carrying their boots.[47] As most of the soldiers had already had extensive fighting experience during the Abyssinian campaign and in Madagascar, more explanation was required as to why these training methods were necessary. *Mazungumzo ya Bwana Kiko* was the key discussion forum in this case. In one fictitious conversation, a soldier declares that this boot-wearing policy might be an attempt to bully the *askaris*.[48] Although *Bwana Kiko* explains to him that the Japanese soldiers were able to move silently in the bush precisely because they did not wear boots, the soldier replies: 'You are right, sir, but I do not want to wait. I don't like route marches and daily training'.[49]

The soldier linked his answer to another problem: the waiting around and lack of understanding as to why they were not being transferred to the front immediately. At this point in the conversation, *Bwana Kiko* becomes sterner: 'Are you a soldier or a normal citizen?'. He then resorts to a mode of explanation that he (or the editors) consider suitable for the 'African' mind – the agrarian circle. He compares route marches with seeds that will bear fruits, or equals military training with the farmer's daily care for his field. The argument finishes by demanding the soldier to perform these tasks without complaint as he knows that he will one day face the enemy. This example does not only reveal the comparison of military aspects with civilian experience as a discursive strategy, but also hints at a lack of confidence in the orders of the British officers. The 11th (EA) Division Progress Report No. 4 gives a lengthy account of the lack of sympathy between the African ranks and their British leaders. Both sides were made responsible. Obviously, a number of British soldiers did not possess the required qualities. Their sudden promotion to the rank of a sergeant together with a feeling of power over the African ranks made some of them arrogant and even racist.[50] In particular, the more educated *askaris* were reported to have become more difficult to handle.[51] Consequently, it was the British ranks who were asked to treat the African soldiers under their command with more respect.

Another discursive strategy to counteract disciplinary problems was the use of the African voice in the troops. Contrary to *Askari*, the vernacular newspaper of the East Africa Command, it was not the *Askari Mzee* or senior KAR soldier who tried to teach his junior comrades, but soldiers of all age groups. In his letter to the editor, Lance Corporal Joel Warui urged his comrades:

> To all my friends who are on this island, I want to say two words – 'Adabu' [correct behaviour – KB] and 'Tabia' [character – KB]. My comrades who are here are not children, but some of us have a very bad character. If you have to do foolish things that have nothing to do with proper behaviour, then wait until you return and do them at home. Be thoughtful and respectful, show your bravery and we will win.[52]

The reference to key words of the East African (coastal) concept of proper behaviour was one of the more prominent discursive strategies employed to instil discipline. They were carefully implanted into the military code of good behaviour in the military discourse. Arguably, it was exactly this interface that provided fertile ground for the influence of other key words. In his letter to the editor, British driver Maurice Margeson argued that *upendo* (love), by which he meant the love for 'our King' (*mfalme wetu*), was what welded soldiers of the Empire together. *Umoja* (unity) is derived from the fact that soldiers on active service have only one father – King George. He also reminds the readership that *utii* (obedience) is the backbone of a successful army. By applying the 'we are all in the same boat' strategy, the author makes use of a powerful linguistic device, the primary mode of which addresses the readership as part of the Allied Forces.[53] Lack of mail, money, and tobacco are problems shared by ranks from all parts of the Empire and thus work as a unifying argument. The same is true for the shared aversion to being far from home. Raising this topic, Margeson emphasizes the importance of *akiba* (saving money) and *barua* (letters).[54]

Saving and writing letters were evidently given top priority by the editors, as they were impressed upon in almost every issue in 1943–44. Money in particular remained a 'source of mingled mystery and dismay to African ranks', since a rupee was worth Sh.1 Cts 50 but bought only about '25 cents worth of goods by East African standards'.[55] Apart from a table comparing East African currency with that of Ceylon, the second issue of *Heshima* left it once again to *Bwana Kiko* to explain how to handle the pay book or who to turn to for assistance. He asks the soldiers not to waste their money or risk being cheated, but to save it for their families. The motto is 'Certainly, the pay book never lies!'.[56] Cases of spending money recklessly are usually reported in connection with leisure activities, e.g. the use of expensive rickshaws instead of buses and trams, the cheaper means of transport. Although occasionally alluded to, prostitution was never openly discussed. However, the authorities were obliged to pass legislation against money-making tricks, which were reported to have been practiced on *askaris* in search of female company.[57]

The significance of *barua* (letters) for the soldiers was clearly recognized by the military authorities, and *Heshima* provided a channel for critique and questions concerning the delay of home mail or censorship. Delayed mail was a constant issue on both sides of the Indian Ocean. *Heshima* put the blame exclusively on the *askaris* themselves, arguing that the address must have been wrong. Given the fact that the soldiers had to cope with a new and highly complex system of postal arrangements, this may have been true for the initial phase of their stay.[58] However, mail from East Africa seems to have been off-loaded at Bombay, which was a bottleneck anyway.[59] In order to give voice to soldiers' complaints about the lack of mail from home, *Mambo Leo*, the Kiswahili newspaper of the Tanganyika Territory Government, published an article on the subject. Tabora (Central Tanzania) reacted by passing the complaints on to the District Commissioner, where they were treated as unfounded because the families of the soldiers had used every opportunity to write to them. The letters from Chiefs had a similar function. They not only personalized and authorized news from the home areas, especially with regard to the wellbeing of the soldiers' wives, but were exploited by the editors to remind the *askaris* of their duties. By publishing repeated statements that African Chiefs were doing everything in their power to protect the soldiers' homes and appealing to the latter to be diligent, obedient and brave in crushing their common enemy, *Heshima* created the image of a joint civil and military war effort.[60]

Nevertheless, the joint war effort still had to be achieved first and foremost by the military. For the KAR, with its military hierarchy along racial lines, this meant mutual confidence between the African ranks and their British officers. Archival sources, memoirs by British officers and *Heshima* emphasized an excellent tradition in this respect. Cases of insubordination among the African ranks towards their military (British) leaders were seldom openly discussed. Instead, more general statements were transmitted about the need for respect. In his poem *Tusiharibu Heshima, wakatuita Wajinga* (Don't destroy our honour, they will call us fools) the author, Clerk Stephens M.S. Raphael, urges his comrades:

Heshima tunaipata hakika hapa Ceylon
Tusifanye matata wakatuita wazimwe.
Hamu yangu ninataka uvumilivu yakini.
Tusiharibu heshima, wakatuita wajinga.

Here in Ceylon we will certainly receive honours.
Do not cause trouble so that they can call us fools.
My sincere wish is [that you show] patience.
Don't destroy our honour, they will call us fools.

Heshima ni jambo bora, ndugu zangu sikizeni,

Sio kupigwa bakora au adhabu ya kambini.

Respect is a good thing, listen my comrades,
And neither to receive corporal punishment nor to be confined to barracks.[61]

This poem hints only vaguely at cases of insubordination and its consequences. The onus, however, is unquestionably on the *askari* side. *Mazungumzo ya Bwana Kiko* on the subject of military greetings could indeed be interpreted as a countermeasure to the lack of respect towards military superiors. When asked about the sense (*faida*) of this procedure, *Bwana Kiko* replied that an indication of good behaviour is a benefit in itself and that '[...] every person has to respect the order of his superior'.[62] In contrast to the various allusions to the subject, Major-General Fowkes addressed it in a clear statement published in the final issue of 1943. He voiced his disappointment about discipline among his soldiers, with whom he had had positive personal experiences during the Abyssinian campaign:

> But these days there are too many people in the King's African Rifles who spoil the honour of the East African soldier because they behave in an unacceptable manner that is strictly prohibited. Some of them refuse to go to parades. Others write letters of complaint but are too cowardly to sign them, and some lack respect for their officers. All these things spoil the honour of the East African soldier. You know that before the war these soldiers were greatly respected and their bravery in Somaliland and Abyssinia increased this honour. Don't allow a few ignorant people to destroy this good reputation.[63]

The good reputation of an army is never achieved in the military context only. Amicable relations with the local civil population were not only desirable, but often crucial for both sides. Apart from the strategic necessity of transferring thousands of East African soldiers to the island of Ceylon, their relationship with the Ceylonese population was clear from the very beginning: as strangers in Ceylon, they should do nothing to spoil the good reputation of the East African contingents.[64] In order to familiarize the soldiers with the new area, the editors published extensive information about its physical geography, infrastructure, ethnographic composition, agriculture, education, religion, and animal life. The text pointed out that Ceylon was not part of India and that its inhabitants were Singhalese and not Indians. Such explicit statements seem to have been necessary for two reasons. First, relations with 'Indians' were overshadowed by the somewhat negative reputation of 'Indians' in East Africa – their prominent economic position made them suspect. Second, the well-known fighting qualities of Indian soldiers in the Empire troops made the need to assist them in defending their own country somewhat incomprehensible, at least from the *askaris* point of view. As further explanation was required in this direction, the editors re-addressed the topic:

> Another confused idea is sometimes heard: why have we come to protect India against the Japanese? Are they unable to protect themselves? The answer is that we are not here to protect India. We are not in India. We are in Ceylon. We are not only protecting Ceylon itself, but also indirectly our own country, for by staying here we bar the Indian Ocean passage to the Japs, so that they cannot penetrate to our side. Remember this when you discuss it among yourselves.[65]

Furthermore, the original text asked the soldiers to learn from the Ceylonese, especially with regard to agriculture and the use of animals.

In order to include them in the discourse on *askaris'* life in Ceylon, *Heshima* launched a letter competition entitled 'Why do I like/dislike Ceylon?'.[66] The winning letter was sent in by Sgt. K. K. Kasumba, who received a prize of 10 Rs. Many of the letters revealed ambivalent attitudes on both sides. While Kasumba stated that African soldiers were not as warmly received as in Abyssinia, others claimed the opposite, stressing that *askaris* were particularly popular with children. The latter was based on individual experiences of some soldiers in North Africa, where the local population had treated them with antipathy (*ukorofi*) and provocation (*uchokozi*). In addition, *askaris* reported cases of racism, although most interpreted such behaviour as 'astonishment at seeing people with black skin'. The editors attempted to compare this 'astonishment' to the fact that Africans had also been shocked when they first saw white people. They explained that the Ceylonese were not yet accustomed to their appearance and compared this encounter with the moment when white people first came to Africa; Africans ran away or fought them. Proper behaviour would help to overcome the shyness of the local people.[67] However, relations with the local population were by no means as easy as the newspaper suggested. Although headquarters in Colombo judged that relations with the local population were on the whole satisfactory, cases of misbehaviour and conflict were reported. Complaints by civil authorities were more or less belittled or seen as 'frenzied efforts of local political leaders' to create the impression of strained relations between the troops and the Singhalese. While good relations were described first and foremost as the result of the patience and good discipline of the *askaris*, negative instances were almost always attributed to the 'fear and ignorance' of the Ceylonese. Thus, the civil and military authorities organized lectures on the soldiers given by East African officers to Ceylonese audiences assembled by government agents. As reported, even petty government officials were not beyond believing that *askaris* were cannibals, married by capture, had tails, and indulged in black magic. In order to counter this alleged ignorance and improve relations, the authorities organized sport sessions, plays and dances as a medium for 'exchanges of talent'.[68] *Heshima* argued in the same direction and, backed up by photographs, reported on cultural and sporting events, or on Islamic festivals where East African soldiers as believers were included.[69]

In addition, Progress Report No. 3 points to the fact that some petty government clerks 'looked with such contempt on their now numerous African visitors', that they were ready to draw a small emolument by renting out their womenfolk for prostitution.[70] However, prostitution never became an explicit topic and was merely hinted at in reports about the low VD rate or in repeated reminders that most *askaris* had good wives at home.

Apart from the subject of (good) relations off duty, the soldiers enquired about the war effort of the Ceylonese. Allegedly for security reasons, the editors revealed nothing about the existence of the Ceylon Light Infantry, which grew from one to five battalions during the Second World War, and also saw out-of-area deployment as garrison units on the Cocas Keeling Island and as combat units in South East Asia.[71] A joint action was reported only once and then in a more egalitarian mode – the photograph of a bridge built by European, Indian, Ceylonese, and East African Pioneer Units.[72] Instead, *Heshima* emphasized contributions by the civil population, especially with regard to cash crops and rubber.[73]

Although the editors addressed various questions relevant to relations between *askaris* and the local population and even provided space to critical voices, the editors carefully avoided burning issues. This might explain the gradual disappearance of the relevant texts and the growing invisibility of the Ceylonese in the newspaper.

Conclusion

This chapter has argued that apart from providing the *askaris* with information about the war and about home, Heshima's primary aim was discipline. Repeated references to the good reputation of The King's African Rifles were combined with the East African (coastal) cultural concept of *heshima*, which not only includes a code of good behaviour but above all, mutual respect. In pursuit of this course, an increasingly egalitarian mode of discourse was introduced, whereby soldiers were addressed as an integral part of the Allied Forces. They were not only invited to voice their concerns and participate in the discourse, but were reminded first and foremost of their duties. Apart from the editors, these reminders were voiced by military superiors, civil authorities and, in growing numbers, by the soldiers themselves. Although this inclusion of disparate voices seems to indicate a 'democratic change' in the propaganda directed towards the services, the content and discursive strategies employed reveal its ultimate aim: A disciplined, well-trained African soldiers. Substantial changes in the newspaper propaganda had to wait until 1945, when the African soldier was primarily addressed as a well-educated 'civic soldier' and the bearer of hope with regard to the construction of 'new' post-war African societies.

Notes

1 Edmett, 6 August 1941, Public Relations: Future of PR, PRO CO 875/11/1, p. 22.
2 2/4th KAR, War Diary, February 1942, PRO WO 169/7027. Also see T. Parsons, *The African Rank-and-File. Social Implications of Colonial Military Service in the King's African Rifles, 1902–1964*, Oxford: James Currey, 1999, pp. 203–6.
3 Parsons, *African Rank-and-File*, p. 29.
4 Plan for Propaganda for East Africa, PRO INF 1/564.
5 Major-General Fowkes, Training Instructions No. 3, 22 June 1943, PRO, WO 172/ 3985, p. 4.
6 The East Africa Command stretched 'from Northern Rhodesia (inclusive) to Eritrea (inclusive) and from the Indian Ocean to the Congo (including the Katanga Province) and the frontiers of A.E.F. (Afrique Équatorial Francais)', Centralised Control of Publicity and Propaganda in East Africa (1941–42), PRO INF 1/552.
7 The Principal Information Officer, Sir Geoffrey Northcote, was responsible for the coordination of the propaganda work with authorities in Uganda, Tanganyika Territory, Nyasaland (today's Malawi), Northern Rhodesia (today's Sambia), Kenya and in the so-called Occupied Enemy Territory (Italian Somaliland).
8 Whitehall to Munroe, 18 November 1941, PRO INF 1/552.
9 Planning Committee, Plan for Propaganda for British East Africa (1943–44), PRO INF 1/564.
10 Usill to Northcote, 7 October 1943, PRO INF 1/554.
11 Usill to Huxley, 2 December 1943, PRO INF 1/554.
12 Sabine to Usill, 2 September 1943, 'It was noted that under new arrangements which have been agreed with the East Africa Command, the Principal Information Officer would no longer have any responsibility for propaganda and information towards troops within the Command and East African troops outside the Command'. Centralized Control of Publicity and Propaganda in East Africa (1942 – 43), PRO INF 1/553.
13 War Diary 11th (EA) Division, Intelligence Section 1943, PRO WO 172/4000.
14 11 (EA) Division Progress Report No. 2, 16 August to 7 September 1943, App. 6, p. 2, PRO WO 172/3985.
15 'A' Branch, HQ, 11th (EA) Division, Ceylon 1943, PRO WO 172/3986.
16 In 1943–44, *Heshima* was printed by C.A.C. Press, Colombo. 1945 issues were printed on high gloss paper by the Statesman Press, Calcutta.
17 M. Anglo, *Service Newspapers of the Second World War. An Illustrated History*, London: Jupiter Books Ltd, 1977, p. 17.
18 Headquarters published the Chinyanja monthly *Ulemu*, which was designed for the Nyasaland and Northern Rhodesian.
19 Lieutenant J. Batson, editor, described the demanding condition under which the newspaper was produced as follows: '[…] the editorial "office" roof was a truck tarpaulin and the table was a crate – and also the fact that the heat was so intense that even duplicating ink specially manufactured for the Tropics melted to the consistency of almost water. Ants did their best to ruin paper stocks'. J. Batson to Director, Imperial War Museum, 23 December 1943, IWM K 58106, published in Imperial War Museum (eds), *Union Jack. A Scrapbook. British Forces' Newspapers 1939–1945*, London: HMSO, p. 252.
20 M. Said, *The Life and Times of Abdulwahid Sykes (1924–1968). The Untold Story of the Muslim Struggle against British Colonialism in Tanganyika*, London: Minerva Press, 1998, p. 55.
21 11th (E.A.) Division Progress Report No. 2, 16 August to 7 September 1943, PRO WO 172/3985.

22 'Kuna Waafrika wengi [...] ambao hawapendezwi na sinema za Kizungu. Kwa hiyo ni haki ya kuwazuia, maana wanacheka tu.' Maswali na Majibu, *Heshima*, 27 July 1945, p. 6.
23 Education Directive, 13 July 1943, G Branch (E.A.) Division, Ceylon. 11th Division, PRO WO 172/3985.
24 Northcote to Cameron, 14 August 1942, PRO INF 1/552.
25 War Diary, 1/ 4 KAR, 1942 (Jan-Dec) Ceylon, PRO WO 169/ 7032.
26 Education Directive, 13 July 1943, G Branch (E.A.) Division, Ceylon. 11th Division, PRO WO 172/3985.
27 Future of Public Relations (1941), PRO CO 875/11/1.
28 S. Bhattacharya, *Propaganda and Information in Eastern India 1939–45. A Necessary Weapon of War*, Richmond: Curzon Press, 2001, p. 180.
29 Wakaguzi wa Barua, *Heshima*, 27 October 1943, p. 6.
30 T. Parsons, 'Dangerous Education? The Army as School in Colonial East Africa', *Journal of Imperial and Commonwealth History* 28, No.1, 2000, p. 113.
31 G. Hanley, *Monsoon Victory*, London: Collins, 1946, p. 30.
32 Parsons, 'Dangerous Education?', p. 113.
33 'Kiingereza ni lugha inay ojulikana zaidi kuliko zote duniani, na hata Ceylon wengi wanajua. Kama unataka kuwa rafiki na watu utakaowakuta hapa auch nchi nyingine ni vizuri ujifunze Kiingereza kidogo.' Kwa Wasomaji, *Heshima*, 11 August 1943, p. 2.
34 'Hii ndiyo mara ya kwanza ya "Heshima", gazeti amablo limetengenezwa kusaidia askari wa Afrika Mashariki walioko Ceylon.', Usomaji wa Bwana Mkubwa, *Heshima*, 4 August 1943, p. 2.
35 Of the numerous positive comments by African soldiers, I would like to quote one by Lance Corporal Gabriel Thuma. 'This newspaper is like our ears [listen] back and forth in time, in that it provides us with home news and news of the military affairs that lie ahead of us.' [Gazeti hili ni kama masikio yetu ya nyuma na mbele, yaani inatupasha habari za nyumbani na za mbele mambo ya vita yanayotungoja.] Barua za Askari, *Heshima*, 8 September 1943, p. 7.
36 'Mabwana, Makarani, Walimu, ama Maorderli wa Posta ambao kazi yao ni kuangalia shida zenu, hasa mishahara, kuongoza tepe, livu, na shauri za barua', Tangazo juu ya barua, *Heshima*, 15 December 1943, p. 2.
37 Editorial, *Heshima*, 15 September 1943, p. 2.
38 'Sisi watu wa Afrika ya Mashariki' Kwa Wasomaji, *Heshima*, 4 August 1943, p. 3.
39 Achim von Oppen has pointed out in a personal communication (May 2006) that a pipe is a typical attribute of a high-ranking British administrative officer in East African cartoons.
40 Letters to the editor asked about *Bwana Kiko*'s unit and even invited him personally to come and have talks. In 1945, a picture of a British officer with a huge pipe was published close to the text.
41 Adui yetu, *Heshima*, 17 November 1943, p. 6.
42 JAMBO, one of the army newspapers for British personal of the KAR, printed cartoons that gained fame among the troops. Whether African rank and file also had regular access to the paper is unknown. Cross-references were only found between the various military and partly civilian newspapers in Swahili.
43 'Wazungu wawili ambao kazi yao ni kupiga picha za askari wetu wakati wa rutek ama mafundisho, na halafu wakati tutakapokwenda vitani.' Wapigapicha wa Vita, *Heshima*, 12 January 1944, pp. 8–9.
44 Training instructions, G Branch 11th Division (E.A.) Division, 2 March 1943, PRO WO 172/3985.
45 On 5 April 1942, Colombo was attacked by over 300 aircraft from Japanese carriers.

46 '[...] kisha twende kuwashambulia shetani hawo Wajapani katika maficho yao ya majani.' Sababu tatu kwa nini tumekuja Ceylon, *Heshima*, 11 August 1943, p. 7.
47 'The object is for the feet of the African to be kept hard so that he can operate barefoot if necessary, at the same time to ensure that he has a good pair of boots he can wear at any time. [...] Infantry will wear boots for one whole day each week and march at least 10 miles in boots at least twice a month. [...] unit orders will provide for native ranks to walk barefoot for fixed periods daily or weekly as appropriate.' Training instructions No. 4, G Branch (E.A.) Ceylon Division, Policy Wearing of Boots and Shirts or Blouses by African Ranks, 10 July19 43, PRO WO 172/3985, p. 3.
48 Similarly annoying was the wearing of long 'shapeless' trousers that reminded the soldiers of female or prison clothing. Mazungumzo ya Bwana Kiko, *Heshima*, 27 October 1943, p. 4.
49 'Kweli Bwana maneno yako ni kweli, lakini mimi sitaki kungoja. Sipendi kazi ya ruteki na training kila siku.' Mazungumzo ya Bwana Kiko, *Heshima*, 22 September 1943, p. 7.
50 11th (E.A.) Division Report No. 4, 8 October to 7 November 1943, PRO WO 172/3985, p. 4.
51 For the topic *army education and its consequences* see Parsons, 'Dangerous Education?', p. 113.
52 'Kwa rafiki zangu, mnapokaa ndani ya kisiwa hiki napenda kumtajia maneno mawili haya "Adabu" na "Tabia". Wenzangu mliofika hapa hakuna mtoto lakini wengine miongoi mwetu wana tabia mbaya; kama unataka mambo ya ujinga yasiyo na adabu ngojea murudi kwetu mkayafanye. Muwe wataalamu wanyenyekevu, onyesheni ushujaa wenu na tutafaulu.' Barua za Askari, *Heshima*, 27 October 1943, p. 7.
53 By means of pronominal deixis in the first person plural (hortative), news about the Allied Forces' movements verbally include African soldiers. Mentioning that *Bwana Kiko* also suffers from the shortage of tobacco creates a sense of unity with other soldiers who smoked.
54 Barua toka 18194 Driver E, Maurice Margeson, in: *Heshima*, 1 September 1943, p. 12.
55 11th (E.A.) Progress Report No. 2, 16 August to 7 September 1943, PRO WO 172/3985.
56 'Nakubali, paybook haisemi uwongo.' Mazungumzo ya Bwana Kiko, *Heshima*, 11 August 1943, p. 12.
57 11 (E.A.) Progress Report No. 2, 16 August to 7 September 1943, PRO WO 172/3985.
58 11 (E.A.) Division Security Instructions No. 16, 9 July 1943, Postal Arrangements, PRO WO 172/3985.
59 11th (E.A.) Division Report No. 4, 8 October to 7 November 1943, PRO WO 172/3985, p. 4.
60 However, the *askari* were known to challenge chiefly authority when they were on leave, often by force. Good behaviour on leave was a hotly debated issue in *Askari*, the Kiswahili weekly published by the East Africa Command. A systematic study of this topic has yet to be carried out.
61 M.S. Raphael, Tusiharibu Heshima, Wakatuita Wajinga, *Heshima*, 24 November 1943, p. 6.
62 'Kila mtu lazima aheshimu amri ya mkubwa wake.' Mazungumzo ya Bwana Kiko, *Heshima*, 8 December 1943, p. 5.
63 'Lakini siku hizi katika jeshi la Afrika ya Mashariki kuna watu wengi kupita kiasi wanaoharibu heshima ya askari wa Afrika ya Mashariki kwa sababu wanaofuata njia zinazokatazwa za kuleta mashtaka. Wengine katika hawa wanakataa kwenda

parade, wengine wanaandika barua ya kushtaki lakini wanaopgopa kuandika majina yao chini, wengine hawana adabu mbele ya Mabwana Ofisa yao. Mambo haya yote yanaharibu heshima ya askari wa Afrika ya Mashariki. Mnajua ya kwamba kabla ya vita askari hawa walikuwa na heshima nyingi na mashujaa yao huko Somaliland na Abyssinia yameongeza sana heshima hiyo. Msikubali watu wachache wajinga kuharibu sifa njema hiyo.' Barua hii ya Siku Kuu ya Christmas, *Heshima*, 24 December 1943, p. 4.

64 'Kama wageni katika Ceylon tusifanye kitu kibaya cha kuharibu heshima yetu.' Kwa Wasomaji, *Heshima*, 4 August 1943, p. 3
65 Editorial, *Heshima*, 29 September 1943, p. 2.
66 Kwa nini napenda Ceylon. Kwa nini sipendi Ceylon, Shindano la barua, *Heshima*, 11 August 1943, p. 5.
67 'Waafrika ni wageni hapa na Wasilon hawajawazoea. Wazungu walipofika mara ya kwanza Afrika Waafrika walitoroka ama kupigana. Sasa weusi wamewazoea wazungu, hawatoroki Vilevile mkifanya mambo vizuri hapa Wasilon watazoea na hawatakimbia tena.' Barua za Askari, *Heshima*, 8 December 1943, p. 6.
68 11th (E.A.) Division Progress Report No. 3, 8 September to 7 October 1943, PRO WO 172/3985, pp. 4–5.
69 As the Army only provided services for Christians, Muslims were taken care of by the local Imams. The 1943–44 issues of *Heshima* concentrated far more on news about Muslim soldiers than about their Christian comrades.
70 11th (E.A.) Division Progress Report No. 3, 8 September to 7 October 1943, PRO WO 172/3985, p. 5.
71 Sri Lanka Army (2006), History of the Sri Lanka Light Infantry Regiment. Online available http://www.army.lk/history.php (accessed 4 September 2007).
72 Habari za Nchi, *Heshima*, 1 September 1943, p. 7.
73 Barua ya Askari, *Heshima*, 24 November 1943, p. 6.

Bibliography

Published material

Anglo, M., *Service Newspapers of the Second World War. An Illustrated History*, London: Jupiter Books Ltd, 1977.
Bhattacharya, S., *Propaganda and Information in Eastern India 1939–45. A Necessary Weapon of War*, Richmond: Curzon Press, 2001.
Hanley, G., *Monsoon Victory*, London: Collins, 1946.
Heshima, 1943–45.
Parsons, T., 'Dangerous Education? The Army as School in Colonial East Africa', *Journal of Imperial and Commonwealth History*, 28, No.1, 2000: 112–34.
——, *The African Rank-and-File. Social Implications of Colonial Military Service in the King's African Rifles, 1902–1964*, Oxford: James Currey, 1999.
Said, M., *The Life and Times of Abdulwahid Sykes (1924–1968). The Untold Story of the Muslim Struggle against British Colonialism in Tanganyika*, London: Minerva Press, 1998.

Part II
Subalternity, race and the transgression of moral boundaries

4 Discourses of exclusion and the 'convict stain' in the Indian Ocean, c. 1800–1850

Clare Anderson

Introduction

In recent years, the historiography of the British presence in India has grown to include an impressive set of literature on marginal communities, including soldiers, prostitutes, orphans, vagrants, and 'loafers'.[1] This work has been significant in drawing out some of the social complexities of colonial settlement and expansion, particularly during the era of 'high imperialism' at the end of the nineteenth century. In this, it is strongly suggestive of the processes through which orientalist discourses on and of the Indian 'other' were produced through reference to social, economic, and cultural structures in the British metropole. Non-elite British communities were also orientalized within complex webs of power that both reinforced the social – and eventually racial – exclusivity that both underlay colonial governance and took empire back home.[2]

This chapter will examine the escape and migration of Australian convicts, ex-convicts, and free settlers during the late eighteenth and early nineteenth centuries as a means of extending our understanding of India and the Indian Ocean more broadly as 'spaces of disorder' through which colonial discourses of exclusion were constructed. It is also through an exploration of their experiences that aspects of what Peter Linebaugh and Marcus Rediker describe as 'the many-headed hydra' of proletarian life, and the open challenge they sometimes posed to British authority, can be discussed in the Indian Ocean context.[3] The colonial authorities either returned escaped convicts to the penal settlements in Australia or sent them back to England to face charges of returning from transportation. Escape was a capital offence, but most usually convicts faced re-transportation and transfer to the harsher regime of a penal station. The fate of ex-convicts and free settlers was more complex, for they embodied and represented Australia's 'convict stain'. British colonial administrators were ambivalent about their social desirability, and in practice they retained their status as felons long after serving their sentence. A discussion of the 'convict stain' thus reveals something of subaltern practices of resistance, the social complexities of the British presence, and the production of culturally exclusive social boundaries in the Indian Ocean colonial context.

Convicts escaped from Botany Bay and residing in Calcutta

In 1800, the colonial authorities in the Bengal Presidency produced a list of *Convicts and Other Persons Escaped from Botany Bay and residing in Calcutta, with their period of residence and their occupation*.[4] The list gave a surprisingly detailed account of fifteen women, eleven men, and six children living in the city. It identified explicitly three of the women as escaped convicts: Elizabeth Harvey, who had been transported to New South Wales on the first fleet (*Friendship*), Mary Ann Fielding (*Indispensable*), and Mary Bryant (*Britannia*).[5] The women had escaped to Calcutta on board the *Marquis Cornwallis*, and were living in Rada Bazaar with three men from the same ship, Duncan Campbell, Thomas Brading, and William Reid. The men – probably ex-convicts – had been given permission to leave the colony, and it is likely that they had been complicit in the escape of their female partners.

Another woman on the 1800 Calcutta list was first fleet convict Mary Radford, who had left Botany Bay in 1796 for Amboyna (Ambon Island in modern Indonesia, then a British possession). She went to Calcutta three years later, probably after the death of her husband, master of the East India Company artillery band. Elizabeth Marshall, also an ex-convict, had been in the city since 1796. It seems that she had spent some time in French Ile de France (later British Mauritius) before travelling to India on a Dutch ship. A third time-expired convict, Sarah Young, arrived in Calcutta in 1798, later marrying a cooper. At least two of the men detailed, John Wisehammer and Richard Manly, had also served sentences of transportation in Australia. However, there is no evidence that any of the others had convict antecedents.[6] One, James Roll, had arrived in Calcutta from the northwest coast of America, having been employed as a carpenter on board several ships sailing between the Cape, America, and India. Another, Thomas Smith, had worked his passage from Botany Bay as a ship steward. Elizabeth Wise had spent time in Batavia before settling in Calcutta. Margaret Holt and her husband had migrated to Australia as free settlers. After he died, she went first to Bencoolen and later to India. In their experience of colonial islands and enclaves across the Indian Ocean, these men and women were part of what Rediker has described in the Atlantic context as a 'huge, boundless, and international' world.[7] Turn-of-the-century Calcutta was a vibrant multicultural port city, and many of those listed in 1800 lived in the area around Lal Bazar. Rada Bazar, where the three escaped convict women and their male companions had fled, housed most of the Europeans living in the city, including James and Eliza Scott and their three children, alongside the Armenian and Portuguese communities. Mary Radford lived on Cossiatola Street. Doomtollah, where Elizabeth Wise resided with her husband Edward Sweeney, together with Richard Manly and Elizabeth Davis, was a Jewish and Parsi area. Moorghihatta, home to Thomas Smith, John Wisehammer, Sarah Merchant, and Thomas Tuck, was the site of the Portuguese market.[8]

These time-expired convicts and free migrants were models of respectability. Most followed a trade, as artisans, tradesmen, retailers or servants. John Potrie was a tailor, John Wisehammer and James Roll were carpenters, and Richard Manly a bookbinder. James Scott and Thomas Smith were licensed retailers of spirits. Elizabeth Davis was a midwife employed by a Dr Dick. Thomas Tuck was a servant. Where the list added personal comments on individuals, it described them as peaceable, quiet, industrious, and well behaved. Most of the women were either married or in stable relationships with European partners. There were no hints that any were of 'bad character' or working in the sex trade, the accusation so often levelled at female convicts in Botany Bay.[9] Most female convicts remained in Australia after their sentences expired, with only a small minority returning to their homes in Britain or Ireland. Many had formed personal attachments or found employment in the colony, which meant that they did not wish to go back. Even if they did, it was difficult for them to save enough money to pay the cost of their passage.[10] Some of the women on the 1800 Calcutta list had travelled to India with partners in military service. Mary Radford is a case in point. Another woman, Sarah Merchant, had first travelled to Pondicherry with a Company soldier, going on to Calcutta after she was widowed. Other women found new partners in India. In 1800, four were cohabiting with harbour pilots, underlining the intensely maritime nature of the world in which they all lived, moved and worked.

Despite the apparent respectability of these ex-convict and free migrant settlers, they were faced with hostility from the British authorities, for they brought with them the Australian 'convict stain'. In the colonial world, New South Wales was viewed widely as a degraded society. Europeans with criminal records embodied the moral shortcomings of metropolitan life, therefore challenging ideological claims that colonialism was a civilizing presence. In the context of sensitivities about British colonial status (and their social if not racial superiority), the 'convict stain' proved remarkably enduring.[11] For these reasons, the East India Company did not want time-expired convicts settling in the city. In 1800 it issued a proclamation ordering the return to New South Wales of the escaped convicts, and prohibiting any person who had ever been transported as a convict from landing in Bengal, under threat of deportation. The Governor-General wrote of ex-convicts as 'persons from whose establishment in these possessions the most prejudicial consequences are to be apprehended both to the British character and interests', and requested that ships sailing between New South Wales should not embark them.[12] There is no record of the deportation of any of the time-expired men and women resident in Calcutta in 1800, and migration from Australia continued.[13] However, at least one of the escaped convicts, Mary Ann Fielding, was returned to England, for there is a record of her trial on a charge of returning from transportation.[14]

The response of the colonial authorities to the settlement of ex-convicts was part of a broader effort to monitor closely all Europeans not employed in the service of the Company. From at least the 1780s, a *List of European Residents* was kept in Bengal and sent to the court of directors in London on an annual basis, for careful inspection.[15] In addition, the masters of ships were obliged to produce a list of all Europeans on board when they arrived and left the port of Calcutta, and were responsible for any discrepancies. Passengers wishing to stay in India were obliged to register with the master attendant or face deportation.[16] A significant minority of British settlers had been employed formerly in military service. Many were also skilled craftsmen, and worked as silversmiths, jewellers, and carpenters. Others became traders.[17] However, administrators feared that if they fell sick, lost their jobs or went out of business they would become a financial and social burden. Worse still, they might take military service with competing Indian elites. Though British society in India was not homogeneous, the illusion that it was had to be maintained. Poor Europeans could bring the 'ruling race' into contempt.[18] Company administrators viewed 'poor whites', as they were generally known, with suspicion, and vagrants as a menace.[19]

From the end of the eighteenth century, the colonial authorities confined unemployed Europeans within the limits of Fort William.[20] They also admitted European paupers to hospital.[21] These policies removed socially disruptive individuals from the visible parameters of the British community. The behaviour of Europeans was also subject to strict regulation. For instance, the Company took measures to control the often violent conduct of drunken European sailors in port. There was always a surplus pool of seamen in Calcutta, ready to replace the dead or sick, and therefore keep the cost of shipping down.[22] On discharge from their ship, sailors headed for the area around Lal Bazar, and indulged in the eating houses, grog shops, and brothels there.[23] Fights broke out frequently, so much so that in 1788 the Company directed that crew could not come ashore in possession of knives or anything that might be used as a weapon. Ships' captains were obliged to provide security for them.[24]

The vagrancy of settler women was a particularly alarming prospect for the colonial authorities, as they might turn to the sex trade as a means of generating income. Though we know little about white prostitution in late eighteenth- and early nineteenth-century India, there is plenty of evidence to suggest that in Britain and early colonial Australia women who sold sex were accepted within their own plebeian communities. However, middle-class observers saw them as sources of immorality and contagion.[25] Women's sexuality took on a further dimension in colonial settings, as potentially the social and economic alliances and transactions in which they engaged traversed community borders. Though elite men engaged in sexual relationships with Indian women, from the eighteenth century boundaries began to emerge around notions of 'Britishness' and 'whiteness'.[26] The regulation of sex became part of the politics of empire, with what Kathleen Wilson describes as the 'debased femininities' of subaltern women – indigenous, slave, migrant, plebeian – mutually inflecting and constituting a gendered metropolitan and colonial social order.[27]

Escape and migration in the Indian Ocean

Sydney was a cosmopolitan city, increasingly centred at the hub of Indian Ocean trading networks. As John Molony notes in his study of the first generation of Australians born to immigrant parentage, children raised in Sydney grew up in a global world. The daughter of one First Fleeter, Elizabeth Harris, married a Calcutta merchant in 1812, leaving for India and returning a few years later. Her husband died, so she returned to England and married the wealthy emancipist shipowner and merchant, John Underwood, who had been trading between New South Wales, China and India for some years. Her son, John Lang, also ended up in Calcutta, sailing for India with his wife and two children in 1842.[28] Australian settlers, whether convict or free, looked not only to the bush, but also out across the water as a focus for their dreams of mobility and freedom.[29] During the first decade of the nineteenth century, two vessels called at Sydney harbour each month, providing multiple opportunities for escape.[30] Two hundred ships passed through Prince of Wales Island each year.[31] Between 1815 and 1822 thirteen vessels sailed from Australia to Mauritius, about two per year. By the early 1830s, this figure had risen to about sixteen per year. Between 1829 and 1832, no fewer than 47 ships arrived.[32] Commissioner Bigge in his inquiry into New South Wales commented that escape to the island would increase as trade between Australia and Mauritius grew.[33] In 1818, the colonial secretary of New South Wales suggested that all ships sailing from Australia should be mustered on arrival in colonial port cities as a means of detecting escapees.[34] By the 1820s, the Sydney Port Regulations required that commanders of all vessels give written notice of their departure at least ten days before setting sail. The list of passengers could then be checked against convict indents, to ensure that ex-convicts' sentences had expired and no escapees were on board.[35] Nevertheless, convicts stowed away, assumed aliases and worked the passage, or struck a deal with captains short of hands. The constant movement of people across the sea to Sydney – sailors, soldiers, officials, labourers – assisted escape in other ways too, for it created vast flows of information upon which convicts drew, transforming the ocean into a source of knowledge as well as a space for the projection of liberty.[36]

Though no formal records were kept during the early nineteenth century, in 1823 Commissioner Bigge's inquiry reported that between 1803 and 1820 over 250 convicts had attempted to escape by ship, and almost a quarter of them were never seen again.[37] A further dimension to convict escape was the seizure of vessels, or acts of piracy.[38] Both the Bigge reports and the later Molesworth select committee on transportation (1837–38) mentioned favoured convict destinations: New Zealand, South America, and the Pacific Rim. Escaped convicts also settled on various islands in the Bass Straits.

Bigge reported that in 1818 officials discovered a boat built by a party of convicts employed in seal fishery in the Bass Straits at George Town, near Launceston (Van Diemen's Land). Convicts made regular trips to offshore islands, and knew the waters well. Seal fishery in the Bass Straits was so affected by convicts escaping to India that its productivity declined, and it was subsequently relocated to the New Zealand coast and Macquarie Island.[39] The story of Mary Bryant, who escaped to East Timor, is well known.[40] Convicts also escaped to South and Southeast Asia, jumping ship in ports like Calcutta, Batavia, and Penang (Prince of Wales Island). In 1815, convict James Smith was turned over to the police in Calcutta. They put him on board a ship heading for New South Wales, but he absconded again when it called at Penang.[41] In 1817, three more women from New South Wales – Elizabeth Finlay, Amelia Barker and Ann Helling – were discovered secreted on board a ship bound for Calcutta. They were returned to Australia on the ship *Frederick*, which also carried seven British soldiers sentenced to transportation to New South Wales for offences in India, and ten Indian convicts destined for the East India Company's penal settlement at Bencoolen.[42] Eight escapees were discovered in Calcutta in one single year, 1820. Like James Smith, two of them – James Ledlow and John Willis – absconded in Penang on their way back to New South Wales.[43]

Escaped convicts were also arrested in the Mascarene island colony of Mauritius, which was a popular port of call for ships sailing from Australia to Britain. In 1819, for instance, a 20-year-old woman named Catherine Ruby, who had absconded from Sydney on the *Port Sea,* was arrested in Port Louis and returned to Australia. The clerk of the ship, Joseph Clark, had hidden her on board.[44] In 1822, William Demett was found hidden on the *Mary* a few days after it had left Hobart (Van Diemen's Land). He admitted that he was a convict, and stated that he had got on board by swimming underneath the ship's bow and climbing up the cable. On arrival in Port Louis he again absconded, but was arrested and returned to Australia.[45] Another man, John Meldrum was discovered hidden on the *Countess of Harcourt* a month after its departure from Sydney in 1829. When the ship docked off the coast of Mauritius, Meldrum was placed in irons, but he managed to remove them and swim to shore. He was picked up by the police two weeks later.[46] Subsequently, if the Mauritian authorities had the slightest suspicion that a new arrival was a convict, they contacted their counterparts in Australian for verification of identity.[47] This perhaps explains why in the post-Bigge period, despite enhanced opportunities, proportionately fewer convicts absconded.[48] Nevertheless, a group of escaped Van Diemen's Land convicts made it to Fiji in 1854.[49] Two convict women, calling themselves 'Rose' and 'Rosetta', turned up in Ceylon in 1855.[50] Into the 1860s, the Australian authorities circulated descriptive lists of absconders around the colonies.[51]

In the colonial archive, convict perspectives on escape emerge invariably through the mouths of the officials recording their stories: captains, crew, fellow passengers, the police, and other officials. Sometimes only the tiniest fragments of their escape and arrest survive, in the form of bills of payments to ships that agreed to take them back to Australia. Often, escaped convicts remain completely nameless in these financial transactions.[52] And yet the actions of absconders form their own sort of dialogue. The devastation of the loss of and separation from former social networks is sometimes forgotten as central to how convicts experienced transportation. In his evidence to the Molesworth committee, Lieutenant-Governor George Arthur wrote of the hopeless escape attempts made by convicts:

> if there were further proof wanting to show the irksomeness, and the extreme penalty of transportation, it is the desperate attempts that some of these men have made to get away ... they have placed themselves in casks, and under packages, and have suffered most excruciating pains.[53]

John Stoodley, who was found hidden on board the ship *Aligator* in Port Louis, told one of the ship's crew on the way from Sydney that he had not received his wages from his master. The assistant commissioner of police in Port Louis, James Reader, had visited New South Wales previously, staying with Stoodley's master, port master Isaac Nichols. He recognized Stoodley, and claimed that during one of his visits he had heard him tell Nicholas that 'he had no business to strike his prisoner servants but report them to the Police to get them punished'.[54] The convict Benjamin Castle[55] was discovered on board the *Boyne*, about a month after it set sail from Sydney for Bombay in 1839. At first he refused to speak, but later admitted that he was a Sydney convict who had been employed by the owner of the The Three Tons, a public house on King's Street. He swam to the ship a week before it sailed, and was helped on board by its crew. The captain of the ship secured him, but twice he removed his fetters. The second time, he jumped overboard on the coast of Cannanore (South India) and tried to swim to shore. When the ship docked in Bombay, Castle told the police magistrate that he longed to see his parents again. Pictures of a woman, a boy, and the initials 'RF', tattooed on his arm, speak movingly of the kin networks he had left behind.[56]

James Doran was shipped to New South Wales on the *Atlas* in October 1819. He was aged 25 and a literate man, having been employed as a 'clerk'. Doran served the first year of his sentence in the commissariat department, presumably as a writer, and was then assigned to the prominent Sydney merchants, Wollstonecraft and Berry. His gentlemanly status apparently secured him the support of dozens of eminent businessmen, civil servants and clergymen, as a result of which he received the promise of a conditional pardon from Governor Brisbane. In 1827, however, he was reconvicted for smuggling liquor. Governor Darling relinquished the promise of pardon and sent him to Wellington Valley, a remote convict settlement in New South Wales. Doran petitioned for a more lenient sentence, writing of the 'privations and sufferings' to which he was being subjected, but his plea was denied. Eighteen months after his arrival at Wellington, Doran escaped, apparently with the assistance of his friends, John Raine, Richard Kemp and Edward Lee, who were later put on trial. Doran himself was last seen heading for Mauritius on the *Bona Vista*. The ship was wrecked on its journey to the island, nine days after setting sail. It was presumed by the Mauritian authorities that Doran had drowned, though records show that all on board were saved and sent on to Batavia. We do not know what became of Doran.[57]

Occasionally escaped convicts were sent back to England where they faced trial on the charge of returning from transportation, but most usually they were shipped back to Australia where men faced the public humiliation of flogging and the chain gang or transfer to a penal station. In 1829, for example, two men and one woman escaped to Bombay on the *Phoenix*. The (unnamed) female convict escaped from police custody shortly after arrival, from where she disappeared without trace. The men were shipped back to Australia. At least one of them (Edward Powers) made it to Van Diemen's Land, for he was put on trial for absconding in January 1830. He was found guilty and sentenced to 12 months in irons, first in the penal station at Macquarie Harbour and later in Port Arthur. Only in 1835 was he returned to the public works gang in Hobart.[58] In another extraordinary case, during the early 1820s, Philip Cato stowed away to Mauritius on the *Governor Phillip*, and then worked his passage back to Liverpool on the *Mary*. In 1827, he was retried for a second offence and shipped to Hobart under the name Robert Collins. As a returned absconder, he too was confined at Macquarie Harbour.[59]

Time-expired convict men and women also took advantage of communication networks, and tried to make new lives for themselves beyond the confines of Australia's shores.[60] Frequent shipping links made Mauritius especially appealing to ex-felons wishing to leave Australia, at least partly because it was so difficult to save enough money for the passage back to Britain or Ireland. By the 1830s, about 16 ships a year sailed between the colonies.[61] One time-expired man, John Bell, claimed that he had surreptitiously boarded a ship to Port Louis 'because of the pregnancy of a female'.[62] Time-expired convict James Moreton, who went clandestinely from Van Diemen's Land to Mauritius in 1824, wrote of the £60 passage money required for the voyage to England: 'that is a great deal of money for a man to raise who has nothing but what he gets by his work'.[63] However, as in India at the beginning of the century, ex-convicts and their families enjoyed a far from enthusiastic reception. In 1829, the chief secretary to the government of Mauritius wrote of the island being overrun with vagabonds from 'New South Wales and elsewhere'. He urged the deportation of European migrants without means of subsistence.[64] And yet there were tensions between the skills time-expired convicts undoubtedly possessed and their status as ex-felons. As chief of police John Finniss wrote of cooper

Patrick Hastings later that year: 'However desirable it may be to encourage persons of his Trade to settle here I fear the admission of time-expired convicts would be liable to many objections'. As a result, the Mauritian government asked the Australian authorities not to allow time-expired convicts to sail for the island.[65] Only one such man appears to have been granted a licence to remain in Mauritius during the first half of the nineteenth century. Daniel Kelly was a mason, and had been time-expired for some seven years before his arrival in Mauritius in 1832. That he had his ten-year-old daughter with him perhaps rendered him open to sympathy.[66] Three years later John Roche was not so lucky. The government turned down his request for a shop licence, and asked him to leave the colony.[67] Later that year, it shipped the 'violent and dangerous' time-expired convict Daniel Brophy back to New South Wales.[68]

Conclusion

Though the status of escaped convicts, time-expired convicts, and free migrants from Australia was quite different, the response to their presence across the Indian Ocean during the first half of the nineteenth century reveals a great deal about British society and the construction of social boundaries of exclusion in the colonial context. Local authorities shipped convict absconders back to the Australian penal settlements as soon as possible, for their escape signified a threat to imperial governance and their presence challenged the illusion of British social and moral superiority in the colonies. All plebeian people embarking for the colonies in Australia carried this 'convict stain' with them, and they were greeted with hostility and suspicion whether they had served sentences of transportation or not. Further, the response of British officials to the arrival of ordinary men and women from Australia is revealing of colonial attitudes to plebeian mobility more broadly. The ocean itself represented a 'space of disorder' in this respect, for it was a place of sometimes uncontrolled movement and migration. Cultures of exclusion in the colonial context thus had an important maritime, as well as social, dimension.

Acknowledgements

This work emerged from a series of chance findings in British, Australian, Indian, and Mauritian archives. I am indebted to staff in the Archives Office of Tasmania (AOT), India Office Library, London (IOL), National Archives of Mauritius (MA), National Archives of India (NAI), National Archives, Kew (NA) and Tamil Nadu State Archives, Chennai (TNSA). An earlier version of this chapter appeared in the *Journal of Australian Colonial History* 3, 2, 2001, and I would like to thank the editor David Roberts for allowing republication of some of the material here. Most of all, I am grateful to the National Maritime Museum for the award of the Caird

Senior Fellowship during 2006–7, which allowed me to develop further my work on the cultural dynamics of Indian Ocean voyaging.

Notes

1. D. Arnold, 'European Orphans and Vagrants in India in the Nineteenth Century', *Journal of Imperial and Commonwealth History* 7, 2, 1979: 104–27; S. De, 'Marginal Europeans and the white underworld in colonial Bombay', *Jadavpur University Journal of History* 16, 1995–96: 32–56; S. C. Ghosh, *The Social Condition of the British Community in Bengal, 1757–1800*, Leiden: Brill, 1970; H. Fischer-Tiné, 'Britain's Other Civilising Mission: Class-prejudice, European "Loaferism" and the Workhouse System in Colonial India', *Indian Economic and Social History Review* 42, 3, 2005: 295–338; H. Fischer-Tiné, '"White Women degrading themselves to the lowest depths" – European Networks of Prostitution and Colonial Anxieties in British India ca. 1870–1914', *Indian Economic and Social History Review* 2, 2003: 163–90; A. Ganachari, '"White Man's Embarrassment" – European Vagrancy in Nineteenth-Century Bombay', *Economic and Political Weekly* 37, 2, 2002: 2477–85; C. J. Hawes, *Poor Relations: The Making of a Eurasian Community in British India 1773–1833*, London: Routledge Curzon, 1996; P. J. Marshall, 'British Society in India under the East India Company', *Modern Asian Studies* 31, 1, 1997: 89–108; P. Sinha, *Calcutta In Urban History*, Calcutta: Firma K.L.M., 1978; P. Stanley, *White Mutiny: British Military Culture in India, 1825–1875*, London, 1998; R. K. Renford, *The Non-Official British in India to 1920*, New Delhi: Oxford University Press, 1987.
2. C. Hall and S. O. Rose, eds, *At Home With the Empire: Metropolitan Culture and the Imperial World*, Cambridge: Cambridge University Press, 2006; P. Levine, ed., *Gender and Empire*, Oxford: Oxford University Press, 2004.
3. P. Linebaugh and M. Rediker, *The Many-Headed Hydra: Sailors, Slaves, Commoners, and the Hidden History of the Revolutionary Atlantic*, London: Verso, 2000.
4. NAI Home (Public) Original Consultation, 3 July 1800, no. 7: List of convicts and other persons escaped from Botany Bay and residing in Calcutta, with their period of residence and their occupation, 2 July 1800 (all subsequent references to this list refer to this document).
5. See P. Robinson, *The Women of Botany Bay: a reinterpretation of the role of women in the origins of Australian society*, Sydney: The Macquarie Library, 1988, pp. 281, 287: Elizabeth Harvey (*alias* Hervey/Harvy) NSW *per Friendship*, 1788, Mary Ann Fielding, NSW *per Indispensable*, 1796, Mary Briant (*alias* Brian), NSW *per Britannia*, 1798. Two Mary Bryans were included in *Governor Hunter's Assignment List, return of convict women in the services of Officers or other Households, 1798*, Archives Office of New South Wales (AONSW), COD197, SZ767, pp. 155–57. The first was in the service of a Bryan Egan, the second was married to a George Patfield.
6. Both men received seven-year sentences, Wisehammer in Bristol and Manly in Middlesex (AONSW Bound Indents, 1786–99). It is more difficult to trace convicts with common names: for instance, eight Thomas Smiths and two James Scotts were transported to New South Wales between 1787–91. Therefore, it is possible that some of the other men detailed on the 1800 list were also time-expired convicts.
7. M. Rediker, *Between The Devil And The Deep Blue Sea: Merchant Seamen, Pirates, and the Anglo-American Maritime World, 1700–1750*, Cambridge: Cambridge University Press, 1987, p. 10.

8. J. Long, 'A Peep Into the Social Life of Calcutta During the Second Half of the 18th Century', reproduced in P. Thankappan Nair, *A Tercentenary History of Calcutta, Vol. II: A History of Calcutta's Streets*, Calcutta: Firma K.L.M., 1987, pp. 18–19.
9. J. Damousi, *Depraved and Disorderly: Female Convicts, Sexuality and Gender in Colonial Australia*, Cambridge: Cambridge University Press, 1997.
10. K. Daniels, *Convict Women*, St Leonards: Allen and Unwin, 1999, pp. 237–38.
11. M. Sturma, *Vice In A Vicious Society: crime and convicts in mid nineteenth-century New South Wales*, St Lucia: University of Queensland Press, 1983.
12. NAI Home (Public) Original Consultation, 3 July 1800, nos 5–6. See also W.S. Seton-Karr, *Selections from Calcutta Gazettes*, Calcutta: O.T. Cutter, 1864, p. 55 and G. Karskens, '"This spirit of emigration": the nature and meanings of escape in early New South Wales', *Journal of Australian Colonial History* 7, 2005: 32.
13. A. Atkinson, *The Europeans in Australia, A History: Vol. I*, Oxford: Oxford University Press, 1997, pp. 130–31.
14. Robinson, *The Women of Botany Bay*, p. 259 (n. 22). Fielding's sentence of death was commuted to life (re-)transportation. See also AONSW Bound Indents, Mary Ann Fielding *per Nile*, 1801. There are no trial records of the other two women, who may have died before reaching England.
15. NAI Home (Public) Original Consultation, 11 March 1783, no. 4. See also *British Social Life in Ancient Calcutta (1750 to 1850): During the second half of the 18th Century by the Rev. James Long and During the first half of the 19th Century by J. H. Stocqueler*, edited with notes by P. Thankappan Nair, Calcutta, Firma K.L.M., 1983, pp. 47–48.
16. NAI Home (Public) Original Consultation, 25 June 1788, no. 38.
17. NAI Home (Public) Original Consultation, 28 January 1788, nos 5–6.
18. Arnold, 'European Orphans and Vagrants in India', 124.
19. See footnote 2. The *Calcutta Gazettes* contain frequent references to European crimes and misdemeanours: Seton-Karr, *Selections from Calcutta Gazettes*, A.C. Das Gupta, *The Days of John Company; Selections from Calcutta Gazettes 1824–1832*, Calcutta: Superintendent of Government Printing, 1959.
20. NAI Home (Public) Original Consultations, 24 April 1789, no. 8A; 1 May 1789, no. 2.
21. See, for example NAI Home (Public), Original Consultation, 12 May 1794, no. 18.
22. Arnold, 'European Orphans and Vagrants in India', p. 115.
23. Thankappan Nair, *A Tercentenary History of Calcutta, Vol. II*, p. 509.
24. NAI Home (Public) Original Consultation, 25 June 1788, no. 38.
25. T. Henderson, *Disorderly Women in Eighteenth-Century London: Prostitution and Control in the Metropolis, 1730–1830*, London: Longman, 1999, pp. 42–43, 194. Michael Sturma argues that in colonial Australia the perception that convicts engaged in 'lewd conduct' originated in the conflict between bourgeois sensibilities and working-class practices (*Vice in a Vicious Society*). See also J.R. Walkowitz, *Prostitution and Victorian Society: Women, class, and the state*, Cambridge: Cambridge University Press, 1980; K. Daniels, 'Prostitution in Tasmania during the transition from penal settlement to "civilized" society', in K. Daniels, ed., *So Much Hard Work: Women and Prostitution in Australian History*, Sydney: Fontana, 1984, pp. 15–86; K. Reid, *Gender, Crime and Empire: convicts, settlers and the state in early colonial Australia*, Manchester: Manchester University Press, 2007.
26. D. Ghosh, *Sex and the Family in Colonial India: the Making of Empire*, Cambridge: Cambridge University Press, 2006.
27. K. Wilson, 'Empire, Gender, and Modernity in the Eighteenth Century', in Levine, ed., *Gender and Empire*, p. 44. On sex and the politics of empire, see

P. Levine, 'Sexuality, Gender, and Empire', in Levine, ed., *Gender and Empire*, pp. 134–35.
28 J. Molony, *The Native-Born*, p. 78 and 169–77.
29 J. Molony, *The Native-Born*, p. 34. Grace Karskens makes a similar point in *The Rocks: Life in Early Sydney*, Melbourne: Melbourne University Press, 1997, p. 19, ch. 16.
30 J. Molony, *The Native-Born*, p. 32. These included coal ships bound for India.
31 G. Leith, *A Short Account of the Settlement, Produce, and Commerce, of Prince of Wales Island, in The Straits of Malacca*, London: J. Booth, 1804, pp. 52–53, 89–91.
32 E. Duyker, *Of the Star and the Key: Mauritius, Mauritians and Australia*, Sylvania: Australian Mauritian Research Group, 1982, pp. 23–24.
33 J. T. Bigge, *Report of the Commission of Inquiry on the Judicial Establishments of New South Wales (1823)*, Adelaide: Libraries Board of South Australia, 1966, p. 79.
34 MA RA121. J. Campbell, secretary to government New South Wales, to G.A. Barry, secretary to government Mauritius, 3 March 1818.
35 J. T. Bigge, *Report of the Commissioner of Inquiry into the State of the Colony of New South Wales (1822)*, Adelaide: Libraries Board of South Australia, 1966, pp. 54–55.
36 On the circulation of knowledge, see C. A. Bayly, *Empire and Information: Intelligence gathering and social communication in India, 1780–1870*, Cambridge: Cambridge University Press, 1996; and Linebaugh and Rediker, *The Many-Headed Hydra*.
37 Bigge, *Report of the Commission of Inquiry (1823)*, p. 79.
38 I. Duffield, '"Haul away the anchor girls": Charlotte Badger, tall stories and the pirates of the "bad ship *Venus*"', *Journal of Australian Colonial History* 7, 2005: 35–64.
39 Bigge, *Report of the Commission of Inquiry (1823)*, pp. 55–56; Bigge, *Report of the Commissioner of Inquiry (1822)*, pp. 47, 79; PP 1837 XIX (518), p. 1 ff: Report from Select Committee appointed to inquire into the System of Transportation (Molesworth Committee). See also Hurst, *Great Escapes*, pp. 148–49; 'Escape: Essays on Convict Australia', special edition of *Journal of Australian Colonial History* 7, 2005.
40 C. H. Currey, *The Transportation, Escape and Pardoning of Mary Bryant*, Sydney: Angus and Robertson, 1963. Robert Hughes also discusses the case of Mary Bryant in *The Fatal Shore: A History of the Transportation of Convicts to Australia, 1787–1868*, London: Collins Harvill, 1987, pp. 205–9.
41 IOL P/131/60 (Bengal Judicial Consultation 2 May 1815). W.B. Bayley, acting secretary to government Bengal, to the sheriff of Calcutta, 25 April 1815.
42 IOL P/132/57 (Bengal Judicial Consultation 28 March 1817). Extract of proceedings, law department, 25 March 1817. Elizabeth Finlay, *per Experiment*, 21 September 1809 and Amelia Barker, *per Minstrel*, 4 June 1812 (Robinson, *The Women of Botany Bay*, pp. 296, 315). Both women were sentenced to seven years' transportation, Finlay in Monoghan and Barker in York. AONSW Bound Indents (4/4004). Ann Helling could not be traced.
43 IOL P/134/21 (Bengal Judicial Consultation 25 April 1820). Campbell to C. Lushington, secretary to government Bengal, 6 January 1820.
44 MA RA125. report of the general police office, Port Louis, 16 February 1819; MA Z2A16. Report of A.W. Blanc, deputy secretary to government, 22 February 1819.
45 MA RA263. Report of F. Goulburn, colonial secretary's office Sydney, 21 May 1824; MA Z2A 20. Declaration of [Captain] William Kneale, 7 November 1821.
46 MA Z2A49. Report of Barry, 19 February 1829; MA RA409. Report of J. Finniss, chief of police, 2 February 1829, enclosing a declaration of the ship's crew, 23 January 1829.

47 See, for example, correspondence between W. Austen, chief police magistrate Hobart, and Finniss, 31 July 1836 (MA Z2A100). For the case of Jane Henry, alias Marie Wilkinson, alias Jane New, escaped from the female factory at Parramatta, said to be bound for Port Louis on the *Eliza*, see MA Z2A54. F. Rossi, principal superintendent of police Sydney, to Finniss, 24 July 1829. She was not found on board (Finniss to Rossi, 26 September 1829). Daniels discusses Jane New in *Convict Women*. Shortly before her escape, she wrote to her 'dear husband': 'I hear that you are in Parramatta; I hope and trust that you will get an order to come and see me, for I am almost out of my mind at not seeing you' (p. 135).
48 Atkinson, *The Europeans in Australia*, p. 115.
49 AOT CSO24/257/10635 and CSD 1/28/33. Colonial secretary's office, Van Diemen's Land, 30 October 1854, report of Captain Fitzgerald, H.M. ship *Calleope*, Port Jackson, 31 December 1854.
50 AOT CSD1/76/203. Female convicts absconded to Ceylon, July 1855 – January 1856.
51 For example TNSA Judicial, 5 July 1867, 55–66. List of [56] Convicts who are supposed to have escaped from the Colony [Western Australia] since 1 June 1850.
52 For details of these payments, see, for example, the Mauritian Blue Books (PRO CO172 series).
53 Molesworth Committee, Evidence of George Arthur, 30 June 1837.
54 MA RA56. Blanc, commissioner of police, Port Louis, to F. Rossi, acting deputy secretary to government, 9 January 1815, enclosing 'Extracts from the Log Book of the Schooner *Aligator*, Captain Joseph Savigny, from Port Jackson, 5 and 6 September 1814' and report of James Reader, first assistant commissioner of police Port Louis, 8 January 1815. Stoodley was from Devon where he was sentenced to life transportation in March 1811. AONSW Bound Indents (4/4004) John Stoodley *per Guildford* (1) 12 January 1812. Isaac Nichols was a wealthy emancipist dealer, shipowner, landowner, and civil servant. See Karskens, *The Rocks*, p. 228.
55 Castle was a brick maker from Northampton by trade. He was sentenced to life for housebreaking and was shipped to Sydney on the *Norfolk* in 1837. AONSW Bound Indents, 37–516 Benjamin Castle *per Norfolk*, 12 February 1837.
56 IOL P/402/33 (Bombay Judicial Consultation 15 May 1839). J.A. Forbes, senior magistrate of police Bombay, to J. P. Willoughby, secretary to government Bombay, 4 May 1839, enclosing statements of George Richardson, captain of the *Boyne*, 3 May 1839, and Benjamin Castle, 5 May 1839. Details of Castle's tattoos are noted in AONSW Bound Indents, 37–516.
57 I am indebted to David Roberts for discussions on James Doran. The papers regarding James Doran are at: Letters Received (Colonial Secretary), 1828, State Records of New South Wales (SRNSW), Bundle 4/2001. Doran's 1827 petition is also reproduced at MA RA121. Petition of James Doran Prisoner for life *per* ship *Atlas*, 24 July 1827. The survival of the passengers from the wrecked *Bona Vista* is noted by C. Bateson, *Australian Shipwrecks; Including Vessels wrecked en route to or from Australia and some strandings, Vol. 1: 1622–1850*, Sydney: A.H. and A.W. Reed, 1972, p. 80. More details of the formative years of Wellington Valley can be found in D. A. Roberts, '"A sort of inland Norfolk Island?" Isolation, Coercion and Resistance on the Wellington Valley Convict Station, 1823–26', *Journal of Australian Colonial History*, 2, 1, 2000: 50–72.
58 A few details of the escape can be found in the IOL: P/400/23 (Bombay Judicial Consultations 4/18 February 1829). J. Cuzins, commander of the *Phoenix*, to C. Norris, secretary to government Bombay, 22 January 1829, report of C. Norris, 14 February 1829. See also 431 Edward Powers *per Surrey* (1816) and *Elizabeth* (1825) AONSW bound indents, AOT, Con 31 and CS01/509/11138. I

thank Hamish Maxwell-Stewart for the New South Wales and Tasmanian archive references.
59 I thank Hamish Maxwell-Stewart for the story of and archival references to Philip Cato/Robert Collins: 782 Robert Collins *per Governor Ready*, AOT, Con 31/6.
60 A. Atkinson, 'The Pioneers Who Left Early', *Push From The Bush* 29, 1991, 110–16. Atkinson calculates that around one-third of first fleet men left the colony, and between 7 and 40 per cent of women (p. 113).
61 Duyker, *Of the Star and the Key*, pp. 23–24.
62 MA RA263. Report of J. Finniss, 22 December 1824.
63 MA RA261/263. Petition of John Moreton, 4 July 1824 and report of Finniss, 14 May 1824.
64 MA Z2A49. Barry to Finniss, 21 March 1829.
65 MA RA399/121. Report of Finniss, 12 March 1829, Alexander Macleay, colonial secretary Sydney, to Barry, 21 October 1829. Hastings was from Limerick, and was sentenced to seven years' transportation in 1822. He was a cooper by trade. AONSW 4/4008 305–15 Patrick Hastings *per Brampton*, 22 April 1823.
66 MA RA469. Finniss to G.F. Dick, secretary to government Mauritius, 13 October 1832.
67 MA Z2A84. Dick to Finniss, 10 April 1835.
68 MA Z2A85. Dick to Finniss, 9 October 1835.

Bibliography

Printed material

Arnold, D., 'European Orphans and Vagrants in India in the Nineteenth Century', *Journal of Imperial and Commonwealth History* 7, 2, 1979: 104–27.
Atkinson, A., 'The Pioneers Who Left Early', *Push From The Bush* 29, 1991: 110–16.
——, *The Europeans in Australia, A History: Vol. I*, Oxford: Oxford University Press, 1997.
Bateson, C., *Australian Shipwrecks; Including Vessels wrecked en route to or from Australia and some strandings, Vol. 1: 1622–1850*, Sydney: A.H. and A.W. Reed, 1972.
Bayly, C. A., *Empire and Information: Intelligence gathering and social communication in India, 1780–1870*, Cambridge: Cambridge University Press, 1996.
Bigge, J. T., *Report of the Commission of Inquiry on the Judicial Establishments of New South Wales (1823)*, Adelaide: Libraries Board of South Australia, 1966.
——, *Report of the Commissioner of Inquiry into the State of the Colony of New South Wales (1822)*, Adelaide: Libraries Board of South Australia, 1966.
Currey, C. H., *The Transportation, Escape and Pardoning of Mary Bryant*, Sydney: Angus and Robertson, 1963.
Damousi, J., *Depraved and Disorderly: Female Convicts, Sexuality and Gender in Colonial Australia*, Cambridge: Cambridge University Press, 1997.
Daniels, K., *Convict Women*, St Leonards: Allen and Unwin, 1999.
——, 'Prostitution in Tasmania during the transition from penal settlement to "civilized" society', in K. Daniels, ed., *So Much Hard Work: Women and Prostitution in Australian History*, Sydney: Ed. Fontana, 1984, pp. 15–86.
De, S., 'Marginal Europeans and the white underworld in colonial Bombay', *Jadavpur University Journal of History* 16, 1995/96: 32–56.
Duyker, E., *Of the Star and the Key: Mauritius, Mauritians and Australia*, Sylvania: Australian Mauritian Research Group, 1982.

Fischer-Tiné, H., 'Britain's Other Civilising Mission: Class-prejudice, European "Loaferism" and the Workhouse System in Colonial India', *Indian Economic and Social History Review* 42, 3, 2005: 295–338.

——, '"White Women degrading themselves to the lowest depths" European Networks of Prostitution and Colonial Anxieties in British India ca. 1870–1914', *Indian Economic and Social History Review* 40, 2, 2003: 163–90.

Ganachari, A., '"White Man's Embarrassment" – European Vagrancy in Nineteenth-Century Bombay', *Economic and Political Weekly* 37, 2, 2002: 2477–85.

Ghosh, D., *Sex and the Family in Colonial India: the Making of Empire*, Cambridge: Cambridge University Press, 2006.

Ghosh, S. C., *The Social Condition of the British Community in Bengal, 1757–1800*, Leiden: E. J. Brill, 1970.

Hall, C., and Rose, S. O., eds, *At Home With the Empire: Metropolitan Culture and the Imperial World*, Cambridge: Cambridge University Press, 2006.

Hawes, C. J., *Poor Relations: The Making of a Eurasian Community in British India 1773–1833*, London: Routledge Curzon, 1996.

Henderson, T., *Disorderly Women in Eighteenth-Century London: Prostitution and Control in the Metropolis, 1730–1830*, London: Longman, 1999.

Hughes, R., *The Fatal Shore: A History of the Transportation of Convicts to Australia, 1787–1868*, London: Collins Harvill, 1987.

Leith, G., *A Short Account of the Settlement, Produce, and Commerce, of Prince of Wales Island, in The Straits of Malacca*, London: J. Booth, 1804.

Levine, P., ed., *Gender and Empire*, Oxford: Oxford University Press, 2004.

Linebaugh, P. and Rediker, M., *The Many-Headed Hydra: Sailors, Slaves, Commoners, and the Hidden History of the Revolutionary Atlantic*, London: Verso, 2000.

Long, J., 'A Peep Into the Social Life of Calcutta During the Second Half of the 18th Century', reproduced in P. Thankappan Nair, *A Tercentenary History of Calcutta, Vol. II: A History of Calcutta's Streets*, Calcutta: Firma K.L.M., 1987, pp. 18–19.

Marshall, P. J., 'British Society in India under the East India Company', *Modern Asian Studies* 31, 1, 1997: 89–108.

Molony, J., *The Native-Born: the first white Australians*, Melbourne: Melbourne University Press, 2000.

Nair, Thankappan P. (ed.), *British Social Life in Ancient Calcutta (1750 to 1850): During the second half of the 18th Century by the Rev. James Long and During the first half of the 19th Century by J.H. Stocqueler*, Calcutta, Firma K.L.M., 1983.

Rediker, M., *Between The Devil And The Deep Blue Sea: Merchant Seamen, Pirates, and the Anglo-American Maritime World, 1700–1750*, Cambridge: Cambridge University Press, 1987.

Reid, K., *Gender, Crime and Empire: convicts, settlers and the state in early colonial Australia*, Manchester: Manchester University Press, 2007.

Renford, R. K., *The Non-Official British in India to 1920*, New Delhi: Oxford University Press, 1987.

Roberts, D. A., '"A Sort of Inland Norfolk Island?" Isolation, Coercion and Resistance on the Wellington Valley Convict Station, 1823–26', *Journal of Australian Colonial History* 2, 1, 2000: 50–72.

——(ed.), *Escape: Essays on Convict Australia*, Armidale, NSW 2005, special edition of *Journal of Australian Colonial History* 7, 2005.

Robinson, P., *The Women of Botany Bay: a reinterpretation of the role of women in the origins of Australian society*, Sydney: The Macquarie Library, 1988.

Sinha, P., *Calcutta In Urban History*, Calcutta: Firma K.L.M., 1978.
Stanley, P., *White Mutiny: British Military Culture in India, 1825–1875*, London: Hurst, 1998.
Sturma, M., *Vice In a Vicious Society: crime and convicts in mid nineteenth-century New South Wales*, St Lucia: University of Queensland Press, 1983.
Walkowitz, J. R., *Prostitution and Victorian Society: Women, class, and the state*, Cambridge: Cambridge University Press, 1980.

5 Flotsam and jetsam of the Empire?
European seamen and spaces of disease and disorder in mid-nineteenth century Calcutta

Harald Fischer-Tiné

> Choleraic drains, a life-destroying sun, drugged brandy, brothels exceeding in beastliness the pictures of Juvenal, robbery under the name of discount and charges on Bills and Notes, hospitals and cemeteries – these are the comforts, with which India welcomes Christian sailors [...] Till our sailors ashore are cared for as well as when afloat, till the sailor is made as much an object of public concern as the soldier, Christianity will continue to be disgraced and humanity outraged in every Indian port.[1]

Introduction

On 12 August 1858 the 'white town' of Calcutta presented an unusual sight. Thousands of Europeans lined the roads in order to welcome sailors of the '*Shannon*'s Naval Brigade' returning from Lucknow, where they had been engaged in suppressing the 'Mutiny' cum rebellion for several months.[2] To see the 'respectable' portions of Calcutta's European population cheering a crowd of seamen was completely unheard of. For decades, the relationship between the wealthier part of British India's white society and the infamous seaman 'Jack Tar' had been ambiguous, as British seafaring men possessed the reputation of being a source of annoyance, trouble and even shame rather than pride – at least when they were on shore. Their proverbial affinity for drink and prostitution, their notoriously 'unruly conduct' and their often cruel behaviour towards the 'natives' turned these particular representatives of Britain's working classes into a threat against the ideological substructures of British rule. In the eyes of the colonial administration their alleged lack of discipline and 'reckless and irrational ways' brought them close to the 'uncivilized natives', a fact regarded as highly disturbing in a colonial setting based on the ideology of racial difference and – at least partly – informed by notions of a civilising mission supposedly entrusted to the British by providence. The relationship between the white establishment in the 'second capital of the Empire'[3] and the European sailors who frequented the city was thus highly problematic. In contradistinction to other low-class groups of 'white' society – European orphans, prostitutes and vagrants for instance – the problems arising from their presence in Indian seaport towns could not be easily solved by the 'politics of making invisible'. It was impossible to deport these white misfits or institutionalize them in asylums, workhouses[4] or segregated red-light districts,[5] as their labour was vital to the empire. In this respect, 'Jack' was quite similar to 'Tommy', the British Soldier, who often posed similar problems in the garrison towns of British India:[6] his presence was indispensable for the imperial project and yet at the same time threatened to undermine it.

In this chapter, I shall explore this contradictory phenomenon by focusing on Calcutta in the 1850s and 1860s. There are three reasons for this choice of place and time: first, Calcutta was the most important seaport, the seat of British administration and arguably the most 'European' of all Indian cities. Second, during the period under survey the sense of vulnerability of British colonial society was extremely high because of the traumatic experience of the Indian Rebellion. Issues of imperial prestige and legitimacy of rule were hence of critical interest and one can expect that 'in-between' groups caused even greater anxieties than under normal circumstances. Third, for various reasons, the number of European seamen on shore rose dramatically during these years and the 'sailor problem' became so pressing that the colonial authorities were preoccupied with its solution for years. In the process they produced an abundance of sources that allow us a wonderful insight both into the life-world of European seamen ashore and the ideological paradigms and practical dilemmas of imperial administration.

After giving a brief sketch of the historical, geographical, and statistical background of these 'spaces of disorder', the chapter opens with the narrative of two events that were mainly responsible for the emergence of a 'sailor problem' in British India's most important seaport town: first, the recruitment and subsequent dissolution of 'Naval Brigades' during the Indian Mutiny; second, a cyclone which devastated the Bengal Coast in 1864 and destroyed dozens of ships in the harbour, thus causing the distress of more than a thousand sailors stuck on shore. The next section examines how growing official concern about these developments was translated into attempts to collect and categorize knowledge about the potentially dangerous 'sailor class'. The official discourse on sailors' contacts with the 'corrupting' influences of indigenous society, on their criminal or violent behaviour and on issues of hygiene and disease is discussed in this context. Finally, the chapter analyzes in greater detail the various discursive strategies and practical measures employed by clergymen and colonial officials to solve the problem. Particular emphasis is placed on the convergence of the categories of race and class by analyzing the analogies and overlaps between efforts of 'reclaiming' the 'ignorant, inexperienced, unlettered seaman'[7] with the colonial agenda of educating and 'improving' the colonized population. The argument brought forward here is that the othering of European mariners can hence be aptly described as an 'internal orientalization'.

Rebellions, hurricanes and the emergence of a 'sailor problem'

The setting: Calcutta and its European seafarers

The decades following the consolidation of the rule of the East India Company, witnessed a massive increase in overseas exports.[8] As a result, the number of European and American vessels sailing to Calcutta also grew. In turn, this had a considerable effect on the overall composition of the city's 'white' community.[9] As the entire fleet of the East India Company and most of the ships owned by private merchants were manned by European crews,[10] white seamen on shore formed a significant part of white society in British India's premier city from the late eighteenth century, when the total number of Europeans in Calcutta was still comparatively small. But even by the middle of the nineteenth century, when the 'white' population had grown tremendously, the 'sailor element' was still important. The statistics of the Chamber of Commerce reveal that during the year 1863–64 1,216 European and American ships entered the port of Calcutta.[11] As the vessels were manned with an average of 17–25 sailors, the total number of European seamen passing through in just one year has been estimated at 27,500.[12] The majority of these men would only spend a couple of weeks in Calcutta, staying mostly on board their ships and paying only occasional visits to the town itself. But over the year, 15–20 per cent of them belonged to the 'floating population of the city'. The first reliable census of Calcutta's European population dating from 1866 lists the total number of permanent European inhabitants at about 11,000 against more than 2,000 sailors who were 'transient members of white Calcutta'.[13] According to other sources, this number could even double during seasonal peak times.[14] Thus, it seems reasonable to assume that the average sailor population must have been around 3,000; 300–500 of them were unemployed or 'distressed' seamen, sailors without affiliation to one of the ships lying in harbour who would stay for several months or even longer in the city.[15] Among them were a high number of deserters, as many sailors tried to escape the severe and often cruel regime on board ships. In the 1850s and 1860s, desertion was particularly popular among American sailors as there was no legal basis for their extradition to American authorities.[16] It is also clear that many men were provoked to desert by commanders eager to save money by replacing them through cheap Indian *lascars*.[17] Apprehended deserters and seamen who had refused the discharge of their duty – 'the only means by which a dissatisfied seaman c[ould] hope to get clear of his ship'[18] and also often a conscious act of resistance against injustice or brutal treatment by ships' officers – were sent to the House of Correction. They represented a significant portion of those stuck ashore.[19] Jobless seamen not confined to jail were usually residing either in the Sailor's Home or private boarding houses concentrated in the Bow Bazar area and the lanes off Lal Bazar Street (popularly known as 'Flag Street' because of the string of flags across the street showing the way to punch-houses, cheap eating-places and brothels).[20] There were also a noteworthy number of seamen being compelled to extend their sojourn in Calcutta as they were lying ill in one of the city's hospitals or in the lunatic asylum.

At quite an early stage, seamen on shore were regarded as 'loafers occasionally rambling over the country disgracing the British name and weakening the Hands of the Government'.[21] Complaints against the sailor population continued to appear occasionally in the press throughout the early nineteenth century,[22] but it was only in the wake of the events of 1857–58 that the problem took on so threatening a dimension as to call for government intervention.

'The terror of friends as well as foes?'[23] – the Indian Naval Brigades

In the weeks following the outbreak of the mutiny in Meerut and Delhi on 10 May 1857, an uneasy feeling prevailed among the European and perhaps even more so among the Eurasian inhabitants of Calcutta.[24] Governor-General Canning hence agreed reluctantly to raise volunteer corps among the civil population to protect the 'white' and 'mixed-race' residents.[25] Additionally, more than 350 seamen residing in the boarding houses were put on alert to assist the police in case of need.[26] Hundreds of sailors belonging to the merchant ships lying in the Hughli were landed and 'mounted guard over the public buildings'.[27] In June and July the first units of Indian Navy seamen arrived in Calcutta. Shortly afterwards three ships from the Royal Navy reached the port.[28] On 14 August the first 'Naval Brigade' consisting of 408 sailors and Marines from the HMS *Shannon*,[29] proceeded to Lucknow to assist the Army in the suppression of the rebellion.[30] Several other detachments of seamen, partly raised from merchant ships, left Calcutta in the subsequent weeks, after the men having received only superficial military training.

While the 'regular' Naval Brigades were reinforced continually by the crews of warships belonging to the Indian or Royal Navy,[31] the Government of Bengal kept on recruiting sailors from the merchant marine to form additional 'irregular' naval detachments, some of them not serving as combat forces but as 'Police Brigades' up-country or in Calcutta. Thus, by the middle of 1858 there existed more than a dozen 'Naval Brigades' of various sizes and backgrounds. It is difficult to estimate the total number of these troops, but by July 1859, when quite a few of them had already been disbanded, there were still 1,178 regular and 666 'irregular' seamen employed in the Lower Provinces of the Bengal Presidency.[32] It might be safely assumed that there were between 2,000 and 2,500 seamen under arms in Northern India and Burma by the end of 1858.[33]

It has been pointed out by various military historians that the manpower and arms of the Naval Brigades proved a valuable asset for the British in the various campaigns of 1857–59, and that these detachments therefore had a substantial share in the suppression of the mutiny.³⁴ However, before long it became apparent that not only the hearts of 'native budmashes' were terror-stricken owing to the presence of the Naval Brigades: the auxiliary troops also caused considerable trouble for the colonial authorities as well as for the wider European and Indian public. Part of the problem arose from the fact that the Brigades attracted apparently 'adventurers' and other persons of 'dubious character', as a contemporary police report illustrates:

> for some months past the Officers of the Indian Navy have enlisted, in Fort William, a large number of men for service in the interior. The pay and bounty of this Brigade being large, and considerable license being expected at the *Mofussil* stations to which detachments are sent, the service has been to a certain extent popular, and numbers of deserters from the mercantile shipping and Army are consequently enlisted by the officers of the Brigade, who, I am sorry to say, omit altogether taking precautions by making enquiries into the previous employment of those they receive.³⁵

Some of the Brigades thus became a refuge for deserters and sailors who had jumped ship.³⁶ What made matters even more complicated was the fact that the legal status of these troops was not clear. In most cases they were backed by the military authorities, which caused bitter complaints by the Commissioner of Police in Calcutta.³⁷ It was also highly disputed how the men could be punished by their officers, as the naval laws did not apply to seamen ashore and some officials warned that the 'advisability of inflicting corporal punishment upon Europeans in the present state of the country, [wa]s [...] very questionable'.³⁸

Quite predictably, therefore, men of this background, 'not being amenable to martial law, or accustomed to strict discipline', proved to be 'uncontrollable'³⁹ particularly when they were quartered in remote *Mofussil* towns. In a letter to *The Englishman*, an Indian Christian from Buxar complained in January 1859 that '[s]ome of the Naval Brigade men around this place are becoming quite intolerable,' and proceeded to explain that it was 'quite common for them to force themselves even at the hours of 12 and one in the night into the houses of respectable families' to harass the women and insult the male family members as 'niggers'.⁴⁰ The behaviour of the seamen eventually caused 'respectable' Indian inhabitants to write petitions to the Government of Bengal, praying to rid them of their protectors.

But even in Calcutta itself the conduct of the Naval Brigades was far from exemplary. The detachment on the Mint Guard for instance, was found to be 'in the habit of committing robberies on native shop-keepers' and had to be stopped by the police.⁴¹ On the whole, the regular detachments seem to have been less frequently involved in 'criminal' or 'uproarious' incidents,⁴² but even there the military authorities were constantly anxious to improve the state of discipline.⁴³ As already conveyed, matters were even more problematic with the irregular 'Police Brigades', composed of merchant seamen who had never been brought under the restraints of military discipline. These troops soon became infamous throughout the Province and were despised as 'a set of thieves and vagabonds'[44] by one of their fellow countrymen. Significantly, they were considered to be 'the terror of friends as well as foes'[45] even in the English press.

Given the difficulties in maintaining discipline even when the seamen were under the close supervision of their officers, it is understandable that some officials were anxious about the fate of the seamen after their Brigades had been dissolved. In March 1859 the Lieutenant-Governor of Bengal suggested that the Government of India should charter ships to convey the discharged Naval Brigadiers immediately to Australia or Britain, as the 'ill-consequences' of their staying on in Calcutta would be 'great'.[46] The situation in Calcutta port was indeed tense already because next to the growing number of seamen waiting to be shipped, there were hundreds of white grooms who had come from Australia or South Africa in charge of horses and failed to find work in India. The city was thus flooded with 'idle' working-class Europeans. One might speculate that the official anxieties were additionally fed by the memories of experience in the metropolis where soldiers and sailors dumped on the streets after the end of the Napeloeonic wars had caused considerable problems.[47] The Commissioner of Police painted a rather gloomy picture of the possible consequences of a further influx of seamen:

> I look forward with some apprehension to the discharge in Calcutta of at least 600 more seamen, most of them raised in a hurry, and many of them of the very worst character. As long as they have money, nothing worse perhaps will ensue than drunken quarrels in the streets; but when they are destitute of cash and credit, [...], I should not be surprised, if gangs were formed for the purpose of robbery. As far as Calcutta is concerned, the European Police is in my opinion strong enough to put up a summary end to anything of that kind, if such should be attempted; but there is nothing that I know to prevent Europeans from plundering in the *Mofussil* with impunity. All that is wanted are persons to put it into their imaginations and to lead them, and I know those who are well able to do both.[48]

He shared the view that immediate deportation was the only viable method of averting such a scenario. In April and May 1859 the situation indeed came to an alarming head with about 1,200 unemployed Europeans loitering around the Bow Bazar area and sleeping on the *Maidan*. In early May 1859 the Calcutta public was shocked when an article of an English Missionary, published in the *Bengal Hurkaru*, depicted in detail the sad state of affairs regarding the 'destitute and homeless Europeans' in the city.[49] There were several cases of theft and robbery committed by Europeans, but the police eventually managed to handle the situation by 'placing patrols of European

Police on the *maidan* and in all the lanes inhabited by desperate characters, and by exercising a strict surveillance over those known as *Loafers*'.[50]

Within a few months the agglomeration of distressed seamen was reduced to the normal number of about 400.[51] The Government had to deport only very few sailors (mostly seriously ill or mentally deranged men);[52] the majority could find employment on a ship comparatively quickly as the trading activities reached a tremendous intensity soon after the end of the Great Rebellion. Some of those who had to wait longer to be hired were accommodated in the Alms House, which received special grants from the Government for this purpose. Besides, a considerable number of ex-naval-brigadiers were encouraged to enlist in the regular army.[53]

The expected breakdown of law and order thus did not take place, but nonetheless the colonial Government as well as the public had become aware of the potential threat posed by the 'sailor class'. The enthusiastic reception accorded to the *Shannon*'s Brigade remained but a brief episode without consequences for the public esteem of European sailors among their reputable countrymen. Quite the reverse: distrust of this group had even grown owing to the events of 1857–59. Only a few years later 'distressed' European seamen came once again to the focus of public opinion. This time the growing sensitivity towards the 'spaces of disorder' inhabited by them would lead to massive interference by the colonial Government.

After the storm: the 1864 cyclone and the growing concern about the 'state of sailors in Calcutta'

In early October 1864 the coastal areas lining the Bay of Bengal were hit by a cyclone that proved to be devastating for the capital of British India. According to a Government source, an estimated 50 people lost their lives in the city and the surrounding areas and several thousand houses and huts were destroyed.[54] The port area was affected considerably. One eyewitness wrote that the damage inflicted on the buildings and parks of the city 'absolutely paled in insignificance'[55] when compared with the scenes he witnessed on the river bank.[56]

As many as 36 vessels were completely destroyed and 96 severely damaged by the storm.[57] The effect on shipping and commercial activities for the next months was described as 'most disastrous' by an official of the Marine Department.[58] Hundreds of seamen lost their ships and their numbers added to the usual pool of those kept on reserve to replace incapacitated seamen, casualties and deserters. Within a couple of days the total number of unemployed and shipwrecked sailors rose to more than 1,000, almost equalling that of the post-mutiny year 1859.[59] As the trade came to a near standstill for several weeks following the catastrophe and the chances of finding work at sea were slim, the situation in the Bow Bazaar and Lal Bazaar areas once again became tense. Given their experience of the dissolution of the Naval Brigades, the port authorities were anxious to prevent the distress of the sailor population from rising to a point where scenes of begging and petty crime would occur again. Consequently, many of the shipless seamen were recruited for repair works on board the damaged ships and were thus enabled to 'make their own terms'.[60] Additionally, 50 sailors were taken on by the police to protect wrecked property and prevent the plunder of ships cast ashore. But the colonial authorities were well aware of the fact that these measures provided only temporary solutions for the 'sailor problem', and at an early stage the Commissioner of Police reminded the Government that '[a]s soon as the present demand for labour ceases, some steps must be taken to send home the sailors who have lost their ships'.[61] Sharing his view, the Master Attendant sought various ways to get rid of the labour surplus. Ninety-five sailors were sent home at the expense of the Board of Trade, 68 men had their passage paid by the Cyclone Relief Fund, 30 were sent to Bombay to join the Royal Navy, and 187 were shipped for nominal wages by captains who had entered a special agreement to the effect that the seamen had to work part of their passage. The legal basis for the immediate deportation of 'distressed seamen' at Government expense was provided by the Merchant Shipping Act (1854),[62] which had grown out of a concern of the British Government to extend its control on the Mercantile Marine and improve the living and working conditions of merchant seamen.[63]

However, the costly deportations failed to provide a durable solution to the problem. Already, in June 1865, the Shipping Master complained that the port of Calcutta was again 'greatly overcrowded with British Merchant Seamen, most of whom are in the greatest distress imaginable'.[64] Nonetheless, the fact that the authorities took to such unusual and expensive measures betrays that the official paranoia regarding the seamen's alleged propensity to 'disorderly behaviour', which had been aroused for the first time in the post-mutiny period, was still alive.[65] According to one source, ten per cent of the 500 seamen still unemployed by July 1865 were 'hardened loafers' who did not intend to find work at all, causing instead constant annoyance for the public through their begging tours in Calcutta's White Town. The Shipping Master went so far as to call for legal innovation in the form of 'a clause giving me power to take such loafers up and send them home at the public expense' as this would be the only 'means of keeping good order amongst them'.[66]

As a result of the constant trouble caused by the city's distressed sailor population, the Lieutenant-Governor of Bengal eventually asked the Sanitary Commission in August 1865 to produce a report on the 'State of the Sailors in Calcutta'.[67] The Commission, it was hoped, would not only find out the causes of the high unemployment rates but also provide information on their actual living conditions and their state of health. Major Malleson, who headed the working group, submitted the results of his detailed enquiry to the Government in Bengal in February 1866.[68] Meanwhile, a number of articles on the same topic had appeared in the press.[69] The interest in the life-world of European sailors that had first been sparked off by the events of the mutiny thus clearly reached a peak after the Calcutta cyclone. 'Jack Tar' had become an object of official enquiry, scholarly study and public curiosity alike. As one official put it: 'to judge Jack aright and to deal with him aright, we must have some data to go upon, – we must know something about him'.[70]

'Drunkenness, disease and disorder': Imperial anxieties and the ethnographic gaze upon the fringes of 'white' society

Hygiene, health and mortality

One issue touched upon in the Malleson Report, as well as in many other publications, was the health of the sailors. Already during the crisis of 1859 the high death-rate prevailing among this group had been a major concern for the colonial authorities. Along with his apocalyptic vision of hordes of sailors turning to brigandage, the Commissioner of Police, Calcutta had also warned the government of the 'mortality which must ensue among the men [...], turned loose in the hot weather, most of them at first with money, among the liquor shops, bazars and sinks of iniquity'.[71] Such apprehensions seemed to be confirmed by the results of an official enquiry into the death rates of the various communities residing in Calcutta that was undertaken immediately after the end of the mutiny.[72] This so-called Macpherson Report stated that European seamen were the section of white colonial society with the highest mortality, cholera being the single most important cause of death. According to Macpherson, no fewer than 76 per cent of the European cholera victims belonged to the city's floating sailor population.[73] All of a sudden, issues of health and infection were no longer discussed primarily with regard to the densely populated 'native suburbs' or 'bustees', which had long been perceived as 'seats of diseases destructive of individual happiness and of life',[74] as they were inhabited by 'people who apparently delight in filth and dirt'.[75] Such 'seats of diseases' had now also been discovered in the 'White Town' – albeit on its fringes and in parts of it that were usually not frequented by members of the 'respectable' European community.[76] In a rhetoric reminding one of Victorian literature depicting the dirt and depravity of the industrial cities of England,[77] Calcutta's Bow Bazar and Lal Bazar areas came to be portrayed as 'the most hateful haunts in the world for Jack Tar'.[78] According to a Christian missionary writing in the *Friend of India*, even the 'most infamous purlieu of Wapping or Ratcliff Highway [wa]s clean and respectable compared with Flag Street'.[79]

In an influential booklet published in 1864, Norman Chevers, surgeon of the Bengal Army and professor of medicine in the College Hospital presented the results of his survey on the mortality of European seamen. His calculations, based on figures for the years 1853–64, resulted in the estimate of a 'terrible and, in the present day unexampled, death-rate of 96.48 in every thousand annually', which was 'a very near approach to annual decimation, or total extinction in ten years'.[80] Like Macpherson, he also pointed to the high number of cholera victims among the European seafaring population. The reference to cholera inevitably raised issues of hygiene and sanitation, as by mid-nineteenth century it was accepted knowledge that the contamination of air and drinking water through 'filth' and 'night soil' were the causes of the disease.[81] In drastic terms, Chevers hence denounced the housing of sailors in the vicinity of Lal Bazar:

> The manner in which European sailors are lodged and 'done for' in most of the boarding-houses in Flag Street and the adjoining lanes is most disgraceful, and [...] hence arises much of the worst diseases occurring among seamen on shore. The whole neighbourhood is extremely ill-drained. The cause alone would be sufficient to render these lodging houses pestilential. About one and a half years ago, there was one of the most frequented of these houses where you would see a row of sailors seated early every morning before the door, enjoining the air immediately over one of the worst open sewers in the town. That house sent five cases of malignant cholera into Medical College Hospital in one week.[82]

In the judgment of other officials, the unsanitary housing conditions were further aggravated by the supposed absence of personal cleanliness among the 'sailor class'.[83]

Recent scholarship has pointed to the fact that from about the 1830s onwards the prevalence of diseases and epidemics in India was no longer regarded as a natural outcome of the region's climate, but increasingly understood as a product of the 'social conditions, habits and morals, of the population', in other words, of their 'defective' civilization.[84] The relative paucity of epidemic outbreaks in Europe thus seemed to underscore not only the advanced scientific and medical knowledge but also the moral superiority of the colonizers. Consequently, the twin project of imperial medicine and sanitation became a 'tool of empire' and cornerstone of the rhetoric of Britain's civilizing mission in India.[85] The discovery of enclaves of putridity and disease in parts of the 'white town' of a colonial metropolis, then, was more than disturbing for the colonial authorities, as it laid bare the mockery of such legitimizing claims.[86] The myth of the existence of the neat boundaries between the lifestyles of 'white', 'mixed-race', and 'native' inhabitants of Calcutta seemed additionally damaged when the average diet of those staying in these boarding-houses was revealed to a wider audience: Norman Chevers informed his upper-class readership that the food served to the sailors was 'generally bad', mostly consisting of 'the diseased bazaar pork, which none but the very poorest willingly eat'.[87]

An even greater blow to claims to the moral superiority of the 'imperial race' resulted from the seamen's drinking habits, which were also considered to be partly responsible for the frightening death-rate. The excessive consumption of alcohol had been a problem in the British navy for a long time,[88] and the propensity to drink was certainly part of the image of the sailor current in contemporary elite discourse, where he was usually portrayed as morally weak and easily influenced by all sorts of temptations. In a colonial setting, his alleged lack of self-restraint made 'Jack' very similar to the 'natives' in the eyes of many upper-class observers. This trope of racial boundary-crossing is also important in a more direct sense, as it was widely assumed that the worst effects of alcohol abuse did not arise of the consumption of 'pure and sound European brandy' – sailors were given their daily rations of Rum or grog on board ships as part of their regular diet – but of 'country liquor'. It was understood that liquor sold in native shops was not only 'drugged with several powerful narcotics' but also 'doctored to the point of giving cholera to him who swallows it almost as certainly as a pistol fired into the mouth blows the head off'.[89] Hence, several medical experts proposed to prohibit the selling to Europeans of 'that most intoxicating and deleterious of all drinks, the native Rum or "Doasta"'.[90]

However, this line of argument did not remain uncontested. Some critics soon pointed to the results of an official enquiry conducted in 1858 where it had been 'conclusively prov[en]' that the excessive drunkenness and its results' among Europeans resorting to the native shops 'was due rather to the quantity than the quality of the liquor drunk in them'.[91] Accordingly, official endeavours to remedy this evil pursued a double strategy. On the one hand the authorities tried to control the quality of alcoholic beverages and regulate the access to liquor stores (particularly the 'native' ones) by granting fewer licences[92] and restricting the opening hours.[93] On the other hand, attempts to educate seamen, to persuade them to be 'moral and religious' and abstain from heavy drinking were encouraged. Norman Chevers himself tried to convince an audience of sailors of the advantages of temperance by invoking their manly pride as well as their fear of God:

> You are not poor men: you are, as a body, rich in health and in an amount of strength and manly beauty such as is granted by Providence to scarcely any other race under the sun. Your Father, who made you in His image cares for and loves you in that equal measure in which he cares for and loves all His children; and you violate his law and hopelessly separate yourselves from him when you deface His image in this abominable disease and death which drunkenness engenders.[94]

The debate about another issue directly linked to questions of health, hygiene and mortality was similarly shaped by strong moral overtones. An inclination to visit brothels was as much part of the popular image of the seafaring population as his fancy for liquor.[95] The official concern about the sailors' health, therefore, also included anxieties about the spread of venereal diseases.[96] Such fears were additionally fed by the new scientific interest in the 'sailor class'. A medical officer who accompanied a large party of sailors from Calcutta to Assam in 1863 discovered that 90 per cent of them had contracted syphilis during their stay in the port.[97] Here, again, the close physical involvement with 'natives' was held largely responsible for the contamination of the seamen as the majority of them visited Indian prostitutes, rather than the few and expensive European and 'Eurasian' sex-workers available. As Philippa Levine and others have shown, even the concept of venereal diseases was affected by racial ideology. It was not only widely held that 'native' women were the main carriers of syphilis and gonorrhoea because of their low standards of hygiene, it was also supposed that such diseases were much more dreadful if they were contracted not from European but from 'Oriental' women.[98]

The 'natural' affinity of sailors to prostitution was taken for granted to the extent that even the Seamen's Chaplain of Calcutta port believed it to be 'a matter of impossibility' to prevent them from 'launching in the wildest debauchery' once they were ashore.[99] In consequence, appeals to the moral feelings of the sailors alone did not seem a promising way to avoid the 'death from a disease that must be nameless'.[100] Both Norman Chevers and the Malleson Report accordingly recommended the introduction of a lock-hospital system as the only viable measure to protect the health of European sailors.[101] Their suggestion met with official acclaim and a law to that effect was eventually enacted in 1867.[102]

Crime and 'disorderly' behaviour

Seamen's health was not the only concern of the colonial authorities. Even before the official interest in the sailor population had led to an increased effort in data collection about drunkenness, disease and debauchery, another facet of the seafarers' behaviour had been the object of statistics compiled by the colonial government: their 'disorderly' or even criminal conduct. In the context of the Naval Brigades, we have already seen that European crime was a topic that could provoke mild hysteria in official circles, particularly when the victims were natives and the credibility of Britain's self-proclaimed civilizing mission was at stake.

As far as Calcutta is concerned, the sources leave no doubt that the sailors' unenviable notoriety in this regard was not completely unfounded. They were indeed largely responsible for the high crime rates among Europeans. In 1855, for instance, the magistrate tried more than 500 cases in which seamen were involved. Next to the more obvious breaches of marine law like 'wilful neglect of duty',[103] 'disobedience' or 'desertion', there were 248 sailors involved in violent assaults, several of them resulting in loss of life. The Police Commissioner of Calcutta observed 'that in four of the nine manslaughters, and five of the eight cases of cutting and wounding, the offenders were sailors sojourning at this port'.[104] It is also remarkable that in 1864 as many as 12 out of 21 inmates of the prison in Ootacamund – one of the few jails that had been especially constructed to accommodate European long term-convicts – were former sailors, sent over from Calcutta.[105] The number of imprisoned seamen in the Houses of Correction in Bombay and Calcutta was even higher, which made some officers worry about the 'slight terror that the Jail has for sailors'. N. Oliver, the Magistrate of Police in Calcutta, gave an insightful explanation for this fact:

> It may be that seamen feel no moral degradation in the imprisonment which, in some cases they know they scarcely deserve […] they care little for the physical inconveniences of the prison, which can hardly exceed those they have been subjected to in their filthy quarters aboard on board third class ships – bad food and constant "bully ragging" as they term it.[106]

The frequent occurrence of crime soon resulted in special Police controls with the aim of disarming sailors of their 'clasp knives and other offensive weapons'.[107] Nevertheless, drunken brawls in the 'punch-houses' remained quite common, as did disputes over money in the brothels, which were also often the causes for quarrels and punch-ups, sometimes even for murder.[108] Given that seamen usually had been confined under (sometimes appalling conditions) on board their ships for three or four months when they arrived in the port, and that most of them had been subjected to a brutalizing disciplinary regime, including the frequent use of the lash, their aggressive behaviour and the high crime rates should not be surprising. Significantly, violence against officers and fellow sailors occurred quite commonly both on the ship and in the port.[109] However, equally notorious were the incidents of violence against the Indian population, which – it would certainly not be too bold to speculate – presumably served as acts of compensation and often went hand in hand with excessive drinking. Thus, in 1858, a party of sailors lynched a Bengali tavern-keeper whom they suspected of selling poisonous liquor by hanging him from Kidderpore Bridge.[110] The violence could also be completely arbitrary. The following is a rather typical example:

> On the 18th of February a party of sailors, ripe for mischief, were parading a part of town most infrequently visited by persons of their class, and were amusing themselves by striking more or less every person passing them, or destroying the articles (water jars &c,) they carried. At length they entered a liquor shop and called for liquor, which on getting they refused to pay for, at the same time destroying the bottle it was served in, by throwing it at the vendor and decamping.[111]

There are dozens of references to similar cases in the police reports. This particular excursion, it ought to be added, ended in a clash with Malayan seamen and the murder of an Indian *chaukidar* (watchman) who had dared to interfere to end the dispute. However, the sailor accused of the deed was eventually acquitted by the English magistrate.

Given the frequent occurrence of such atrocious crimes (and the notoriously mild punishment received by European perpetrators), the question arises as to how the indigenous population did react to such incidents? Was the official *angst* that the 'disorderly' behaviour of the seafaring specimens of the ruling race might endanger the slender basis of British power a mere product of colonial imagination? There are at least some indications that this was not the case. As far as we can judge from articles in the 'native' press,[112] the elite section of the Indian population in the seaport towns affected by the problem was well aware of the misdemeanours committed by European seamen and condemned them in the strongest terms. Already, decades before unemployment had become a mass phenomenon in Indian ports, the British had realized what effect the presence of 'drunk and disorderly' Europeans could have for their missionary aspirations. The account of one Reverend Wilson, a clergyman living in Bombay during the 1830s and 1840s, marvellously illustrates this point:

> In the discharge of my duties as a Missionary to the heathen, I go to the high-ways and hedges to invite sinners to come to the marriage supper of the Son of God; I announce the glad tidings of Salvation through our crucified Redeemer, and I speak of the sanctifying influence of his gospel. As I proceed in my discourse my attention is frequently directed to a gang of drunken sailors or soldiers, bearing the Christian name, staggering along the streets in a state of intoxication; and I am sneeringly asked by the natives. "Would you like to become us like these your kindred?" I need not to tell you [...] what my answer is. [...] The unbelievers triumph; and it is the promise of God alone, which can sustain me and enable me to repeat my message.[113]

As there is a paucity of direct evidence, one can ultimately only hypothesize that Britain's cultural civilizing mission was affected by such incidents in the same manner as the Christian one. What is beyond doubt, however, is the fact that most British administrators were firmly convinced that the 'sailor question' contributed to the erosion of the colonizers' prestige. How, then, did British officials try to come to grips with a dilemma threatening to acquire imperial dimensions?

Bringing 'Jack Tar' within the pale of civilization: practical and discursive strategies to solve the 'sailor problem'

The events of the 1850s and 1860s had brought the fate of distressed seamen to the notice of a wider public, but initiatives to improve the lot of European sailors had a much longer history in Calcutta. As early as 1827, the Seamen's Friend Society was founded with the aim of contributing to the spiritual welfare of sailors arriving in the port.[114] In 1852, a Seamen's Mission was founded for the same purpose.[115] It entertained two 'floating churches', one of which, however, was destroyed during the 1864 cyclone.

More pragmatic considerations had led to the inauguration of the Sailor's Home in Lal Bazar Street in July 1837,[116] only two years after the first such institution in the British Empire had opened its doors in London.[117] The institution had been opened with a view to protect seamen from 'imposition and extortion'; it offered refuge for unemployed, shipwrecked or distressed sailors up to a period of 25 days. The rules and regulations of the Home placed emphasis on discipline and the observance of fixed times for meals and prayer, leaving no doubt that the institution should provide an alternative to the 'anarchy' prevailing in private boarding-houses.[118] In spite of its ostensibly secular character, the promotion of the inmates' 'moral, intellectual and professional improvement' was also mentioned in the objects of the institution.[119] Referring to the United Kingdom, Alston Kennerley has pointed to the fact that this blending of issues of 'material' and 'moral welfare' was typical of nineteenth-century Sailors' Homes, as they came 'from the same stock' as the missionary societies and the temperance movement.[120] The Home was shifted to a new location in 1865, partly because the building had become too small to accommodate the ever-growing number of distressed seamen and partly because it was situated 'in the very centre of the touters' hell',[121] which had provoked constant criticism both from medical officers and missionaries.

A strong moral and paternal element is also evident in some of the 'simple measures of control and precaution'[122] recommended by the Malleson Commission. The different suggestions were characterized by a common aim to protect the victimized seaman from those who could cause him the most harm: greedy commanders, vile boarding-house keepers and, last but not least, his own 'lower instincts'. They included, among others, the intensification of control and the provision of reliable statistics about the sailors through a system of registration, the reduction of the number of seamen ashore by a prohibition of discharging European Sailors in the port,[123] the appointment of a Marine Magistrate who would 'keep a constant watch'[124] over them and, last but not least, the introduction of a vagrancy law. The strict regulation of the opening hours of liquor stores and punch-houses already referred to above can also be seen in the same light.

Most of the proposed measures were never adopted by the Government of Bengal due to financial and political constraints, but perhaps more intriguing than the practical steps suggested were the discursive strategies employed in the elite discourse on 'Jack Tar'. An analysis of the texts produced on European seamen in the period under study shows that there are two main varieties of interpretation regarding the distress and 'moral state' of the sailors.[125] On the one hand they were epitomized as helpless victims: either of their commanders and officers whose authority over them 'may be likened to that of a parent over a child'[126] or of villainous boarding masters, crimps, pimps or liquor vendors. They were perceived as simply lacking the intelligence and 'character' to defend themselves against injustice, resist temptations or even think for themselves. Having described the miserable sanitary conditions and moral dangers existing in the Lal Bazar area, one writer invokes the parental feelings of his educated countrymen, explaining to them that, 'sailors will not think of these facts, but the better educated portion of the community ought to think a little for them'.[127] In a similar vein, another author remarked that 'Jack may fairly claim protection against the evil influence which he himself cannot resist'.[128] The Magistrate of Police, Bombay offered an explanation for this state of affairs that was widely accepted in official circles:

> The majority of the seamen are totally uneducated and being for the greater part of their lives shut up within the narrow compass of a ship, are perhaps less able to form an opinion and act for their own advantage than other persons employed on shore in the same stages of life.[129]

Narratives of this kind suggested that the sailor was ultimately not responsible for his deeds. Not surprisingly, the search for scapegoats played a crucial role in this trope. We have already seen that contact with natives and particularly with *dalals* (touts) and prostitutes was interpreted as moral (and often also physical) contamination. It was also believed that European and Eurasian 'crimps' 'harpies' and 'land-sharks' were critical in corrupting the seamen morally and ruining their health. The keepers of private boarding-houses were frequently depicted as ruthless parasites.[130] According to one statement they cared for the sailors 'only so long as they could make money out of him'; in order to achieve their goal they would 'encourage him to drink and get drunk on their premises; and [...] when his funds are exhausted they turn him out, beggared, into the streets'.[131] Moreover, almost all the boarding-houses were situated in the red-light area around Flag Street. The amusements so easily available in this vicinity further contributed to the sailors becoming 'depraved, vicious, self-abandoned' and, ultimately, 'the tempters and destroyers of others'.[132] To sum up this line of argument: the seaman was, at bottom, 'good-hearted but led astray',[133] he only stood in need of parental guidance and protection by the members of the European elite. And so it was ultimately the responsibility of 'men of educated minds and refined tastes and full purses' to do their 'utmost to improve Jack's character'.[134]

There was, however, a second narrative converging with first the one in so far as both portrayed seamen as immature and barely able to speak for themselves. But, instead of being perceived as 'good-hearted', they were held to be 'hopelessly degraded and irreclaimably vicious'.[135] For this reason, they were portrayed in a language much more reminiscent of the depictions of 'insubordinate natives' rather than those of innocent children. One of the experts interviewed for the Malleson Report pronounced his view that sailors:

as a class, [...] are insolent, wasteful, insubordinate, and slothful. All will admit, that the active, quiet, respectful seaman of a quarter of a century since is now rarely met with, and how different a being in his place. In self-defence, then, it is necessary to adopt measures effective and so possibly extreme, to prevent what otherwise will be a periodical and increasing nuisance, expense and danger to this community.[136]

This was the same sort of class distrust that had stirred up the paranoia after the dissolution of the Naval Brigades. Sailors, according to this strand of opinion, were potentially perilous and hence it was regarded as necessary for the colonial government to react with a strong hand to suppress their misdemeanours.

Such a perception reminds one of the contention recently brought forward by Peter Linebaugh and Marcus Rediker in the context of the late eighteenth century 'revolutionary' Atlantic. They argue that the multi-ethnic 'motley crews' of sailors found creative ways of resisting authorities and posed a threat to existing hierarchies.[137] In the light of this line of reasoning, their violent behaviour as well as their frequent transgression of racial boundaries also acquire a new meaning: they could well be read as outright challenges to the colonial order of things.

Promoters of this view repeatedly tried to underline their argument by pointing to police statistics. The sailors, they maintained, possessed a 'natural' tendency to commit breaches of discipline, to conspire against their officers, to work out 'mischievous plans' and resort to 'vicious courses' in order to avoid the lawful discharge of their duty.[138] Small wonder that the advocates of this stance were convinced that 'strict control' had to be 'kept over the sailor; if an effort be made to bring him within the pale of civilization'. Only then, their argument ran, would it be possible 'that he will become a better citizen and a better man'.[139]

It must be admitted that such extreme statements are quite rare. Public (i. e. European elite-) opinion seems to have mostly oscillated between the two poles just described. Sometimes there were even conscious attempts to reconcile the seemingly contradictory positions. Several writers tried to divide the sailor class into two parts: the 'seamen proper', i.e. a sailor on board his ship, as opposed to the flotsam and jetsam of the sailor population 'living an idle life on shore'. All the positive qualities of 'Jack Tar' (his manliness, his courage, his naïve honesty) were ascribed to the former and all his 'defects of character' to the latter. Reflecting on the crime statistics, one observer notes that:

> *drunkenness* and confinement of seamen on shore is more than is double that of those who are on the river. For *assault*, which so often grows out of drunkenness, the proportion, though somewhat less, is still sadly against the man on the shore. But the third class of *theft* tells a melancholy tale how the idleness of shore life leads to graver crime.[140]

The solution thus seemed to be simple: the sailors needed only to be kept to their ships, protected from the temptations of the port and particularly from the degenerating influences of native society, and 'disease, crime and pauperism' would be 'greatly diminished'.[141] At the same time, one might want to add, the colonized population would be saved from being confronted with elements of British/European societies that could have made them ask questions about the civilizational superiority of the 'ruling race' and the legitimacy of the British *Raj*.

Conclusion

Ports, we have been reminded of late, are 'multi-purpose interfaces' and hence basically about 'bringing things *and people* together'.[142] In a colonial make-up, ports thus do not only play a pivotal role because of their economic significance but also as 'zones of contact'.[143] In the South Asian context, the 'bringing together' of indigenous and European societies and civilizations was doubtlessly most intense in Calcutta. It was here, in the place where British presence was strongest, that not only a large but also a politically and culturally influential portion of the Indian population got in touch with the colonizers and formed their opinion about them.[144] The history of Calcutta Port, therefore, has aptly been described as the 'history of the forces and movement which have shaped modern India'.[145] As soon as colonial rule began to be legitimised with civilizational, moral or even racial superiority, 'prestige' became a crucial ingredient for the stability of the *Raj*. In such a constellation, groups among the port city's 'white' population who could cast a shadow of doubt on the myth of the colonizers' 'natural' supremacy were difficult to handle.

The case of distressed European seamen in Calcutta during the 1850 and 1860s has provided an excellent example of a 'colonial predicament' caused by such an in-between group. On the one hand, sailors were vital for the military dominance and economic exploitation of India, on the other, their presence ashore tended to create serious problems. Their role in the suppression of the mutiny illustrated this ambivalence. Within a time span of a few months, sailors were first hailed by their 'respectable' fellow countrymen as heroes and saviours of the empire and then feared as vandals 'of the very worst character' who posed a serious threat to their reputation, life and property.

The mass unemployment of the 1860s disclosed the deep class divide within British colonial society conspicuously. In many ways, distressed European seamen were treated and talked about by the members of the colonial elite as those segments of the 'native' population that were deemed 'dangerous'.[146] In both cases the first reaction to the perceived threat was to collect scientific data, compile statistics and ascertain control over the group in question. Next, colonial authorities would penetrate the 'spaces of disease and disorder' inhabited by the said community, trying to transform its members through sanitary measures, medical treatment, moral advice and, if necessary, policing.

Moreover, our case study has offered a fine illustration for a process which might be aptly described as an internal 'orientalization'.[147] This 'orientalization' had two aspects: first, the sailors were essentialized as a class and denied individual agency. Second, they were not accepted as responsible human beings, able to act rationally and speak for themselves but either perceived as good-hearted 'children of the sea'[148] in need of parental guidance or condemned as a 'drunken, reckless, mutinous lot'[149], who had to be disciplined. Especially in the latter discourse, they were often treated like 'insubordinate natives'. Their bodily exposure to a predominantly Indian environment when they were on shore, the supposedly degenerating impact of Indian food, liquor and physical contact with 'native' prostitutes and *dalals* seemed to substantiate a view that placed the seaman outside the pale of civilization. The fact that schemes to relieve the distressed sailors coupled practical measures with attempts at uplifting them morally, or even Christianizing them, is, thus, hardly surprising.

Finally, it should be noticed that the plans to confine the seamen on board ship alluded to in the last section, can be read as a prelude to the policy of institutionalization and segregation later applied to European 'women of ill-fame', criminals and vagrants. However, in the case of European sailors it was an impracticable strategy, and 'Jack Tar' continued to be an occasional source of discomfiture for the white colonial elite until the end of the *Raj*.

Acknowledgements

Earlier versions of this chapter were presented at the 18th European Conference on Modern South Asia in Lund (Sweden) on 9th July 2004 and at the school of Social Sciences, Jawaharlal Nehru University, New Delhi on 27 September 2004. Many thanks to Navina Gupta, Franziska Roy, Clare Anderson, Ravi Ahuja, Michael Mann, Gopalan Balachandran, Ian Kerr as well as Radhika Singha and her MA students at JNU for their critical comments. The following abbreviations indicate archival locations: OIOC: Oriental and India Office Collections of the British Library [now: Asia, Pacific and Africa Collections]; OIOC, IOR: Oriental and India Office Collection, India Office Records, British Library, London; NAI: National Archives of India, New Delhi; WBSA: West Bengal State Archives, Calcutta.

Notes

1 *The Friend of India*, 6 April 1865, pp. 392–93.
2 G. L. Verney, *The Devil's Wind. The Story of the Naval Brigade at Lucknow from the Letters of Edmund Hope Verney and other Papers concerning the Enterprise of the Ship's Company of H.M.S. Shannon in the Campaign in India*

1857–1858, London: Hutchinson, 1956, pp. 156–59. Cf. also R. Brooks, *The Long Arm of the Empire. Naval Brigades from the Crimea to the Boxer Rebellion*, London: Constable, 1999, pp. 27–28.

3 R. V. Krishna Deb, *The Early History and Growth of Calcutta*, Calcutta: Romesh Chandra Ghose, 1905, p. 1.

4 D. Arnold, 'European Orphans and Vagrants in India in the Nineteenth Century', *Journal of Imperial and Commonwealth History* [hereafter *JICH*] 7, 2, 1979: 104–27.

5 T. Hubel, 'In Search of the British Indian in British India: White Orphans, Kipling's Kim and Class in Colonial India', *Modern Asian Studies* [hereafter *MAS*] 38, 1, 2004: 227–51; P. Levine, 'Erotic Geographies. Sex and the Managing of Colonial Space', in H. Michie and R. R. Thomas (eds), *Nineteenth Century Geographies. The transformation of space from the Victorian age to the American century*, New Brunswick, NJ and London: Rutgers University Press, 2003, pp. 149–60, p. 152; H. Fischer-Tiné, '"White Women Degrading Themselves to the Lowest Depths": European networks of prostitution and colonial anxieties in British India and Ceylon ca. 1880–1914', *Indian Economic and Social History Review* 40, 2, 2003: 163–90, especially pp. 183–84; and the same author's '"The greatest blot on British rule in the East" – 'Weißer Sklavenhandel' und die britische Kolonialherrschaft in Indien (ca. 1870-1920)', *Comparativ. Leipziger Beiträge zur Universalgeschichte und vergleichenden Gesellschaftsforschung* 13, 6, 2003: 114–37, especially pp. 131–37.

6 W. S. Seton-Karr, *Selections from Calcutta Gazettes* (Repr. in 9 Vols.), Vol. III, Calcutta: Bibhash Gupta, 1987 [1867], p. 181. Cf. also D. Peers, 'Privates off Parade: Regimenting Sexuality in the Nineteenth Century Indian Empire', *The International History Review* 20, 4, 1998: 823–55; and the same author's 'Sepoys, Soldiers and the Lash: Race, Caste and Army Discipline in India, 1820–50', *JICH* 23, 2, 1995: 211–47; P. Stanley, *White Mutiny. British Military Culture in India 1825–1875*, London: Hurst, 1998.

7 Statement of Police Commissioner Schalch; in G. B. Malleson, 'The State of the Sailors in Calcutta', Appendix III, with OIOC, IOR: P/437/29, Government of India, Home Department Proceedings [hereafter GoI, Home Dept. Progs.], Marine 1866, No. 18.

8 Cf. P. Banerjee, *Calcutta and its Hinterland*, Calcutta: Progressive Publ., 1975, pp. 25–26.

9 For the social impact the increase in trade had on Calcutta see also *The Friend of India*, 7 April 1859, pp. 315–16. A comprehensive account of the early development of Calcutta's Port can be found in N. Mukherjee, *The Port of Calcutta. A Short History*, Calcutta: Commissioners for the Port of Calcutta, 1968, pp 18–37.

10 L. Barnes, *Evolution and Scope of Mercantile and Marine Laws relating to Seamen in India*, New Delhi: Maritime Law Association of India, 1983, p. 27. The term 'European' stands in need of some clarification. In Anglo–Indian administrative jargon, 'European' usually included Americans and Australians. A list dating from 1882 gives us an idea about the composition of the 'European' seafaring population: Britain, the USA, Germany, Portugal, Sweden, Norway, Russia, Denmark and France were the most important countries of origin. Cf. *Report on the Working of the Calcutta Shipping office and of the Shipping Offices At the several Outports, for the year 1882–83*, Calcutta: unknown publisher, 1883, p. 15.

11 Anonymous [i.e. John Cave-Browne], 'Sailor Life in Calcutta', *The Calcutta Review* 40 (1865), 452–66, especially p. 455. There were considerable seasonal variations with 75 ships arriving in May against 157 vessels entering the port in October.

12 *The Friend of India*, 7 April 1865, p. 392.

13 P. Marshall, 'The White Town of Calcutta under the Rule of the East India Company', *MAS* 34, 2, 2000: 307–31, especially p. 309.
14 N. Chevers, *On the Preservation of the Health of Seamen, especially those frequenting Calcutta and the other Indian Ports etc.*, Calcutta: Military Orphan Press, 1864, p. 39.
15 Anonymous, 'Sailor Life in Calcutta', pp. 461–63.
16 N. P. Jacobs, Consul-General USA, for British India to G. B. Malleson, in G. B. Malleson, 'The State of the Sailors in Calcutta', Appendix III, p. xxiv.
17 A contemporary official report gives the following example: '[T]he Captain of a Collier, arriving here in the middle of the hot weather, wished to get rid of his European Crew. No other means appeared to him so unobjectionable to effect this object as to direct them to discharge the coals. Now, this is a kind of hard work, which in this country is always performed by coolies, both on the grounds of humanity and economy. I was, nevertheless a lawful order of the Captain and as such the crew were bound to obey it. The first day, however, some of the men refused, the next day more, the third day the entire crew. This was the great object of the Captain. He at once brought a charge against his crew for disobedience of orders; they were convicted and imprisoned. The result was that [...] the Captain was relieved from the expense of supporting his crew during his stay in port, that expense falling upon the Government'. Cf. MALLESON, 'The State of the Sailors in Calcutta', pp. 8–9. Cf. also ibid., Appendix I, Statement of J. H. Branson, Magistrate Southern division, pp. ii–iii.
18 NAI, Home Dept., Judl., Nos 16–19, 11 March 1859, Letter No. 644: W.C. Crawford, Senior Magistrate of Police to the Government of Bombay [hereafter GoBom], to GoBom, Judl. Dept., 23 October 1858.
19 In 1855, for instance, 486 of the inmates of the House of Correction were sailors who had been convicted for the breach of marine laws. OIOC, IOR: P/173/9, Government of Bengal [hereafter GoBeng], Marine Dept. Progs., 1862, A-77: 'Statement of the Number of European Seamen sentenced to Imprisonment in the Calcutta House of Correction for Refusal of Duty on Board Ship from 1st January 1856 to 31st December 1861'.
20 P. Thankhappan Nair, *A History of Calcutta's Streets*, Calcutta: KLM, 1987 (A Tercentenary History of Calcutta, Vol. II), p. 501. The atmosphere of these boarding-houses has been captured in Kipling's famous 'Ballad of Fulta Fisher's Boarding House'. Cf. R. Kipling, *The Collected Poems of Rudyard Kipling*, Ware: Wordsworth Editions, 2001, pp. 43–44.
21 J. Long, *Calcutta in the Olden Time. Its localities and its people*, (Repr.), Calcutta: Sanskrit Pustak Bhandar, 1974, p. 87.
22 See for instance Letter by 'Aclaus' to the editor of the *Calcutta Journal*, 27 April 1820, in S. Das (comp.), *Selections from the Indian Journals, Vol. II., Calcutta Journal*, Calcutta: K. L. Mukhopadhyay, 1965, pp. 169–70. and R. Ray Choudhury (ed.), *Glimpses of Old Calcutta (Period 1836–50)*, Bombay: Nachiketa Publ., 1978, pp. 14, 68 and 106.
23 *The United Service Gazette*, 15 January 1859, on the *Shannon*'s Naval Brigade.
24 The following is based on C. R. Low, *History of the Indian Navy (1613–1863)*, Vol. II, London: R. Bentley and son, 1877, pp. 431–37.
25 OIOC, European Manuscripts [hereafter MSS.Eur.] B. 241.
26 OIOC, IOR: P/213/50, GoBeng, Marine Dept. Progs, 1859.
27 Low, *History of the Indian Navy*, p. 431. Among the objects guarded by these auxiliary troops was the Governmental Palace, The Mint and, last but not least, the Nawab of Oudh who had been brought to Calcutta immediately after the outbreak of hostilities.
28 W. L. Clowes, *The Royal Navy. A History from the Earliest Times to the Death of Queen Victoria*, Vol. VII, London: Sampson Low, Marston & Co., 1903, p. 138.

The Royal Navy vessels had been despatched from Hong Kong by Rear-Admiral M. Seymour to help in quelling the rebellion.
29 The second major Royal Navy Brigade was formed out of the crew of the HMS *Pearl*, which was despatched to Gorakhpur district in mid-September 1857. Cf. E. A. Williams, *The Cruise of the Pearl round the World. With an Account of the Operations of the Naval Brigade in India*, London: R. Bentley, 1859, p. 73.
30 The most detailed account of the *Shannon*'s Brigade's activities can be found in E. H. Verney, *The Shannon's Brigade in India. Being some account or Sir William Peel's Naval Brigade in the India Campaign of 1857–1858*, London: Saunders, 1862. Cf. also C. W. Rowbotham, *The Naval Brigades in the Indian Mutiny 1857–58*, London: Printed for the Navy Records Society, 1947 (Publications of the Navy Records Society, Vol. lxxxvii), pp. 1–50.
31 See for instance NAI, GoI, Home Dept., Publ., Consultations, Nos 95–104, 28 May 1858: 'Raising of additional Brigades and despatch of detachments to Eastern Bengal' and OIOC, IOR: P/213/49, GoI, Marine Consultations, Sep.–Dec. 1858, Files Nos 2–3, 10 September 1858: 'Reporting arrival at Calcutta of the steamer *Dalhousie* from Madras and Singapore with 189 seamen, volunteers for service in the Indian Navy'.
32 OIOC, IOR: P/213/50, GoI, Marine Consultations, 1859, Files Nos 11–17, 21 July 1859: 'On the subject of the cost of the several regular and irregular Naval Brigades now employed in the Lower Provinces'.
33 C. R. Low gives a total number of 1,828 officers and men employed between August 1857 and May 1860 when the last detachment was disbanded. However, he seems to be referring to the regular units only. Cf. Low, *History of the Indian Navy*, p. 492.
34 Rowbotham, *The Naval Brigades in the Indian Mutiny*, p. ix. For a more recent example see R. Brooks, 'Naval Brigades into India: The relief of Lucknow 1857–59' in P. Hore (ed.), *Seapower Ashore: 200 Years of Royal Navy Operations on Land*, London: Chatham Pub in association with the National Maritime Museum, 2001, pp. 130–45.
35 NAI, GoI, Home Dept., Marine Consultations, 21 January 1859, File Letter No. 1046: S. Wauchope, Commissioner of Police [hereafter CoP], Calcutta to A. R. Young, Secy. to GoBeng, 2 December 1858.
36 For an example see shipping case No. 409, 27 November 1858, 'John P. Fox, Master of the British ship Anne Royden, versus William Parkinson, articled seamen of the same', ibid.
37 '[N]ot only the Masters of ships but the mercantile community generally, are in a state of irritation at the encouragement held out to desertion from the shipping in the River, by the officers in charge of the Indian Naval Brigade, supported as it is supposed by the Government, and at the downright opposition they meet with when any attempt is made to bring deserters to justice', ibid., S. Wauchope, CoP, Calcutta to A. R. Young. Cf. also OIOC, IOR: P/213/50, GoI, Marine Consultations, 1859, File No. 53, 21 July 1859, Letter No. 1001: S. Wauchope, CoP, Calcutta to Lieut.-Col. O. Cavenagh, Town Major, Fort William, 22 November 1858.
38 NAI, GoI, Home Dept. Progs, Publ., No. A-43, 5 February 1858: Letter No. 47, Officiating [hereafter Offg.] Magistrate, Rangpore to GoBeng, 22 December 1857.
39 Low, *History of the Indian Navy*, p. 431.
40 *The Englishman*, 15 January 1859, p. 2.
41 OIOC, IOR: P/213/50, GoI, Marine Consultations, 1859, Letter No. 48: Brigadier W. G. Brown, commanding at Calcutta to S. Wauchope, CoP, Calcutta, 30 November 1858.

42 Williams, *The Cruise of the Pearl*, pp. 303–4. Particularly the *Shannon*'s Brigade was praised by various officers as a 'sober, quiet and [...] well conducted body of men'. See for instance Clowes, *The Royal Navy*, p. 143. Nonetheless, six seamen belonging to the Brigade had to be punished for robbery committed while on duty in Sassaram in April/May 1858. Cf. Rowbotham, *The Naval Brigades in the Indian Mutiny*, p. 45.

43 Low, *History of the Indian Navy*, p. 470 fn.

44 OIOC, IOR: P/213/50, GoI, Marine Consultations 1859, File No 6., Letter No, 14: Lieutenant H. Jackson, Indian Navy [hereafter I.N.], Commanding No. 3, Indian Naval Brigade to C.D. Campbell, Senior Officer, I.N. at Calcutta, 20 January 1859.

45 *The United Service Gazette*, 15 January 1859; quoted in Rowbotham, *The Naval Brigades in the Indian Mutiny*, p. 45.

46 OIOC, IOR: P/213/50, GoI, Marine Consultations 1859, File No. 20, 8 April 1859, Letter No. 1365: A. R. Young, Secy. to GoBeng to C. Beaden, Secy. to GoI, 1st March 1859, ibid.

47 Thus, in 1815 the Government had felt the need to appoint a 'Committee of inquiry into the state of mendicity and vagrancy in London'. Cf. J. Marriot, *The other Empire. Metropolis, India and Progress in the colonial Imagination*, Manchester and New York: Manchester University Press, 2003, pp. 51–52 and 71–72.

48 OIOC, IOR: P/213/50, GoI, Marine Consultations 1859, File No. 22, Letter No., 167, 25 February 1859: S. Wauchope, CoP, Calcutta to the Secy. to GoBeng.

49 *Bengal Hurkaru*, 4 May 1859. Cf. also WBSA, Genl. Dept. Progs, 19 May 1859, No. 38, Letter No. 974: V.H.W. Grey, Secy. to GoI, Home Dept. to A. R. Young, Secy. to GoBeng, 11 May 1859.

50 *Report on the State of the Police of the Town of Calcutta for 1859–1860 (With figured statements and comparative statements for 1858–1859 and 1859–1860)*, Calcutta: unknown publisher, 1861, p. 4.

51 OIOC, IOR: P/213/50, GoBeng, Marine Dept. Progs., No. 20, 8 July 1859, Letter No. 3811: A. R. Young, Secy. to GoBeng to W. Grey, Secy. to GoI, 17 June 1859.

52 The following is such a typical case: 'John Waters came out to India in the *Imperatrice Eugenie* from which ship he deserted and entered the Naval Brigade. Had a coup de soleil and his mind is weakened by that and excessive drinking.[...] This man was sent by me some months ago to the Lunatic Asylum, but discharged almost immediately on the ground that he was not mad but only suffering from slight derangement of mind caused by excessive drinking'. Cf. OIOC, IOR: P/173/5, Fort William, Marine Dept. Progs., 1859, No. 4, 25 August 1859, Letter No. 662: S. Wauchope, CoP, Calcutta, to GoBeng, 5 August 1859.

53 See OIOC, IOR: P/213/50, GoBeng, Marine Dept. Progs, No. 20, 8 July 1859, Letter No. 3811: A. R. Young, Secy. to GoBeng to W. Grey, Secy. to GoI, 17 June 1859.

54 N.N. (ed.), *A Brief History of the Cyclone at Calcutta and Vicinity, 5th October 1864*, Calcutta: Cutter, 1865, p. 3. Cf. also P. Ghose, 'Scientific Study in Calcutta: The Colonial Period', in S. Chaudhuri, *Calcutta. The Living City. Vol. I, The Past*, (Repr.) Delhi 1999, pp. 195–202, p. 199. For a detailed survey of the effects of the cyclone cf. also J. E. Gastrell and H. F. Blanford, *Report on the Calcutta Cyclone on the 5th of October 1864*, Calcutta: Military Orphan Press, 1866 and OIOC, IOR: P/173 GoBeng, Marine Dept. Progs. 1864, A-13–43, November 1864.

55 M. Massey, *Recollections of Calcutta for over half a Century*, Calcutta: Thacker, Spink and Co., 1918, p. 32.

56 Ibid., p. 33.
57 N.N. (ed.), *A Brief History of the Cyclone at Calcutta*, p. 12.
58 J.G. Reddie, *Annual Report of the Marine Department and Dockyard under the Government of Bengal for 1864–65*, Calcutta: Bengal Marine Department, 1865, p. 3.
59 OIOC, IOR: P/213/57, GoI, Home Dept. Progs., Marine, 1865 February 1865, A-No. 61, Letter No. 308: J.G. Reddie, Master Attendant, Calcutta to A. Eden Secy. to GoBeng, 28 January 1865.
60 OIOC, IOR: P/173/15, GoBeng., Marine Dept. Progs., 1865, A-No. 29, Letter No. 1287: V. H. Schalch, CoP, Calcutta to GoBeng, 17 October 1864. Cf. also N.N. (ed.), *A Brief History of the Cyclone at Calcutta*, pp. 21–22.
61 OIOC, IOR: P/213/57, GoI, Home Dept. Progs., Marine, 1865, February 1865, A-No. 61, Letter No. 308: J.G. Reddie, Master Attendant, Calcutta to A. Eden Secy. to GoBeng, 28 January 1865.
62 Barnes, *Evolution and Scope of Mercantile and Marine Laws*, p. 29.
63 In spite of the fact that the measures were thus sanctioned by law, J. Reddie, the Master Attendant, had to admit that it was no easy task to arrange for the deportation of the seamen, as many of them had previously been in the House of Correction and commanders were 'naturally averse to carry away Seamen of this description'. OIOC, IOR: P/173/15, GoBeng, Marine Dept. Progs., 1865, No. 41: Capt. A. Caw, Shipping Master to J.G. Reddie, Master Attendant, 12 December 1864.
64 OIOC, IOR: P/437/29, GoI, Home Dept. Progs., Marine, 1866, A-No. 29, Letter No. 135: A. Caw, Shipping Master to Board of Trade, Marine Dept., London, 30 June 1865.
65 Tellingly, the Commissioner of Police, Calcutta warned the Government in June 1865 that the 'state of things is not only most distressing but may prove dangerous to the welfare and the quiet of the town'. Cf. WBSA, Genl. Dept. (Marine) Progs., July 1865, No. 26, Letter No. 1094: V.H. Schalch, CoP, Calcutta to GoBeng, 30 June 1865.
66 Ibid., Letter No. 30: A. Caw, Shipping Master to GoBeng, 7 July 1865.
67 Ibid., No. 18. May 1866, Letter No. 115: J.M. Cunningham, Sanitary Commission of Bengal to GoBeng, 9 February 1866.
68 Malleson, 'The State of Sailors in Calcutta'.
69 Cf. for instance Anonymous, 'Sailor Life in Calcutta', *The Friend of India*, 14 April 1864, pp. 399–400.; *The Friend of India*, 22 September 1864, p. 1061; *The Friend of India*, 6 April 1865, pp. 392–93; *The Friend of India*, 27 April 1865, p. 483; and Chevers, *On the Preservation of the health of Seamen*.
70 Anonymous, 'Sailor Life in Calcutta', p. 453.
71 OIOC, IOR: P/213/50, GoI, Marine Consultations 1859, File No. 22, Letter No., 167, 25 February 1859: S. Wauchope, CoP, Calcutta to the Secy. to GoBeng.
72 H. M. Macpherson, *On the Mortality of Calcutta during the twenty years ending 1860*, Calcutta: s.n., s.a. [1861?].
73 Ibid., p. 206.
74 'Report of the Fever Hospital Committee, 1840', cited in M. Harrison, *Climates and Constitutions. Health, Race, Environment and British Imperialism in India 1600–1850*, Delhi-Oxford: Oxford University Press, 1999, p. 160. See also WBSA, Genl. Dept. Progs, February 1865, Nos. 51–52, and S. N. Mukherjee, '"A City of Splendid Palaces and Dingy Streets": Fiction as History', in ibid., *Calcutta. Essays in Urban History*, Calcutta: Subarnarekha, 1993, pp. 49–69, especially pp. 62–64.
75 Anonymous, 'Calcutta in 1860', *The Calcutta Review*, 34, 1860, 280–312, cf. p. 287. Cf. also *First Annual Report of the Sanitary Commission for Bengal*, Calcutta: Military Orphan Press, 1865, pp. 83–84.

76 *The Friend of India*, 14 April 1864, p. 400. For background information on the social geography of Calcutta see S. Chattopadhyay 'Blurring boundaries: the limits of 'white town' in colonial Calcutta', *Journal of the Society of Architectural Historians* 59, 2, 2000: 154–79; and M. Kosambi and J.E. Brush, 'Three Colonial Port Cities in India', *The Geographical Review* 78, 1, 1988: 32–47, cf. pp. 42–46.
77 Cf. D. Pick, *Faces of Degeneration. A European Disorder ca. 1848–1918*, Cambridge: Cambridge University Press, 1989, pp. 189–202. For Victorian conceptions about the alleged interrelation between physical wretchedness and immorality see also C. Hamlin, 'Providence and Putrefaction: Victorian Sanitarians and the Natural Theology of Health and Disease', *Victorian Studies*, 28, 1985: 381–412, particularly pp. 402–4 and A. S. Wohl, *The Eternal Slum. Housing and social policy in Victorian London*, (Repr.) New Brunswick: Transaction Publ., 2002 [London 1977], pp. 179–99. For a famous (though slightly later) example cf. W. Booth, *In Darkest England and the Way Out*, London etc.: International Headquarters of the Salvation Army, 1890, especially p. 16.
78 *The Friend of India*, 14 April 1864, pp. 399–400.
79 Ibid., p. 400. Cf. also H. E. A. Cotton, *Calcutta Old and New. A historical and descriptive handbook to the city*, Calcutta: W. Newman, 1907, pp. 214–15.
80 Chevers, *On the Preservation of the Health of Seamen*, p. 40. Chevers' calculations were later criticized as much too high by other observers [Cf. *The Calcutta Review*, 40, 1865, p. 465.]. Nonetheless, they were often cited in official documents as well as in the press.
81 M. Harrison, *Public Health in British India. Anglo–Indian Preventive Medicine 1859–1914*, Cambridge: Cambridge University Press, 1994, pp. 204–6. For the role of Calcutta as the 'capital of cholera' see also D. Arnold, 'The Indian Ocean as a disease zone, 1500–1950', *South Asia* 14, 2, 1991: 1–21, especially pp. 10–11.
82 Chevers, *On the Preservation of the Health of Seamen*, p. 42.
83 Malleson, 'The State of Sailors', p. 3.
84 Harrison, *Climates and Constitutions*, Chap. 4. See also M. Ramanna, 'Perceptions of Sanitation and Medicine in Bombay, 1900–1914', in Fischer-Tiné, H. and Mann, M. (eds), *Colonialism as Civilizing Mission. Cultural Ideology in British India*, London: Anthem, 2004, pp. 205–25, especially pp. 206–8; B. Pati, '"Ordering" "Disorder" in a Holy City: Colonial Health Interventions in Puri during the Nineteenth Century', in ibid. and Harrison, M (eds), *Health, Medicine and Empire. Perspectives on Colonial India*, Hyderabad and London: Sangam Books 2001, pp. 270–98; D. Arnold, *Colonizing the Body. State Medicine and epidemic Disease in 19th Century India*, Berkeley, Los Angeles, CA: University of California Press, 1993, pp. 183–92 and the same author's 'Cholera and Colonialism in British India', *Past & Present*, 113, 1986, 118–51.
85 Harrison, *Public Health in British India*, pp. 228–30. Cf. also D. Arnold, *Science, Technology and Medicine in Colonial India*, Cambridge: Cambridge University Press, 2000 (New Cambridge History, III.5) pp. 85–86.
86 The problematic relationship between civilizing aspirations and the sanitary realities of Calcutta had become an important topic by the early 1860s. Writing in 1864, Sir John Strachey, president of the Sanitary Commission for Bengal, declared the 'the state of the Capital of British India [...]' to be 'a scandal and disgrace to a civilized Government'. Cited in *First Annual Report of The Sanitary Commission for Bengal*, p. 83. Cf. also Anonymous, 'Calcutta in 1860', pp. 280–81.
87 Chevers, *On the Preservation of the health of Seamen*, p. 43.
88 Cf. for instance C. Lloyd, *The British Seaman 1200–1860. A social survey*, London: Collins, 1968, pp. 254–56.
89 Chevers, *On the Preservation of the health of Seamen*, p. 37. Cf. also L. Sykes (ed.), *Calcutta Through British Eyes, 1690–1990*, Delhi.: Oxford University

Press, 1992, pp. 47–48. For an account of similar rumours in Bombay see M. K. Joyce, *An Exposure of the Haunts of Infamy and Dens of Vice in Bombay. Collected from Facts*, Bombay: 'Bombay Gazette' Press, 1854, p. 3. Joyce, a former police officer describes the degree of 'intemperance' prevalent among European sailors in Bombay and mentions that Indian liquor-shop owners had reacted to the strong demand by offering a cheap brand of arrack mixed with chillies and opium under the label 'Sailor Jack'.
90 Malleson, 'The State of Sailors', p. 3. Cf. also Chevers, *On the Preservation of the health of Seamen*, Appendix B, 'Adulterated Liquor sold to Sailors and Soldiers in the Bazars of Calcutta', pp. 62–64.
91 Ibid., p. 2.
92 This decision was disputed as the 366 licensed liquor shops that existed in the city in 1862 were an important source of income for the Government. Thus, the Calcutta Police Report notes in 1863 that 'there is a constant struggle between the *Abkarry* [tax on liquor] authorities and the Police, the former endeavouring to increase by every possible means the number of shops, and consequently their revenue, and the latter to keep them out'. *Report on the State of the Police of the Town of Calcutta and its Suburbs For 1862–63*, Calcutta: unknown publisher, 1863, p 4.
93 Ibid., pp. 3–4.
94 Chevers, *On the Preservation of the health of Seamen*, p. 38.
95 J. Malley, *Our Merchant Ships and Sailors*, London: Vacher and Sons, s.a. [1876], p. 63–64. Cf. also Lloyd, *The British Seaman*, pp. 246–47.
96 P. Levine, *Prostitution, Race and Politics. Policing Venereal disease in the British Empire*, New York-London: Routledge, 2003, pp. 285–86.
97 Chevers, *On the Preservation of the health of Seamen*, Appendix C, 'The Dangers to which Soldiers and Sailors are exposed in the Bazars of Calcutta', p. 68. See also OIOC, IOR: P/173/9, GoBeng, Judl. Dept. Progs., 1862, A-74, March 1865, Letter No. 1666, 15 February 1864: A. Turnbull, Secy. to the Justices of Peace of Calcutta, to S.C. Bailey, Secy. to GoBeng.
98 Levine, *Prostitution, Race and Politics*, pp. 85–86. and J. Whitehead, 'Bodies Clean and Unclean: Prostitution, Sanitary Legislation and Respectable Femininity in Colonial North India', *Gender and History* 7, 9, 1995: 41–63, esp. pp. 41–42.
99 Malleson, 'The State of Sailors', Appendix III, Statement of Rev. A. L. Mitchell, Seaman's Chaplain, Port of Calcutta, p. x.
100 *The Friend of India*, 6 April 1865, p. 393.
101 Chevers, *On the Preservation of the health of Seamen*, p 51. In a later publication the same author severely criticized the abolition of the lock-hospital system in 1883, as it resulted in a significant increase venereal diseases among European seamen. Cf. N. Chevers, *A Commentary on the Diseases of India*, London 1886.
102 S. Banerjee, *Dangerous Outcast. The Prostitute in 19th Century Bengal*, Calcutta: Seagull Books, 1998, p. 65.
103 In the five years from 1856 to 1861 altogether 1522 seamen were sentenced to imprisonment in the Calcutta House of Correction for 'refusal of duty' alone. Cf. OIOC, IOR: P/173/9, GoBeng, Judl. Dept. Progs., 1862, A-77.
104 *Report on the State of the Police of the Town of Calcutta For 1855 (With figured statements and comparative statements for 1854 and 1855)*, Calcutta 1856, p. 3.
105 OIOC, IOR: P/147/4, GoBeng, Jail Dept. Progs., Nov. 1864, No. 82: 'Statement of Prisoners in the European Jail Ootacamund'.
106 NAI, GoI, Home Dept. Progs., Judl., No. 65, 29 July 1859: N. Oliver, Magistrate of Police, Calcutta to W. Crawford Senior Magistrate of Police, Bombay, 13 April 1859.

107 *Report on the State of the Police of the Town of Calcutta For 1861–62 (With figured statements and comparative statements for 1860–61 and 1861–62)*, Calcutta: unknown publisher, 1862, p. 3. See also WBSA, GoBeng, Judl. Dept. Progs., No. A-113–17, 6 January 1859: Prevention of Sailors from going out with their knives.
108 The case of Frank Fowles, a sailor on board the American ship *Eliza*, is quite characteristic of such a crime. He killed the mother of a prostitute called 'Bebee Jaun'. When the woman asked him to go elsewhere, because he did not have enough money to pay for her daughter's sexual services, 'Fowles took from his pocket a pistol, and without saying anything presented it in the direction of the mother; the pistol exploded and the old woman was shot in the head, and shortly after died'. However, he was convicted of manslaughter and not murder as it was presumed 'that he presented the pistol to the woman more with intent to frighten than to shoot her'. *Report on the State of the Police of the Town of Calcutta For 1860–61 (With figured statements and comparative statements for 1859–60 and 1860–61)*, Calcutta: unknown publisher, 1861, pp. 16–17.
109 Cf. *Report on the State of the Police of the Town of Calcutta and its Suburbs For 1862–63*, p. 4 and OIOC, IOR: P/433/10, GoBeng, Judl. Dept. Progs., Jan-March 1866 Feb. A-116–18, March 1866, A-1–2: 'Murder by an American sailor on board ship'.
110 Cotton, *Calcutta Old and New*, p. 222.
111 *Report on the State of the Police of the Town of Calcutta for 1855*, p. 16.
112 Banerjee, *Dangerous Outcast*, p. 52. For an example from Bombay see *Bombay Samachar*, 9 June 1868, in *Report on Native Papers, Bombay*, 1868.
113 *Proceedings of a Meeting for forming a Temperance Society, held in the Town Hall of Bombay etc.*, Bombay: Printed at the Courier Press by Sorabjee Dorabjee, 1834, p. 10. Cf. also P. Spear, *The Nabobs: A Study of the Social Life of the English in Eighteenth-Century India*, (Repr.) London-Dublin: Curzon Press, 1980 [1932], pp. 59–60; and T. Raychaudhuri, 'Transformation of Indian Sensibilities: The West as Catalyst', in ibid., *Perceptions, Emotions, Sensibilities. Essays on India's Colonial and Post-colonial Experiences*, New Delhi: Oxford University Press, 1999, pp. 3–21, cf. p. 7.
114 *Thacker's Bengal Directory*, 1869, Calcutta: Thacker, Spink and Co., 1868, p. 203.
115 Ibid.
116 *The Englishman*, 6 July 1837.
117 For the history of the early British institutions see also W. H. Hall, *Sailors' Homes, Destitute Sailors' Asylums and Asylums for aged Seamen, Their Origin & Progress*, s. l., 1852, p. 10.
118 *Bengal Directory and Annual Register 1858*, Pt. XI, Calcutta: Bengal Hurkaru Press, 1858, p. 107. See also Anonymous, 'Sailor Life in Calcutta', p. 461. We know from other sources that the home – at least in the first years of existence – did not live up to these expectations and was a centre of 'liquor traffic' characterized by the 'prevalence of disorder and intoxication'. Cf. T. Atkins, *Reminiscences of Twelve Years' Residence in Tasmania and New South Wales; Norfolk Island and Moreton Bay; Calcutta, Madras and Cape Town; the United States of America and the Canadas*, s. l. [Malvern]: 'Advertiser' Office, 1869, pp. 91–92.
119 *Bengal Directory and Annual Register 1858*, pp. 106–7.
120 A. Kennerley, 'Seamen's Missions and Sailors' Homes: Spiritual and Social Welfare Provision for Seafarer in British Ports in the Nineteenth Century, with some Reference to the South West', in S. Fisher (ed.), *Studies in British Privateering, Trading Enterprise and Seamen's Welfare, 1775–1900*, Exeter: Exeter University Publications, 1987, pp. 121–50, cf. pp 147–48. See also Hall, *Sailors' Homes, Destitute Sailors' Asylums and Asylums for aged Seamen*, pp. 6–7.

121 *The Friend of India*, 6 April 1865, p. 393.
122 OIOC, IOR: P/437/29, GoI, Home Dept. Progs, Marine, 1866, No. 18, Letter No. 115: J. M. Cunningham, Offg. Secy. to Sanitary Commission for Bengal to A. Eden, Secy. to GoBeng, 9 February 1866.
123 A reaction to the widespread practice by commanders of European ships to get rid of their expensive European crew discussed above.
124 Cf. Malleson, 'The State of the Sailors in Calcutta', Appendix I, Statement of J. H. Branson, Magistrate Southern division, pp. ii–iii.
125 For surprisingly similar results see a recent German study about the historical evolution of stereotypes regarding sailors: T. Heimerdinger, *Der Seemann. Ein Berufsstand und seine kulturelle Inszenierung (1844–2003)*, Köln-Weimar-Wien: Böhlau 2005.
126 Malleson, 'The State of the Sailors in Calcutta', Appendix I, p. xi.
127 *The Friend of India*, 14 April 1864, p. 400.
128 Malleson, 'The State of Sailors', Appendix II, 'Memorandum of Rev. J Cave-Browne, Cathedral Chaplain and Chaplain of the General Hospital on the want of official sanitary measures for our seamen while in the Port of Calcutta', p. vi.
129 NAI, GoI, Home Dept. Progs, Judl., Nos. 16–19, 11 March 1859. Letter No. 644: W.C. Crawford, Senior Magistrate of Police to the Government of Bombay, to GoBom, Judl. Dept., 23 October 1858.
130 This trope was also current in metropolitan discourse on sailors. Cf. C. Dixon, 'The Rise and Fall of the Crimp, 1840–1914', in S. Fisher (ed.), *British Shipping and Seamen, 1630–1960. Some studies* (Exeter Papers in Economic History, No. 16), Exeter: University of Exeter, 1984, pp. 49–67, see p. 65.
131 Malleson, 'The State of Sailors', p. 11. The official distrust of the boarding-house keepers had also other reasons. In some cases they were apparently involved in helping British soldiers to desert and getting employment as deck hands on board ships sailing to Europe. Cf. NAI, GoI, Home Dept. Progs., Judl., A-37–42, Oct. 1876: 'Desertion of Soldiers of the 40th Regiment and the part taken by Kelly, a boarding house-keeper in their embarkation'.
132 Ibid., Appendix III, Statement of Rev. A. L. Mitchell, Seaman's Chaplain, Port of Calcutta, p. xiii.
133 Malley, *Our Merchant Ships and Sailors*, p. 63.
134 Anonymous, 'Sailor Life in Calcutta', p. 466,
135 Ibid.
136 Ibid., Appendix III, p. xxv. The trope of a progressing moral corruption of European seamen from a 'golden age' where they had been obedient and respectful can also be found in earlier as well as in later writings. Cf. for instance Reverend H. Jeffreys in his speech 'Intemperance: root of crime, disease and poverty' held in Bombay, 13 November 1834, in *Proceedings of a Meeting for forming a Temperance Society, held in the Town Hall of Bombay etc.*, p. 9; Malley, *Our Merchant Ships and Sailors*, p. 63 and W. H. Hood, *The Blight of Insubordination. The Lascar Question and rights and wrongs of the British Shipmaster*, London: Spottiswoode & Co., 1903, pp. 17–18.
137 P. Linebaugh and M. Rediker, *The Many-headed Hydra. Sailors, slaves, commoners and the hidden history of the revolutionary Atlantic*, London-New York: Verso, 2001, pp. 214–21.
138 OIOC, IOR: P/173/9, GoBeng, Marine Dept. Progs., 1862, No. A-73: H.W.I Wood, Secy. to Bengal Chamber of Commerce, to E.H. Lushington, Secy. to GoBeng, 20 January 1862. Cf. also NAI, GoI, Home Dept. Progs., Judl., No. 65, 29 July 1859: 'Imprisonment of Seamen at Bombay and Calcutta'; N. Oliver, Magistrate of Police, Calcutta to W. Crawford Senior Magistrate of Police, Bombay, 13 April 1859.
139 Malleson, 'The State of Sailors', p. 21.

140 Anonymous, 'Sailor Life in Calcutta', p. 463.
141 Malleson, 'The State of Sailors', Appendix II, Memorandum of Rev. J. Cave-Browne, Cathedral Chaplain and Chaplain of the General Hospital on the want of official sanitary measures for our seamen while in the Port of Calcutta, p. vi.
142 A. Jarvis, 'Port History: Some Thoughts on Where it Came from and Where it Might be Going', in L. Fischer and A. Jarvis (eds), *Havens and Harbours. Essays in Port History in Honour of Gordon Jackson*, St. John's, Newfoundland: International Maritime Economic History Association, 1999 (Research in Maritime History No. 16), pp. 13–34, pp. 14–15. [Italics H. F.-T.]
143 The Model of the 'contact zone' has been successfully introduced and developed in M. L. Pratt, *Imperial Eyes: Travel Writing and Transculturation*, New York 1992.
144 Marshall, 'The White Town of Calcutta', pp. 307–8.
145 B. B. Ghosh, 'Foreword', in Mukherjee, *The Port of Calcutta*, p. ix.
146 There is a vast literature on 'thugs' and 'criminal tribes'; the more important titles include: R. Singha, 'Providential Circumstances: The 'Thuggee'-Campaign of the 1830s and Legal innovation', *MAS* 27, 1, 1993, 83–146; J. Pouchepadass, 'Criminal tribes of British India: a repressive concept in theory and practice', *International Journal of Asian Studies* 2,1, 1982, 41–59; M. Radhakrishna, *Dishonoured by History: 'Criminal Tribes' and British Colonial Policy*, Hyderabad etc.: Orient Longman, 2001; R. Tolen, 'Colonizing and Transforming the Criminal Tribesman. The Salvation Army in British India', in J. Terry and J. Urla (eds), *Deviant Bodies. Critical Perspectives on Difference in Science and Popular Culture*, Bloomington, Indianapolis, IN: Indiana University Press, 1996, pp. 78–107; M. Brown 'Race, Science and the Construction of Native Criminality in colonial India', *Theoretical Criminology* 5, 3, 2001, 345–68; and M. Fourcade, 'The So-called Criminal Tribes of India. Colonial violence and traditional violence', in D. Vidal with G. Tarabout, and E. Meyer (eds), *Violence/Non-Violence. Some Hindu perspectives*, New Delhi: Manohar, 2003, pp. 143–73.
147 That the techniques of 'orientalization' could obviously be applied to members of the 'occidental' lower classes makes a renewed discussion of the meanings and usefulness of the concept seem worthwhile.
148 Anonymous, 'Sailor Life in Calcutta', p. 461.
149 Ibid., p. 453.

Bibliography

Manuscript sources

British Library, Oriental and India Office Collection (OIOC, now: Asia, Pacific and Africa Collections).
European Manuscripts (MSS.Eur.).
Oriental and India Office Collection, India Office Records, British Library, London (*OIOC, IOR*).
Fort William, Marine Department Proceedings, 1859.
Government of Bengal, Marine Department Proceedings, 1859–65.
Government of Bengal, Jail Department Proceedings, 1864.
Government of Bengal, Judicial Department Proceedings, 1862 – 1866.
Government of India, Home Department Proceedings, Marine, 1865–66.
Government of India, Marine Consultations, 1858–59.

National Archives of India, New Delhi (*NAI*).
Government of India, Home Department, Marine Consultations, 1858–59.
Government of India, Home Department, Public, Consultations 1858.
Government of India, Home Department Proceedings, Judicial, 1859.
West Bengal State Archives, Calcutta (WBSA).
Government of Bengal, General Department Proceedings, 1859–65.
Government of Bengal, Judicial Department Proceedings, 1859.

Published material

Anonymous [i.e. Cave-Browne, John], 'Sailor Life in Calcutta', *The Calcutta Review*, 40, 1865: 452–66.
——, 'Calcutta in 1860', *The Calcutta Review*, 34, 1860: 280–312.
——, 'Sailor Life in Calcutta', in *The Friend of India*, 14 April 1864.
Arnold, D., *Science, Technology and Medicine in Colonial India*, Cambridge: Cambridge University Press, 2000 (New Cambridge History, III.5).
——, *Colonizing the Body. State Medicine and Epidemic Disease in 19th Century India*, Berkeley, Los Angeles, CA: University of California Press, 1993.
——, 'The Indian Ocean as a disease zone, 1500–1950', *South Asia* 14, 2, 1991: 1–21.
——, 'Cholera and Colonialism in British India', *Past & Present*, 113, 1986: 118–51.
——, 'European Orphans and Vagrants in India in the Nineteenth Century', *Journal of Imperial and Commonwealth History* 7, 2, 1979: 104–27.
Atkins, T., *Reminiscences of Twelve Years' Residence in Tasmania and New South Wales; Norfolk Island and Moreton Bay; Calcutta, Madras and Cape Town; the United States of America and the Canadas*, s. l. [Malvern: 'Advertiser' Office], 1869.
Banerjee, P., *Calcutta and its Hinterland*, Calcutta: Progressive Publications, 1975.
Banerjee, S., *Dangerous Outcast. The Prostitute in 19th Century Bengal*, Calcutta: Seagull Books, 1998.
Barnes, L., *Evolution and Scope of Mercantile and Marine Laws relating to Seamen in India*, New Delhi: Maritime Law Association of India, 1983.
Bengal Hurkaru (Calcutta), 1859.
Booth, W., *In Darkest England and the Way Out*, London: International Headquarters of the Salvation Army, 1890.
Brooks, R., 'Naval Brigades into India: The relief of Lucknow 1857–59' in P. Hore (ed.), *Seapower Ashore: 200 Years of Royal Navy Operations on Land*, London: Chatham Pub in association with the National Maritime Museum, 2001, pp. 130–45.
——, *The Long Arm of the Empire. Naval Brigades from the Crimea to the Boxer Rebellion*, London: Constable, 1999.
Brown, M. 'Race, Science and the Construction of Native Criminality in Colonial India', *Theoretical Criminology* 5, 3, 2001: 345–68.
Chattopadhyay, S., 'Blurring boundaries: the limits of 'white town' in colonial Calcutta', *Journal of the Society of Architectural Historians* 59, 2, 2000: 154–79.
Chevers, N., *A Commentary on the Diseases of India*, London: J. & A. Churchill 1886.
——, *On the Preservation of the Health of Seamen, especially those frequenting Calcutta and the other Indian Ports etc.*, Calcutta: Military Orphan Press, 1864.
Clowes, W. L., *The Royal Navy. A History from the Earliest Times to the Death of Queen Victoria*, Vol. VII, London: Sampson Low, Marston & Co., 1903.

Cotton, H. E. A., *Calcutta Old and New. A historical and descriptive handbook to the city*, Calcutta: W. Newman, 1907.
Das, S. (comp.), *Selections from the Indian Journals, Vol. II., Calcutta Journal*, Calcutta: K. L. Mukhopadhyay, 1965.
Dixon, C., 'The Rise and Fall of the Crimp, 1840–1914', in Fisher, S. (ed.), *British Shipping and Seamen, 1630–1960. Some studies* (Exeter Papers in Economic History, No. 16), Exeter: University of Exeter, 1984, pp. 49–67.
First Annual Report of the Sanitary Commission for Bengal, Calcutta: Military Orphan Press, 1865.
Fischer-Tiné, H., '"White Women Degrading Themselves to the Lowest Depths": European networks of prostitution and colonial anxieties in British India and Ceylon ca. 1880–1914', *Indian Economic and Social History Review* 40, 2, 2003: 163–90.
——, '"The greatest blot on British rule in the East" – 'Weißer Sklavenhandel' und die britische Kolonialherrschaft in Indien (ca. 1870-1920)', *Comparativ. Leipziger Beiträge zur Universalgeschichte und vergleichenden Gesellschaftsforschung* 13, 6, 2003: 114–37.
Fourcade, M., 'The So-called Criminal Tribes of India. Colonial violence and traditional violence', in Vidal, D. with Tarabout, G. and Meyer, E. (eds), *Violence/Non-Violence. Some Hindu perspectives*, New Delhi: Manohar, 2003, pp. 143–73.
Gastrell, E. and Blanford, H. F., *Report on the Calcutta Cyclone on the 5th of October 1864*, Calcutta: Military Orphan Press, 1866.
Ghose, P., 'Scientific Study in Calcutta: The Colonial Period', in Chaudhuri, S., *Calcutta. The Living City. Vol. I, The Past*, (Repr.) Delhi 1999, pp. 195–202.
Ghosh, B.B., 'Foreword', in Mukherjee, N., *The Port of Calcutta. A Short History*, Calcutta: Commissioners for the Port of Calcutta, 1968, pp. 1–12.
Government of Bombay, *Report on Native Papers*, Bombay, 1868.
Heimerdinger, T., *Der Seemann. Ein Berufsstand und seine kulturelle Inszenierung (1844–2003)*, Köln-Weimar-Wien: Böhlau 2005.
Hall, W. H., *Sailors' Homes, Destitute Sailors' Asylums and Asylums for aged Seamen, Their Origin & Progress*, s. l., 1852.
Hamlin, C., 'Providence and Putrefaction: Victorian Sanitarians and the Natural Theology of Health and Disease', *Victorian Studies* 28, 1985: 381–412.
Harrison, M., *Climates and Constitutions. Health, Race, Environment and British Imperialism in India 1600–1850*, Delhi and Oxford: Oxford University Press, 1999.
——, *Public Health in British India. Anglo-Indian Preventive Medicine 1859–1914*, Cambridge: Cambridge University Press, 1994.
Hood, W.H., *The Blight of Insubordination. The Lascar Question and rights and wrongs of the British Shipmaster*, London: Spottiswoode & Co., 1903.
Hubel, T., 'In Search of the British Indian in British India: White Orphans, Kipling's Kim and Class in Colonial India', *Modern Asian Studies* 38, 1, 2004: 227–51.
Jarvis, A. 'Port History: Some Thoughts on where it Came from and Where it Might be Going', in Fischer, L. and Jarvis, A. (eds), *Havens and Harbours. Essays in Port History in Honour of Gordon Jackson*, St. John's, Newfoundland: International Maritime Economic History Association, 1999 (Research in Maritime History No. 16), pp. 13–34.
Joyce, M.K., *An Exposure of the Haunts of Infamy and Dens of Vice in Bombay. Collected from Facts*, Bombay: 'Bombay Gazette' Press, 1854.
Kennerley, A., 'Seamen's Missions and Sailors' Homes: Spiritual and Social Welfare Provision for Seafarer in British Ports in the Nineteenth Century, with some

Reference to the South West', in Fisher, S. (ed.), *Studies in British Privateering, Trading Enterprise and Seamen's Welfare, 1775–1900*, Exeter: Exeter University Publications, 1987, pp. 121–50.

Kipling, R. *The Collected Poems of Rudyard Kipling*, Ware: Wordsworth Editions, 2001.

Kosambi, M. and Brush, J.E., 'Three Colonial Port Cities in India', *The Geographical Review*, 78, 1, 1988: 32–47.

Krishna Deb, R. V., *The Early History and Growth of Calcutta*, Calcutta: Romesh Chandra Ghose, 1905.

Levine, P., 'Erotic Geographies. Sex and the Managing of Colonial Space', in Michie, H. and Thomas, R. R. (eds), *Nineteenth Century Geographies. The transformation of space from the Victorian age to the American century*, New Brunswick and London: Rutgers University Press, 2003, pp. 149–60.

——, *Prostitution, Race and Politics. Policing Venereal Disease in the British Empire*, New York adn London: Routledge, 2003.

Linebaugh, P. and Rediker, M., *The Many-headed Hydra. Sailors, slaves, commoners and the hidden history of the revolutionary Atlantic*, London and New York: Verso, 2001.

Lloyd, C., *The British Seaman 1200–1860. A social survey*, London: Collins, 1968.

Long, J., *Calcutta in the Olden Time. Its localities and its people*, (Repr.), Calcutta: Sanskrit Pustak Bhandar, 1974.

Low, C.R., *History of the Indian Navy (1613–1863)*, Vol. II, London: R. Bentley and son, 1877.

Macpherson, H.M., *On the Mortality of Calcutta during the twenty years ending 1860*, Calcutta: s.n., s.a. [1861].

Malleson, G.B., 'The State of the Sailors in Calcutta', Appendix III, [in OIOC, IOR: P/437/29, GoI, Home Department Proceedings, Marine, 1866].

Malley, J., *Our Merchant Ships and Sailors*, London: Vacher and Sons, s.a. [1876].

Marriot, J., *The other Empire. Metropolis, India and Progress in the colonial Imagination*, Manchester and New York: Manchester University Press, 2003.

Marshall, P., 'The White Town of Calcutta under the Rule of the East India Company', *Modern Asian Studies* 34, 2, 2000: 307–31.

Massey, M., *Recollections of Calcutta for over half a Century*, Calcutta: Thacker, Spink, 1918.

Mukherjee, N., *The Port of Calcutta. A Short History*, Calcutta: Commissioners for the Port of Calcutta, 1968.

Mukherjee, S. N. '"A City of Splendid Palaces and Dingy Streets": Fiction as History', in idem, *Calcutta. Essays in Urban History*, Calcutta: Subarnarekha, 1993, pp. 49–69.

N.N. (ed.), *A Brief History of the Cyclone at Calcutta and Vicinity, 5th October 1864*, Calcutta: Cutter, 1865.

Pati, B., '"Ordering" "Disorder" in a Holy City: Colonial Health Interventions in Puri during the Nineteenth Century', in ibid. and Harrison, M (eds), *Health, Medicine and Empire. Perspectives on Colonial India*, Hyderabad and London: Sangam Books 2001, pp. 270–98.

Peers, D., 'Privates off Parade: Regimenting Sexuality in the Nineteenth Century Indian Empire', *The International History Review* 20, 4, 1998: 823–55.

——, 'Sepoys, Soldiers and the Lash: Race, Caste and Army Discipline in India, 1820–50', *Journal of Imperial and Commonwealth History* 23, 2, 1995: 211–47.

Pick, D., *Faces of Degeneration. A European Disorder ca. 1848–1918*, Cambridge: Cambridge University Press, 1989.

Pouchepadass, J., 'Criminal tribes of British India: a repressive concept in theory and practice', *International Journal of Asian Studies*, 2, 1, 1982: 41–59.
Pratt, M.L., *Imperial Eyes: Travel Writing and Transculturation*, London: Routledge, 1992.
Proceedings of a Meeting for forming a Temperance Society, held in the Town Hall of Bombay etc., Bombay: Printed at the Courier Press by Sorabjee Dorabjee, 1834.
Radhakrishna, M., *Dishonoured by History: 'Criminal Tribes' and British Colonial Policy*, Hyderabad: Orient Longman, 2001.
Ramanna, M., 'Perceptions of Sanitation and Medicine in Bombay, 1900–1914', in Fischer-Tiné, H. and Mann, M. (eds), *Colonialism as Civilizing Mission. Cultural Ideology in British India*, London: Anthem, 2004, pp. 205–25.
Raychaudhuri, T., 'Transformation of Indian Sensibilities: The West as Catalyst', in idem, *Perceptions, Emotions, Sensibilities. Essays on India's Colonial and Post-colonial Experiences*, New Delhi: Oxford University Press, 1999.
Ray Choudhury, R. (ed.), *Glimpses of Old Calcutta (Period 1836–50)*, Bombay: Nachiketa Publications, 1978.
Reddie, J.G., *Annual Report of the Marine Department and Dockyard under the Government of Bengal for 1864–65*, Calcutta: Bengal. Marine Department, 1865.
Report on the State of the Police of the Town of Calcutta and its Suburbs for 1862–63, Calcutta:, 1863.
Report on the State of the Police of the Town of Calcutta for 1861–62. (With figured statements and comparative statements for 1860–61 and 1861–62), Calcutta: s.n., 1862.
Report on the State of the Police of the Town of Calcutta For 1860–61. (With figured statements and comparative statements for 1859–60 and 1860–61), Calcutta: s.n., 1861.
Report on the State of the Police of the Town of Calcutta For 1859–1860. (With figured statements and comparative statements for 1858–1859 and 1859–1860), Calcutta: s.n., 1861.
Report on the State of the Police of the Town of Calcutta For 1855. (With figured statements and comparative statements for 1854 and 1855), Calcutta: s.n., 1856.
Report on the Working of the Calcutta Shipping office and of the Shipping Offices At the several Outports, for the year 1882–83, Calcutta: s.n., 1883.
Rowbotham, C.W., *The Naval Brigades in the Indian Mutiny 1857–58*, London: Printed for the Navy Records Society, 1947 (Publications of the Navy Records Society, Vol. lxxxvii).
Seton-Karr, W. S., *Selections from Calcutta Gazettes* (Repr. in 9 Vols.), Vol. III, Calcutta: Bibhash Gupta, 1987 [1867].
Singha, R., 'Providential Circumstances: The 'Thuggee'-Campaign of the 1830s and Legal innovation', *Modern Asian Studies* 27, 1, 1993: 83–146.
Spear, P., *The Nabobs: A Study of the Social Life of the English in Eighteenth-Century India*, (Repr.) London-Dublin: Curzon Press, 1980 [1932].
Stanley, P., *White Mutiny. British Military Culture in India 1825–1875*, London: Hurst, 1998.
Sykes, L. (ed.), *Calcutta Through British Eyes, 1690–1990*, Delhi: Oxford University Press, 1992.
Thankhappan Nair, P., *A History of Calcutta's Streets*, Calcutta: Firma KLM, 1987 (A Tercentenary History of Calcutta, Vol. II).
The Calcutta Review (Calcutta), 1865.
The Englishman (Calcutta), 1837 – 1859.

The Friend of India (Calcutta), 1864 – 1868.
The United Service Gazette (Ottawa), 1859.
Tolen, R., 'Colonizing and Transforming the Criminal Tribesman. The Salvation Army in British India', in Terry, J. and Urla, J. (eds), *Deviant Bodies. Critical Perspectives on Difference in Science and Popular Culture*, Bloomington and Indianapolis, IN: Indiana University Press, 1995, pp. 78–107.
Verney E. H., *The Shannon's Brigade in India. Being some account or Sir William Peel's Naval Brigade in the India Campaign of 1857–1858*, London: Saunders, 1862.
Verney, G. L., *The Devil's Wind. The Story of the Naval Brigade at Lucknow from the Letters of Edmund Hope Verney and other Papers concerning the Enterprise of the Ship's Company of H.M.S. Shannon in the Campaign in India 1857–1858*, London: Hutchinson, 1956.
Whitehead, J., 'Bodies Clean and Unclean: Prostitution, Sanitary Legislation and Respectable Feminity in Colonial North India', *Gender and History* 7, 9, 1995: 41–63.
Williams, E. A., *The Cruise of the Pearl round the World. With an Account of the Operations of the Naval Brigade in India*, London: R. Bentley, 1859.
Wohl, A. S., *The Eternal Slum. Housing and social policy in Victorian London*, (Repr.) New Brunswick: Transaction Publishers, 2002 [London 1977].
Various eds, *Bengal Directory and Annual Register 1858*, Pt. XI, Calcutta: Bengal Hurkaru Press, 1858.
——, *The Bengal Directory [Thacker's Directory]*, 1869, Calcutta: Thacker, Spink and Co., 1868.

6 'Degenerate whites' and their spaces of disorder

Disciplining racial and class ambiguities in colonial Calcutta (c. 1880–1930)

Satoshi Mizutani

Introduction: empire and the question of racial and class ambiguities

In contrast to the preceding three decades, during which Britain's middle class firmly established their economic dominance and social prestige both at home and abroad,[1] the 1880s–90s emerged as an era of domestic social unrest and imperial insecurity. The rise of new international powers such as the German Empire and the United States, with their rapidly growing industrial and military strength, was seen to threaten the hitherto incontestable ascendancy of the British Empire. The mounting fear of loss in the fierce imperial competitions with rival foreign powers was characteristically conjoined with the domestic anxieties over 'racial fitness', and nowhere was this to be more explicitly evident than in the heated debate concerning the poor quality of recruits for the British troops fighting in the Boer War (1899–1902).[2] At the turn of the century, the ruling order was forced to contend with the lingering existence of the urban poor and with their 'otherness', which Henry Mayhew had graphically sketched decades earlier in his influential *London Labour and the London Poor* (1861–62). Mayhew had not only described the lives of London's indigent populations but sought to direct the public's attention to an ironizing effect they had upon Britain's 'civilizing mission' overseas. He wrote:

> indeed, the moral and religious state of these men is a foul disgrace to us, laughing to scorn our zeal for the "propagation of the gospel in foreign parts," and making our many societies for the civilization of savages on the other side of the globe appear like a "delusion, a mockery, and a snare," when we have so many people sunk in the lowest depth of barbarism round about our very homes. It is well to have Bishops of New Zealand when we have Christianized all our own heathen; but with 30,000 individuals, in merely one of our cities, utterly needless, mindless, and principleless, surely it would look more like earnestness on our parts if we created Bishops of the New-Cut and sent "right reverent fathers" to watch over the "cure of souls" in the Broadway and the Brill.[3]

Such a passage betrays an ambivalent relationship between imperialist racism and bourgeois classism, between colonial civilizing mission and philanthropy at 'home'. Imperial civilizing, for Mayhew, could never have been just an overseas affair at a time when the British had not yet civilized the impoverished 'heathens' of their own nation. Exclusion of Britain's paupers from the sphere of civilizing would only return with a vengeance, relativizing white racial prestige, and thus ultimately undermining the very legitimacy of British colonial rule. The ever-escalating problem of the urban poor was seen as a 'racial' question in its own right, and it was partly in order to regenerate the racial fitness of Britain's white population that constant efforts were to be made, by both the state and private sectors, at alleviating urban pauperism throughout the late nineteenth and early twentieth centuries. And characteristic of those endeavours against urban pauperism was their ideological grounding in biomedical and statistical modes of thought, which in turn gave rise to the very idea of 'social science'.[4]

Despite these endeavours, however, what Mayhew had called 'barbarians' were to find their wretched existence well into the new century, with their perceived menace to social order recognized more as a specifically *urban* problem than ever before. Writing in 1902 in the preface to his book, *The Heart of Empire* (1902), Charles Masterman was compelled to repeat the same self-contradictoriness of the civilizing mission that Mayhew had invoked earlier. While civilizing the rest of the globe, the British middle class had hardly managed to regenerate those poor who lived right in the centre of empire, to the extent that their pauperization presented itself in 'all its sordid, unimaginable vastness as insoluble as ever'.[5] The British Empire was facing a major challenge from within its 'white' population inhabiting the slums of the great capital city: its substantial proportion seemed to be rapidly decaying into a sheer state of 'degeneration', instead of constituting the core of the imperial body politic. There had emerged, according to Masterman, a 'New Town type' that was 'physically, mentally, and spiritually different from the type characteristics of Englishmen during the past two hundred years': 'the future progress of the Anglo-Saxon Race' and, by extension, its imperial domination of the world, would depend upon how this type of people were brought back into civilization.[6]

Such a sense of crisis over the 'residuum' of London had been widely shared among the middle class, which resulted in the evolution of the sort of social surveys epitomized by Charles Booth's *Life and Labour of the People in London* (1892–97). The shocking findings of the statistical and ethnographic data provided by such surveys spurred responses from both the increasingly interventionist state and private agents of philanthropy such as General Booth's Salvation Army. Pauperism commissions were appointed, while various measures of urban poverty relief, such as agricultural colonization and emigration, were experimented upon, with differing degrees of success.[7]

This bourgeois conceptualization of the urban pauper can never be fully accounted for without registering the cultural impact of Britain's colonial encounters with non-European peoples overseas. As the above quote from Mayhew's book aptly shows, the emergent middle class affirmed their prestige through inferiorizing both their class and colonized subalterns simultaneously.[8] Through disseminating such ideas as 'wandering tribes', Mayhew referred to the perceived otherness of colonized subjects whilst simultaneously illuminating an alarming alienation of the metropolitan poor from the rest of British society, a move with lingering influences on the next generations.[9] But this centripetal discourse of otherness did not terminate once it hit the metropole. Rather, those ideas and practices regarding the urban poor flowed outwards too, from the centre of empire to its peripheral corners, where they were conjured up by colonial white communities in countering the increasing pauperization of their less-privileged members. In various contexts of European colonialism, whether British, Dutch, French or German, 'the poor-white question' and 'the Eurasian question' (the problem of miscegenation and of mixed populations) loomed larger than we have imagined.[10]

As far as the British Empire was concerned, the 1913 Select Committee on the Poor-White Question in South Africa, for example, asserted, 'the efficacy of the ideology of racism as a means of exerting control over Africans is challenged by the behavior of poor whites'.[11] In British India, such a perceived threat to white racial rule had been articulated as early as 1859, when Bishop Cotton of Calcutta declared, 'If a generation calling themselves Christians and descended wholly or partly from European parents, grow up in ignorance and evil habits, the effect on the Mohamedan and Heathen population will be most disastrous'.[12] Underlying such a sense of crisis was an increasing demographical fragmentation of India's white population along both class and racial lines: by the late nineteenth century, nearly one-quarter of the whites living in India were regarded as 'poor whites', and the mixed-descent 'Eurasians' (numbering more than 150,000 by the 1930s) had come to be known for their immense collective pauperization.[13] The poverty of these groups, situated ambiguously around the edges of colonial white society, became hardened into a chronic state and survived into the twentieth century, threatening to compromise the ideological legitimacy of white minority rule. Motivated by such a perceived predicament of European prestige in the midst of colonized natives, the colonial state and philanthropists assisted one another, launching a score of pauperism commissions, often with a quasi 'social-scientific' approach to indigence not dissimilar to the sort that had been adopted in Europe and North America.

In colonial and postcolonial studies, it is only recently that the aforementioned colonial incarnations of anti-pauperism measures have attracted serious attention. They deserve further historical examinations all the more for the complex questions they raised about the particular social order Europe's bourgeoisies sought to fashion within an increasingly *global* circuit of social formations. The 'problems' identified were partly about class and partly about race, often in extremely confounding ways that defied (and still continue to defy) ready simplification. The aim of the current chapter, which looks at one example of such problems of colonial pauperism, – the pauperism of 'Domiciled Europeans' and 'Eurasians' in late British India –, is precisely to explore such complex bounds of bourgeois social order at the age of empire. Such order, as the essay will seek to show, would become intelligible only through a holistic approach, advocated by Frederic Cooper and Ann Stoler, to the transcontinental dynamics of social and ideological interrelations, which bring together metropole and colony under a single analytic framework.[14]

European pauperism: its perceived danger and rationale for colonial intervention

Following the Reports of the Select Committee on the Colonization and Settlement (1858–59), it had been officially held that only certain privileged layers of British society were considered good enough to be in colonial India and rule the 'teeming millions' of the colonized population. And these ruling whites, including officials, capitalists, professionals and (if more ambiguously) missionaries, defined and maintained their whiteness through their self-chosen isolation from the social and environmental fabrics of the subcontinent.[15] Even though their colonial career could last for a long time (for several decades in cases), the elite classes never regarded India as their permanent place of abode. Instead, they almost paranoically counted on the metropole for social and cultural resources in order for them and their children to remain 'respectable'. Their colonial residence would make sense only insofar as it was meant as a temporary sojourn. As Elizabeth Buettner correctly observes, Britons in India were, as a rule, *transients*, who would travel back to the British Isles as soon as their colonial career came to an end.[16]

The problem was that there existed those people of white descent who shared neither the aforementioned idea of being transient nor the socio-economic means required for its materialization. In fact, the post-rebellion India witnessed more people who might well be called 'poor whites' than Britons of respectable standing. The majority of these stemmed from the subaltern soldiering class, whose modes of behaviour and sense of morality were notoriously different from those of their civilian counterparts.[17] But even among the civilians, there existed those whites, such as low-paid marine sailors and railway engineers, whose social and economic conditions were far from stable. What bothered the colonial authorities was that these groups easily became rootless wanderers in India, reduced, in the worst cases, into vagrants with their spectacular visibility at the heart of colonial society. To counter any further increase of these 'poor whites', they sought to regulate reckless immigration and wipe out the already existent 'undesirable' immigrants by institutional confinement and, ultimately, by repatriation.[18]

But despite these efforts, the British ruling class did not always succeed in making 'poor whites' leave India. Instead, they allowed the latter to inscribe some permanent traces of white pauperism and of miscegenation, giving birth to a 'seriously depressed class' despite their being 'Christian by birth'. These subaltern white populations made India their permanent domicile, allowing their progenies as well as themselves to be collectively labelled as 'Domiciled Europeans' with a sense of social inferiority often attached thereto.[19] Domiciled Europeans were mostly of British extraction, though they also included Europeans of other nationalities, such as French or Portuguese. They often, if not invariably, merged through miscegenation into the mixed-race population, or the 'Eurasians',[20] who had, by the 1830s, come to form a distinct community rooted in India.[21]

The colonial existence of both Domiciled Europeans and Eurasians appeared as a blatant contradiction to the racial and class constitutions of whiteness in British India in this period. Middle-class Britons, on their part, sought to maintain their racial hygiene, social prestige as well as cultural refinement through a geographical distancing from certain social and environmental milieus of colonial India, especially those epitomized in the plains.[22] The European hill stations in the northern mountain regions, which mushroomed from the mid-nineteenth century onwards, were often idealized as the only space where the British could recover and nurture their whiteness, which was easily damaged, so it was believed, by a prolonged stay in India's plains.[23] But, ultimately, even the hill stations were not regarded as ideal as the British Isles. Of course, it was not that middle-class colonials were always able to enforce in a strict fashion this geographical self-isolation. (Their retreat to the hills as well as the furlough leave to Europe were often few and far-between). Nevertheless, it is crucial to note, – and especially in view of our present interest in colonial whiteness –, the extent to which the affirmation of bourgeois self rested on a belief that colonial cities in the plains like Calcutta would never be their proper place to live, let alone their permanent domicile where they would spend the rest of their married lives and raise their offspring across generations.[24] It was partly against this backdrop that Domiciled Europeans and Eurasians became permanently stigmatized: they were condemned not only because of their class and racial origins but also because of their colonial domicile and urban residence.

Moreover, the distinction in terms of domicile was of fundamental importance when and where white membership and access to the commensurate privileges were concerned. In terms of racial descent, they were (albeit not always fully) 'white', but, due to their cursed place of domicile, neither Domiciled Europeans nor Eurasians were regarded as qualified members of the white establishment. At this juncture these two groups came to be collectively called as 'the domiciled community' and treated as such on many crucial occasions. To be sure, in some respects (especially in terms of racial composition), the two were not the same, nor did they always see each other as their kith and kin. Nevertheless, they appeared to resemble each other in certain significant ways, particularly in their ambiguous distance from the 'home-born' British and in their almost chronic state of economic deprivation.[25] In socio-legal terms, 'the domiciled' were not 'European British' but 'native'. The majority of them attended so-called European schools located throughout British India, which usually excluded natives. But, in fact, attendance at these special schools was taken *not* as a proof of their acquired 'Europeanness' but merely as an irrevocable submission to their much-stigmatized state of being 'domiciled'. Though many members of the community had jobs in the state-related sectors, especially in the subordinate positions of the civil and railway services, equally many suffered unemployment.[26] British India's demand for white labour was always limited, if not non-existent, due to the abundance of cheap labour readily drawn from the extensive native population. Even in the civil and railway services, it was more economical and politically expedient to use native labour wherever possible. Moreover, the upward mobility for the domiciled community within these services were limited because they were not 'home-born', and thus not considered fit for the higher positions. It was against this complex historical background that the domiciled community ended up causing so-called 'European pauperism'.

European pauperism in colonial Calcutta was extraordinary not only for its degree and nature in the objective sense but also for the ways in which it became perceived. It was as though Henry Mayhew's nightmare of internal 'barbarism' saw its reincarnation, requiring the same 'cure of souls'. For Bishop Cotton, the Metropolitan of the Anglican Church in India, the visible pauperization of the domiciled community was nothing less than an imperial crisis from within. He declared:

> it is nothing less than a national sin to neglect a class of persons who are our fellow-Christians and fellow-subjects, whose presence in India is due entirely to our occupation in the country, but who, unless real efforts are made for their welfare, are in great spiritual and moral danger.[27]

This had been voiced in the wake of the 1857 revolt, when there was a recognized increase in the number of impoverished whites and Eurasians, filling the Calcutta slums. Despite their white descent, these people were very far from being called 'civilizers': instead, they were so destitute and socially marginalized that they themselves need to be 'civilized', or, in Mayhew's phase they were 'our own heathen'. Like Mayhew, Cotton pointed to how the poor might emerge as 'a foul disgrace to us', thus requiring vigilant attention and control. What was different in the colonial context was that such a 'disgrace' bore an even more urgent connotation. For unlike Mayhew's London poor, the domiciled poor in colonial India exhibited themselves right in the midst of 'propagation of the gospel in foreign parts'.

In a country like India where a handful of whites governed the vast majority of natives, a visible manifestation of internal class disparities was feared to immediately damage the racial order of colonial society. Hence, it was with even a greater sense of urgency that the colonial authorities and philanthropists took to this ambiguous task of 'civilizing' the domiciled-European and Eurasian poor. The Viceroy, Lord Canning, to whom Cotton had made this remark, took his view seriously.[28] He agreed that the domiciled community had a special claim upon their non-domiciled British fellows, as it was nothing but the colonial presence of the latter that made them come into being in the first place. Or in Canning's words, 'The presence of a British Government has called them into being'.[29] What underlay such a move towards inclusion was a perceived threat of the community's poverty, which seemed to be growing so endemic.

What both Cotton and Canning were afraid of were the ways in which this phenomenon of pauperism might emerge as a scandal to British imperial prestige. Although non-domiciled Britons did not see members of the domiciled community as their equals, it remained the case that the latter had been perceived as an inseparable part of the white body politic. Certain portions of the community might have acquired darker complexions and succumbed to modes of living that actually appeared more 'Indian' than 'European'. But they had not been assimilated into any of the various Indian communities, Hindu, Muslim or otherwise. Being English-speaking and, moreover, Christian, the domiciled community was usually seen by the rest of Indian society as an appendage to the colonizing community. At this juncture, the colonial authorities contended that the non-domiciled British in India ought to put their domiciled brethren under their tutelage in order to abate the negative political consequences the latter could possibly cause. The announcements by Cotton and by Canning both left a long-lasting impact on the formation of British attitudes towards the domiciled community. Philanthropy-minded Britons shared their ambiguous sense of responsibility and urged the non-domiciled British community at large to take the plight of its domiciled counterpart as its own problem. *The Friend of India* proclaimed that members of the domiciled community 'may be of bad character, they may be idle, they may be drunkards – but they are countrymen and they call themselves Christians'.[30] It would be better, as the newspaper noted, *not* to conceive of these people as a distinct group, but to integrate them, to some extent at least, into the British community.[31] For neglecting them had already been:

> creating a race lower than any other known in India, and that pleases some people, but it is exceedingly dangerous, for it (which cannot be reached on any general principle) reacts on other portions of the same race.[32]

To prevent such degeneration from going further, the affluent British should assume a responsibility for the well-being of their less fortunate kin.

Diagnosing a 'social ill': degree and nature of impoverishment

How, in practice, could the British save their domiciled brethren from pauperism – what could the former do to rehabilitate the latter economically? During the first three decades of Crown rule, educational initiative expanded significantly. By the mid-1870s there was a widespread recognition among the colonial educationalist circle that the Government should play a central role in trying to reduce European pauperism by aiding the educational efforts of missionaries. Joseph Baly, the Archdeacon of Calcutta, made a crucial contribution for systematizing the education of India's domiciled community. His efforts bore fruit in the form of the European Education Code, drafted in Bengal in 1883. Back then, there were hopes that education would be able to equip domiciled children with practical knowledge and skills and so enable them to compete successfully with educated Indians. Both government and private employers would be happy to take them; all would be able to find employment one way or another. The new education system, however, was not as effective in countervailing European pauperism as its promoters had hoped. Not only was it impossible to remove illiteracy, but it was also always extremely difficult to find employment even for those who attended school.

By the beginning of the 1890s, it seemed increasingly clear that the British could not solve European pauperism merely by creating schools: an urgent and more specific form of intervention was required. It was the District Charitable Society, a governmental institution to supervise British philanthropic work, that made a move towards such intervention (May 1887). H. Beverley, the Society's President, issued a circular to the parishes of the Church of England asking for cooperation in 'an attempt to procure trustworthy information regarding the extent of pauperism among the Christian poor of this city'.[33] By this time, the British ruling classes were convinced that the Government had to commit itself more fully to relieve the further pauperization of the domiciled community. As *The Statesman* declared: 'The Government has not given the community the least assistance or encouragement. [...] Why should so much be done for the conquered race and literally nothing for those who are the kith and kin of the British?'.[34] To dismiss the domiciled community from the Government's responsibilities would eventually 'reflect discredit on the national name'.[35] It was in this context of a highlighted awareness of national crisis that the District Charitable Society approached the Government on the subject of European pauperism in February 1891. Together with the Eurasian and Anglo-Indian Association, which also approached the Government in early March, the Society engaged the Lieutenant-Governor of Bengal to appoint a Commission to enquire into the question of indigence among Calcutta's domiciled community. In response, Resolution No. 479 (18 April 1891) appointed a representative Committee 'to enquire into the extent and nature of the poverty and destitution which prevail in the town of Calcutta among

Europeans and Eurasians, and other matters connected therewith'.[36] Thus the 'Pauperism Committee' [hereafter PC] was launched with Sir H. L. Harrison as the chair. The Board of the Committee had prominent figures from the European philanthropic circle, including government officials, educationalists, missionaries, social workers and lawyers. It also had certain representatives of the Eurasian and Anglo-Indian Associations. The PC had five Sub-Committees: Statistics, Avenues of Employment, Education, Charitable Endowment, and Housing. The Committee elicited the support of a number of Britons in Calcutta, such as policemen, missionaries and private employers who had first-hand experience with members of the domiciled class. The findings of the PC, both quantitative and qualitative, were published in *Report of the Pauperism Committee* (submitted to the Government of Bengal on 3 March 1892). In August of the same year, the Government made its formal reply to the recommendations contained in the *Report*.

The Pauperism Committee

The PC came to many conclusions and offered specific recommendations. Among other things, it found the impoverishment of the domiciled class singularly alarming. As a whole, 7.9 per cent of Britons of pure European descent were found to be in receipt of charitable relief. The Committee noted that 7.9 was a very large percentage, given that the British community was supposedly predominantly upper or middle class, necessarily precluded from any risks of becoming paupers. What they learnt from this was that Britons who belonged to the domiciled group tended very strongly to become paupers; that in India the rate of poor Britons being reduced to pauperism was nearly twice as high as in England and Wales. And even more alarming was the pauperization of the mixed-race population; 22.3 per cent of Eurasians were found to be dependent on European charitable relief. The Committee lamented: '22.3 among Eurasians is an enormous percentage which can scarcely be paralleled in any other community in the world'.[37]

Accompanying these numerical assessments were ethnographic accounts which the Statistics Sub-Committee gathered by interviewing those non-domiciled Britons of the city, such as clergymen, philanthropic agents and police inspectors, who were seen as possessing first-hand knowledge about the domiciled poor. These interviewees told the Committee of the extremely destitute and precarious lives of unskilled casual labourers among the domiciled, especially the poorest portion of Eurasians. The Rev. Nicholas Hengesch, s.j. of the Cathedral Church of Nossa Senhora DeRozario (interviewed on 28 September 1891) noted how many of the poor in question were illiterate.[38] Thomas McGuire, Superintendent of the District Charitable Society's Alms-house (interviewed on 30 September 1891), mentioned 'an excessive proportion of unskilled labour among the Eurasians in Calcutta'.[39] According to these accounts, it was on the jetties that these impoverished men earned their means of subsistence. They worked as trolleymen, tally-clerks or gunners, and because these jobs were sought after also by natives (who required lower living costs and thus lower wages), their daily wages were inevitably kept low. On a monthly basis, the work on the jetties earned them around Rs. 15 or less. And, as Clarence W. Thomas of the District Charitable Society (interviewed on 28 September 1891) pointed out, this was almost a starvation wage considering that the lowest income on which a single man could live in the very poorest way was thought to be Rs. 12 a month. In cases with families to feed, such a wage level would be simply far too insufficient.[40]

The PC argued that in the face of such a critical condition of their domiciled brethren, middle-class Britons had a special responsibility: 'The circumstances of the Indo-European [i.e. domiciled] community are such as equitably entitle them to special and exceptional consideration at the hands of the Indian Government'.[41] The Committee also claimed that the degree of impoverishment was such as to necessitate urgent state involvement. As its 'Avenues of Employment' Sub-Committee wrote:

> We think that the condition is such that philanthropic help cannot effect any permanent good. It is an evil of large magnitude, and we would very respectfully remark that the only possible remedy lies in the Government giving the subject their full consideration and taking the action which the case demands. We think that the situation is one that has passed out of the sphere of self-help or the help which any other than the Government can give. To us it appears that when all avenues of employment are closing round a community and the pauperism found among them is represented at least as being 16.57 per cent, or one pauper for every six Europeans and Eurasians taken together, the question becomes a political question, and State interference is necessary.[42]

What practical measures should the Government take in order to discharge such responsibility to the domiciled paupers? The PC doubted that the Government could easily help the latter to find employment within the British establishments, whether governmental or commercial. In this respect, the Committee's view differed from that of Archdeacon Baly. The Committee acknowledged their indebtedness to the educational efforts of Archdeacon Baly, who after all was *the* person who brought the case of European pauperism before the Government.[43] But, unlike Baly, members of the PC thought that school education offered only a partial solution. Though appalled by the extent to which the domiciled had declined economically, Baly still believed that the British could somehow transform its rising generations into employable youths and save the community as a whole from future unemployment. Members of the PC, however, found this view too optimistic:

the difficulty is experienced now more acutely than it was when the Archdeacon was making his enquiries 11 and 12 years ago, but be that as it may, we beg to place on record our dissent from the statement that all steady, sober, honest, industrious and able-bodied Indo-Europeans can find employment in Calcutta.[44]

The PC found, if reluctantly, that European business employers were not generally keen on taking domiciled persons, especially those from poor families. Even the railways, the biggest employer of the domiciled class since the mid-nineteenth century, would not recruit from the impoverished portion of the domiciled class. For example, in reply to the Committee's inquiry, the Bombay-Baroda and Central Indian Railway claimed:

> the class of persons in whose interest the Pauperism Committee are enquiring are understood to be principally composed of men without a profession or who have been thrown out of employment, and these men can find no work on railways.[45]

The company recommended a creation of special 'Homes' where these men could be given adequate disciplinary training. Disciplinary training, not preferential employment, would be the key to the solution of European pauperism. As another railway company, the Eastern Bengal State Railway, asserted, the whole difficulty was seen to lie in 'the want of thrift and improvident marriages among domiciled Europeans and Eurasians': at best, the domiciled poor might possibly be trained as domestic servants, postmen, or tailors, but emphatically not as railway employees.[46]

It was certainly true that past governments had made considerable use of the domiciled community for colonial administration and public works, and that, as a consequence, the class had grown dependent on the British for employment. But the Committee found that the present situation surrounding these avenues of employment was blatantly hostile to the domiciled class. Their view was that the British should face the fact that the pauperization of their domiciled brethren had already become a constitutional part of colonial Indian society. The kind of general scheme represented by Baly's education policy would be insufficient in addressing this particular problem of pauperism because the former underestimated the latter's depths and complexities in which the entire community had been entangled. Instead, the British in India should develop policies and institutions more specifically targeting the poorer sections of their domiciled fellows. The best the Government could do would be to sanction and generously support welfare efforts to suppress domiciled pauperism.

The Committee saw that it was with the recognition of this harsh reality that the British effort to regenerate their domiciled compatriots must begin. They should discharge their due responsibility by making the domiciled *unlearn* the latter's dependence on them, whilst providing alternative livelihoods outside British establishments. The PC condemned the ongoing practices of relief aid for allegedly making many members of the domiciled class habitual dependants, thus increasing the problem of pauperism instead of solving it. And it recommended establishing a new central organization, the Charity Organization Committee, which would supervise the distribution of relief aid so that it would not produce any more professional mendicants.[47] The Committee also recommended that the Government should launch special employment schemes to provide younger members of the community with fresh opportunities. The Government should sanction the establishment of a special military regiment composed exclusively of domiciled men. This would inculcate the male youths of the community not just in military skills (possibly opening the prospects of a career in soldiering), but also in endurance and self-discipline. The Government should also establish a training vessel in the river Hooghly. The harsh regime on board such a ship would provide them with a disciplined life and a possible career in the field of marine piloting.

The Government's response to these recommendations was not exactly encouraging. Charles Elliot, the Lieutenant-Governor of Bengal, did find that the ideas expressed by the PC possessed the seeds of genuine social reform. But he did not see how the colonial state could justify the spending of public money on policies that targeted one particular community without incurring an accusation of preferential treatment. The domiciled class was certainly an important group but at the same time it was only one of the many 'Native' groups to which the colonial state was equally responsible: 'Government can do nothing more than see that Europeans and Eurasians domiciled in India receive fair treatment, equally with other persons included in the term "natives of India"'.[48] Elliot largely denied financing the new schemes which the Committee had proposed. He ordered that the proposed re-organization of the charity regime, with a central charitable headquarters as its head, was too drastic. Instead of creating a new Charity Organization Committee, the British could continue to rely on the District Charitable Society for supervising the existing charitable societies available in Calcutta.[49] As for the two aforementioned youth-labour schemes, Elliot concluded that the state was not in a position to establish and finance schemes that did not benefit the Indian nation as a whole. There were no pre-existing demands, whether military, economic or otherwise, for domiciled regiments or marine pilots.[50]

The appointment of the PC was undoubtedly significant in that it informed British society of the sheer scale and complexities of European pauperism. It was a vivid illustration of how concerned many middle-class Britons were about their poor relations domiciled in India. But whilst bringing the question of the domiciled poor to the fore, the Committee fell short of convincing the Government of taking any truly radical measures for its solution.

The Calcutta Domiciled Community Enquiry Committee

After the PC ended, the appeal for the establishment of a communal military regiment and of a special vessel for pilot training continued to be made. But the Government remained committed to the view that such schemes would be unjustifiably costly. At the turn of the century the only substantial aid the Government was making for the domiciled class fell in the category of education. But even that was not producing tangible improvements when it came to the immediate relief of European pauperism: in all India there remained about 7,000 domiciled children who received no school education whatsoever. Domiciled paupers concomitantly presented their existence to the British as though to condemn the latter for their prolonged failure to bring the problem under control. Meanwhile, the problem of the domiciled poor had not only remained unsolved but had hardened into a chronic state, making *The Statesman* lament: 'Like the poor, the Eurasian problem is ever upon us'.[51] Increasingly, it was not as an appendix to the European colonial enterprise but as a pool of unfit individuals that the domiciled community were noticed. W. Francis, an ICS officer who was in charge of the Madras branch of the 1901 Census, noted that 'The popular idea that Eurasians are mainly employed as fitters or clerks or on the railways [was] clearly inaccurate'.[52] Most, he observed, were living 'on endowments on their relatives and friends, in convents, in lunatic asylums, in jail or by begging'.[53] The Conference on the Education of the Domiciled Community in India at Simla (1912) concluded that the problem of domiciled unemployment and pauperism was so deep-rooted that the only educational policies that could possibly effect a genuine solution were compulsory education and institutionalization of children in special orphanage-type schools.[54] As of the late 1910s, nothing about the domiciled class had changed for the better ever since the PC was appointed nearly three decades before, and only the danger seemed to have increased. As a missionary organ, the All-India Committee noted:

> There is a community of poor Europeans in the city of Calcutta, unrivalled in any slum in the world of misery and degradation. Here the rate of pauperism is higher than in any community in Christendom.[55]

It was out of the above sense of crisis that, in 1918, another committee, the Calcutta Domiciled Community Enquiry Committee (hereafter CDCEC), was launched. Unlike the PC, this CDCEC was not a Government initiative, but a private one. But it was clearly modelled on the former, with prominent Britons, such as the Right Reverend Bishop Lefroy (Metropolitan of India), J.H. Hechle, and Arden Wood as its founding members. The CDCEC's specific objective was to investigate the living condition of poor Europeans and the people of mixed descent living in Calcutta, and to make recommendations for ameliorating that condition.

The CDCEC re-confirmed that the state of indigence among the domiciled community was at a critical stage. A substantial number within the community lived in poverty and constituted what looked to be an urban 'residuum'. The Sub-Committee on Health and Physique noted that there were great numbers of domiciled persons who 'live below the poverty line and herd together like animals in unspeakably filthy, undrained slums, Indians and Anglo-Indians living side by side in mud and bamboo huts'.[56] What was alarming was that the lives of these impoverished people were so 'un-European' and presented little difference from those of certain poor-native inhabitants of the city. As it was noted: 'This class merges into the pure Indian Christian and a point is reached at which separation is difficult to determine'.[57]

In the CDCEC's view, faced with this plight of their domiciled brethren in Calcutta, the non-domiciled, wealthy Britons must come to their rescue without any delay. Instead of just minding their own career advancement and commercial profit-making, the British community should acknowledge its historical responsibility for the well-being of its impoverished domiciled relations:

> the community exists because of the coming to India of various European peoples and that it is the obvious duty of the immigrant European community to accept the burden of the troubles to which communally it had given birth. Apart from Government assistance in matters like education, comparatively little of the enterprise, the money, and the brains which are the special characteristics of the home-bone European community, would set in motion forces which would provide as speedy a remedy as so complex a problem is susceptible of. In so urging we include those who have made their money in India and who are now enjoying the fruits of their labour in Europe.[58]

But, unfortunately, the Committee found that European employers were almost invariably reluctant to recruit members of the domiciled class: 'The accusations levelled against the Domiciled Community by employers are condemnatory to an exceptional degree'.[59] Of the 61 firms that replied to the circular issued by the Committee, 21 reported that they employed members of the domiciled class.[60] These European managers found that the domiciled were far too undereducated and undisciplined to be recruited. The Committee took this verdict as a fact to be taken seriously. Employment would not be created out of sympathy, as the Committee observed: 'It is of little use appealing to the employer's sympathetic consideration; the business man has little time to enquire into the domestic conditions of the individual'.[61] The Committee argued that the British sympathizers should *not* work on behalf of the domiciled class to win partial treatments from employers. Rather they should work with the domiciled poor in an effort to improve their mental, hygienic and social fitness, with a view to increasing 'the earning capacity of the individual'.[62] After all, 'The community must apply self-help and improve their capacity for work of the natural demand'.[63]

According to the CDCEC, if there was anything that could be asked of British employers, it would be a generous donation of facilities and funds that would serve to improve the living condition of the domiciled youth, many of whom had been forced to live in dreadful slum environs.[64] The CDCED put greater weight, than the PC did, on the amelioration of living conditions. For the former, the problem of the domiciled poor was to a large extent one of environment – it was the slum condition of Calcutta that had shaped their social, cultural and racial selfhood. The effort of non-domiciled Britons to save their domiciled brethren had to start by ameliorating this very condition.

As for employment, the CDCEC largely followed the PC's view that the labour market within the Europe-related sectors, both civil and commercial, had been structurally closed, and that there was nothing practical to be done about it. The Committee expressed its regret that the Government had repeatedly denied the request for offering help to make domiciled youths into soldiers or pilots. Given the steady decline of employment opportunities, the demand for these special labour schemes had only increased.[65] What the British could do was to orient members of the domiciled community towards such occupations as artisanship and low-grade engineering. Employment had to be created in special arenas, as the domiciled were bound to lose both to 'home-born' British elites and to cost-efficient Indian workers.

The impact of reforms and recessions

The CDCEC was only right in observing that it was becoming ever more difficult for the domiciled to obtain state-related jobs. Especially after the re-organization of the Indian Civil Service following the Government of India Act (1919), the situation surrounding government and railway employment was disheartening for most of the domiciled community. Political leaders of the community vehemently complained that its members had been cruelly sacrificed in order to make room for their Indian fellows who had been vigorously empowered under the on-going scheme of political reforms, which gradually veered towards 'Home Rule'. To make matters worse, the 1920s saw an unprecedented problem of unemployment, which hit the already pauperized domiciled class especially hard. The post-war economic boom in 1919 had lured some men of the domiciled class to new businesses. To jump on these opportunities, which promised them larger salaries, they had resigned their appointments on railways or elsewhere. But when the booming economy collapsed in 1923, they were no longer able to return to their previous jobs and were quickly reduced to pauperism.[66] The numerous reports in *The Statesman* about this predicament demonstrates how seriously the colonial authorities took European pauperism. As for 'poor whites', who were not yet recognized as domiciled in India, the British tried to repatriate as many of them as possible. And as far as the domiciled class was concerned, they tried to reach those affected by the crisis through organizations such as the Ex-Services Association and the Anglo-Indian Unemployment Committee [AIUC], the second one of which had been run by the members of the domiciled community themselves.

The economic crisis was widely publicized through British papers such as *The Statesman*, which often quoted from the reports of the AIUC. These reports of the AIUC showed that, in the mid-1920s, Calcutta alone witnessed well over 1,000 people of the domiciled class who would not survive without immediate relief measures. The Committee's first report (covering the period since January 1924) indicated that the Committee had about 2,500 people of the domiciled class under its care.[67] The second report (covering October 1924–March 1925) revealed that the AIUC had on their rolls about 500 unemployed men. With their wives, children and other families included, the total number of people living in absolute poverty amounted to 1,500. Of these people, about 200 received regular weekly monetary relief.[68] The third report (April 1925–December 1925) showed that there were still 300 men and about 600–700 of their family members on the list, of whom 200 were in receipt of monetary relief.[69]

Reforming disorderly subjects: disciplinarian schemes and quests for alternative spaces

Within the frame of the inclusive politics of welfare, concerned British voices represented themselves as anti-racist. They argued that it was the racial prejudice against people of mixed descent that had served to marginalize the domiciled community. Both the PC and the CDCEC urged British society in India to discard stereotypical ideas about domiciled persons. The Secretary of the CDCEC argued it had already been proven that the admixture of blood did not lead to racial degeneration.[70] But this anti-racist gesture did not mean that colonial philanthropists were ready to admit that all problems relating to the domiciled class were caused by social contingencies external to the latter, such that they themselves had nothing to blame for their own impoverishment. On the contrary, they believed that much of the trouble derived from certain intrinsic traits of the domiciled poor themselves and argued that it was the duty of the non-domiciled British to point out these inimical traits. What is striking is the extent to which the views of these poverty commissions were similar to those of the so-called theory of hereditary urban degeneration, which in the 1880s and 1890s received widespread middle-class support in Britain and had institutional expression in various commissions of enquiry into the causes of distress in London. The PC, for one, argued that genuinely concerned Britons should not shy away from these 'defects', simply 'owing to the fear of wounding susceptibilities'.[71] Negative and painful as it might be, it was a 'duty' of Europeans to address the issue. The CDCEC argued along similar lines. It was a 'disagreeable

'Degenerate whites' and their spaces of disorder   171

task', but 'to enumerate some of the failings' was necessary so long as the employers of labour accused them.[72]

On the basis of statistical, sociological and anthropological analyses into the minute details of everyday lives, the PC asserted the following: because they inherited the blood of Europeans, the domiciled had too much of a 'pride of race'.[73] It was the 'defects of character more or less connected with this sentiment [of racial pride]' that 'seriously interfere[d] with Indo-Europeans in the struggle for work'.[74] As they were too proud of themselves, they characteristically disliked manual labour even when they led an impoverished living. And the poverty just became worse, because they went on spending to satisfy their vanity. In the PC's view, this false pride was built into the psyche of domiciled individuals to the extent that it was 'almost impossible to inculcate providence among persons thus circumstanced'.[75]

Such a view of the domiciled person as innately vain and indolent was also found in the academic discourse of Edgar Thurston, a renowned ethnologist and Superintendent of the Madras Government Museum. According to Thurston, the domiciled man was sickly prone to the love of luxury and pleasure. As a result of his characteristic 'want of thrift', there was a 'widespread tendency to allow expenditure to exceed income'.[76] Thus, the domiciled man became indebted, losing his credibility as an employee, and inevitably became unemployed.[77]

The above notion of false economic consciousness is nowhere better articulated than in the views presented by John MacRae in *The Calcutta Review* (1913). As a missionary based in Calcutta, he was well known for his enthusiastic commitment to the problem of pauperism among the domiciled community. MacRae's basic idea was that the pauperization of Calcutta's domiciled class was chiefly due to certain problems in the mental constitution of its members. Their poverty was not a real kind of poverty and the domiciled poor not genuinely a poor people: 'It does not seem real poverty. It occasions a strange lack of a sense of the value of things'.[78] To be sure, there were certain other factors too, such as the harsh climate and bad sanitary conditions, which might have helped to impoverish the domiciled, but these were nothing special, common to any other cases of poverty. When it came to the domiciled community, the real cause of its pauperization was an incapability of its members of knowing who they really were, and by extension, their tendency to mimic the ways of the British elites. According to MacRae, the domiciled could not recognize their difference from their non-domiciled brethren and, because of their racial connection with them, mistakenly assumed that they too could enjoy the latter's affluent life-style. Most 'British' in India were (at least by definition) 'bourgeois': they did not include a model working-class people from whom the domiciled might possibly learn an art of honest and humble living. As a result, the domiciled class took as its model what was actually a group of 'temporarily detached fragments of a large and complete organisation'.[79] The domiciled class ended up emulating the wealthy though they themselves were nothing but the indigent. MacRae wrote:

> It is to organise life on an artificial and not a real basis, it is to live a life out of harmony with the true facts of existence. The roots of the Anglo-Indian are not sufficiently deep in reality [...] He starts from a false position and his life is spent among shadows. He fails, of one thing, to distinguish between necessities and luxuries.[80]

According to this view, the 'British' in India and their 'domiciled' brethren occupied fundamentally distinct positions in the social order of colonial society. For MacRae, the only effective remedy for domiciled pauperism was to make the domiciled recognize this distinction. The British, on their part, should not simply assist them by giving aid too readily. They should rather try and discipline the domiciled into embracing the fundamental differences between them. As he said, 'Any attempt to help the Anglo-Indian socially or economically must begin by recognising this difference'.[81]

British philanthropists also thought that hygienic negligence fostered in the 'slum condition' had inscribed an inexorable mark on the body and mind of the domiciled. As the Secretary of the CDCEC wrote, 'the children of slum parents will have slum tendencies, irrespective of blood and country'.[82] One of such inimical 'slum tendencies' was early marriage. British observers were appalled by its degree and understood it as a major contribution to European pauperism. In 1891, *The Statesman* wrote that 'early and improvident marriages' were one of the greatest causes of pauperism and 'one of the most important services which the Eurasian and Anglo-Indian Association and similar societies can perform lies in discouraging such marriages'.[83] William Forbes-Mitchell, a self-claimed expert on the problem of the domiciled community, asserted that early marriages had 'done more to degenerate and abase the race than any other influence'.[84] Many took early marriage as one of the symptoms of the 'innate' improvidence of the domiciled.[85] Edgar Thurston remarked that the results were too frequently disastrous, with 'a plethora of children, brought up in poverty, hunger, and dirt; but little to earn and many to keep; domestic unrest; insolvency; and destitution'.[86] He also attributed early marriage to an 'innate' immorality of the domiciled: 'I may hazard a guess that it is because they have not acquired the power to "subordinate animal appetite to reason, foresight, and prudence"'.[87]

But others thought that early marriage was itself a direct consequence of the slum environment in which the domiciled poor lived. The CDCEC's Sub-Committee on Health and Physique reported that most early marriages were the inevitable result of over-crowded living conditions: 'In many cases lads and girls of 14 to 18 years of age are sleeping in the same hut, with the inevitable result that the girls are ruined morally and physically at an early age'.[88]

'Degenerate whites' and their spaces of disorder 173

Because of the housing conditions of the slums, immoral sexual relations were said to have often led to incest. As a consequence, the Sub-Committee wrote, 'we have succeeding generations of weaklings, diseased and weak-minded poverty-stricken people'.[89] In their view, the question of Calcutta's domiciled paupers was 'not only the legacy of bye-gone progenitors, but the consequence of the utterly unwholesome conditions in the recent and present generations'.[90]

In order to check these psychological and hygienic tendencies among the domiciled class, a number of suggestions were made. As far as the psychological side was concerned, the British thought it necessary to regulate access to charitable relief. The organization of various European charitable efforts was necessary not just to extend the ground covered but in order to distinguish between those who were really in need of relief and those who were not. It was as important to exclude from the scheme of charity those who volunteered to live on charity even though they were able-bodied. In fact, charity had been criticized for giving relief far too readily and indiscriminately. Such a way of giving out relief did not solve pauperism but increased it by nurturing among the poor a disregard for labour. As MacRae noted: 'to give money is usually not to strike at the roots of poverty but to water them'.[91] Charity did not help the poorer classes of the domiciled to become independent but rather enabled them to live as 'parasites'.[92] The PC recognized this problem of charitable aid only too well. It warned that pensions or doles had been given in ways that:

> destroy all spirit or love of independence and respect which springs from a person being self-supporting, but not sufficient to obviate the necessity of seeking further help elsewhere, and thereby converting the recipient into a skilful and professional mendicant.[93]

The PC identified the psychological factor as the prime cause of pauperism and in that connection criticized the existing mode of charitable relief. By failing to take the psychological dimension into account, European relief efforts were positively fostering the pauperization of the domiciled class.

What was ultimately thought necessary was to introduce a 'scientific' view of the phenomenon of pauperism. Calcutta was said to be a backward place, where the old conception of poverty, represented in the 1834 Poor Law in England, had still been observed. The charitable system of the colonial periphery had to be upgraded to the metropolitan standard, and one vital thing that had to be done urgently was the application of a more strict set of criteria to include only the deserving poor.[94] To counter pauperism, it was imperative not to help those who were just lazy or too proud to stain their own hands. These people had to be disciplined in reformatory and educational institutions, instead of being spoiled by charity. And in certain cases, coercive institutionalization in the alms house or workhouse should be done to subject the paupers to a thorough process of confinement and discipline.

Thus, both the PC and the CDCEC recommended a stronger degree of the institutional confinement of the domiciled poor in the alms- and workhouses.[95]

With regard to hygienic problems, nothing would be more important than European support for the effort to ameliorate living environments. This concern was addressed particularly explicitly by the CDCEC, which took housing as the most important of all problems. As its Sub-Committee on Housing observed:

> If living conditions remain such that physical health and moral family life are difficult or impossible, efforts to raise the community by improved education and other means are bound to be largely infructuous.[96]

Such ugly conditions would inevitably cause a hygienic and sexual degeneration of the domiciled class, and for this the poor themselves were hardly to blame.[97] The non-domiciled British community should assume responsibility and provide them with better housing. The Sub-Committee especially noted that rents were excessively high even for the relatively well-to-do sections of the domiciled class. At rents within the means of the poor, sanitary and decent accommodation could hardly be obtained. Thus, the Sub-Committee recommended that European capitalists and charities combine their capital and energies to construct new buildings. For this, endeavour should be made to establish a trust or registered association. For the better classes, houses of economical construction should be built on the cheapest land obtainable and rented at Rs. 50 to Rs. 100 a month. The Government should exercise compulsory powers for acquiring suitable land in large blocks. For the poorest classes, tenement dwellings should be built by European capital. Charitable funds should help the tenants pay the rents.[98]

Alternative ways of living

Along with the organization of charity and improvement of racial hygiene, colonial efforts to alleviate the pauperization of the domiciled community pointed to more radical measures as well. British officials were increasingly convinced that the question at hand would remain unsolved unless they could remove the domiciled poor from the social and economic context of the city altogether. The reasons were multiple. First, the psychological 'trait' of the domiciled – namely the supposed tendency of mimicking Europeans whilst despising Indians – would not be completely removed so long as they lived among the two groups. Second, their hygienic 'degeneration' would not be avoided unless the domiciled grew up outside the urban slums of Calcutta or other urban centres. Third, the city did not provide its domiciled inhabitants with any new avenues of employment: welfare policies would not ultimately solve the question of pauperism so long as no employment was forthcoming.

And fourth, their impoverished existence would not be shielded from the eyes of colonized subjects as long as they lived among them. In view of these problems, the British thought it necessary to isolate the domiciled poor from the social and cultural influences of the city. And they also saw it indispensable to somehow coordinate social relocation with education, vocational training, and employment. Throughout the late colonial period, British philanthropic circles considered several schemes to realize this synthesis of isolation and labour. As mentioned earlier, these schemes, among others, included military and marine training, agricultural resettlement, and emigration. It is worthwhile to look at the proposed measures in greater detail.

Regimental discipline

The idea of creating a military regiment entirely and solely composed of domiciled-class youth derived from a concern that men of this class characteristically lacked discipline and a healthy attitude to labour. A Calcutta mercantile company, Anderson, Wright & Co., wrote to the PC that it had employed several such men but found them particularly unsatisfactory, and therefore would no longer employ them even on an experimental basis. It supported the idea of forming a military regiment because, it argued, 'the best chance of making men of them would be to place them under military discipline'.[99] Another company, Whitney Brothers, wrote similarly in favour of a military regiment, as 'The training they would receive would go a long way in teaching them self-reliance and habits of industry'.[100] European capitalists were generally sympathetic to the plight of the domiciled community, but they would not employ the latter for charity. These opinions exercised a decisive influence on the PC's decision to recommend to the Government the formation of a military regiment.[101] Seeing that almost all avenues of employment had been closed, the Committee came to regard the special regiment as 'the only one remedy at all adequate to the disease'.[102] The disciplinary aspect of the regiment scheme would provide a promising philanthropic solution to the question of European pauperism.

An isolated and disciplined environment of regimental life would eradicate from domiciled youth all the undesirable traces of family and communal life. The special regiment would continue to subject them to institutional discipline even after their post-schooling years. As the PC remarked: 'the pernicious home-influences which have been so often referred to would be intercepted and precluded from undoing the effects of school-life'.[103] Once institutionalized, they would be taught the ethic of a labouring life, an alleged lack of which had made them unemployable to begin with. It would also prevent early marriages: 'Service with a regiment will check, if not entirely put a stop to, the improvident marriages which young men are now only too ready to contract'.[104] A period of discipline and supervision may also reform the minds and bodies of those who had already become loafers and paupers.[105]

Marine training

Along with a special military regiment, the PC thought that the creation of a government-sanctioned training vessel would alleviate the social and economic plight of the domiciled poor. The Committee recommended a scheme for a training-ship on the River Hooghly modelled after institutions of a similar nature found in British waters. Those British concerned with European pauperism thought that the sort of training provided by a training vessel would offer an ideal period of institutional discipline and would possibly lead the trainees to a related career afterwards. Life on a training vessel would help domiciled youth to acquire self-discipline, and it would also enable a necessary isolation from their families.

But the problem with the proposed scheme was that it was not expected to automatically prepare the domiciled trainees for an employment in piloting. As far as the recruitment policy of the colonial pilot service was concerned, there had traditionally been a more favourable atmosphere towards domiciled pilots than towards their Indian counterparts. But by the late 1870s, the domiciled had been rigidly excluded from this service, due to a policy of Europeanization whereby the authorities preferred those home-born Britons trained at a metropolitan institution. Because of the 'inferior' environment and education facilities India offered, the domiciled were regarded as not fit enough for this service. In theory, domiciled youth could still try and join the service by going to the metropole to be trained on a British training vessel, but in practice few of them could afford it. Thus, the proposal by the Committee was rejected by Charles Eliot on the grounds of impracticality. The Lieutenant-Governor noted, rightly enough, that it would not guarantee the participants employment opportunities after their training.[106] After discharge, the trainees would return to the world of indigence from whence they came.

Despite the aforementioned problems, the idea of pilot training continued to prove appealing in European philanthropic circles. Aside from the claim for the state-sanctioned creation of a special ship in India,[107] pleas were also made for allowing individual domiciled youths to be trained together with British trainees in British waters. A decade after the PC, the authorities finally conceded to this plan a scheme for sending, on an experimental basis, a certain number of selected boys to some training-vessels operating in British waters. In 1906–08, about 20 domiciled youths were sent to a British training-vessel, *Southampton*, from a famous orphanage called St. Andrew's Colonial Homes, and several of them did succeed in obtaining a career in piloting.[108]

Agricultural communes

An alternative way of isolation and disciplining was the idea of relocating the lives of such domiciled persons in the cities to distant places in or even

'Degenerate whites' and their spaces of disorder   177

outside of India. The possible efficacy of agricultural re-settlement in alleviating unemployment and pauperism was recognized from as early as the end of the eighteenth century, and at least by the mid-1870s, inscribed itself firmly in public awareness. One of the self-help efforts of the 'associations' of the domiciled, the first of which was established in Calcutta in 1876 was to promote the agricultural settlement of the poorer members of the community. Concerned Britons responded to this with a great interest. Many thought that it could (and should) be a field for Governmental support. As a form of philanthropy, it appeared to offer a radical solution to European pauperism. It would permanently remove the domiciled class from their urban dwellings, where all their problems were supposedly engendered.

In 1876, the newly founded Eurasian and Anglo-Indian Association asked the Government to sanction an agricultural scheme in the countryside. This elicited a favourable response from the British community, as it would offer: 'a fair chance of raising the "poor whites" and Eurasian population from the depths of misery and degradation into which that unfortunate class had been allowed to sink'.[109] Though the proposed scheme did not see fruition, it did gain certain sympathy within government circles, notably Richard Temple, the Lieutenant-Governor of Bengal. In Southern India, D. S. White, the President of the Anglo-Indian and Domiciled-European Association of Southern India, worked energetically and by the early 1880s created the Whitefield and Sausmond Colonies near Bangalore, and the Southern Eurasian Colony in Mysore. Agricultural settlement was not confined to the hill tracts alone. In 1921, a penal colony on the Andaman Islands was abandoned. It was decided that the Islands would be transformed into a free settlement, with a peasant population now added to native and convict populations. The Ex-Services Association helped a few ex-soldiers of the domiciled class to settle on the Islands as agriculturalists, with monthly doles, servants, free outfits, passages, rations, lodgings and land grants. This 'Andaman Scheme' intended to ease the ensuring pressure of the economic slump in the early 1920s. In addition, in the early 1930s, a 'utopian' colonization scheme for the domiciled class was started in Bihar, and was named the McCluskiegunge Colony, after E.T. McCluskie, a prominent activist of the domiciled community.

But there was still concern that the domiciled poor were not fit for agricultural settlement. Such a scheme would require a strong initiative on the part of the intending settlers. It was only out of a negative reason (namely, that their lives in the urban areas were shuttered) that domiciled setters took up an agricultural life. While acknowledging their possible use, *The Friend of India*, and *Statesman* wrote of the domiciled people who were to be involved in the agricultural schemes initiated by D. S. White:

> are they, either physically or morally, a class of men who would be expected to succeed in a calling where unremitting labour, hard and often unthankful [...] is required?[110]

And commenting on the Andamans scheme, *The Statesman* lamented that the settlers had been drawn 'from too limited a class and subjugated to demoralising influences from the onset'.[111] On this, even the leader of the domiciled community, Henry Gidney, had to agree:

> it does not follow, of course, that Anglo-Indians are incapable of sustained physical effort, but it seems that the men selected to take part in these experiments have not all been of the right class.[112]

Moreover, agricultural schemes were often poorly funded. Writing about such plans in southern India, *The Madras Times* pointed out that a want of funding was an obstacle as the association could not always raise enough capital.[113] Also lacking was a dissemination of knowledge/skills and an organized guidance to use them properly. Cannon Russell Payro, reporting on the 12 men installed in the Andamans, said the failure of these makeshift colonists was attributable to a lack of guidance. Material provision was necessary but it was not everything.[114]

In spite of these difficulties, however, the idea of agricultural settlement remained popular among certain colonial philanthropists. Agriculture would give the poorer classes of the domiciled community a chance for a fresh start. The cool climate enjoyed by most agricultural colonies, such as Whitefield, would do much to restore the domiciled from the 'degeneration' of their body, considered inevitable in the plains of India.[115] Agricultural settlement would also offer an ideal social context for discipline, especially in the absence of both 'superior' Europeans to ask for help and of 'inferior' Indians to depend on for domestic work. Now they would have to be self-reliant, which would naturally orient them towards a spirit of independence and love of labour. As *The Statesman* observed: 'some of our "loafing" population might honourably redeem the wretched life they lead in our cities'. Through 'humbling themselves to honourable toil' in the upland district, they would come to denounce their 'invincible repugnance' to menial labour.[116] They would get rid of their 'false pride'[117] and learn the 'dignity of labour'.[118]

Emigration

Along with agricultural re-settlement, there were attempts to send domiciled youths to other parts of the British Empire, such as South Africa, Australia and New Zealand, and install them as farmers or menial labourers. These were largely 'self-help' efforts by the associations of the domiciled community, but many British were also involved, sometimes making their own initiatives. In Madras, for instance, the Madras Emigration Society was established and run by prominent members of the city's British community. The emigration scheme of the Friend-in-Need Society was also mooted by Europeans.[119] In Bengal, the Scottish missionary, the Rev. John Graham, enthusiastically encouraged and assisted the pupils of his St. Andrew's Colonial Homes to emigrate to British settler colonies, in particular Australia and New Zealand. By the mid-1930s, Graham sent more than fifty to New Zealand, eleven to Australia, four to the United States, one to South Africa.[120] There were hopes that, in such 'setter colonies', where the land had been tilled by Europeans, members of the domiciled class would forget their old dislike of manual labour and start a new life as labouring settlers. As *The Englishman* observed:

> It may be that this prejudice against a person engaged in manual labour which exists amongst all classes of Anglo-Indian society [i.e. British society in India] has done a good deal to foster a dislike to it amongst Eurasians who are extremely susceptible to anything like contempt or reproach. In Australia this feeling does not exist.[121]

In spite of such enthusiasm, the fact remained that many practical problems presented themselves to the idea of overseas settlement. The emigration of domiciled persons was not related to imperial territorial expansion in any positive sense. Nor was it indented as a way to supply labour to areas where there were perceived shortages. There was no intrinsic economic demand and, as such, there existed rigid barriers in the labour market. Labour competition existed in other British colonies as well, in ways that would disadvantage the domiciled class of British India. In South Africa, the domiciled would not qualify to enter the Imperial British East Africa Company, which was just as selective when it came to recruitment. On the other hand, India's domiciled youths would not be needed as menial labour in a labour market that was already full of working-class labourers.[122] In Australia, there was already a large presence of Chinese labour, which would easily undersell the domiciled workforce.[123] And, particularly in Australia, there also existed an issue of racism towards mixed-race persons, whose 'brown-ness' was frowned upon.[124] In any case, it appeared difficult to send abroad members of the domiciled class in large numbers. The CDCEC had read with interest the plan of a proposed scheme for colonization in British East Africa. But they thought that 'it would be difficult to make such a scheme, or indeed any other scheme for emigration, successful on a sufficiently large scale to affect the conditions of the Domiciled Community'.[125] The domiciled class had little capital when they wanted to start out a new farm or an industry of their own. They would be as unfit a labourer abroad as in India, as *The Statesman* wrote:

> it would be a fatal mistake of any clerks, or persons unaccustomed to work, to venture to either country, as the first [Australia] requires hardy, sturdy colonists with a little capital; and in the second [South Africa] the labour market is contested, and there is not the slightest opening for a young man without a grade.[126]

The fact that emigration was continually considered as an alternative, in spite of all these foreseeable problems, was itself a testimony to the graveness of the domiciled's employment situation in India. That non-domiciled Britons continued to support these 'self-help' efforts reflected a sober pessimism that no place in British India could be found for their domiciled brethren: their life had to belong elsewhere. Such perspectives on emigration were well articulated in a pamphlet by the Rev. O. Younghusband, written in the wake of the political reforms starting in the late 1910s. He insisted upon 'abolishing' the very presence of the domiciled community in India. For him, tackling unemployment and pauperism by philanthropic or educational measures was ultimately insufficient as long as it was done in India. He argued that the issue of European pauperism in India could be solved only by removing the children of the domiciled class from that country and then transferring them to other British overseas territories. As the repeatedly elected President of the Domiciled Community of Northern India, Younghusband attended one of the Committees of the Montagu-Chelmsford Reforms (1919). Then he realized that the existence of the domiciled community in the post-Reform India found no positive meanings either from the European or Indian point of view.[127] In any case, he thought, the domiciled class was not a self-wanted community; most remained domiciled in India only because they could not afford to leave.[128] He insisted that it was important to educate the new, rising generation of the domiciled community in order to make them suitable for the 'export scheme', which he had undertaken as his own task. Younghusband defined it as a responsibility of the Government to provide necessary conditions for carrying out the actual transplanting of young domiciled youths of British India across the different dominions of the British Empire:

> it would be best to take an interest in keenly spirited boys in Hill Schools so that they may not become poor whites, to take an interest in them both for their own sakes and for the future of the British Empire, to give them financial and other encouragement so that they may play a useful and valuable part in the building up of the young Dominions Overseas.[129]

In reality, none of the four schemes above can be said to have been successful, let alone being enough to solve domiciled pauperism. But the very fact that they emerged as possible alternatives at all demonstrated the severity of the problem at hand. Under these schemes, labour and discipline would complement each other as a means to transform the attitude of the domiciled towards labour. And this disciplinary transformation was itself conditioned by a possibility of social and physical relocation, whether by institutionalization or by migration. What those radical measures would purport to achieve was to remove the domiciled from the labour competition in colonial society, and from the problematic dialectic of colonizer/colonized, out of which they had allegedly developed their characteristic dependency and misguided self-understanding. Non-domiciled Britons believed that in supporting these schemes they were committing themselves to a worthy imperial cause. James Luke, for one, defined the institution of marine training as a 'modest contribution towards the solution of the ['Eurasian'] problem', a problem which 'has long been a puzzle to the Government of India'.[130] And still earlier, in the late 1870s, Richard Temple, acknowledged the effort at internal migration as 'one of the most important measures' [that can possibly solve] 'a difficulty which has been puzzling the brains of the most astute of Her Majesty's representatives in this country'.[131]

Concluding remarks: urban pauperism in the colony and the metropole

What do our explorations of the question of Calcutta's domiciled poor tell us about the bourgeois social order in the age of empire? How and why did the question of pauperism threaten the British vision of class and racial hierarchies? The attitudes of middle-class Britons towards their poor relations domiciled in India were immensely complex and were not always so coherent as to allow any simplistic historiographical reductions. Still, some of these complexities and ambivalences might be able to be untangled by bringing both European and colonial experiences of urban pauperism under a single framework of analysis. It is with a brief attempt in this direction that I wish to conclude this chapter.

In the colonizing context, the sort of social order the ruling authorities sought to forge was first and foremost a racialized order. The key to such order was a high degree of segregation between colonizer and colonized, or 'civilizer' and 'civilized', and for legitimatizing such segregation, it was the idea of environment, or 'milieu', that was particularly cherished at the time. As was pointed out in the early pages of this chapter, especially from the mid-nineteenth century onwards, it was almost a shared article of faith that white residents from Britain must remain as aloof as possible from the environs of the Indian plains. Ultimately, the 'whiteness' of Britons would be guaranteed only through a social connection with the metropole. It was partly this uniquely colonial configuration of whiteness that served to alienate both Domiciled Europeans and Eurasians from the province of an authentic whiteness: born and bred in India, they were no longer regarded as meaningfully tied to the 'civilized' milieu of British society found on the other side of the globe.

But the exclusion of the domiciled population, and of its pauperized section in particular, cannot simply be explained in terms of *country* of domicile alone. As mentioned at the beginning of this chapter, Britain's middle class had already located their 'inferiors', or 'others', within the confines of the United Kingdom, particularly in its densely populated metropolis, London. Spatial self-segregation, in fact, was not uniquely a colonial phenomenon. In Victorian London, its middle-class residents had gradually moved out of the city centre towards the suburbs, creating therein the 'healthy' and 'refined' environs that suited their bourgeois standards, whilst geographically disconnecting themselves from the inner-city slums allegedly inhabited by so-called 'degenerates'.[132] The various stereotypes enumerated in this paper appear to indicate that India's domiciled poor also came under such a schema of urban segregation with similar ideologies and practices. Reformist interventionists, both governmental and philanthropic, saw their domiciled clients not simply as a population having 'gone native' but simultaneously as one exhibiting all the symptoms of slum environs. To this extent, the origins of British attitudes towards India's domiciled poor can be traced to the late-Victorian and Edwardian class attitudes. Domiciled Europeans and Eurasians were essentially a land-less population and their collective pauperization could easily lead to the creation of slums, as was just observed in the case of Calcutta. And this characteristically slum condition gave fertile ground for the domiciled poor to be thrown into the bourgeois networks of urban-poverty control, which had been going thorough substantial modernization in Britain. As far as the poorest members of Calcutta's domiciled community were concerned, the colonial observers disparaged them not simply because of their colonial domicile but also because of their utter immersion in an *urban* milieu. The extent to which this was the case can be seen not only in the highly stereotypical descriptions of the domiciled poor, but also in those kinds of policy measures, such as agricultural colonization and marine-training schemes, which were meant to eradicate their 'traits' which were seen as particularly 'urban'.

In fact, some of the collective disciplinary measures discussed in this chapter look never remote from those that had been practiced in the British context. Marine training, for instance, had long been instituted as one way of preventing pauperized children from becoming delinquents or criminals. At the beginning of the twentieth century, roughly around the same time as James Luke advocated a 'training-ship institution' for India's domiciled children, marine training was taken up by the National Incorporated Association for the Reclamation of Destitute Waif Children (or more famously known as Dr Barnardo's Homes).[133] Farm colonies had also been established in some European countries like Germany, Denmark and Holland with a specific aim of sheltering and reforming the unemployed.[134] In Britain, the idea was famously adopted by the founder of the Salvation Army, General Booth.[135] In what Booth called 'Farm Colonies', those slum inhabitants who were otherwise regarded as 'unemployables' would be relocated to the countryside, learning agricultural skills whilst diluting themselves of the malicious influences of their previous urban existence. Champions of more 'social-scientific' kinds of philanthropy, such as Charles Booth, were not so optimistic about the possible reformatory effects of such agricultural colonies. But even they were to praise the Hadleigh Farm, an agricultural colony in Essex established by the Salvation Army as a useful anti-slum measure.[136] Thus, in Britain, as well as in India, agricultural re-settlement was supposed to give the urban poor of white descent a chance to geographically isolate themselves from the alleged causes of 'degeneration' and thereafter acquire the ethic of labouring life. Finally, emigration had also been conceived, just as in British India, as the final resort. In fact, General Booth's farm colonies had been designed as none other than a preliminary step to the wholesale emigration of the residuum, which was the final goal of his entire scheme in the first place. Hadleigh, for one, evolved into a farm-training institution meant specifically for those emigrating overseas, especially after 1905.[137]

In order for the British ruling classes to alleviate the question of the inner-city slums, it was overseas colonies that were often recalled as the ultimate destination for unemployable urban paupers. This policy of emigration as a way of displacing urban poverty is undoubtedly one of the most important dimensions of the relationship between empire and class. But our study on Calcutta's domiciled poor sheds light on another, lessknown dimension: it shows one instance where an overseas colony was not a solution to the question of urban poverty but rather a problematic ground for its re-incarnation. British colonial cities, ranging from Calcutta through Madras to Johannesburg, required as much politics against the urban poor, as did London.[138] In such a context, London provided Calcutta's white community with an important model case as to how the problem of urban pauperism could be dealt with in a modern, 'social-scientific' way.

From a wider perspective, the re-incarnation of anti-poverty policies in colonial Calcutta may be taken to indicate what Ann Stoler has identified as certain vulnerabilities inherent in imperial rule itself. According to Stoler, the instabilities of colonial social order were inevitably caused by an often heterogeneous composition of colonial white populations, whose origins, in turn, could be traced to class divisions characteristic of European bourgeois societies. In a racialized context of colonial rule, both the question of 'poor whites' and that of miscegenation, which were often inseparable from one another, presented a major affront as the presence of impoverished and racially mixed whites problematically blurred the boundaries between colonizer and colonized. Racism, as Stoler insightfully argues, was most intense around areas of class and racial ambiguities, and it operated in ways that identified and disciplined those whose whiteness was deemed dubious.[139] Calcutta's white community was a case *par excellance* where such an internal politics of race was deployed. The very existence of the domiciled poor contradicted the class and racial orders of bourgeois society. And furthermore, being situated right at the heart of the colonial encounter, the internal threat posed by 'our own heathen' was even more substantial and urgent than Henry Mayhew would have imagined from the far-off metropole.

Notes

1 For the rise of the middle class in Britain, see, for example, E. Hobsbawm, *The Age of Capital: 1848–1875*, New York: Vintage Books, 1996.

2 On the Boer War, see, R. Soloway, 'Counting the Degenerates: The Statistics of Race Deterioration in Edwardian England', *Journal of Contemporary History*, 17, 1982: 137–64.
3 Quoted in G. Himmelfarb, *The Idea of Poverty: England in the Early Industrial Age*, London: Faber and Faber, 1984, pp. 327–28.
4 On the 'social-scientific' approach to urban poverty, see, R. Nye, 'The Bio-Medical Origins of Urban Sociology', *Journal of Contemporary History*, 20, 1985: 659–75. For a comprehensive overview of the Social-Darwinist and eugenicist discourses of national fitness, see Bernard Semmel's pioneering work on 'social imperialism', B. Semmel, *Imperialism and Social Reform: English Social-Imperial Thought, 1895–1914*, London: Faber and Faber, 1960.
5 C. Masterman, *The Heart of Empire: Discussions of Modern City Life in England with an Essay on Imperialism*, London: Fisher Unwin, 1902 [reprinted in J. Marriott and M. Matsumura (eds), *The Metropolitan Poor: Semi-Factual Accounts, 1795–1910, vol.3, People of the Abyss, 1885–1910*, London: Pickering & Chatto, 1999, p. 225.
6 Ibid., pp. 226–27.
7 For an overview of the conceptual and ideological meanings of 'residuum' and 'urban degeneration', see G. Jones, *Outcast London*, New York: Pantheon, 1984.
8 It should be pointed out here that this inferiorizing process was also a gendered affair, where those who had the upper hand were not just white and bourgeois but were also male. See, for example, C. Hall, *White, Male and Middle Class*, New York: Routledge, 1992.
9 Mayhew was not the first in representing the 'racial' otherness of the poor. Susan Thorn's work shows how missionaries in the late eighteenth and early nineteenth centuries brought back colonialist vocabularies of racial demarcation to describe the perceived exoticness of the domestic underclass whom they wished to 'civilize'. S. Thorn, '"The Conversion of Englishmen and the Conversion of the World Inseparable": Missionary Imperialism and the Language of Class in Early Industrial Britain', in A. Stoler and F. Cooper (eds), *Tensions of Empire: Colonial Cultures in a Bourgeois World*, Berkeley, CA: University of California Press, 1997, 238–62.
10 It is Ann Laura Stoler's seminal writings that have inspired many students of colonialism, including myself, into inquiring into the nature of these 'questions' across the continents. See A. Stoler, *Race and Education of Desire*, Durham, NC: Duke University Press, 1995 and the seminal articles now collected in A. Stoler, *Carnal Knowledge and Imperial Power*, Berkeley, CA: California University Press, 2002.
11 *South Africa, Report of the Minutes of Evidence to the Select Committee of the House of Assembly on European Employment and Labour Conditions*, Cape Town: SC9, 1913, quoted in S. Parnell, 'Creating Racial Privilege: the Origins of South African Public Health and Town Planning Legislation', *Journal of Southern African Studies*, 19, 1993, 471–88, p. 475.
12 Quoted in 'Children of the Poor', *The Friend of India [Weekly]*, 2 June 1864, p. 594.
13 It was David Arnold who first pointed out this high proportion of 'poor whites' and 'Eurasians' among British India's white population in the late nineteenth and early twentieth centuries. See D. Arnold, 'European Orphans and Vagrants in India in the Nineteenth Century', *The Journal of Imperial and Commonwealth History*, 7, 1979: 104–27. For more recent studies, see, H. Fischer-Tiné, 'Britain's Other Civilising Mission: Class-prejudice, European "Loaferism" and the Workhouse System in Colonial India', *Indian Economic and Social History Review*, 3, 2005: 295–338. S. Mizutani, 'Constitutions of the Colonising Self in Late British India: Race, Class and Environment', *Zinbun: Annals of the Institute for Research in Humanities, Kyoto University*, 38, 2005: 21–75.

14 See the introduction to their edited book, F. Cooper and A. Stoler, 'Between Metropole and Colony: Rethinking a Research Agenda' in Stoler and Cooper, *Tensions of Empire*, pp. 1–56.
15 Mizutani, 'Constitutions of the Colonising Self', pp. 24–29.
16 E. Buettner, *Empire Families*, Oxford: Oxford University Press, 2004.
17 On these soldiers, see D. Peers, 'Privates off Parade: Regimenting Sexuality in the Nineteenth-Century Indian Empire', *The International History Review*, 20, 1998: 823–54.
18 On the Vagrancy Act, see Arnold, 'European Orphans and Vagrants', p. 120.
19 The domiciled Europeans included Europeans of other nationalities (such as French or Portuguese) though, mostly, they were of British extraction.
20 The author is well aware that a careless use of these two terms, 'Domiciled European' and 'Eurasian', would not be unproblematic. First of all, historically, there were certain alternative names by which these groups of people were called. This was especially true of people of mixed-descent, who were called 'Indo-Europeans', 'half-castes', and so forth, as well as 'Eurasians'. Second, these terms were often laden with certain class and racist sentiments of derogatory nature. It was partly because of this that the leaders of the 'associations' representing these two groups insisted, since the end of the nineteenth century, that the mixed-race community be given a new nomenclature 'Anglo-Indian', a term which had hitherto been used to denote non-domiciled Britons living in the subcontinent. As a result, since 1911, people of mixed-descent with European blood on the paternal line have officially been called 'Anglo-Indians'. It is mainly for the sake of stylistic simplicity that, despite these historical complexities, I will use 'Domiciled European' and 'Eurasian', and without the parentheses, throughout this chapter.
21 For the earlier history of Eurasians, see C. Hawes, *Poor Relations: The Making of a Eurasian Community in British India, 1773–1833*, Richmond: Curzon Press, 1996.
22 The dominant scientific view of the day was that an uncontrolled exposure to the tropical climate, and, to the environment of the plains more generally, would make Britons 'degenerate'. See, M. Harrison, *Public Health in British India: Anglo-Indian Preventive Medicine 1859–1914*, Cambridge: Cambridge University Press, 1994, pp. 36–59.
23 On the practical and ideological roles of European hill-stations see, D. Kennedy, *The Magic Mountains: Hill Stations of the British Raj*, Berkeley, CA: University of California Press, 1996.
24 Children were sent off to Britain in their early ages. For a detailed study of this practice and its social and political implications, see Buettner, *Empire Families*.
25 Mizutani, 'Constitutions of the Colonising Self', pp. 61–73.
26 On the employment of the domiciled by the railway companies, see D. Arnold, 'White Colonisation and Labour in Nineteenth-Century India', *The Journal of Imperial and Commonwealth History*, 11, 1983: 133–58. and L. Bear, 'Miscegenations of Modernity: constructing European respectability and race in the Indian railway colony, 1857–1931', *Women's History Review*, 3, 1994: 531–48.
27 Quoted in 'Children of the Poor'.
28 The passage had appeared in Cotton's call for a state intervention in the education of the domiciled community.
29 *Review of Education in India in 1886*, Calcutta: Government of India, 1888, p. 294.
30 *The Friend of India [Weekly]*, 28 April 1864, 451.
31 'East Indians', *The Friend of India [Weekly]*, 22 September 1864, 1067–68.
32 'A Loafer', *The Friend of India [Weekly]*, 1 June 1871, p. 628.
33 *Report of the Calcutta Domiciled Community Enquiry Committee,1918–19*, Calcutta: Bengal Secretariat Press, 1920 [*Report of the CDCEC* hereafter], p.173.

34 G. Potenger, 'Letters to the Editor; The Eurasian Question', *The Statesman [Weekly]*, 28 June 1890, p. 1.
35 'Pauperism in Calcutta', *The Statesman [Weekly]*, 24 January 1891, 3.
36 *Report of the Pauperism Committee*, Calcutta: Bengal Secretariat Press, 1892 [*Report of the PC* hereafter], p. 1.
37 *Report of the PC*, p. 3.
38 Ibid., p. xiii.
39 Ibid., p. xv.
40 Ibid., p. xiii.
41 Ibid., p. 12.
42 Ibid., p. lviii.
43 Ibid., p. 12.
44 Ibid., p. 16.
45 Ibid., p. lxii.
46 Ibid., p. lxiv.
47 Ibid., p. 9, 17.
48 Ibid., p. 3.
49 'General Department, Miscellaneous – no. 2263, Calcutta, 8 August 1892, RESOLUTION' in *Proceedings of the Lieutenant-Governor of Bengal, General Department – Miscellaneous, Calcutta, September 1892* (Oriental and India Office Collections of the British Library [hereafter OIOC]; P/4089), p. 4, 9.
50 Ibid., pp. 4–7.
51 'The Eurasian Problem', *The Statesman [Weekly]*, 13 April 1899, 5
52 *The Census of India, 1901: vol. XV: Madras: Part I – Report*, Madras: Government of India, 1902, pp. 204–5.
53 Ibid., p. 205.
54 Though the Government did not in the end endorse the recommendation for compulsory education.
55 The All-India Committee, *'The European of India': A responsibility and an opportunity*, in M. Turner (ed.), *An alien in his own country*, London: (publisher unknown), 191-, collected in *Pamphlets* (OIOC P/T/314), pp. 3–4.
56 *Report of the CDCEC*, p. 141.
57 Ibid., p. 135.
58 Ibid., p. 2.
59 Ibid., p. 134.
60 Ibid., p. 138.
61 Ibid., p. 137.
62 Ibid., p. 137.
63 Ibid., p. 138.
64 Ibid., p. 22, 138.
65 The Sub-Committee for Employment was of the opinion that the Government should re-consider the formation of both a special communal regiment and a scheme of marine training in India. Regarding military recruitment, it said: 'all who have the interest of the community at heart regret that Government should have vetoed the proposal. All the arguments brought forward by the Pauperism Committee in favour of military employment appear to have acquired added strength during the laps of years' (ibid. p. 138).
The General Committee acknowledged the importance of both schemes but differed somewhat on the question of military regiment. It did find military recruitment useful, but, unlike the Sub-Committee, argued that the recruitment of individuals to the British Army would be better than the formation of a regiment. Ibid., p. 21, 138.
66 'Unemployment in Calcutta', *The Statesman [Weekly]*, 18 September 1924, 4.
67 'Living in Poverty', *The Statesman [Weekly]*, 4 December 1924, 19.

68 'Anglo-Indians and Unemployment', *The Statesman [Weekly]*, 4 June 1925, 19.
69 'Relief of Distress: Anglo-Indian Unemployment Problem', *The Statesman [Weekly]*, 11 February 1926, 24.
70 Jean Finot's *Race Prejudice* (London: Archibald Constable, 1906) argued that racial differences were 'almost entirely due to passing social conditions and not to innate racial characteristics', and that the 'scientific' theory that admixture of blood must necessarily lead to racial degeneration had already been refuted. *Report of the CDCEC*, pp. 43–44.
71 *Report of the PC*, p. 8.
72 *Report of the CDCEC*, p. 134.
73 *Report of the PC*, p. 5.
74 Ibid.
75 Ibid.
76 E. Thurston, 'Eurasians of Madras and Malabar', *Madras Government Museum: Bulletin*, 2, 1898, 69–164, p. 76.
77 Ibid.
78 J. MacRae, 'Social Conditions in Calcutta – 1: The Problem for Charity among the Anglo-Indian Community', *The Calcutta Review*, 1, 1913, 84–94, p. 91.
79 Ibid, p. 92.
80 Ibid, p. 91.
81 J. MacRae, 'Social Conditions in Calcutta – 2: The Problem for Charity among the Anglo-Indian Community', *The Calcutta Review*, 1, 1913, 351–71, p. 352.
82 *Report of the CDCEC*, p. 43.
83 'Pauperism in Calcutta', p. 3.
84 W. Forbes-Mitchell, 'Letter to the Editor: The Eurasian Problem and Missionary Employment', *The Statesman [Weekly]*, 28 November 1891, 1. Elsewhere Forbes-Mitchell also said, 'If the pauperised Eurasian and Anglo-Indian are to rise, they must avoid all selfish indulgences of early and imprudent marriages'. W. Forbes-Mitchell, 'The Gospel of the Regeneration of An Anglo-Indian and Eurasian Pauperism – I.', *The Statesman [Weekly]*, 31 October 1891, p. 1. About ten years later, this view on early marriage was reproduced in his book, W. Forbes-Mitchell, *The Gospel of Regeneration of the Anglo-Indian and Eurasian Poor*, Calcutta: Thacker, Spink & Co., 1900, p. 77.
85 For instance, Robert Joseph Carbery, the Vice-President of a charity organization (St. Vincent de Paul) replied to the PC, saying, 'They [Eurasians] marry early now. [...] I do not consider these early marriages as a sign of prosperity, but of improvidence'. *Report of the PC*, p. xiv.
86 Thurston, 'Eurasians of Madras and Malabar', p. 75.
87 Ibid.
88 *Report of the CDCEC*, p. 142.
89 Ibid., p. 142.
90 Ibid., p. 143.
91 MacRae, 'Social Conditions in Calcutta – 2', p. 363.
92 MacRae, 'Social Conditions in Calcutta – 1', p. 93.
93 *Report of the PC*, p. 10.
94 Ibid., p. 11.
95 Ibid., pp. 75–100. and *Report of the CDCEC*, pp. 26–30.
96 *Report of the CDCEC*, p. 73.
97 Ibid., p. 74.
98 Ibid., p. 79.
99 *Report of the PC*, p. lxvii.
100 Ibid., p. lxxiv.
101 Ibid., p. lix.
102 Ibid., p. 14.

103 Ibid.
104 Ibid.
105 Ibid., p. 15.
106 'General Department, 8 August 1892, resolution', p. 7.
107 The Sub-Committee on Employment of the CDCEC took up the subject of establishing a training ship in the Hooghly as having been suggested before the PC, and expressed its wish 'to bring this proposal forward again as one of their definite recommendations'. *Report of the CDCEC*, p. 138.
108 For a brief account of the role of St. Andrew's Colonial Homes, see S. Mizutani, 'Historicising Whiteness: from the Case of Late Colonial India', *Australian Critical Race and Whiteness Studies Association Journal*, 2, 2006: 1–15, p. 10.
109 *The Friend of India [Weekly]*, 15 January 1876, 44–45, p. 44.
110 'The Southern Eurasian Colony', *The Friend of India, and Statesman [Weekly]*, 9 January 1883, 46–47.
111 'Anglo-Indian Colonisation Schemes', *The Statesman [Weekly]*, 8 May 1924, 3.
112 'Anglo-Indians in the Andamans', *The Statesman [Weekly]*, 14 August 1924, 3.
113 *The Madras Times [Weekly]*, 26 February 1890, 5.
114 'Anglo-Indians in Andamans: Lack of Experience', *The Statesman [Weekly]*, 3 April 1924, 10.
115 *The Statesman [Weekly]*, 27 July 1899, 20.
116 *The Statesman [Weekly]*, 11 September 1875, 830.
117 'Sir Richard Temple and Hill Colonization', *The Statesman [Weekly]*, 22 January 1876, 76.
118 'The Southern Eurasian Colony', p.46
119 L. Caplan, *Children of Colonialism: Anglo-Indians in a Postcolonial World*, Oxford: Berg, 2001, p. 132.
120 J. Graham, 'The Education of the Anglo-Indian Child', *Journal of the Royal Society of Arts*, 83, 1934, 22–46, pp. 36–37.
121 *The Englishman [Weekly]*, 23 August 1884, p. 10.
122 'The Prospects of Eurasians in Africa', *The Statesman [Weekly]*, 23 August 1890, 2.
123 'Eurasian Emigration ', *The Statesman [Weekly]*, 26 September 1879, 839–40.
124 W. Wood and A. Francis, 'Letter to the Editor: Anglo-Indians and Australia', *The Statesman [Weekly]*, 13 June 1912, 7. The criteria that had been laid down by the Minister of the Interior was that Eurasians of three-quarters white parentage would be allowed to land if they were in sound health, of good character and in possession of a British passport. See, 'Kalimpong Homes Look Ahead', *The Statesman [Weekly]*, 10 February 1938, 13.
125 *Report of the CDCEC*, p. 138.
126 *The Statesman [Weekly]*, 31 January 1891, 3.
127 O. Younghusband, 'The Domiciled Community in India", in *Pamphlets, vol. 72* (OIOC; T/722), pp. 4–5.
128 Ibid., pp. 5–6.
129 Ibid., p. 7.
130 Luke, 'A Training-Ship Institution', p. 333.
131 'Sir Richard Temple and Hill Colonization', p. 76.
132 D. Ward, 'The progressives and the urban question: British and American responses to the inner city slums 1880–1920', *Transactions of the Institute of British Geographies*, 9, 1984: 299–314. See also P. Mazumdar, 'The Eugenicists and the Residuum: the problem of the urban poor', *Bulletin of the History of Medicine*, 19, 2, 1980, 204–15; and S. Koven, *Slumming: Sexual and Social Politics in Victorian London*, Princeton, NJ: Princeton University Press, 2004.

133 In 1899, various 'homes' for destitute children were legally incorporated under the name of 'the National Association for the reclamation of Destitute Waif Children', but the new institution was more famously known as 'Dr Barnardo's Homes' named after the reputed philanthropist, Thomas John Barnardo (1845–1905). The Homes allied itself since 1901 with Watts Naval School in Norwich. But, in fact, despite its name, the school was not so much a 'naval school' as a training institution for destitute children. As *The Times*, reporting in December 1901, emphasized the difference: 'this cannot be a "naval training school" in the usually accepted meaning of the term; it is to be, we assume, a school for training boys to follow the calling of the sea, and particularly in the mercantile marine'. 'Gift of A Marine Training School', *The Times*, 28 December 1901, 9. The Navy was not always willing to draw recruits from the poorest population, a problem that also fell upon India's domiciled youth seeking employment in it.
134 For a contemporary account of farm colonies across Europe, see J. Mavor, 'Labor Colonies and the Unemployed', *The Journal of Political Economy*, 2, 1893: 26–53.
135 For details see H. Fischer-Tiné, 'Global Civil Society and the Forces of Empire: The Salvation Army, British Imperialism and the Pre-history of NGOs (ca. 1880–1920)', in S. Conrad and D. Sachsenmaier (eds), *Competing Visions of World Order: Global Moments and Movements, 1880s–1930s*, New York: Palgrave-Macmillan, 2007, 29–67.
136 J. Brown, 'Charles Booth and Labour Colonies, 1889–1905', *The Economic History Review*, 21, 1968: 349–36, p. 357. For a good summary of General Booth's colonization and emigration schemes, see also, C. Spence, 'The Landless Man and the Manless Land', *The Western Historical Quarterly*, 16, 1985, 397–412, pp. 397–99.
137 Spence, 'The Landless Man and the Manless Land', p. 399.
138 In Madras, the 'Anglo-Indian' community today is still deeply embedded in a culture of philanthropic aid that mirrors the legacies of colonial politics that had been aimed at the domiciled poor. See L. Caplan, 'Dimensions of Urban Poverty: Anglo-Indian Poor and Their Guardians in Madras' in *Urban Anthropology*, 25, 1996: 311–49, and L. Caplan, 'Gifting and Receiving: Anglo-Indian Charity and its Beneficiaries in Madras', *Contributions to Indian Sociology*, 32, 1998: 409–31. In Johannesburg (British South Africa), the infamous racial segregation policy, starting in the name of 'city planning' in the 1910s, was necessitated partly by a perceived need to solve the question of 'poor whites'. See Parnell, 'Creating Racial Privilege'. The acute anxieties over this poor-white question led to an extensive 'scientific' survey by the Commission of Investigation into the Poor-White Question, commissioned by the Carnegie Corporation in 1929. See, M. Bell, 'American Philanthropy, the Carnegie Corporation and Poverty in South Africa', *Journal of Southern African Studies*, 26, 2000: 481–504.
139 See her essays on the white communities in the Dutch East Indies in Stoler, *Carnal Knowledge and Imperial Power*.

Bibliography

Published material

Arnold, D., 'European Orphans and Vagrants in India in the Nineteenth Century', *The Journal of Imperial and Commonwealth History* 7, 2, 1979: 104–27.
——, 'White Colonisation and Labour in Nineteenth-Century India', *The Journal of Imperial and Commonwealth History* 11, 2, 1983: 133–58.

Bear, L., 'Miscegenations of Modernity: constructing European respectability and race in the Indian railway colony, 1857–1931', *Women's History Review* 3, 4, 1994: 531–48.

Bell, M., 'American Philanthropy, the Carnegie Corporation and Poverty in South Africa', *Journal of Southern African Studies* 26, 3, 2000: 481–504.

Brown, J., 'Charles Booth and Labour Colonies, 1889–1905', *The Economic History Review*, 21, 2, 1968: 349–36.

Buettner, E., *Empire Families*, Oxford: Oxford University Press, 2004.

Caplan, L., 'Dimensions of Urban Poverty: Anglo-Indian Poor and Their Guardians in Madras', *Urban Anthropology*, 25, 4, 1996: 311–49.

——, 'Gifting and Receiving: Anglo-Indian Charity and its Beneficiaries in Madras', *Contributions to Indian Sociology*, 32, 2, 1998: 409–31.

——, *Children of Colonialism: Anglo-Indians in a Postcolonial World*, Oxford: Berg, 2001.

Cooper, F. and A. Stoler, 'Between Metropole and Colony: Rethinking a Research Agenda' in A. Stoler and F. Cooper (eds), *Tensions of Empire: Colonial Cultures in a Bourgeois World*, Berkeley: University of California Press, 1997.

Fischer-Tiné, H., 'Britain's Other Civilising Mission: Class-prejudice, European "Loaferism" and the Workhouse System in Colonial India', *Indian Economic and Social History Review* 42, 3, 2005: 295–338.

——,'Global Civil Society and the Forces of Empire: The Salvation Army, British Imperialism and the Pre-history of NGOs (ca. 1880–1920)', in S. Conrad and D. Sachsenmaier (eds), *Competing Visions of World Order: Global Moments and Movements, 1880s–1930s*, New York: Palgrave-Macmillan, 2007, pp. 29–67.

Forbes-Mitchell, W., *The Gospel of Regeneration of the Anglo-Indian and Eurasian Poor*, Calcutta: Thacker, Spink & Co., 1900.

Graham, J., 'The Education of the Anglo-Indian Child', *Journal of the Royal Society of Arts* 83, 1934: 22–46

Hall, C., *White, Male and Middle Class*, New York: Routledge, 1992.

Harrison, M., *Public Health in British India: Anglo-Indian preventive medicine 1859–1914*, Cambridge: Cambridge University Press, 1994.

Hawes, C., *Poor Relations: The Making of a Eurasian Community in British India, 1773–1833*, Richmond: Curzon Press,1996.

Himmelfarb, G., *The Idea of Poverty: England in the Early Industrial Age*, London: Faber and Faber, 1984.

Hobsbawm, E., *The Age of Capital: 1848–1875*, New York: Vintage Books, 1996.

Jones, G.S. *Outcast London. A study in the relationship between classes in Victorian society*, New York: Pantheon, 1984.

Kennedy, D., *The Magic Mountains: Hill Stations of the British Raj*, Berkeley, CA: University of California Press, 1996.

Koven, S., *Slumming: Sexual and Social Politics in Victorian London*, Princeton, NJ: Princeton University Press, 2004.

MacRae, J., 'Social Conditions in Calcutta – 1: The Problem for Charity among the Anglo-Indian Community', *The Calcutta Review*, 1, 1913: 84–94.

——, 'Social Conditions in Calcutta – 2: The Problem for Charity among the Anglo-Indian Community', *The Calcutta Review*, 1, 1913: 351–71.

Masterman, C., *The Heart of Empire: Discussions of Modern City Life in England with an Essay on Imperialism*, London: Fisher Unwin, 1902, [reprinted in J. Marriott and M. Matsumura (eds), *The Metropolitan Poor: Semi-Factual Accounts, 1795–1910, vol.3, People of the Abyss, 1885–1910*, London: Pickering & Chatto, 1999].

Mavor, J., 'Labor Colonies and the Unemployed', *The Journal of Political Economy* 2, 1893: 26–53.
Mazumdar, P., 'The Eugenicists and the Residuum: the problem of the urban poor', *Bulletin of the History of Medicine*, 54, 2, 1980: 204–15.
Mizutani, S., 'Constitutions of the Colonising Self in Late British India: Race, Class and Environment', *Zinbun: Annals of the Institute for Research in Humanities, Kyoto University*, 38, 2005: 21–75.
Mizutani, S., 'Historicising Whiteness: from the Case of Late Colonial India', *Australian Critical Race and Whiteness Studies Association Journal* 2, 1, 2006: 1–15.
Nye, R., 'The Bio-Medical Origins of Urban Sociology', *Journal of Contemporary History* 20, 4, 1985: 659–75.
Parnell, S., 'Creating Racial Privilege: the Origins of South African Public Health and Town Planning Legislation', *Journal of Southern African Studies* 19, 3, 1993: 471–88.
Peers, D., 'Privates off Parade: Regimenting Sexuality in the Nineteenth-Century Indian Empire', *The International History Review* 20, 4, 1998: 823–54.
Report of the Calcutta Domiciled Community Enquiry Committee, 1918–19, Calcutta: Bengal Secretariat Press, 1920.
Report of the Pauperism Committee, Calcutta: Bengal Secretariat Press, 1892.
Review of Education in India in 1886, Calcutta: Government of India, 1888.
Semmel, B., *Imperialism and Social Reform: English Social-imperial Thought, 1895–1914*, London: Faber and Faber, 1960.
Soloway, R., 'Counting the Degenerates: The Statistics of Race Deterioration in Edwardian England', *Journal of Contemporary History*, 17, 1,1982: 137–64.
Spence, C. C., 'The Landless Man and the Manless Land', *The Western Historical Quarterly*, 16, 4, 1985: 397–412.
Stoler, A. L., *Race and Education of Desire*, Durham, NC: Duke University Press, 1995.
Stoler, A. L., *Carnal Knowledge and Imperial Power*, Berkeley, CA: California University Press, 2002.
The Census of India, 1901: vol. XV.: Madras: Part I – Report (1902) Madras: Government of India.
The Englishman [Weekly], 1884.
The Friend of India [Weekly], 1864–76.
The Friend of India and the Statesman [Weekly], 1883
The Madras Times [Weekly], 1890.
The Statesman [Weekly], 1875–1938.
The Times [London], 1901.
Thorn, S., '"The Conversion of Englishmen and the Conversion of the World Inseparable": Missionary Imperialism and the Language of Class in Early Industrial Britain', in A. Stoler and F. Cooper (eds) (1997) *Tensions of Empire: Colonial Cultures in a Bourgeois World*, Berkeley, CA: University of California Press, 1997.
Thurston, E., 'Eurasians of Madras and Malabar', *Madras Government Museum: Bulletin*, 2, 1898: 69–164.
Ward, D., 'The progressives and the urban question: British and American responses to the inner city slums 1880–1920', *Transactions of the Institute of British Geographies*, 9, 3, 1984: 299–314.

7 Hierarchies of subalternity
Managed stratification in Bombay's brothels, 1914–1930

Ashwini Tambe

Introduction

On a February night in 1917, a woman named Akootai was murdered after she tried to escape the brothel where she worked, on Duncan Road in Bombay. Her brothel keeper Syed Mirza and his two accomplices tortured her before they killed her, as a warning to other brothel inmates. They beat her in front of the other inmates with fists, a curry stone and a metal yard measure, and branded her with lit matches; they forced her to drink her supervisor's urine, and bathe in scalding water.[1] The specifics of this case – the grisly forms of torture, the brothel keeper's Pathan identity, and his victim's valiant attempted escape – generated a great deal of press coverage. Yet when the police force was criticized for its failure to detect and prevent such cases, Bombay's Police Commissioner F.A. M. Vincent pleaded that it could not be expected to control this 'class with its low state of evolution'.[2]

That same year, a police inspector in Vincent's department was investigated for wrongdoing of a different kind. Inspector Favel, termed the 'right hand man' of the previous police commissioner S. M. Edwardes, was found guilty of routinely extorting money and gifts from pimps, mistresses, and workers in European brothels in Kamathipura; collecting commissions when such brothels changed hands; sharing brothel profits; and availing of free sexual services.[3] When a European prostitute tried to escape brothel life with the aid of an outsider, Favel obstructed them with blackmail and threats of deportation. At the end of the investigation, Favel was asked to resign.

These two episodes – one characterized by very little police attention, and the other by extraordinary police involvement – exemplify the stratification at the heart of state control of prostitution in late colonial Bombay. While police scrutinized, and even socialized, with upper rung European prostitutes, they viewed Indian prostitutes as a de-individuated mass. When asked to enforce laws against the transporting and bondage of prostitutes, Bombay's police responded with strategies of elaborate differentiation between races and classes of brothels, and effectively altered the scope of the law. These modes of differentiation exemplify the divided character of the British colonial state: although it utilized modern technologies of surveillance in attending to European segments of the subaltern population in colonized settings, entire strata of subaltern Indians escaped its gaze. Although it claimed to possess jurisdiction over all its subjects, the colonial state actually represented a very hollow shell of authority before many in the Indian underclass. In a Foucauldian sense, then, it combined aspects of the modern state – focused on controlling a 'population' and wielding strategies of individuation and surveillance – with those of the pre-modern territorial state.

Urban prostitutes may be considered classic subaltern figures insofar as they were reviled by both the colonial state and nationalist elites. For nationalists, who regularly equated the nation's honour with female purity, prostitutes were useful only as symbols of the subjugation of the country. For the colonial state, urban residential complaints about visible prostitution represented a threat to its moral authority. Prostitutes drew highly selective state surveillance practices, and unlike other subaltern figures who rarely figure in official records, were sporadically the subject of rich and chilling accounts in official sources such as police files, census and survey data and high court trials. This chapter focuses on the selectivity of the colonial state's gaze, and how this selectivity demonstrates the state's tolerance for disorder in particular spaces. I focus in particular on how the state responded to international anti-trafficking conventions, which were meant to curtail the sex trade; I demonstrate how the universalist language of international anti-trafficking conventions was adapted and redirected to serve the requirements of colonial hierarchies.

The idiom of trafficking, which began circulating in the 1910s and 1920s in Europe and North America, supplanted an earlier vein of concerns about 'white slavery.'' Although the term 'traffic' only connoted 'improper dealings' or 'prostitution',[4] the notion of movement across borders – and implicitly of white girls carried from Europe to colonies – lent this new discourse its emotional weight. The first anti-trafficking agreements – signed by the members of the International Society for the Suppression of White Slave Traffic in 1894, 1904 and 1910 – required countries to keep a watch at ports of embarkation, repatriate victims, and criminalize abduction and trafficking.[5] The most influential convention of 1910 specified that anyone who 'procured, enticed, or led away, even with her consent, a woman or girl under age, for immoral purposes, [would] be punished, notwithstanding that the various acts constituting the offense may have been committed in different countries'.[6] The League of Nations adopted this convention as part of its mandate in 1920, and its member nations, including India, had to submit annual reports on how they were reducing trafficking.

The annual anti-trafficking reports that the Bombay government sent to the League of Nations in the 1920s are the main sources analyzed in this chapter, although I also draw on a range of police files, newspaper articles, social workers' records and census tables.[7] The anti-trafficking reports consist of letters from police commissioners summarizing major cases, social workers' reports, and judicial statements. I critically read and compare the voices of missionary and social reform organizations, citizen petitions and police reports to arrive at an assessment of social relations in Bombay's sex trade. While agreeing with Gayatri Chakravorty Spivak's well-founded assertion that it is never possible to fully access subaltern voices, I will nonetheless engage in a mode of 'information retrieval' that allows an analysis of the relationship between the colonial state and prostitutes.[8] In the first part of the chapter, I compare the roles played by European and Indian prostitutes in the city's racialized sexual order. In the second part, I focus on the local police's selective enforcement of League of Nations Conventions: their emphasis on cross-national cases with an attendant neglect of internal trafficking, their legalistic emphasis on third-party procurers, and concern only for victims with no prior history of prostitution.

Racial rankings in Kamathipura

As Bombay became a prominent seaport in the late nineteenth century, its brothels served sailors and received brothel workers from distant parts of the world; it joined a sex trade circuit spanning cities in Asia, South America and Africa.[9] An organized system for directing sailors from ports to licensed brothels was approvingly described by the Chief Medical Officer of Bombay as early as 1885.[10] European and Middle Eastern brothel workers came to Bombay in large numbers after the 1860s, typically travelling through the Suez Canal; they often proceeded southwards or eastwards towards Capetown, Colombo, Hong Kong, Singapore and Shanghai.[11] Japanese and some Chinese brothel workers also arrived to the city, travelling in the opposite direction.[12] Because of its location and eminence as a commercial port, Bombay was a point of entry to other Indian cities; there were more European prostitutes here than Calcutta, Madras and Karachi.[13] Bombay's large population of Europeans made it attractive to the network of suppliers of brothel workers.[14] When anti-trafficking measures were introduced internationally, the Government of Bombay served as the central authority submitting annual reports to the League of Nations, as it was acknowledged to be the primary destination for traffickers in India.[15]

Although the term 'European' was generically used in colonial India to include those who were British, in this context, European prostitutes were specifically of continental origins, particularly French, Polish, Austrian and Russian.[16] The presence of European prostitutes resolved the separate dictates of sexual recreation for British soldiers and sailors, medicalized racism and British national prestige. Although brothels remained legal in India well into the 1920s, inter-racial sex between Indian women and British men was increasingly viewed as a problem. With the growing pervasiveness of a biological construct of race, preserving racial purity and preventing miscegenation became a critical political project.[17] Concerns about venereal disease led to the framing of Indian prostitutes, and indeed all lower class Indian women, as threats to British soldiers: the Commander-in-Chief of the army warned British soldiers against inter-racial sex by stating that 'diseases passed on from one race to another (were) always more severe'.[18] At the same time, British women in India were seen to embody national honour, and British women who turned to prostitution were decried as 'scandals to the nation' and often punished or sent home.[19] Stephen Edwardes, police commissioner of Bombay from 1909 to 1917, declared that without European prostitutes, there would be increasing resort to Indian women, a possibility that 'could not be regarded with impunity by those responsible for the general welfare of India'.[20] As he explained it, 'the growth of European populations, and the government's disapproval of liaisons with Indian women made authorities accept European brothels as a necessary evil. No direct steps were taken to curb [them]'.[21]

European prostitutes in Bombay assumed the status of permanent outsiders, embodying a 'lesser whiteness' than British subjects but an identity that was nonetheless superior to Indian prostitutes. Administrators symbolically distanced themselves from European prostitutes by highlighting the latter's Jewish background. In his description of prostitution in colonial India, for instance, Edwardes repeatedly refers to 'the preponderance of Jewesses in the brothels of Indian coast cities' and the 'Jewish identity of procurers'; at a 1921 League of Nations conference on trafficking, he asked the representative of Jewish Associations why the latter's 'co-religionists' formed the 'majority of the procurers and "fancy men"' who visited Bombay.[22] The actual religious or ethnic identity of European prostitutes in Bombay is perhaps less important than the official insistence that it was 'less white' because it was Jewish or Eastern European. Despite the presence of a local Sephardic community, officials in Bombay drew on the British ideology of Jews as 'foreigners',[23] heightened in Britain after the Russian pogroms;[24] in so doing, they simultaneously configured themselves as a legitimate, settled population.

Although European prostitutes' intermediate racial stratum and outsider status provided a neat resolution of political imperatives, the women had a volatile social presence that required regular police attention. They lived principally in Kamathipura, originally settled by sweepers and construction workers, where their brothels were so conspicuous that a principal street, Cursetji Sukhlaji Street, was known as *safed galli* (white lane).[25] Although there were brothels with Indian prostitutes in Kamathipura, the presence of European prostitutes troubled Indian neighbours considerably. Residents of Kamathipura sent petitions to the police to have the women removed from the area, drawing striking contrasts between Indian and European prostitutes. One set of petitioners who called themselves a group of 'respectable poor' stated that while native prostitutes were 'very little nuisance', European prostitutes created annoyances the likes of which they 'had never witnessed in their lifetime'.[26] Middle-class Indian residents of other neighbourhoods of the city also petitioned the police to drive European women back into Kamathipura, when they set up shop elsewhere.[27] These frank expressions of dismay, marked by hostility for British rule and a nationalist invocation of local female honour, also indicate that Indian residents understood the outsider and subordinate status the state assigned to European prostitutes. Indian residents questioned the continuing official tolerance of such women and their 'disorderly' clientele without fear of retribution; unlike respectable Englishwomen, European prostitutes were fair game. The state responded to these pressures by insistently 'herd[ing] together' European prostitutes in Kamathipura, where surveillance could be focused and disruption to middle-class residents was minimal; police stayed informed of new arrivals and deported prostitutes 'guilty of misbehaviour'.[28]

Surveillance of prostitutes was a feature of state regulation set up under the Contagious Diseases Acts in numerous colonies, but the level of precision in archival information about European prostitutes in Bombay is striking. While Indian constables, who were primarily Marathi-speaking immigrant recruits from neighbouring regions, rarely interacted with European brothel workers, the officers above inspector grade, who were usually British,[29] took an intense interest in the European prostitutes of Kamathipura. They considered themselves privy to the goings-on in European brothels, detailing the numbers, nationalities and even names of European women.[30] Police ranked European brothels into three tiers according to how well conducted they were: the first class consisted solely of European women living in private houses; the second, of women who solicited in the streets; and the third, of women who were grouped along with Japanese and Baghdadi women in Kamathipura.[31] Indian women implicitly figured as the bottom rung in this hierarchy, but the fact that they were not even named as a tier, or as part of a tier, underscores their official invisibility.

European prostitutes reportedly numbered around 100, a far smaller figure than the wildly diverse estimates of Indian prostitutes who officially ranged anywhere from 1,500 to 15,000.[32] Yet European prostitutes were prominently featured in annual and national reports, and even in books that the police wrote.[33] Police commissioners showed familiarity with the names of European brothel workers: in 1930, the commissioner uncovered a case of visa fraud involving a French prostitute who altered her name to re-enter India – he recalled that the name 'Indree Fiscari' was similar to that of a woman named 'Andree Fiscari' who had left Bombay in 1928.[34] The commissioner denied a Romanian woman permission to visit Bombay in 1928 because he reportedly 'knew her to be a prostitute'.[35][36]

Indian brothel workers, in contrast, received far less police attention: their stories rarely made it to the police commissioner's summary letters in annual anti-trafficking reports, and the circumstances explaining their entry into prostitution were rarely elaborated in anti-trafficking report tables. Unlike the carefully named European subjects, Indian brothel workers appear in the records simply termed 'women'. Unlike European brothel workers, Indian brothel workers were far more dispersed across the city, and met with less public revulsion. There were no furious debates between police and residents over where to locate Indian prostitutes.

The very designation of the city's red-light zone demonstrates the selective vision of the colonial state. Census figures for both 1864 and 1871 show high concentrations of prostitutes in parts of Bombay other than Kamathipura, and notably in neighbourhoods populated by working-class Indians, such as Market, Oomburkharee, Phunuswaree and Girgaon.[35] For instance, in 1864, while there were 610 reported prostitutes in Kamathipura, there were nearly twice that number in Girgaon and Phunuswaree, and nearly thrice that number in Market and Oomburkharee.[37] Census figures for 1901 and 1921 also indicate that areas other than Kamathipura such as Khetwadi, Phunuswaree, Girgaon and Tardeo had larger numbers of prostitutes living there.[38] Yet none of these other areas were defined as red-light zones. Kamathipura was the area where European prostitutes first resided, and then were allocated. On the strength of its European residents, Kamathipura was termed the 'prostitutes' zone' by the administration.[39] For instance, a 1917 guide to the street names of Bombay noted: 'Kamathipura is commonly used to denote the prostitutes' quarter'.[40] When police reports referred to brothels, they implicitly meant European brothels.

Police files provide great detail about European prostitutes, indicating their zeal in targeting this population. The Favel case, referred to at the start of this chapter, demonstrates the extent of police surveillance over this group.[41] The statements made before the police by Favel's accomplice, five brothel mistresses, and a brothel client create a picture of a quotidian relationship between the police and European brothel mistresses, in which policemen visited brothels, oversaw the arrival on ships of new brothel workers, and sometimes even owned shares of brothels. Police surveillance not only hung over brothels, it also followed European brothel workers' movements. Women who wished to leave Kamathipura and reside in other parts of the city had to seek police permission. Even making public appearances at the horse races involved bribing Favel, explains one brothel mistress, Mlle. Margot. Rather than facilitating women's escape from brothels, Favel refused to relinquish his authority: when a man named Meyer tried to 'rescue' brothel worker Mary Fooks, Favel forced him to purchase brothel shares, sell him a horse carriage, and even throw him a picnic, in exchange for 'keeping' Fooks as a mistress.[42]

While this inquiry reveals a particularly egregious web of extortion, Inspector Favel was not alone in such activities. Other archived files corroborate the involvement of police superiors in regulating the sex trade. A 1925 letter from the police commissioner of Bombay to the Home Department relates matter of factly that a brothel mistress brought three newly arrived prostitutes from Cairo to the police for registration, and that the deputy commissioner 'raised no objection to their going to the brothel'.[43] Even under an abolitionist climate, after the 1923 Bombay Prostitution Act had made illegal the procuring of women for brothels, and at a time when reports were annually sent to international anti-trafficking bodies, the police continued to have working relationships with European procurers and brothel mistresses. I turn now to examine how police negotiated such contradictions.

Police responses to anti-trafficking conventions

The discourse of trafficking set up a prototypical victim: the needy young girl who was enticed away by promises of respectable work, adventure or marriage. The victims were typically portrayed as being younger than 20, naïvely trustful of strangers, and of peasant or small-town origins.[44] In various ways, police declared European prostitutes in Bombay to be unworthy trafficking victims because they did not conform to this type. A 1920 national report on prostitution in Indian cities declared that all the foreign prostitutes in Bombay 'were prostitutes in their own countries ... long before their arrival in India, and if any of them were victims of the "White Slave" traffic, they have been so victimized long before their arrival in India. The "White Slave" traffic as known in Europe is non-existent in India'.[45] In 1932, the police reported to the League of Nations that 'if a girl comes to Bombay who has already been seduced or been a prostitute then we leave her alone ... no European woman had been allowed to stay as a brothel inmate during the last years who was not already, on her arrival, a prostitute'.[46] According to S.M. Edwardes, European prostitutes entered the 'profession' of their own free will, after serving an 'apprenticeship' in Europe, Constantinople or Egypt; they were 'fallen women' whose 'weak morals' and 'carelessness with money' had led them into vice.[47]

The relative material security of European prostitutes helped Bombay's police cast them as exceptions to the discourse of trafficking. In the course of the Favel inquiry, European brothel mistresses related that they had all been able to save enough money to buy 'half shares' of brothels.[48] They all declared that they had arrived in Bombay as brothel 'girls' and worked as prostitutes from three to nine years before they went on to run brothels.[49] It is not clear how much money European brothel workers charged per customer; however, a doctor who treated venereal diseases in the red-light area reported in 1920 that 'foreign' prostitutes earned on average 1,500 to 2,000 Rs. a month.[50] If we compare the earnings of Indian women in Akootai's brothel in 1917, 3–4 *annas* (half a rupee) per customer, it is obvious that European brothel workers earned considerably larger amounts of money per customer, to be able to save sums as great as 7,000 rupees.[51] European brothels were profitable corporate entities; their value rose over time, as in the case of 392 Falkland Road, whose half-share value rose from 7,000 rupees in 1909 to 11,500 rupees in 1917.[52] Another indication of brothel workers' material circumstances is the description in the 1925 police anti-trafficking report of a French brothel worker who travelled to France to bring back her sister to 'join her' in Bombay; she must have been content enough with her circumstances to travel back and forth to draw her 'sister' in.[53]

Although the police were likely to take a benign view of European prostitutes, the records of local social work organizations such as the Bombay Vigilance Association, and Christian missionary groups such as the League of Mercy and the Salvation Army present a more alarmist picture. These groups took a close interest in monitoring trafficking, and placed a quasi-competitive pressure on the police. Salvation Army officers, by their own account, visited brothels on *safed galli* 'once a week' seeking rescue cases.[54] The League of Mercy, run by British subjects, exclusively sought out and repatriated European brothel workers independently of the police; the group hired a 'rescue worker' trained in England for this purpose.[55] In 1923, for instance, the League of Mercy returned seven girls and two children 'to England'; a mother and two children 'to Africa'; two girls 'to Ceylon'.[56] In the same year, the police report only mentioned the deporting to Russia and Poland of two women who had been practicing prostitution. In 1927, the League of Mercy repatriated to Czechoslovakia a girl 'found living with a Parsee ... in a diseased condition', while the police report for that year mentioned no repatriations.[57] The League of Mercy's higher repatriation figures were driven by a code of female honour that suspected women who travelled alone: in 1926, among the several English girls the group sent back was one who had simply arrived in Bombay 'to marry a man she had never seen'.[58] Directed by stringent notions of moral hygiene that drew on Victorian, Christian and brahminical ideologies, these organizations revealed gaps in police responses.[59]

Bombay police muted the competing voices of social purity organizations by strictly defining the parameters of the term 'trafficking'. They held to a very literal understanding of the 1910 anti-trafficking convention, declaring that trafficking involved a third party transporting the victim across state borders to a brothel or client. In cases brought forward by social workers, they very often declared that third parties were absent. This understanding of trafficking enabled Bombay's police to minimize the scale of the social problem that they were called upon to monitor.

Most importantly, the limited understanding of trafficking allowed the police to overlook trafficking between Indian provinces. Census figures from 1921 reveal that the majority of Indian brothel workers in Bombay were not born in that city.[60] Of the 2,995 reported female prostitutes, only 460 listed their birth district as being Bombay. The others hailed from regions such as Deccan, Ratnagiri and Goa to the south; Hyderabad state to the east; and Delhi, Punjab and Kashmir to the north. Twenty-five women listed Jodhpur as their birthplace, which suggests an organized network was recruiting women from there.[61]

In many ways, Akootai, the murder victim in the case I mentioned at the start of this chapter, was a prototypical trafficking victim. According to her cousin's testimony, she was brought to Bombay from Kolhapur, where her husband lived. She was also living in bondage: brothel keepers confiscated all her earnings, and the boarding, clothes and ornaments were all that she received.[62] Others around her worked under the same conditions: if their earnings were insufficient, they were beaten with rods, a curry stone, an iron nail, or sticks.[63] They were locked in barred rooms on the ground floor of a building, where they received customers both day and night. When they slept, it would be five to a room and under lock and key; they were even accompanied to the toilet. Yet nowhere in the official and journalistic descriptions of the case, was the term 'trafficking' used to describe this case.

The annual reports of the Bombay Vigilance Association, a committee of prominent Indian and English reformists, give a fuller picture than the police of movement between Indian provinces. The reports state that in 1927, 54 girls or women were trafficked from other parts of India into Bombay; in 1928, 65 similar cases emerged.[64] However, in the introduction to the League of Nations submissions for those years, the police commissioner argues that this information was not worthy of reporting to the League of Nations because the cases were 'found not to fall under Articles 1 and 2 of the 1910 Convention', which emphasized cross-border movement.[65] Thus, Bombay police refused to attend closely to trafficking between Indian provinces, and even refused to classify the phenomenon as trafficking.

The Bombay Vigilance Association's records indicate that many Indian girls and women were lured to brothel work in Bombay by deception: its 1929 report mentions false promises of work made to girls, particularly jobs as mill-workers and ayahs (nannies), and its 1927 annual report explains that women who call themselves 'employment agents' often procured girls for brothels.[66] In the questionnaires that the police submitted in those and other years to the League of Nations however, they left blank sections on 'employment agencies', declaring that 'no such agencies have come to light'.[67]

Since the discourse of trafficking focused on third parties who shipped women across national borders, police attention centred on the figure of the foreign pimp. The 'extraditions' and 'repatriation and deportations' sections of the annual police reports to the League of Nations are peppered with voyeuristic details about pimps. The arrest of Luciano la Rosa, labelled a 'well-known international pimp' by the police, is described carefully right down to the 'obscene photographs' of a 'semi-nude' woman found in his possession.[68] In another case, the police followed a man newly arrived from France who described himself as a photographer, but who two days later, 'took his wife to a brothel'. The police arrested the man, but the French consul intervened and urged his release.[69]

Under pressure to demonstrate that they were complying with the League of Nations conventions, but unable to come up with examples of deportations every year, Bombay police turned to reporting cases of 'suspicious aliens'. In the 1928 report, they explain with excitement that they coordinated with police in Marseilles, France, to monitor the movements of four French women who had set sail for Bombay. The women ultimately avoided coming to Bombay, but this fact did not stop the police from reporting the case to the League of Nations. Similarly, in 1929, Bombay police communicated with the British passport control officer in Paris to deny permission to Gaston Guillon and Marie Amandine Poinet to arrive in Bombay. This pair claimed to have been in the hairdressing business in Brazil for 15 years before they set sail for India via France, and Bombay's police were convinced that personal grooming establishments such as 'massage' and 'manicure' services were often a cover for 'disreputable businesses'.[70] Occasionally, the police deported foreign prostitutes as a token measure. As with the deporting of pimps, the more distant the origins of the women, the better the police felt they were doing their jobs. In 1925 the police deported a Polish woman 'who had been practicing prostitution in Singapore and Penang'. In addition, a Russian woman who admitted to carrying on prostitution in Shanghai, Hong Kong and Japan since 1918 was also forced to leave the city. The police related the previous history of the women with fanfare as if indicative of their own competence.[71]

Conclusion

On the whole, Bombay's police were quick to dissociate the prostitution they encountered from that decried in the metropole. Their legalistic approach to the discourse of trafficking enabled convenient emphases and omissions. Their insistence that European prostitutes were not victims of trafficking sustained the racially stratified sexual order that they oversaw in the city. Any possible relevance of anti-trafficking conventions to local European prostitutes, whose outsider status served a useful purpose, was discounted. The language of trafficking also expanded the possibilities for corruption, as police could use the threat of deportation to extract money from European brothel workers and pimps. Most importantly, their interpretation of the international conventions seriously underplayed trafficking within the subcontinent. For the Indian subalterns who might have benefited from some form of anti-trafficking policing, the available law was simply beyond reach, because they remained beneath the threshold of official sight.

Historians of colonialism have fruitfully explored the disjunctions between the needs of colonial and metropolitan states.[72] This chapter has focused on the internal ideological constructs that delimited the governmental reach of colonial states. While acquiescing to the imperial rhetoric of protecting white womanhood implicit in anti-trafficking discourse, the colonial state nonetheless fostered orderly relations among the stratum of European prostitutes that it nurtured. Even as it presented an appearance of enforcing international conventions against trafficking, it overlooked practices of trafficking, and spaces of intense disorder, among an entire substratum of women, due to its heavy racialization of the populations it oversaw.

Acknowledgements

An earlier version of this chapter was presented at the 2004 EASAS meeting in Lund, Sweden, and portions appear in *Gender and Society* 19, no. 2, 2005, pp. 160–79. I am grateful to panel participants at the EASAS meeting for their comments.

Notes

1 High Court of Judicature, Bombay, 2nd sessions, 1917; Home Department, Police A, December 1917, NAI.
2 High Court of Judicature, 1917; Home Department, 1917, pp. 34–36.
3 Judicial Department Proceedings, 6 April 1917, 'Statement from F.A.M. Vincent, Police Commissioner to the Secretary to Government, Judicial Department, Bombay,' File no. 1456-M-3S, pp. 195–203. OIOC.
4 *Oxford English Dictionary*, second edition, Oxford: Clarendon Press, 1933, pp. 2092–93.
5 League of Nations, 'Prevention of Prostitution: A Study of Measures Adopted or Under Consideration Particularly with Respect to Minors,' Geneva: League of Nations, 1943.
6 Home Department 1922, Judicial 58/22, 'Stephen Edwardes' Account of the League of Nations Conference', p. 35. NAI.
7 These sources are drawn from archival research conducted in Mumbai, New Delhi, London, Washington DC and Philadelphia between 1999 and 2002.
8 G.C. Spivak, 'Can the Subaltern Speak?' in *Marxism and the Interpretation of Culture*, ed. C. Nelson and L. Grossberg, Urbana, IL: University of Illinois Press, 1988, 271–313. See also the discussion in A. Loomba, *Colonialism/Postcolonialism*, London: Routledge, 1998, pp. 231–44.
9 See K. Ballhatchet, *Race, Sex and Class Under the Raj: Imperial Attitudes and Policies and Their Critics, 1793–1905*, New York: St. Martin's Press, 1980; D. Guy, *White Slavery and Mothers Alive and Dead: The Troubled Meeting of Sex, Gender, Public Health and Progress in Latin America*, Lincoln, NE: University of Nebraska Press, 2000; G. Hershatter, *Dangerous Pleasures: Prostitution and Modernity in Twentieth Century Shanghai*, Berkeley, CA: University of California Press, 1997; R. Hyam, *Empire and Sexual Opportunity*, Manchester: Manchester University, 1991; P. Levine, *Prostitution, Race and Politics: Policing Venereal Disease in the British Empire*, New York: Routledge, 2003; and E. Van Heyningen, 'The Social Evil in the Cape Colony 1868–1902: Prostitution and the Contagious Diseases Acts' *Journal of Southern African Studies* 10, 2, 1984: 170–97.
10 Government of Bombay. 'Reports of the Working of the Contagious Diseases Act,' Surgeon General's Report, 9 July 1885. OIOC.
11 See H. Fischer-Tiné, 'White women degrading themselves to the lowest depths. European Networks of Prostitution and Colonial Anxieties in British India and Ceylon c. 1880–1914', *Indian Economic and Social History Review* 40, 2, 2003: 163–90; Hershatter, *Dangerous Pleasures*; Hyam, *Empire and Sexual Opportunity*; Levine, *Prostitution, Race and Politics*; and Van Heyningen, 'The Social Evil in the Cape Colony'.
12 Apart from Eastern Europeans, Kamathipura also had a distinct Japanese brothel colony, visited by local Japanese residents – generally numbering around 1,000 – and itinerant Japanese sailors. The Japanese Consulate looked upon this set of women benignly, reporting that many of them 'enjoy(ed) rather happy and comfortable private lives and even devot(ed) their spare time to mental and physical development'. See Home Department Judicial 1932, *Report on the enforcement of trafficking*. Part 1. NAI, p. 16. These brothels drew far less official attention than European ones presumably because their clientele differed.
13 At the turn of the twentieth century, Bombay was reported to have the largest number of European prostitutes in the country, 126 in 1912, in comparison with the reported 50 in Calcutta, two in Madras and six in Karachi. See Home Department, Judicial A, 'Legislative Notes at the All-India Level,' July 1913, p. 221, NAI.

14 There were about 9,000 Europeans (5,000 of whom were male) in Bombay, but around 4,000 in Calcutta and 3,000 in Madras in 1932. See Home Department, Judicial, 914/32, 1932, *Responses to the League of Nations Questionnaire*, p. 25, NAI.
15 Ibid.
16 These specific countries are identifiable through several means: census tables (Government of India, *Census of India 1921*, Volume IX, Part 1, Section 20: *Prostitution in Bombay*, UP) and CDA enforcement reports (Government of Bombay, *Reports of the Working of the Contagious Diseases Act, 1880–1888*. OIOC; MSA; and NAI) listed birthplaces in Europe. A petition to the police by a Kamathipura landlord mentioned German and Italian women tenants (General Department, 1888, vol. 42A, *Petition Submitted to the Governor and President in Council, Bombay, by Inhabitants of Fort, Chowpatti, Khetwadi, and Other Places in Bombay*, 11–13. pp. 227–29. MAI); the last names of Kamathipura petitioners resisting dispersal by the police, such as Polsky, Lukatsky, Puritz, Prevenziano, Greenberg, Erlich, Felman and Stern, suggest Polish, Russian, Italian, and German origins (General Department, 1887, vol. 37, *Petitions Submitted to the Governor and President in Council, Bombay*, pp. 376. MAI). These countries correspond to Hyam's map of the circuits of traffickers, which indicates that women from Russia, Poland, Austria, France and Germany moved, or were moved, to Asia and South America. See Hyam, *Empire and Sexual Opportunity*, p. 144. Many 'sending' countries were sites of state-regulated prostitution: France had in place a system of regulated brothels, which made it an easier recruiting ground, while the Russian Czarist state issued prostitutes a 'yellow card' in place of a passport, which allowed for their easy identification by recruiters, as mentioned in Dyson Carter, *Sin and Science*, New York: Progress Books, 1945.
17 F. Cooper and A.L. Stoler, eds *Tensions of Empire: Colonial Cultures in a Bourgeois World*, Berkeley, CA: University of California, 1997; A. L. Stoler, *Race and the Education of Desire: Foucault's 'History of Sexuality' and the Colonial Order of Things*, Durham, NC: Duke University Press, 1995.
18 Kitchener, 'Memorandum to all Army: "Our Army in India and the Regulation of Vice"'. *Correspondence Between India Office and the British Committee of the International Abolitionist Federation*. 1912, pp. 60. OIOC.
19 D. Kincaid, *British Social Life in India (1608–1937)*, London: Routledge and Kegan Paul, 1973, pp. 43–44; Levine, *Prostitution, Race and Politics*.
20 S.M. Edwardes, *Crime in British India*, New Delhi: ABC Publishing, 1924/1983, p. 81.
21 S.M. Edwardes, *Bombay City Police: A Historical Sketch*, London: Oxford University Press, 1923, p. 85.
22 Home Department 1922, p. 12.
23 Edwardes, *Crime in British India*, p. 77.
24 L. Marks, 'Race, Class and Gender: The Experience of Jewish Prostitutes and Other Jewish Women in the East End of London at the Turn of the Century', in J. Grant (ed), *Women, Migration and Empire*, London: Trentham Books, 1996.
25 Edwardes, *Bombay City Police*, pp. 85–89.
26 General Department 1888a, vol. 42A, Petition Submitted to the Governor and President in Council, Bombay, by Residents of Trimbuk Purushram Street, p. 29. MAI.
27 General Department, 1887, vol. 37, Petitions Submitted to the Governor and President in Council, Bombay, pp. 362–408. MAI; General Department, 1888b, vol. 42A, Petition Submitted to the Governor and President in Council, Bombay, by Inhabitants of Fort, Chowpatti, Khetwadi, and Other Places in Bombay, pp. 11–13. MAI.
28 Edwardes, *Crime in British India*, p. 80; Home Department 1920, Nos 24–29.
29 On the racial composition of Bombay's police force see Rajnarayan Chandavarkar, *Imperial Power and Popular Politics*, Cambridge: Cambridge University Press, 1998.

30 Edwardes, *Crime in British India*, p. 80.
31 Home Department 1920; Edwardes, *Crime in British India*, p. 80.
32 During the enforcement of the CDA from 1870–72 and 1880–88, the number of registered European prostitutes never rose above 75, as compared with the average 1,500 registered Indian prostitutes (see Government of Bombay 1880–88). In 1912, the number of registered European prostitutes in Bombay was pegged at 126 (see Home Department Judicial A 1913); at the end of the First World War in 1920, it had declined to 67, a tiny fraction of the 15,000 Indian women estimated by the police (see Home Department 1920).
33 Edwardes, *Bombay City Police; Crime in British India*; Home Department, 1920.
34 Home Department 1930, File P-133, *Political Department Memo*, 4.
35 Home Department 1928a, File 3338-IX, *Proceedings Relating to the Traffic in Women and Children, League of Nations*, p. 18. MAI.
36 The spellings used here are consistent with the sources; the names have changed since colonial times.
37 See *Census of Island of Bombay*, 1864, Table LX, p.84. UP.
38 In 1921, for instance, there were 779 reported prostitutes in Khetwaree as compared to 896 in Kamathipura. Yet Khetwaree was not described as a red light area, see *Census of India 1921*, Vol. IX, Part 1, Section 20. UP.
39 Home Department 1920.
40 George Sheppard, *Bombay Place-names and Street-names: An Excursion into the By Ways of the History of Bombay City*, Bombay: The Times Press, 1917, p. 84.
41 Judicial Department Proceedings 1917, 195–203.
42 Ibid., pp. 99–100.
43 Home Department 1925, File 8514, *Prostitutes*, p. 89. MAI.
44 Clifford G. Roe, *The Great War on White Slavery or Fighting for the Protection of Our Girls*, Chicago, IL: Clifford G. Roe, 1911, p. 105.
45 Home Department 1920, pp. 24–29.
46 Home Department Judicial 1932, p. 17.
47 Edwardes, *Crime in British India*, pp. 77, 79.
48 Judicial Department Proceedings 1917, 99–102.
49 The average half share cost anywhere from 7,000 to 10,000 Rs. in 1908 (see Home Department 1917, 102). It is hard to gauge the purchasing power of such sums, but the manuscripts also mention other sales which give insight into the rupee's strength: a summer rental for a bungalow in Poona came to 1,500 Rs. and a Victoria (tonga to be driven by a horse) bought from England could be sold for 1,500 Rs. (see Judicial Department Proceedings 1917, p. 100).
50 Home Department 1921b, File 469-IX, 'Questionnaire Reply from Dr. K.S. Patel of Venereal and Skin Hospital, Grant Road' *Report of the Prostitution Committee*. MAI.
51 See the testimony of Phooli, Moti and Paru, (in Home Department 1917), which relate the amounts earned per customer in a Kamathipura brothel.
52 Judicial Department Proceedings, 1917, *Statement from F.A.M. Vincent, Police Commissioner to the Secretary to Government, Judicial Department, Bombay*, 6 April 1917, File no. 1456-M.-3S. OIOC.
53 File P-133. Annual Reports on Traffic in Women and Children for 1924, for Submission to the League Secretariat. MSA.
54 *Indian Social Reformer* 1921b, 'Salvation Army work in Bombay,' October 1921, vol. 32, 9, p. 140. UI.
55 *Indian Social Reformer*, 'Report of the Prostitution Committee,' August 27, vol. 32, 52 1922, p 5. UI.
56 Home Department 1924, File P-35, p. 15.
57 Home Department 1928, File P-133, p. 53.
58 Home Department 1927, File P-133, p. 69.

59 Judy Whitehead, 'Modernizing the Motherhood Archetype: Public Health Models and the Child Marriage Restraint Act of 1929' in *Social Reform, Sexuality and the State,* edited by P. Uberoi, New Delhi: Sage, 1926, pp. 187–209.
60 Government of India, *Census of India 1921.*
61 *Indian Social Reformer,* 1922, p. 7.
62 Phooli relates that 'Accused 1 (Mirza) used to buy them for us because there was no one else who could buy them for us', from Home Department 1917, pp. 128–30.
63 See testimony of Phooli, Moti and Paru, in Home Department 1917, pp. 128–30.
64 Home Department 1928, File P-133; Home Department 1929, File P-133.
65 Home Department 1928a, File 3338-IX, *Proceedings Relating to the Traffic in Women and Children, League of Nations,* p. 47. MAI; Home Department 1929, pp. 47, 61.
66 Home Department 1929, pp. 47–49; Home Department 1927, pp. 102–3.
67 Home Department 1927, p. 51; Home Department 1929, 87; Home Department 1930, p. 65.
68 Home Department, 1927, p. 31.
69 Home Department 1925, p. 7.
70 Home Department 1929, pp. 11–12
71 Home Department 1926, File P-133, p. 85.
72 Cooper and Stoler, *Tensions of Empire.*

Bibliography

Archival material

Abbreviations

OIOC: Oriental and India Office Collections, British Library, London.
MSA: Maharashtra State Archives, Mumbai.
NAI: National Archives of India, New Delhi.
UP: University of Pennsylvania Library, Philadelphia.
UI: University of Illinois-Urbana Library, Urbana-Champaign.

Census of Island of Bombay. 1864. Table LX. UP.
Census of India. 1921. Vol. IX, Part 1, Section 20. UP.
General Department. 1887. vol. 37. *Petitions submitted to the Governor and President in Council, Bombay.* 362–408. MSA.
General Department. 1888a. vol. 42A. *Petition submitted to the Governor and President in Council, Bombay, by residents of Trimbuk Purushram Street.* 29–33. MSA.
General Department. 1888b. vol. 42. *Petition submitted to the Governor and President in Council, Bombay, by Beebee Vaziram.* 227–29. MSA.
General Department. 1888c. vol 42A. *Petition submitted to the Governor and President in Council, Bombay, by inhabitants of Fort, Chowpatti, Khetwadi, and other places in Bombay.* 11–13. MSA.
Government of Bombay. 1880–88. *Reports of the working of the Contagious Diseases Act.* OIOC.
Government of Bombay. 1885. *Reports of the working of the Contagious Diseases Act.* Surgeon General's Report, 9 July. OIOC.
Government of India. 1921. *Census of India,* Section 20, Prostitution in Bombay, Table III. UP.

Home Department. 1917. Police-A, December 128–30. *High Court of Judicature, Bombay, 2nd sessions, 1917, case no.13.* NAI.
Home Department. 1917a. Police-A, December 128–30. *Vincent's memorandum to the Judicial Department, 11 August 1917.* NAI.
Home Department. 1920. Police-A, *Report by E.C. Shuttleworth,* January, Nos 24–29. NAI.
Home Department. 1921. 'Questionnaire reply from Dr. K. S. Patel of Venereal and Skin Hospital, Grant Road.' *Report of the Prostitution Committee.* File 469-IX. MSA.
Home Department. 1922. Judicial, *Stephen Edwardes' account of the League of Nations conference.* NAI.
Home Department. 1924 through 1930. File P-133. *Annual reports on traffic in women and children for 1924, for submission to the League Secretariat.* MSA.
Home Department. 1932. Judicial, *Report on the enforcement of trafficking.* Part 1. NAI.
Indian Social Reformer 1921b. 'Salvation Army work in Bombay.' October 1921, vol 32, 9. UI.
Indian Social Reformer 1922. 'Report of the Prostitution Committee.' August 27, vol 32, 52; supplement p.1–6. UI.
Judicial Department Proceedings. 1917. *Statement from F.A.M. Vincent, Police Commissioner to the Secretary to Government, Judicial Department, Bombay.* 6 April 1917, File no. 1456-M.-3S. OIOC.
Kitchener. 1912. *Memorandum to all army: 'Our army in India and the regulation of vice.'* Correspondence between India Office and the British Committee of the International Abolitionist Federation. OIOC.

Published material

Ballhatchet, K., *Race, sex and class under the Raj: Imperial attitudes and policies and their critics, 1793–1905.* New York: St. Martin's Press, 1980.
Burton, A., *Burdens of history: British feminists, Indian women, and imperial culture, 1865–1915.* Chapel Hill, NC: University of North Carolina, 1994.
Carter, D., *Sin and science.* New York: Progress Books, 1945.
Chandavarkar, R., *Imperial power and popular politics.* Cambridge: Cambridge University Press, 1998
Cooper, F. and A. Stoler (eds), *Tensions of empire: Colonial cultures in a bourgeois world.* Berkeley, CA: University of California Press, 1997.
Edwardes, S., *Bombay city police: A historical sketch.* London: Oxford University Press, 1923.
——, *Crime in British India,* New Delhi: ABC Publishing, 1983 [London 1924].
Fischer-Tiné, H., '"White women degrading themselves to the lowest depths": European networks of prostitution and colonial anxieties in British India and Ceylon c. 1880–1914', *Indian Economic and Social History Review,* 40, 2, 2003: 163–90.
Guy, D., *White slavery and mothers alive and dead: The troubled meeting of sex, gender, public health and progress in Latin America.* Lincoln, NE: University of Nebraska Press, 2000.
Hershatter, G., *Dangerous pleasures: Prostitution and modernity in twentieth century Shanghai.* Berkeley, CA: University of California Press, 1997.
Hyam, R., *Empire and sexuality.* Manchester: Manchester University Press, 1990.

Kincaid, D., *British social life in India 1608–1937*. (Repr.) London: Routledge and Kegan Paul 1973.
League of Nations, *Prevention of prostitution: A study of measures adopted or under consideration particularly with respect to minors.* Geneva: League of Nations, 1943.
Levine, P., 'Venereal disease, prostitution, and the politics of empire: The case of British India', *Journal of the History of Sexuality* 4, 4, 1994: 579–602.
——, *Prostitution, race and politics: Policing venereal disease in the British empire.* New York: Routledge, 2003.
Marks, L., 'Race, class and gender: The experience of Jewish prostitutes and other Jewish women in the East End of London at the turn of the century.' In *Women, migration and empire*, edited by J. Grant. London: Trentham Books, 1996.
Oxford English Dictionary, second edition. 1933. Oxford: Clarendon Press.
Roe, C. G., *The great war on white slavery or fighting for the protection of our girls.* Chicago, IL: Clifford G. Roe, 1911.
Sheppard, G., *Bombay place-names and street-names: An excursion into the by-ways of the history of Bombay city.* Bombay: The Times Press, 1917.
Spivak, G. C., 'Can the subaltern speak?' In *Marxism and the interpretation of culture*, edited by C. Nelson and L. Grossberg. Chicago, IL: University of Illinois Press, 1988.
Stoler, A. L., *Race and the education of desire: Foucault's history of sexuality and the colonial order of things.* Durham, NC: Duke University Press, 1995.
Van Heyningen, E., 'The social evil in the Cape Colony 1868–1902: Prostitution and the Contagious Diseases Acts', *Journal of Southern African Studies* 10, 2, 1984: 170–97.
Whitehead, J. 'Modernizing the motherhood archetype: public health models and the Child Marriage Restraint Act of 1929.' In *Social Reform, Sexuality and the State*, edited by P. Uberoi. New Delhi: Sage, 1996.

Index

11th East Africa (EA) Division 84–86, 91, 97; Abyssinian campaign and 92, 95; education of 88–89; finances of 93; insubordination of 94–95; Intelligence Section of 86; morale of 85, 94; propaganda and 85; reputation of 95; *see also askaris*
1864 Calcutta Cyclone 127, 129, 135
1878–79 Afghan War 60
1901 Census 167

abolitionism 197
Abyssinia 92, 95–96
Act X (1887) *see* Native Passenger Ships Act (1887)
Aden 17, 25, 34, 57, 61
Afghanistan 59, 69
agriculture 20, 23–25, 27, 176–78; *see also* peasantry
agvalas 15, 25, 27–28
Ahmed, M. Rafiuddin 64–65
alien pilgrims 59–60, 70
Alligator 111
All-India Committee 167
Ali, Shaukat 64
Ambon Island *see* Amboyna
Amboyna 106
Andaman Islands 177–78
Anderson, Wright & Co. 175
Anglican Church in India 160; *see also* Church of England
Anglo-Indians 24, 162, 170
Anglo-Indian Unemployment Committee (AIUC) 170
Anjuman-i-Islam 64
Anjuman-i-Khuddam-I Kaba 64
anthropology 3, 18, 26–27, 171
Armenians 106
Arthur, George, Lt. Gov. 111

articles *see* lascars: contracts of
Asiatic Articles *see* Lascar Articles
Asiatic Seamen's Union 32
Askari 92
askaris 84–85, 87, 89–91, 96; literacy of 88; racism and 92, 96
Assam 132
Assolna 32
asylums 122
Atlas 111
Attock 25
Australia: Chinese labour and 179; emigration and 178–79; immigration and 34, 67; Indian Ocean and 1–2; migration from 105–13; sailors and 126; *see also* convicts

baghalahs 21
Baly, Joseph 162, 164–65
Bangalore 177
Bari, Maulana Abdul 64
barivalas 28
Barker, Amelia 110
Basra 68
Bass Straits 109–10
Batavia 106, 110, 112
Bay of Bengal 127
Bedouins 53
Begum of Bhopal 54
Bell, John 112
Bencoolen 106, 110
Bengal 122, 128, 135; convicts and 106–8; domiciled Europeans and 162–63, 178; education and 162; Indian Mutiny and 124–25; lascar recruitment and 17, 22–24; Lieutenant-Governor of 126, 128, 162, 166, 177
Bengal Army 129

Bengal Hurkaru 126
Bengal Mariners' Union 31
Beverley, H. 162
Bhattacharya, Sanjoy 88
Bigge, Commissioner 109–10
Bihar 177
boarding houses *see* lodging houses
Boer War 155
Bombay 20, 32, 64, 134, 192–201; Chief Medical Officer of 194; convicts and 111–12; Hajj shipping and 54, 57; Health Officer of 53, 57, 61–62; House of Correction of 133; maritime labour and 13, 19, 21, 23–24, 26, 28, 194; Police Commissioner of 51–53, 57, 59–60, 135, 192–93, 195, 200; prostitutes and 2, 4, 192–201; Protector of Pilgrims of 52, 57; Sephardic community of 195; Shipping Master of 22, 29; Shipping Office of 27
Bombay Act II (1883) *see* Pilgrim Protection Act (1883)
Bombay Act II (1887) 52
Bombay-Baroda Railway 165; *see also* railways
Bombay Chronicle 64
Bombay Persia Steam Navigation Co. 63; *see also* shipping companies
Bombay Pilgrim Department 52
Bombay Prostitution Act (1923) 197
Bombay Seamen's Union 32
Bombay Vigilance Association 198, 200
Bona Vista 112
Booth, Charles 156, 182
Booth, Gen. 156, 182
Bose, Sugata 1, 57
Botany Bay 106–7
Bow Bazaar 123, 126–27, 129
Boyne 111
Brading, Thomas 106
Brazil 200
Brisbane, Gov. 111
Britain 17, 108; convicts and 105, 107, 112; extraterritoriality and 55–56, 61; immigration and 34; newspapers in 126, 170; poverty in 156
Britannia 106
British Empire 3; economy of 20; infrastructure of 20, 25, 58; religious liberty and 64–65
British Indian passport 67–68
British India Steam Navigation Company (BI) 21–22; *see also* shipping companies

British merchant marine 2, 17, 22–23, 25, 124, 128; Indian Mutiny and 124; lascars and 13–14
Brophy, Daniel 113
brothels 124, 131, 192–201; extortion and 192; police and 192–201.
Bryant, Mary 106, 110
Buettner, Elizabeth 158
Buggalows 21
Burma 84, 88, 92
Burton, Richard 49
Butler, S.H. 63, 66
Buxar 125

Cairo 197
Calcutta 20, 54, 157; Archdeacon of 162; convicts and 106–10; European population of 123; House of Correction in 123, 133; Indian Mutiny and 125; Pilgrim Department of 70; police officers of 126, 129, 132–33; sailors and 4, 13, 19, 21, 23–24, 26–28, 31, 121–24, 132; Sailor's Home 123, 135; Seaman's Chaplain 132; Shipping Master of 13, 22, 128
Calcutta Domiciled Community Enquiry Committee (CDCEC) 167–70, 172, 174, 179
Calcutta Review, The 171
Campbell, Duncan 106
Canada 67
Cannanore 111
Canning, Gov. Gen. 124, 161
Cape Town 34, 194
Castle, Benjamin 111
Cathedral Church of Nossa Senhora DeRozario 163
Cato, Philip 112
Central Indian Railway 165; *see also* railways
Ceylon 92–93, 95–97, 110, 199
Ceylon Army Command 86
Ceylon Light Infantry 97
chambers of commerce 30, 123
Charity Organization Committee 166
chaukidars 133
Chevers, Norman 129–32
Chichgars 22, 28
China 59, 109
Chinyanja 86–87, 89–90
Chittagong 22–23
cholera 50, 57, 129–31
Christianity 24–25, 31; domiciled Europeans and 160–61; prostitutes

and 198–99; sailors and 125, 129, 139; *see also* Goa; missionaries
Church of England 162; *see also* Anglican Church in India
civilizing mission *see* colonial rule
Clark, Joseph 110
class attitudes 4, 181–82
clergymen 122, 163
Circus, R. W., Lt. 86
Cocas Keeling Island 97
Collins, Robert 112
Colombo 34, 86–87, 96, 194
Colonial Office 84, 87
colonial rule: civilizing mission of 61, 107, 121, 130, 132, 134, 137, 155, 156, 161; hierarchies of 3, 122, 157, 161, 183, 192–93.law of 15, 19, 193, 201; legitimacy of 2, 122, 137, 155, 157, 161, 195; stability of 2, 3.
colonial studies 1–3, 157, 201.
compulsory education 167
Conference on the Education of the Domiciled Community in India (1912) 167
Constantinople 198; *see also* Istanbul
Contagious Diseases Acts 196
Continuous Discharge Certificate 33
convicts 2, 4–5; international cooperation and 110; transportation of 111; *see also* escaped convicts; ex-convicts
coolies 14, 24
Cooper, Frederic 158
Coromandel Coast 23
cotton 51, 161
Cotton, Bishop 157, 160–61
Countess of Harcourt 110
Country-wallahs 21
Crawford, Capt. 86
Crimmin, J., Dr. 62
Cuncolim 32
Cyclone Relief Fund 128
Czechoslovakia 199

Dacca 24
dalals 136, 139
Daldis 23
Daman 23
Darling, Gov. 111
dasturi 30
Davis, Elizabeth 106
Deccan 199
Delhi 124, 199
Demett, William 110

Denmark 182
deras 31
Desai, Dinkar 26
De Woronin, Sgt. 86
Dhobi Talao 31
dhonis 21
Dhows 21
differential incorporation 18–19
District Charitable Society 162–64, 166
Diu 23
Doasta 131; *see also* liquor
Dr Barnardo's Homes 182
Domiciled Community of Northern India 180
domiciled Europeans 4, 158, 161, 172; affordable housing and 174; colonial legitimacy and 161, 181; education of 162–65, 167; employment of 160, 169, 180; perceptions of 160–61, 167, 169–70, 172, 177–78, 181–82; poverty of 162, 164, 168–72, 174, 180; social inferiority of 159; solutions for 162, 164–66, 168–69, 171, 175–80, 183; statistics and 163–64, 170–71
Doran, James 111–12
Dutch Java 50–51

East Africa Command 84–86, 92; Principal Information Officer (PIO) of 85, 87
East African Army Education Corps 88
East African Intelligence Centre 85
East African soldiers 2–3, 5, 84, 92; *see also* askaris; King's African Rifles (KAR)
Eastern Bengal State Railway 165; *see also* railways
East India Company 13, 123, 179; convicts and 106–8, 110
East Timor 110
Edwardes, S. M. 51, 192, 195, 198.
Egypt 50, 198
Elliot, Charles, Lt. Gov. 166
English language education 88–89
Englishman, The 125, 179
escaped convicts 105, 110–11, 113; trials of 107, 112
Ethiopia 84, 87
ethnography 129, 156, 163, 171; *see also* racial ideology
Eurasian and Anglo-Indian Association (EAIA) 162–63, 172, 177–78
Eurasians 159, 163, 181; conditions of 167

European: careers of 107; elites 2, 4, 168, 193; domiciled Europeans and 158–59, 162, 168, 183; ex-convicts 105; illegal immigration of 109; official response to 107, 112; pauperism *see* domiciled Europeans; prostitutes *see* prostitutes; relationships of 107; sailors 136, 139, 194; sexual relationships of 108, 194–99, 201; social desirability of 105, 107, 113, 195, 196.
European Education Code 162
Ex-Services Association 170, 177

Favel, Inspector 192, 197–98
feminist studies 3, 194.
Fielding, Mary Ann 106–7
Fiji 110
Finlay, Elizabeth 110
Finniss, John 112
First Engineers 29
First Fleet 109
First World War 13, 15, 17, 25, 50–51, 57, 59, 65, 68
Fiscari, Andree 196
Fiscari, Indree *see* Fiscari, Andree
Flag Street 123, 129–30, 136
Fooks, Mary 197
Forbes-Mitchell, William 172
Foreign Office 60
Fort William 108, 125
Fowkes, Maj. Gen. 92, 95
France 50, 64, 157, 159, 198, 200
Frederick 110
free settlers 105, 108–9; social desirability of 105
free trade 60, 64
French Algeria 50
Friend-in-Need Society 178
Friend of India 129, 161, 177
Friendship 106

Gardner, Katy 17, 27
Genoa 32
George Town 110
Germany 155, 157, 182
ghat serangs 22, 28–29, 31; *see also* shipping brokers
Ghogha 23
Ghuznavi, A. K. 70
Gidney, Henry 178
Girgaon 197
Goa 22–25, 32–33, 199; seamen's clubs in 32; *see also* Christianity

gonorrhoea 132; *see also* venereal disease
Government of India Act (1919) 169
Governor Phillip 112
Graham, John, Rev. 178–79
Guillon, Gaston 200
Gujarat 22–23
Gulf of Khambhat 23

Hadleigh Farm 182
Hajj 3, 49–51, 53, 57, 59, 61; charity and 51, 54; compulsory return ticket and 62–66, 70; conditions of 52, 54, 62–63, 67–68, 70; cost of 52, 62–63; European intervention in 50, 54–55; historiography of 50; statistics and 55, 57; *see also* pauper pilgrims
Hanley, Gerald 88
Hansa Linie 13
Harris, Elizabeth 109
Harrison, Sir H. L. 163
Harvey, Elizabeth 106
Hastings, Patrick 113
Heart of Empire, The 156
Hechle, J. H. 167
Helling, Ann 110
Hengesch, Nicholas, Rev. 163
Heshima 85–87, 89, 92–93; British-*askari* relations and 94; Ceylon and 96; letters and 93–94; reception of 86, 91; role of 89–91, 97; structure of 90
high imperialism 13, 17, 105
Hijaz 2, 49–50, 56–58, 68; restrictions to 66; shipping agents of 54
hill stations 159
Hindustani 14, 16
HMS *Shannon* 121, 124, 127
Hobart 110, 112
Holt, Margaret 106
Home Rule 169
Hong Kong 194, 201
Hood, W. H., Capt. 25
Hooghly River 166, 176
hospitals 129–30
Hughli 124
human trafficking: conventions against 4, 193–94, 198–201; definition of 199–200; measures against 194, 196, 198–200
Hyderabad 60, 199

Ihram 71
Ile de France 106
ILO 29, 31–32
immigration legislation 34, 158

Imperial Legislative Assembly 66
indentured labour 2, 16
India: British society in 108, 195; Department of Education of 63; Foreign Department of 57, 60; Governor-General of 107; Home Department of 57, 197; independence of 14; Jewish communities in 106, 195; Office 62; Parsi communities in 106; working classes 197; Viceroy of 65, 161
Indian Army 25
Indian Civil Service 169
Indian Merchant Shipping Act (1925) 50; amendments to 66
Indian Mutiny 121–22, 125, 127, 158; domiciled Europeans and 160; sailors and 124, 129, 137; volunteers and 124
Indian Navy 124–25
Indian Rebellion *see* Indian Mutiny
Indian soldiers: fighting qualities of 95
Indispensable 106
Indo-Europeans 171
Information Officers 87
International Society for the Suppression of White Slave Traffic 193
Ireland 107, 112
Islamic law 50, 61, 63
Istanbul 50; *see also* Constantinople

'Jack Tar' 30, 121, 129, 135, 139; positive qualities of 137
Jama'tis 23
Janjira 23
Japan 84, 90, 92, 96, 201
Jeelani, S. A. K. 66
Jerusalem 64
Jewish Associations 195
Jhelum 25
Jidda 51–55, 57, 61, 65, 67
Jodhpur 199
Johannesburg 183
Jubilee Indian Pilgrims Relief Fund 61

Kabulis 28, 60
Kamathipura 192, 194–97
Karachi 21, 54, 194
Kashmir 25, 199
Kasumba, K. K., Sgt. 96
Kathiawar 23
Kelly, Daniel 113
Kemp, Richard 112
Kennerley, Alston 135
Kenya 2, 90

Kenya Information Office 87
Kenya Security 85
khalasis 15–16, 22–23
Khan, Muhammad Haji 62
Khandwani Steam Navigation Company 52; *see also* shipping companies
Kharwas 23
Khilafat movement 58, 66, 69
Kidderpore Bridge 133
Kidderpore Docks 27
King George VI 91, 93
King's African Rifles (KAR) 84, 88–89, 91, 93, 97; behavior of 95; British relations with 94
kinship 4, 19, 25, 29, 31, 33
Kiswahili 86–91, 94
Kolhapur 199
Konkani coast 23
kurs 31–33

labour 15–33; catchment areas 17, 20, 22–25, 27, 33
Lakhadive islands 23
Lal Bazaar: convicts and 106; sailors and 108, 123, 127, 129–30, 135–36
Lang, John 109
Lascar Articles 15
lascars 3, 13, 16, 123; contracts of 28–30; definition of 14–15, 17, 25, 34; economic conditions of 19, 21, 26, 28–30, 34; ethnic diversity of 22, 31, 34; living conditions of 15, 26, 30; movement of 29–30, 34; recruitment of 21–22, 24, 27–28, 31; rural origins of 20, 22, 27; statistics and 13
Launceston 110
Layton, Sir Geoffrey, Adm. 86
League of Mercy 198–99
League of Nations 194, 198, 200; human trafficking reports of 193
Ledlow, James 110
Lee, Edward 112
Lefroy, Bishop, Right Rev. 167
Levine, Philippa 132
Life and Labour of the People in London 156
Linebaugh, Peter 105, 137
liquor 130–31, 135
List of European Residents 108
literacy 3, 51, 88, 162, 163
Liverpool 112
lock-hospital system 132; *see also* venereal disease; prostitutes

Index   213

lodging houses 123–24, 130, 135–36; ethnic segmentation of 31; owners of 28–30
London 156, 181, 183
London Labour and the London Poor 155
Lucknow 121, 124
Luke, James 181–82

Mackenzie, Alexander 62
Mackinnon, Mackenzie & Co. 28
Macpherson Report 129–30
Macquarie Harbour 112
Macquarie Island 110
MacRae, John 171–73
Madagascar 84, 92
Madras 20, 183, 194
Madras Emigration Society 178
Madras Government Museum 171
Madras Times, The 178
Maidan 126–27
Maldive islands 23
Malleson, Maj. 128
Malleson Report 129, 132, 135–36
Mambo Leo 94
Manly, Richard 106
Marathi 196
Margeson, Maurice 93
Marine Magistrates 135
maritime 1, 2, 13; censuses 13; maritime legislation 34
Marseilles 200
Marshall, Elizabeth 106
Marquis Cornwallis 106
Marwaris 28
Mary 110, 112
Mascarenhas, Joseph 32
Masterman, Charles 156
maulvi 60
Mauritius 109–10, 112–13; *see also* Ile de France
Mayhew, Henry 155–57, 160, 183
Mazagaon 31
Mazarello, A. 32
McCluskiegunge Colony 177
McGuire, Thomas 163
Mecca 49, 51, 53, 55–56, 64; Sharif of 53, 58, 65, 67
Medina 49, 51, 53, 55–57, 64
Meerut 124
Meldrum, John 110
Memons 54
Merchant, Sarah 106
Merchant Shipping Act (1854) 128
Mijikenda identity 19

Ministry of Information (MOI) 85–86, 88
Mint Guard 125
Mirpur 25
miscegenation 159, 183, 194
miskeen 49, 61, 71
missionaries: European pauperism and 158, 163, 171, 178; prostitutes and 194, 198; sailors and 126, 129, 134–35; *see also* Christianity
modernity 4, 18
Mofussil stations 125–26
Mogul Line 66
Molesworth select committee on transportation (1837–38) 109–10
Molony, John 109
Mombasa 19, 34
Moncrief, L. 52, 56
moneylenders 28–30; *see also* Kabulis; *see also* Marwaris
Monsoon Victory (Hanley) 88
Montagu-Chelmsford Reforms (1919) 180
Moreton, James 112
Moshi *see* Tanganyika Territory
Mowat, James 29
Muslims 25, 31, 59; clergy of 64; Hajj and 50–51, 57, 61, 65; lascars and 22–24; poor whites and 157, 161; public sphere of 64, 71
Muslim League 64
mutawwifs 51, 53, 58, 67–70
Mysore 177

Nairobi 85, 87
Napoleonic Wars 126
National Congress 64
National Incorporated Association for the Reclamation of Destitute Waif Children *see* Dr Barnardo's Homes
nationalism 1, 4, 58, 193; women and 195
Native Passenger Ships Act (1887) 54
Naval Brigades 121–22, 124, 126, 132; dissolution of 127, 137; official response to 127; reputation of 125
Netherlands 50, 64, 106, 157, 182; *see also* Dutch Java
new imperial history 1
New South Wales 106–7, 109–12
New Zealand 109, 178–79
Nichols, Isaac 111
Noakhali 22–23
Northern Rhodesia 90

North Western Provinces Legislative Council 62
North-West Frontier Provinces 24, 59
nullies see Permanent Discharge Certificates
Nyasaland 90

Oliver, N. 133
Omari, Mfaume, Sgt. 86
Oomburkharee 197
Ootacamund 132
orientalism 4, 105, 122, 139
Orientals 30
Ottoman Empire 64; cholera and 57; Hajj and 49, 53, 55, 60–61; passports and 56, 67; Sultan of 56, 58, 61, 63, 71

Pacific Ocean 34
pardah 62
Paris 200
Pasha of Egypt 49
passenger travel 61, 71
Pathans 60
Pauperism Committee 163–64, 169–71, 175; recommendations of 165–67, 173–74, 176
pauper pilgrims 2–3, 5, 49, 57, 60; condition of 62, 70; disease and 50, 55, 57, 62–63, 70; ethnic diversity of 54; perceptions of 57, 63, 71; transportation of 50–53, 57, 59–61, 63–64; see also Hajj; pilgrim passports
Payro, Cannon Russell 178
peasantry 26–27
Penang 110, 201; see also Prince of Wales Island
Peninsular and Oriental Steam Navigation Company (P&O) 16, 21–22, 28, 32–33; Hajj traffic and 62; see also shipping companies
Peradeniya 86
Permanent Discharge Certificates 28
Persia 14, 69
Peshawar 25
phatemaris 21
philanthropy 161–63, 172–74, 178
Phoenix 112
Punuswaree 197
Pilgrim Manual 56
Pilgrim Shipping Bill 62
pilgrim passports 49, 51, 59, 70–71; compulsory system of 50, 55–57, 67;

details of 67–69; see also pauper pilgrims
Pilgrim Protection Act (1883) 54
plantations 2, 16
Platt, Sir William, Gen. 84
Poinet, Marie Amandine 200
Poland 199, 201
Police Brigades 124, 126
police officers 163; extortion and 192, 197, 201; prostitutes and 196–201
Pondicherry 107
Poor Law (1834) 173
poor whites 126, 158; alienation of 157; assistance for 156; pauperization of 157; racial ideology and 108, 155–57, 159
Port Arthur 112
Port Louis 110–12
Port Sea 110
Portugal 23, 106, 159
post-colonial studies 3, 157, 194.
Powers, Edward 112
Prince of Wales Island 109–10; see also Penang
prisoners of war 85
propaganda 3, 5, 84–88; see also *Heshima*
prostitutes 2, 136, 192–201; *askaris* and 97; British men and 194; conditions of 192, 194, 198–99; deportation of 192, 196, 201; European 4, 108, 122, 132, 139, 192, 194–96, 198; Indian 132, 192, 194, 199; statistics and 197, 199; surveillance of 193, 197; see also brothels; human trafficking; venereal disease
punch-houses 124, 135
Punjab 24–25, 28, 199

Qamaran 53, 55, 57, 62

racial ideology 121, 131, 155, 159, 183, 194–96; domiciled Europeans and 170–71, 174, 179, 181; medicine and 130; poor whites and 157, 161; prostitutes and 194–201; venereal disease and 132; white sailors and 134, 137
Rada Bazaar 106
Radford, Mary 106
radio broadcasts 89; see also propaganda
Radio Colombo 89
Rahimtoolah, Ibrahim 68

railways 21, 59, 165, 167, 169; *see also* Bombay-Baroda Railway; Central Indian Railway; Eastern Bengal State Railway
Raine, John 112
Rangoon 34
Raphael, Stephens M. S., Clerk 94
Rasul, Syed 24
Ratnagiri 23, 28, 199
Rawalpindi 25
Razzack, Abdur 55–56
Reader, James 111
recruitment ports 20
Red Army 90
Rediker, Marcus 105–6, 137
Red Sea 49, 53–54, 56
Reid, William 106
Rhino 87
Roche, John 113
Roll, James 106
Rosa, Luciano la 200
Rowlatt agitations 69
Royal Air Force 85
Royal Botanic Gardens 86
Royal Commission on Labour in India (1929) 26
Royal Indian Marine 23, 28
Royal Navy 124, 128
Ruby, Catherine 110
Russia 50, 59–60; anti-Jewish pogroms in 195; passport trafficking and 67; prostitutes from 199, 201
Ryan, Sgt. 86

sailors 2–4, 16, 122, 194; *see also* lascars; white sailors
St. Andrew's Colonial Homes 176, 179
Salvation Army 156, 182, 198
Sanitary Commission 128
sanitary conferences 50, 54; Paris (1894) 61–62; Venice (1892) 61
Sausmond Colony 177
Scindia Steam Navigation Company 21; *see also* shipping companies
Scott, James and Eliza 106
Seamen's Friend Society 134
Seamen's Mission 134
Second Echolon 87
Second World War 14, 21, 84, 88–89, 97
Select Committee on the Colonization and Settlement (1858–59) 158
Select Committee on the Poor-White Question in South Africa (1913) 157
sepoys 14, 25

serangs 19, 27–31; *see also* shipping brokers
sex trade *see* human trafficking; prostitutes
sexuality 108, 194.
Shanghai 194, 201
shipbuilding industry 23
Shipley, Avalon 59
shipping brokers 22, 28–30, 33, 51; abolition of 31; opposition to 31; *see also* Chichgars; *ghat serangs*; *serangs*
shipping companies 14–17, 22, 25–26, 29–30
Simla 167
Singapore 19, 34, 51, 194, 201
Singhalese 90, 96
Smith, James 110
Smith, Thomas 106
smuggling 111
sociology 171
social science 156–57, 182–83
social security measures 33; domiciled Europeans and 165, 170, 174; Hajj pilgrims and 63, 65, 66; unemployment insurance 26
social workers 163, 193, 198–99
Somalia 24, 84, 87, 95
Sopher, David 20
South Africa 15, 126, 178–79
South America 109, 194
Southampton 176
South East Asia Command 91
Southern Eurasian Colony 177
Statesman, The 162, 167, 169–70, 172, 177–79
steamships 2, 19, 21–24, 26–27, 29–30; crews of 25–28, 33; lascars and 3, 16–17; passenger service of 51, 53
Stoler, Ann 158, 183
Stoodley, John 111
Straits Settlement 50, 63
subaltern groups 1, 2, 4–5, 122, 193, 194; historiography of 5, 105, 194; *see also* domiciled classes; maritime labour; poor whites; prostitutes; white sailors
Subaltern Studies 1–3, 194.
Sublime Porte *see* Ottoman Empire
Suez Canal 2, 13, 49, 51
Surat 23
Surat Anjuman-i-Islam 65
Sweeney, Edward 106
Sydney 109, 111
Sydney Port Regulations 109

Sylhet 17, 22, 24, 26–27
syphilis 132; *see also* venereal disease

Tabora 94
Talakpur 27
Takashi, Oishi 64
Tanganyika Territory 86, 90, 94
Tardeo 197
temperance movement 135
Temple, Richard, Lt. Gov. 177, 181
tezkirah marur 55
Thomas, Clarence W. 164
Thomas Cook and Son 52, 58; subsidies and 59; *see also* shipping companies
Thurston, Edgar 171–72
tindals 28
trade unions 17, 19, 25–26, 30, 32–33; serangs and 19, 31; *see also* Asiatic Seamen's Union; Bombay Seamen's Union
transnational history 1, 4
Tuck, Thomas 106
Turko-Balkan wars (1911–13) 62
Turko-Italian wars (1911–13) 62
Turner Morrison and Company 63–64, 65
Turner, Sgt. 86
Tusiharibu Heshima, wakatuita Wajinga 94

Uganda 90
Underwood, John 109
unit censorship boards 88
Unit Education Officers 87
United States 15, 34, 106, 123, 155, 179

vakils 58
Van Diemen's Land 110, 112
Velim 32
venereal disease 97, 131, 194, 198; racial ideology and 132, 194–95
Viceroy's Legislative Council 70

Victorian literature 129
Vincent, F. A. M. 192

Wahiuddin, Haji 71
Wales 163
War Office 84, 88, 91
War Risk Compensations 15
Warui, Joel, L. Cpl. 93
Wellington Valley 111
White, D. S. 177
white sailors 108, 121–23, 139, 194; character of 123, 135–36; complaints against 124, 127, 132; health of 129–31, 194; living conditions of 128–30, 132–33; reputation of 134–37; solutions for 127–28, 133–34, 138; statistics and 123, 129, 137; vagrancy of 135
Whitefield Colony 177–78
whiteness: European pauperism and 158–59, 181, 183; prostitutes and 108, 195; whiteness studies 4; *see also* racial ideology
Whitney Brothers 175
Willis, John 110
Willis, Justin 19
Wilson, Kathleen 108
Wilson, Rev. 134
Wise, Elizabeth 106
Wisehammer, John 106
Wolf, Eric R. 18
Wollstonecraft and Berry 111
women 108, 192–201; national symbolism of 195
Wood, Arden 167
workhouses 122

Yaqub, Muhammad 66
Yemen 53
Young, Sarah 106
Younghusband, O., Rev. 180

Zanzibar 24, 34

For Product Safety Concerns and Information please contact our EU
representative GPSR@taylorandfrancis.com
Taylor & Francis Verlag GmbH, Kaufingerstraße 24, 80331 München, Germany

www.ingramcontent.com/pod-product-compliance
Lightning Source LLC
Chambersburg PA
CBHW052109300426
44116CB00010B/1594